KU-609-794

TERRITORIES, COMMODITIES AND KNOWLEDGES:

LATIN AMERICAN ENVIRONMENTAL HISTORY IN THE NINETEENTH AND TWENTIETH CENTURIES

WITHDRAWN FROM THE LIBRARY UNIVERSITY OF WINCHESTER

KA 0399243 8

Territories, Commodities and Knowledges:

Latin American Environmental History in the Nineteenth and Twentieth Centuries

Edited by
Christian Brannstrom

Institute for the Study of the Americas
Senate House, Malet Street
London WC1E 7HU
Web: www.sas.ac.uk/americas

UNIVERSITY OF WINCHESTER
LIBRARY

UNIVERSITY OF WINCHESTER	
	03092438

British Library Cataloguing-in-Publication Data
A catalogue record for this book is available
from the British Library

ISBN   1 900039 57 5

INSTITUTE FOR THE STUDY OF THE
AMERICAS

Institute for the Study of the Americas, 2004
Senate House
Malet Street
London WC1E 7HU

Telephone: 020 7862 8870
Fax: 020 7862 8886

Email: americas@sas.ac.uk
Web: www.sas.ac.uk/americas

TABLE OF CONTENTS

ACKNOWLEDGEMENTS

Although several colleagues had warned me that editing books was a thankless task, the editing of this book has been rather pleasant because of the generous and friendly nature of the contributors and staff involved. Early versions of several chapters in this book were presented at the 'Workshop on Nineteenth- and Twentieth-century Latin American Environmental History' held at the Institute of Latin American Studies, University of London, 2–3 November 2001, with partial funding from the British Academy (Conference Grant BCG–32852). Michael Redclift supported the application to the British Academy, while Linda Newson, Laura Rival and David Arnold commented critically on the papers presented. Commissioned work submitted by Reinaldo Funes, Nikolas Kozloff and Alejandro Tortolero supplemented the Workshop.

The combined tasks of editing the papers, preparing the maps, translating two chapters into English and writing the introduction occupied much of 2002 and 2003. Fortunately, all of this weathered one international move, two changes in academic affiliation, the birth of a child and arrival of a second PhD in the family. I began editing the chapters while I was Lecturer at the Institute of Latin American Studies (ILAS). Work continued while I taught at the Department of Geography at California State University, Long Beach, where Christine Rodrigue made my year as a part-time lecturer conducive to intellectual production. By the time I was appointed as Assistant Professor in the Department of Geography at Texas A&M University only two chapters had yet to be finalised. The combined enthusiasm of Wendy Jepson and the contributors toward the project represented by this volume helped me through this transitional period.

My affection for ILAS and my former colleagues there has only increased after leaving London. I am especially grateful to James Dunkerley for his consistent support, initially for the Workshop and later for seeing the edited volume to publication. The Workshop went smoothly because the logistics were admirably handled by ILAS staff, especially Tony Bell and Olga Jiménez, and this resulting volume was guided through editing and production by Melanie Jones and John Maher.

College Station, Texas
10 March 2004

NOTES ON CONTRIBUTORS

Stephen Bell is an Assistant Professor in the Department of Geography at the University of California, Los Angeles. Most of his research falls under the broad umbrella of European influence (and its consequences) in southern South America since around 1800. His book *Campanha Gaúcha: A Brazilian Ranching System, 1850–1920* was published by Stanford University Press in 1998. He is currently finishing a study of Aimé Bonpland's career in resource appraisal in the Río de la Plata during the first half of the nineteenth century.

Christian Brannstrom is an Assistant Professor of Geography at Texas A&M University. He has published several research articles in geography and development journals. His present research interests include the historical geography of wood in south-eastern Brazil, the environmental management of globalised agriculture and the development of decentralised water-resources policies.

Reinaldo Funes Monzote received his doctorate in 2002 from the Universitat Jaume I in Spain. His areas of specialisation are Cuban environmental history and history of science. In 2003 he won the Premio al Pensamiento Caribeño for his book *De bosque a sabana: azúcar, deforestación y medioambiente en Cuba, 1492–1926* (Editorial Siglo XXI, 2004). He also is author of the forthcoming book *El despertar del asociacionismo científico en Cuba, 1776–1920*, to be published in Madrid. Currently he directs a research programme at the Fundación Antonio Nuñez Jiménez de la Naturaleza y el Hombre in Cuba.

Stefania Gallini is a Researcher at the Departamento de Investigaciones de la Universidad Central (DIUC) in Bogotá, Colombia, and also teaches at the Universidad Nacional de Colombia. She holds a PhD in Latin American History from the Universitá degli Studi di Genova (2002). Her current project deals with early-twentieth-century meat consumption and production in Colombia.

Nikolas Kozloff is currently Auxiliary Professor of History at Drexel University, Philadelphia, in the Department of History and Politics. He is currently at work revising his PhD dissertation, which deals with oil and environment in Venezuela during the Juan Vicente Gómez period, into a book manuscript.

Karl H. Offen is an Assistant Professor of Geography at the University of Oklahoma. His research interests include political ecology, history of cartography and ethnic identity formation in Latin America. He is the author of articles in *Historical Geography, Human Organization, Ethnohistory* and *Hispanic American Historical Review*.

John Soluri is a member of the History Department at Carnegie Mellon University where he teaches courses on Latin American and environmental history. His current research projects include an environmental history of Tierra del Fuego.

Alejandro Tortolero Villaseñor is Profesor-Investigador at the Universidad Autónoma Metropolitana-Iztapalapa, Mexico. His obtained his PhD in History from the Ecole des Hautes Études en Sciences Sociales in Paris. He specialises in Mexico's economic, ecological and technological history.

Robert W. Wilcox is an Associate Professor of History at Northern Kentucky University. He has published in several journals, including *Agricultural History*, *The Americas*, *Environmental History* and *Fronteiras: Revista de História* (Campo Grande, MS, Brazil). At present he is working on a book manuscript that examines the environmental history of cattle ranching in the Brazilian Centre-West.

LIST OF FIGURES

LIST OF TABLES

UNIVERSITY OF WINCHESTER
LIBRARY

UNIVERSITY OF WINCHESTER
LIBRARY

An Introduction to Latin American Environmental History*

Christian Brannstrom and Stefania Gallini

T his book explores three inter-related questions of Latin America's nineteenth- and twentieth-century environmental history. To what extent was environmental change at the centre of territorial conflicts between nation-states and indigenous peoples or local communities? The territorial expansion of newly independent states, beginning in the early nineteenth century, frequently encroached on territorial claims of indigenous peoples, whose populations were recovering from their seventeenth-century nadir, and local communities that previously had been at the margins of the state and international market economy. Territorial and resource appropriation, which relied on both a politically repressive state apparatus and a sophisticated discursive arsenal of maps and textual representation, affected peoples throughout Latin America, especially in cases where export commodities could be obtained from new territories to satisfy the immense economic appetites of states and entrepreneurs.

What were the environmental implications of the commodities produced in and exported from Latin America? This second question refers to what has been called Latin America's 'second conquest'[1] from 1850 to 1930, when various export booms spread across all of the newly created states. Numerous agricultural and mineral commodities became inextricably linked to the fates of the lands and peoples of Latin America, often dominating state revenue and policies whilst causing deforestation, ecosystem simplification, soil erosion, water contamination, air pollution and risks to human health.

How did new knowledge encourage territorial expansion and production of new commodities? Contemporary understanding of the environment influenced practices, policies and technologies instrumental to commodity booms and territorial expansion. Technological changes and newly introduced organisms reconfigured human-environment relations in many regions. Some scientists tried to slow the pace of exploitative resource uses; many others developed new technologies or introduced new organisms that would increase destructive uses of natural resources, often by further encouraging commodity production or territorial expansion.

*   We are grateful to Karl Offen, Robert Wilcox, John Soluri and Wendy Jepson for their helpful comments on earlier versions of this chapter. All inaccurate and inconsistent points are our own errors.
1   Topik and Wells (1998).

Certainly, the territories-commodities-knowledges framework does not encompass all themes of nineteenth- and twentieth-century Latin America. Urbanisation, industrialisation, natural disasters, environmental perceptions, public policies and popular resistance are discussed toward the end of this chapter but not specifically addressed in this book. Notwithstanding these omissions, the territories-commodities-knowledges framework merges much of the current literature on modern Latin American environmental history. The framework also points to three issues that scholars in the region have perceived as crucial to an environmental understanding of Latin America's past. Thus, we are asserting a particular agenda for Latin America, distinct from literatures for North America, Africa, South Asia and Australia but informed by them. We hope that this framework will stimulate others to contribute to the theory and methods of environmental history practised in Latin America (by Latin Americanists and by scholars from the region).[2] Above all, we want to assess the present status of environmental history in order to place the incipient field of Latin American environmental history in a constructive dialogue with other literatures.

We do not suggest that scholars of Latin American environmental history should follow uncritically either the trajectory or theoretical framework of regional literatures. Nor do we believe that scholars necessarily should search for similar types of primary sources used in different regions. In fact, one of the most interesting developments of the field is precisely the current search for a particular Latin American approach to environmental history, based not only on cultural traditions but also on regional interests and priorities.[3] Thus, our view is that an in-depth reading of other regional literatures should inform and enrich, but not determine, Latin American environmental history. The following section explores several related issues that amount to a multi-dimensional understanding of environmental history. This view, in contrast to a theoretical introduction to the field, is meant to create an operational definition of the field useful to Latin Americanists, not the desiderata of it.

Defining Environmental History

Environmental history may be understood as the study of past interactions of humans with environments. The field of inquiry is sufficiently broad to accommodate scholarly inquiry on topics as diverse as the destruction of the North American bison, colonial forest policies in South Asian forests, soil

2   Castro Herrera argues that there is a difference; see his 'Environmental History (made) in Latin America,' at www2.h-net.msu.edu/~environ/historiography/latinam.htm, accessed 21 March 2003.

3   Castro Herrera is committed to this project; see note 2 and his earlier publication (Castro Herrera, 1997). See also Palacio (2002) and Dean (1992) on this debate.

conservation in East Africa and pre-European agriculture in Middle America.[4] The range of disciplines contributing to environmental history is broad and diverse, because the field is inherently transdisciplinary. In the last decade, for example, major books in the field have been published by historians, geographers, anthropologists, botanists and legal scholars, often under the classification of 'historical geography of the environment' or 'ecological history'.

Disciplining Environmental History

A common way of defining environmental history is to situate it in an academic discipline. In Europe the 'disciplining' of environmental history usually emphasises continuity with *Annales* historians such as Marc Bloch, Lucien Febvre and Fernand Braudel, while in North America continuity with scholars such as Frederick Jackson Turner, James Malin, Samuel Hays and Carl Sauer has been underlined. Indeed, the present field of environmental history owes much to geographers and anthropologists interested in past environments, especially agriculture, and to environmental movements.[5]

Several scholars have moved well beyond the intellectual history approach in establishing normative claims on environmental history, arguing that certain disciplines are best suited to house the field. For example, anthropologists have attempted to separate historical ecology from environmental history, suggesting that the former is more materialist than the latter because it 'reveals a dialectical process in the unfolding' of human-environment changes.[6] Disciplinary barriers have been defended by claiming that most historians do not have 'appropriate credentials to comment on scientific subjects' and seldom collaborate with 'natural scientists'.[7] Similarly unconvincing is the argument that ecological history is focused on 'the natural environment itself', while historical geography and environmental history emphasise 'the human element'.[8] Geographers have lamented mainly that some of the best environmental history has been done 'on topics that historical geographers have either not perceived or ignored'[9] or that geography has '[relinquished] ground to a field like history with no physical underpinnings'.[10]

We believe that the normative definition of environmental history nourishes a never-ending and misleading debate on assigning environmen-

---

4   Isenberg (2000); Sivaramakrishnan (1999); Tiffen, Mortimore and Gichuki (1994); Whitmore and Turner (2002).
5   Crosby (1995), p. 1182; Williams (1994), p. 4; White (1985); Miller and Rothman (1997) p. xiii.
6   Balée (1998), p. 13.
7   Crumley (1998), p. xi.
8   Russell (1997), p. 15.
9   Williams (1994), p. 9.
10   Trimble (1992), p. xvii.

tal history to a single discipline. This approach is the sort of cul-de-sac question that scholars of Latin American environmental history would do well to avoid. In a future academic scenario increasingly dominated by transdisciplinarity, it is to be hoped that environmental history will be acknowledged as a legitimate field for its own sake.

Here we adopt an operational definition of the field, considering as 'environmental history' works of research on past human-environment relations that display some of the following characteristics: reworked spatial scales; environmental readings of written evidence or actual measures of past environments; and attempts to situate nature conceptually within historical research. In our understanding these issues define environmental history far more than disciplinary credentials.

Reworking Spatial Scales

Rather than focus exclusively on political entities such as countries or states, environmental historians frequently make drainage basins, vegetation regions and biological organisms the object of historical research. For scholars studying drainage basins, analysis focuses on changing uses of river water and the creation of river infrastructure, such as dams or irrigation canals, in addition to changing land uses in the entire catchment, which necessarily affect the quantity and quality of the main river course. In particular, the Columbia River basin of western North America has inspired two significant studies, whilst the Rhine River has been the topic of a recent 'eco-biography'.[11] Other environmental historians have focused on contiguous areas of vegetation, such as forests, or organisms, such as fisheries or animal herds.[12]

Environmental historians have also reworked conventional geographical scales by focusing on biological organisms, especially plants, and the implications of their inter-regional transfer. In Latin America, the foundational work was on the 'Columbian Exchange' and the implications of the 'portmanteau biota' of European animals, plants and pathogens.[13] More recent work has stressed specific crops, such as the movement of rice cultivars and technology from Africa to the Americas, the global history of the *Eucalyptus* genus (native to Australia but planted throughout Latin America for fuel or soil conservation) and the rubber tree (native to Amazonia).[14] Several other

11   Taylor (1999); White (1995b); Cioc (2002).
12   For fisheries, see McEvoy (1986); Bogue (2000); McCay (1998); for animal herds, see Isenberg (2000); for US forests, see Williams (1989); Whitney (1994); for British forests, see Rackam (1980; 1996); for South American forests, see Dean (1995); Miller (2000); Aagesen (1998); McNeill (1986); for global forests, see Williams (2003).
13   Crosby (1972; 1986).
14   On rice, see Carney (2001); for eucalytus, see Tyrrell (1999); Doughty (2000); on rubber, see Dean (1987).

studies have focused on the role of individuals and imperial powers in stimulating inter-regional exchanges of plants, animals and pathogens.[15]

Evidence

As they redefine the spatial scale of research, environmental historians have widened considerably the range of evidence used in historical analysis by engaging in environmental readings of familiar sources or by using entirely novel sources. Some environmental historians rely primarily on written evidence and oral testimony, while others primarily use evidence collected in field settings such as sediment particles or preserved pollen. Documentary evidence includes written materials (travellers' and settlers' accounts, gazetteers, local histories, emigrant guides, legal documents and scientific literature), graphical materials (maps, photographs, drawings and paintings), statistical series and manuscript materials (land survey records and farm account books, for example). Disturbance histories and analysis of stand structure and tree form comprise field evidence for the study of past forests; archaeological evidence and analysis of sediment and pollen in lake-core sediments are examples of field evidence. Bias, of course, is inherent to each type of evidence.[16]

What are the implications of this epistemological divide between written and field evidence? Some topics of environmental history are inherently transdisciplinary, demanding competence in reading written sources, which are often spread across several archives located in different countries, as well as a solid grasp of 'scientific' or 'technical' literatures of specialists in water, soil, vegetation, wildlife, pollution or other issues. Other topics may require obtaining new evidence directly from the environment, which requires environmental fieldwork to complement archival research. However, written and field sources testify to different aspects of environmental phenomena.[17] Field evidence is often useful in establishing parameters of environmental change, but does not establish the social, economic or political causes for change. Similarly, written evidence of environmental phenomena is not always sufficient to describe and quantify the location, pace and intensity of environmental changes. Bridging the gap between written and field evidence requires considerable training, resources and inter-disciplinary support.

Written and field evidence for environmental history come from myriad sources. Historians interested in environmental ideas might rely exclu-

---

15 Arnold (1996); Dunlap (1999); Griffiths and Robin (1997); Grove (1995; 1997); MacKenzie (1990); see also Wilcox (this volume); Soluri (this volume); and Bell (this volume).
16 Whitney (1994), pp. 10–38.
17 Brannstrom (this volume).

sively on careful analysis of published and unpublished texts of a handful of key protagonists.[18] On the other side of the continuum, studies of the environmental impacts of land uses might rely exclusively on measurements of the environment itself, using analyses of aerial photographs or river-borne sediments.[19] A wide middle ground exists between these extremes. To take two Latin American examples, environmental historians have studied changes in vegetation by using sixteenth-century accounts of land grants and vegetation in Central Mexico and early twentieth-century records of land surveyors in south-eastern Brazil.[20] For other scholars, written records attesting to economic activities, which had important influences on the environment, and state regulation of economic or environmental issues, have formed the evidentiary basis of important studies. Such written sources include records of private firms, individual capitalists and local, regional or national governments. Many key works in North American environmental history have made innovative use of a wide range of similar written sources.[21]

Nature in Environmental History

All environmental histories contain a set of assumptions (usually implicit) about how nature is interpreted and understood, and about the dynamics of nature when (or if) humans could not influence it. To explore what environmental historians mean by 'nature' is to open a wide-ranging discussion.[22] However, the position of nature in environmental history illuminates some interesting present trends in the field. We discuss four. First, it has become popular to claim that the environment is 'fundamental' to, and the 'centre stage' of, human history. How do scholars situate 'nature' with respect to human affairs? Second, the debate between technocentrism and ecocentrism has influenced scholarship in environmental history, with the effect of prioritising research. Third, environmental historians have varying positions on the 'usefulness' of their scholarship. Should environmental history serve present-day concerns? This 'presentist' tendency points to a fourth trend, environmental history's uneasy position with regard to environmental public policy. Should environmental history be

---

18   Pádua (2002).
19   Tiffen, Mortimore and Gichuki (1994); Klepeis and Turner (2001); O'Hara, Street-Perrot and Burt (1993); Sluyter (2002).
20   Butzer and Butzer (1997); Brannstrom (2002); Endfield and O'Hara (1999); Sluyter (2002).
21   Cronon (1991); McEvoy (1986); Fiege (1999); Brechin (1999).
22   The degree to which 'nature' is socially constructed and the dynamics of nature independent of human intervention merit lengthy discussion, but adequate treatment in this introduction is impossible. On social construction, see Demeritt (1998; 2002); Cronon (1995); Soulé and Lease (1995); on 'new ecology', see Zimmerer (1994).

tightly connected to public policy debates? These polemics are embedded in far-reaching debates with large literatures, but here we limit the analysis to works of environmental history.

Positioning nature in environmental history has a normative effect on the practice of environmental history. At one extreme, Donald Worster has pleaded for abandoning 'the common assumption that human experience has been exempt from natural constraints'.[23] Andrew Isenberg goes further in suggesting that environmental history should emphasise 'nonhuman nature' as 'a dynamic agent in human history'.[24] If we accept that humans are not 'exempt from natural constraints', then to what degree are humans constrained by nature? Richard White argues that 'nature does not dictate' human activities, but only '[sets] limits to what is humanly possible'. Accordingly, White claimed that environmental history should make 'the reciprocal influences of a changing nature and changing society' its central theme.[25]

Does nature have agency? According to one environmental historian, the environment 'influenced the course of events by means of both its own independent dynamism and its characteristic responses to human impact across a range of activities'.[26] It follows, then, that environmental history should focus on 'how the environment has shaped human cultures over time' and 'the effects of human activity on nature itself'.[27] But if nature 'shapes' society, then human agency should be reconsidered toward a 'less anthropocentric and less arrogant' understanding.[28]

Other scholars do not suggest causality or reduced human agency, but claim 'centre stage' for the environment. Frequently cited is William Cronon's claim that environmental history should place at centre stage 'a cast of nonhuman characters', such as plants and wildlife, that are only at 'the margins of historical analysis if they are present in it at all'.[29] Moving along the other extreme, and backing away from any suggestion that the environment has agency, Gordon Whitney argues that the field should 'document the environmental changes of the past and determine the factors responsible for their occurrence'.[30] Another step away from the prioritisation of nature is the argument that 'labour, property, exploitation and social struggle' should be centre stage.[31] This suggestion matches the idea that placing nature at 'centre stage' fails 'to grasp how human beings have historically known nature through work'.[32]

23   Worster (1990b), p. 1088.
24   Isenberg (2000), p. 11.
25   White (1985), p. 335.
26   McEvoy (1986), pp. 14–5.
27   Steinberg (1991), p. 11.
28   Steinberg (2002), pp. 819–20.
29   Cronon (1983), p. vii.
30   Whitney (1994), p. 8.
31   O'Connor (1997), pp. 29, 13.
32   White (1995b), p. x; White (1995a), p. 172.

The discussion about prioritising human and non-human agency leads directly to the debate usually understood as technocentrism versus eco-centrism. Technocentrism refers to the belief in society's ability to solve environmental problems; adherents to this belief tend to be reformist politically and tend to have faith in science and modern technology. By contrast, ecocentrism is often associated with the idea that natural systems are models for human societies; lack of faith in modern technology, 'deep ecology' views on humans' place within (not separate from) nature and a radical political agenda also characterise ecocentrism.[33]

Technocentrism and ecocentrism are certainly not 'hard, fast and mutu-ally exclusive categories', as each contains significant currents and counter-currents, grounded in historical debates.[34] Nevertheless, environmental histories should be interrogated on this issue, as one's position on this ide-ological debate may influence how studies are crafted, which sources are prioritised and how they are interpreted. One recent study, for example, argued that the past 5,000 years of human history could be considered to be 'human "macro parasitic" activity' similar to 'a malignant cellular process'.[35] Other ecocentric environmental historians have stressed the evils of science and technology. The author of an Australian environmen-tal history criticises the idea that 'science, technology and economic growth contained the capacity to provide permanent solutions to all gen-uine problems of life or thought, to all questions of human worth'.[36] Somewhat less broad is the argument that technological innovations of the twentieth century have 'lulled' society 'into thinking that nature can be dominated at will, seduced by our seemingly invincible ability to conquer the environment'.[37] Not all ecocentrist environmental historians, however, would argue that humans are parasites. Some simply argue that nature should provide a model for human behaviour and social formations. It fol-lows that the task of environmental history should be to '[help] people find again the coherence, pattern and integrity of nature, to help locate the realm of nature into which we can once more put our human history'.[38]

Situated on the other side of the debate, an openly 'anthropocentric' environmental historian admits that his book on the twentieth-century world omitted several instances of environmental changes 'simply because they have little to do with human history'.[39] A somewhat different version

33   This debate is best understood as a continuum of complex and often contradictory
       ideologies; see Pepper (1996).
34   *Ibid.*, p. 37.
35   Chew (2001), pp. 1, 173.
36   Lines (1991), p. 279.
37   Steinberg (1991), p. 271; see also Bevilacqua (2001, chapter 1; 2002).
38   Worster (1990a), p. 1147.
39   McNeill (2000), p. xxv.

of anthropocentrism is to accept that the human-modified landscape is not 'departure or degradation', but rather is 'a new environment, a new ecological system, that has been created and formed' as a 'new, hybrid landscape'.[40] Thus, on the one hand, environmental history may consider humans as parasites, whilst on the other, environmental change without humans is not part of environmental history at all.

The ecocentrism-technocentrism tension has real implications for writing environmental histories. A telling example comes from the Latin American literature, in the case of two books about the Brazilian Atlantic Forest. Before publishing *Broadax and Firebrand*, Warren Dean had argued that environmental 'externalities' and 'degradation' were 'the most consequential of human activities'; consequently, the role of environmental history was to 'dispel the hollow triumphalism of all former interpretation of our common and conflictive past'.[41] Later, Dean argued that forest history was invariably a history of 'exploitation and destruction' that 'reflects so strikingly [human] improvidence and parasitism'.[42] A few years later, another historian of the Brazilian Atlantic Forest emphasised 'utilisation' — 'poor' utilisation and 'overutilisation' — of the forest, arguing that environmental damage resulted from barriers to productive use.[43] In *Fruitless Trees*, which is firmly on the technocentric side of the continuum, Shawn Miller questions historical analysis guided by the ecocentric idea that 'non-human life has the same rights to life, liberty and habitat as humans'.[44] The ideological divide between Dean and Miller explains divergent interpretations of colonial forest policies implemented by the Portuguese in Brazil. For Dean, the policies were conservationist because they restricted access to forests; in Miller's view, *de jure* restrictions had the opposite effect because they prevented the development of a responsible timber industry and encouraged the poor use of forests.

Besides the axes of human and non-human agency, and the technocentrism-ecocentrism debate, other polemics guide and prioritise research in environmental history. One is the degree of involvement environmental history should display with respect to present-day concerns. By one account, an 'urgent sense of advocacy' informed environmental history since the early 1970s, as scholars felt an 'obligation to alert the public to the character and consequences of ecological devastation, historical and contemporary'.[45] Several scholars go beyond that and suggest that environmental history should identify when societies crossed 'fundamental

40 Fiege (1999), pp. 8–9.
41 Dean (1992), p. 13.
42 Dean (1995), pp. 5–6.
43 Miller (2000), p. 6.
44 *Ibid.*, p. 7.
45 Miller and Rothman (1997), p. xv.

thresholds' leading to present environmental crises.[46] Presentism also appears in accounts that show how today's environmental concerns have been present 'since time immemorial' and are not 'merely a newfound goal of twentieth-century environmentalists'.[47]

Other environmental historians are less comfortable with presentism. Environmental history's 'moral concern' comes in for criticism for its 'tendency to produce precautionary tales' and suggesting that 'only a miracle has preserved life on this planet, and that all environmental change has been for the worse'.[48] A critic of the 'doomsday' approach of 'post-Earth Day environmental histories' has implicated their 'single-minded focus on human folly' that 'runs the risk of creating a biased view of history'.[49] Other critics argue that presentist environmental history searches for past 'success stories', when in fact 'there is no golden age, pre-capitalist, pre-Christian or pre-historic, to return to'.[50] Yet another scholar takes pride in rooting out examples of the 'Apocalypse Then' scholars who support the idea that 'humans went wrong from the Neolithic revolution onwards'— especially agriculture, which 'started the dry rot of the world'— and for whom 'ecological degradation explains almost everything'.[51] Pulitzer-prize winning scholar Jared Diamond uses the environmental history of past civilisations to argue that environmental 'stress' and 'overpopulation' are causes of terrorism.[52]

What are the practical implications of presentism in environmental history? In Latin America, one key issue is the degree to which past knowledge of indigenous land uses should inform present agricultural policies. In the early 1990s, evidence from lake-core sediments in Michoacán, Mexico, revealed high levels of soil erosion prior to the arrival of Spaniards. The study's authors concluded that pre-European agriculture would not 'solve the problem of environmental degradation', while a sympathetic commentator went on to dismiss the use of indigenous agriculture as 'an ideal norm for the future'.[53] Other scholars of indigenous agriculture, however, have been more enthusiastic about interpreting past indigenous agriculture. A rather extreme view is that past indigenous

---

46   Pfister and Brimblecombe (1990), p. 1; see also Bevilacqua (1998).
47   Zupko and Laures (1996), p. 8.
48   White (1990), pp. 1114–6.
49   Whitney (1994), pp. 3, 337.
50   Smout (2000), pp. 3–4.
51   MacKenzie (1997), p. 7. In White's (2001, p. 105) view, the lustre of 'Whiggish' and 'declensionist' environmental history has faded recently, as scholars have become more 'sympathetic' to agricultural and urban landscapes.
52   Diamond (2003), pp. 44–5.
53   O'Hara, Street-Perrot and Burt (1993), p. 50; Butzer (1993), p. 17. Other studies relevant to the debate include Butzer and Butzer (1997); Endfield and O'Hara (1999); Melville (1994); and Whitmore and Turner (2002).

resource uses are 'footprints' that might become 'a blueprint for the future'.[54] More balanced is the idea that knowledge of indigenous agriculture is essential to reach 'a compromise between the general sustainability' of indigenous systems and the 'high productivity objective' of modern agriculture.[55] Indeed, the inspiration for much research on past agricultural systems, or on present-day indigenous peoples thought to use relatively unchanged agricultural practices, may be found in a concern for improving agricultural productivity whilst avoiding modern chemical and fossil-fuel inputs.

Presentism in environmental history is closely related to the imperative of being 'useful' to public policy debates. Several environmental historians are enthusiastic about the field becoming tightly connected to public policy concerns, effectively overwhelming Cronon's suggestion to only 'offer parables about how to interpret what may happen' with regard to human-environment relations.[56] Enthusiasts claim that 'the future prosperity and vibrancy of environmental history' is contingent upon the field's 'explicit purchase on important policy questions'.[57] Responding to the need to guide environmental history along 'useful' conceptual lines, the proposed 'organisational' approach would be the means to create an 'applied' field.[58] Indeed, several environmental histories are useful to policy debates. Forest policies for the northeastern USA 'must develop from an understanding and consideration' of forest history.[59] The history of the destruction of the Atlantic Forest is a warning against decimating Amazonian forests.[60] Recent historical research in African environments vigorously challenges the 'received wisdoms' and 'environmental crisis narratives' that support public policies.[61]

In summary, environmental history has used new geographical scales that frequently cross political boundaries. Environmental historians utilise myriad sources of evidence, ranging from written sources to field-based measures of the environment itself. However, the field's most contentious aspects regard the rather simple question of nature in environmental history. In particular, there is significant discussion on whether the field should stress human or non-human agency. Environmental historians are not removed from tensions between ecocentric and technocentric ideolo-

---

54　Lentz (2000), p. 504. Less strident claims may be found in recent studies of pre-Columbian fish weirs and ponds in lowland Bolivia (Erickson, 2000) and agricultural land uses in Brazil's Upper Xingu (Heckenberger et al., 2003).
55　Denevan (2001), pp. 305–6.
56　Cronon (1993), p. 17.
57　Dovers (2000a), p. 131; see also Dovers's (2000b, p. 13) criticism of 'policy *ad hocery* and amnesia'.
58　Uekoetter (1998), p. 40.
59　O'Keefe and Foster (1998), p. 19; Foster (2002).
60　Dean (1995), pp. 6, 364.
61　Leach and Mearns (1996); Bassett and Crummey (2003).

gies, which inevitably influence how research problems are framed and pursued. Finally, environmental historians have strong views on how 'useful' the field should be to present-day issues and the desired relevance of environmental history to public policy debates. It is against this background that the studies of Latin America's nineteenth- and twentieth-century environmental history in this volume are framed.

Territories, Commodities, Knowledges: a Research Framework

A common concern of most chapters is the focus on export commodities, a traditional field of historical research in Latin American studies. To present Latin American environmental history to an academic audience familiar with political, social or economic history — which prevails in the analysis of such a topic — may prove a difficult task. Resistance to conceptualising the environment as 'co-operative partner'[62] in shaping historical processes often has been quite strong. Social or political historians sometimes feel uncomfortable when facing methodologies foreign to their classic tool kit, such as radiocarbon dating of sediments or pH levels in soils to evaluate environmental changes. But there is one field of research where Latin Americanists may easily grasp the capability of environmental history to produce original results, deeper understanding and new stimulating questions: Latin America's nineteenth- and twentieth-century export economies.

Although export commodities have long been important to Latin American studies, the environment has rarely been investigated as an important actor or variable. Instead, it usually plays the role of passive backdrop or undifferentiated stage upon which historical events occur. This is surprising because natural resources are the very object of these narratives. A significant example of the marginal role of the environment is the recent and otherwise very insightful *Second Conquest of Latin America*, which is entirely devoted to a reappraisal of the export boom (1850–1930) through the cases of oil, henequen and coffee.[63] Although nature is indisputably a powerful force in making these products available for exploitation, determining the need for technological innovations and influencing cost of extraction or production,[64] environmental matters are limited to framing remarks rarely connected to the argument. In fact, in *Second Conquest* environmental issues are conceived neither as interpretative tools nor as potential sources for a new glimpse of a familiar topic.

---

62   Bevilacqua (1996), p. 9.
63   Topik and Wells (1998).
64   This is not intended as an exhaustive list of questions raised by an environmental history perspective.

An important task of Latin American environmental history, therefore, is to open a category of analysis previously hardly explored. Coffee, cocoa, beef, sugar, wheat, henequen, bananas, rubber, guano, nitrates, copper, petroleum, gold and timber and other extractive and agricultural resources that Latin America exported have their own history.[65] They are not separate histories, but are interrelated with territorial expansion and knowledge appropriation, in addition to the better-known history of states, workers, economies, institutions, infrastructure and technologies. However, focusing on export commodities should not be a goal unto itself; rather, it should be instrumental to understanding two deeper questions regarding the territorial and environmental aspects of commodity production.

First, it is imperative to study the degree to which territories and their environments determined the form, period and possibilities of extractivism and agro-exports. In this book, Offen takes up this issue with regard to eastern Nicaragua, showing the environmental limits on the ability of outside actors to exploit resources. Similarly, Soluri details the different US and British responses to banana diseases, while Wilcox's chapter indicates how the *cerrado* of central Brazil limited the suitability of European cattle and favoured South Asian Zebu cattle.

A second question refers to the environmental impacts of integration of territories and their environments into world markets, including both material and cognitive transformations of nature. Several chapters in this book support the importance of studying material and perceptual transformations. Offen's chapter stresses the importance of geographical imaginations in shaping resource economies of eastern Nicaragua. Kozloff's chapter studies the effects of the Venezuelan oil boom on one Lake Maracaibo village, Lagunillas. Funes's chapter details the deforestation of Cuba's centre-eastern forests by large sugarcane mills. Tortolero's chapter indicates how private firms undertook lake drainage in central Mexico. Soluri discusses 'shifting plantation agriculture' as a strategy of US firms in Central America to avoid pathogens. Bell's paper focuses on the role of a prominent individual in exchanging biological materials.

In addressing these two questions, environmental histories can count on several advantages over more conventional approaches. On a pragmatic level, the vast (and diverse) historiography helps frame local topics in broader perspectives.[66] This is important to escape the risk of writing ster-

65 For a synthesis of mining, see Dore (2000); for the Amazon rubber boom (1860–1920), see Dean (1987); Weinstein (1983); Barham and Coomes (1996); Stanfield (1998); for cattle ranching, see Amaral (1998); Bell (1998); Zarrilli (2001); González (2001); Williams (1986); Wilcox (this volume); for bananas, see Marquardt (2001; 2002); and Soluri (this volume); for Cuban sugarcane, see Dye (1998); Díaz-Briquets and Pérez-López (2000); Funes (this volume).

66 To cite only two influential books, see Bulmer-Thomas (1994) and Cardoso and Pérez Brignoli (1981).

ile microhistories unable to contribute to a deeper understanding of the changing relations of human societies and the environment.[67] And the very nature of the topic, that is, exporting natural resources, means that the existing literature provides basic environmental information, although more detailed data are less abundant than the large literature would suggest.

Many types of sources are useful to an environmental history of export commodities, such as custom registers, diplomatic reports, commercial records of shipping companies and statistics compiled by trading houses. Authors in this book make creative use of diplomatic correspondence (Offen), personal letters (Bell), agronomic-zoological literature (Funes; Wilcox), botanical papers (Soluri) and local archives (Gallini; Kozloff; Tortolero; Brannstrom). The sources for environmental history thus reveal another aspect of our research framework: export economies (or the willingness to foster them) prompted the fledging Latin American states to build scientific institutions and infrastructure for gathering environmental knowledge. Numerous national or regional bureaucracies produced environmental knowledge required to assist policy makers and supported institutes for agricultural development, geographical and geological survey, meteorological forecasting and the census, among others.[68] Thus, the 'commodity lottery' influenced not only the relative position of the exporting countries in the world economy,[69] but also the realistic chances of doing environmental history by creating a paper trail with relevant information.

Another advantage is apparent at a broader theoretical level. To focus on the nineteenth- and twentieth-century increase in export commodities in Latin America is quite pertinent for scholars convinced that the rise of capitalist mode of production in Latin America — generally coinciding with export economies — was a driving force of modern environmental change.[70] To this extent environmental history might refresh the longstanding but rather stagnant debate about capitalism in Latin America and US imperialism, as well as a newer claim regarding the role of US consumers in affecting the environment in other countries. A promising beginning point for in-depth research is Richard Tucker's argument that 'the steaming mugs on American breakfast tables were connected with the machetes and hoes' that cleared land in the Andes for coffee. Similarly, the US coffee habit was 'key to the ecological transformation' in late-nineteenth-century southern Brazil. Not limiting his argument to forested envi-

---

67   This is Radkau's warning (Radkau, 1993, pp. 128–9). The reference to microhistory should not be interpreted as underestimation of such an approach. Carlo Ginzburg (1980) has convincingly shown the kind of universal knowledge that a microhistory is able to produce.

68   Restrepo (1984); Dean (1989); McCook (2002); Eakin (1999).

69   Bulmer-Thomas (1994), p. 15.

70   See Melville (1997); Tucker (2000); McNeill (2000).

ronments, Tucker also claims that US beef demand in Mexico's 'fragile northern drylands' had 'significant long-range ecological consequences'.[71]

Amongst the advantages of environmental history in pursuing a territories-commodities-knowledges framework also lies a danger. Collaboration with a well-established historiography might lead to the assumption that periods, actors and questions meaningful in economic or political history are pertinent to environmental history. Italian historian Piero Bevilacqua argues that the classic European historical watersheds, such as 1945, do not seem to carry the same significance for European environmental history.[72] The same concern is relevant to Latin America. Until solid empirical research is carried out, there is insufficient reason to assume that traditional time frames (i.e., independence from Spain), actors (i.e., peasants, urban residents or women) and questions (i.e., Latin America's failure to pursue sustained and just development) are necessarily meaningful to Latin American environmental history.[73]

Territories: States, Peoples, Environments

In many regions of Latin America, the nineteenth and twentieth centuries were dominated by territorial struggles between nation-states and indigenous peoples, with conflicts usually focusing on access to environmental resources. The first three chapters in this book explore different aspects of this issue. Offen's chapter focuses on the content and the effects of nineteenth- and twentieth-century elite discourses about people and environments of the Mosquitia of eastern Nicaragua. At least two ironies permeated Mosquitia's environmental history. Not only did the imperative of the weak Nicaraguan state to 'incorporate' Mosquitia depend on significant capital investment by foreigners, but the discourses meant to encourage foreign investment necessarily overlooked basic environmental limitations to export-based resource economies. In addition, the 'geographical imagination' about natural resources and ethnicities in Mosquitia encouraged the development of gold, rubber and mahogany extraction, which in turn produced various environmental impacts.

Gallini's chapter re-appraises the impact of coffee expansion and Liberal reforms on indigenous land and communities in Guatemala by

71 Tucker (2000), pp. 209, 188, 309; see also Dore's (2000, pp. 6, 20–2) argument that less 'human immiseration' in Latin America's mining industry has been associated with 'massive environmental destruction'. Important works on consumption include Mintz (1985), Jiménez (1995) and Soluri (this volume).

72 Bevilacqua (2001), p. 77.

73 At the same time, it may not be particularly useful to frame Latin American environmental history in the evolutionary model outlined by Castro Herrera (1994). Theoretically, Gadgil and Guha's (1993, pp. 49–53) modes of production/modes of resource use is very promising, but then they tend to apply it in the same way as the former.

focusing on the case of a Maya-Mam community and the increasing appetite of regional elites over the indigenous agro-ecosystem. The chapter concludes that the multi-causal process of ecological marginalisation of the indigenous community was a key factor in depleting its economic and political complexity. The concluding remarks suggest turning attention to the ecological assessment of land loss, rather than quantification, whilst assessing the impact of export commodities and nation-state expansion over indigenous actors. Territory is also at the centre of Kozloff's chapter, which recounts the story of a town on the shores of Lake Maracaibo, Venezuela, that had the misfortune of being located above the country's premier hydrocarbon basin. In response to catastrophic explosions, political elites advanced ideas including moving the entire village and improving environmental regulation of the petroleum industry.

Commodities: Export Booms and the Environment

The next three chapters explore environmental aspects of Latin America's nineteenth- and twentieth-century export booms. Amongst numerous potential cases three are addressed. Funes's chapter details the massive expansion of Cuba's sugar industry following the establishment of US military government in Cuba, which caused rapid destruction of forests in Camagüey, east-central Cuba. Much land cleared for sugarcane eventually proved unsuitable and an aggressive African quickly shrub spread over the region's former sugarcane fields.

The case of the forest-savanna region of south-eastern Brazil, presented by Brannstrom, reveals the environmental impact of cotton and soybean production during the twentieth century. The issue raised here is how to measure the impact of destructive land uses by comparing evidence presented by vegetation and sedimentation. Emerging from the case study is the question of how different types of environmental history support competing public policy models for the environment.

Tortolero's chapter relates the export boom in Porfirian Mexico to central Mexico's waterscape — its lakes and wetlands. Foreign investors, equipped with modernist ideologies, drained numerous shallow lakes, which were prized not only for their fertile soils but also for supply of irrigation water and potential role in improving urban health. Several businesses were established to take advantage of the *Porfiriato*'s imperative for water control. As Tortolero suggests, thousands of displaced peasants were eager recruits in the revolutionary movement that would transform Mexico in the early twentieth century.

Knowledges: New Technologies and Organisms

The final three chapters focus on the technologies and biological introductions of the nineteenth and twentieth centuries. A common theme in these chapters is the development of scientific institutions, within and outside the state, that helped adopt exogenous technologies and exotic organisms to new contexts. In particular, agencies for public health and agriculture began to develop a significant presence in Latin America during the late nineteenth century, and were significant in identifying and responding to environmental concerns.[74]

Wilcox centres his analysis on how South Asian Zebu cattle came to dominate ranches in the central Brazilian savanna (*cerrado*). Frequently criticised by supporters of European breeds, Zebu proved extraordinarily well suited to the region's climate and ranching practices. As Zebu became more common, so did Zebu's many 'elbows', such as exotic forage and wire fencing. Significantly, Brazilian ranchers not only relied on Zebu for colonising Amazon rainforest regions in the 1970s, but also exported Zebu to other Latin American countries.

Soluri identifies how US and UK banana interests pursued two fundamentally different strategies for coping with banana diseases. US firms, which owned vast areas of coastal Central American floodplains, opted to abandon infected fields or pursue a 'flood-fallow' system. This 'shifting plantation agriculture' contrasted with the UK strategy for Caribbean islands, where land was much less abundant. UK scientists went on extended collecting trips to find resistant germplasm that could offer disease protection to commercially cultivated bananas.

In Bell's chapter, the issue of knowledge is approached quite differently. The analysis evaluates the work of a single individual, the eminent French botanist Aimé Bonpland, who had a long career in southern South America. After participating in Alexander von Humboldt's famous travels in equatorial America, Bonpland was influential in translating and shipping biota to European colleagues, and for his role in introducing European plants into South America.

Themes for Future Research

Certainly, there are several issues that this book does not explore. These include urbanisation, industrialisation, resistance to environmental transformations, social and historical dimensions of 'natural' disasters, environmental public policies and environmental perceptions. Twentieth-century urbanisation and industrialisation should be high on the agenda of the region's environmental history. The growth of cities affected not only the surrounding

---

74   McCook (2001); Eakin (1999).

environment (food, water, fuel, construction materials and land), but created several urban environmental issues, such as water and air pollution, traffic congestion and transport improvements. Unlike the stereotype of Latin America being dominated by mega-cities, such as Mexico City and São Paulo, these concerns also apply to more numerous medium-sized cities. Despite a rich tradition of urban history, the environmental history of Latin American cities is poorly understood.[75] Although there is significant work on present-day urban environmental issues,[76] few historical studies have used the 'ecological footprint' concept to study the reliance of cities on their resource hinterlands for provision of food, water, fuel and construction material.[77] In Europe and North America several studies indicate the promise of urban environmental history.[78] As one historian noted, 'A society may be characterised by the contents of its drains, water-closets, grave yards or chimneys.'[79] Recent studies have focused on pollutants, such as DDT, and issues of water supply, sewage disposal, industrial waste disposal and solid waste removal in US cities.[80]

How did people respond to appropriation of their environmental resources by the state or individual capitalists? Although this question has not been thoroughly explored in environmental history of Latin America, other literatures emphasise the power of individual agency and collective identity, suggesting that local actors are actively involved in struggles over resources.[81] In South Asian environmental history, where the forest bureaucracy of the colonial state controlled nearly one-quarter of the subcontinent's territory, the issue of resistance dominates the literature. Histories of environmental resources are intimately linked with the power to determine which groups had access to resources.[82] Similarly, African environmental history is 'essentially corrective and anti-colonial' in approach, often emphasising 'African initiative in the face of European conquest and capitalist exploitation'.[83] Latin American historiography is rich in references to indigenous resistance, women's struggles, labour movements and political conflict. Environmental history of the region would enrich its understanding by tackling these issues.[84]

75   Exceptions include Lipsett-Rivera (1993); González (1999); Dussel and Herrera (1999); Musset (1999).
76   Hardoy, Mitlin and Satterthwaite (1992); Pezzoli (1998); Ezcurra et al. (1999).
77   Constanza (2000); Wackernagel (1998).
78   Luckin (1986); Gandy (2002); Davis (1998); Brechin (1999); Hays (1998, pp. 69–100; 2001).
79   Brimblecombe (1987), p. 1.
80   Dunlap (1981); Sheail (1985); Russell (2001); Tarr (1996); Colten and Skinner (1996).
81   For example, see Peluso and Watts (2001).
82   Gadgil and Guha (1993); Rangarajan (1996); Grove, Damodaran and Sangwan (1998); Arnold and Guha (1995); Sivaramakrishnan (1999).
83   Beinart (2000), p. 270; Beinart and McGregor (2003); Dovers, Edgecombe and Guest (2003).
84   A promising beginning is Lindsay-Poland's (2003) environmental analysis of the US military presence in Panama and insights in Martinez-Alier (1991).

Although several chapters discuss policies (Funes; Offen; Gallini; Wilcox; Brannstrom; Tortolero), we do not provide in-depth analysis of nineteenth- and twentieth-century environmental (or environment-related) polices. Certainly, several recent studies of Latin American environmental history include policies as one important variable. Colonial Portuguese policies for the Brazilian Atlantic Forest are a case in point, with Dean's conservationist interpretation contrasting with Miller's characterisation as destructive.[85] South Asian and African studies often focus on colonial policies directed toward forest and soil resources.[86] Similarly, studies in Latin America could make past policies the explicit focus of analysis. Perhaps scholars could draw on studies of contemporary environmental policies that stress political economy, competing models or discursive strategies.[87]

Notwithstanding the frequency of their occurrence and the seriousness of their social and environmental consequences, natural catastrophes and disasters remain outside the focus of this book. In Latin America, scholars have studied severe natural disasters occurred during the colonial period,[88] emphasising social or economic phenomena embedded in events usually portrayed as products of nature. Recently, scholars have studied hurricanes in Cuba and El Niño's many implications.[89] The topic is both important and accessible in terms of primary sources and should be included in the future agenda of Latin American environmental history. This would require transforming events such as volcanic eruptions, earthquakes, hurricanes and climate phenomena such as El Niño into historical subjects that permit analysis of the relations amongst people, power and the environment.

Finally, a significant issue we address only partially is that of environmental perceptions. How did people understand and represent environments? Why did perceptions change? This question has motivated significant studies focusing on European ideas toward nature.[90] In Latin America, studies of European ideas on New World nature and elite perceptions of water in colonial Mexico, the Brazilian Pantanal and slave-holding-environmental relationships in Brazil have begun to build a fascinating literature.[91] In this volume, the question of environmental perception is an underlying aspect of several chapters. In Offen's chapter, we see how perceptions guided territorial expansion in eastern Nicaragua. Gallini discusses how Guatemalan elites and foreigners constructed an idyllic

---

85   Dean (1995); Miller (2000).
86   Beinart (2000); Beinart and McGregor (2003); Grove, Damodaran and Sangwan (1998); Arnold and Guha (1995); Dovers, Edgecombe and Guest (2003).
87   Silva (1997); Hajer (1995).
88   García Acosta (1996).
89   Pérez (2001); Caviedes (2001); Davis (2001).
90   Glacken (1967); Coates (1998).
91   Costa (1999); Musset (1999); Pádua (2002); Gerbi (1985); Stepan (2001).

notion of Guatemala's Costa Cuca that poorly represented the region's environment, but well suited the idea that coffee was a 'natural' fit to the region. In Tortolero's chapter, we find that the idea of wetlands as unhealthy places was a critical aspect of the *Porfiriato*'s drainage stratagem. Much of Wilcox's paper details the development of ideas that favoured European or South Asian cattle breeds to be the 'Brazilian' cattle breed.

Prospects

The suggested territories-commodities-knowledges research framework focuses on the inter-related phenomena that transformed Latin America's diverse lands and peoples during the nineteenth and twentieth centuries. The framework draws attention to the territorial aspects of state consolidation, the commodities that supported new states and the knowledges that buttressed both territorial expansion and commodity production. We recognise, however, that important issues remain outside this framework. For example, urbanisation and industrialisation had dramatic environmental effects in Latin America, especially after the Second World War. A synthesis of these phenomena requires many detailed case studies before a broader picture may emerge.

Our operational definitions of environmental history are drawn mainly from literatures outside Latin America. This is intended to enrich and inform Latin American studies of environmental history, rather than to determine its trajectory. Issues such as one's ideas about 'nature' are present, implicitly or explicitly, in environmental histories. Placing these debates in the open encourages discussion about how ideologies of nature-society relations influence scholarship. It is with this broad notion of environmental history in mind that we hope to encourage interdisciplinary collaboration amongst scholars interested in the many promising areas for future research in Latin America.

PART I

Territories: States, People, Environments

CHAPTER 1

A Maya Mam Agro-ecosystem in Guatemala's Coffee Revolution: Costa Cuca, 1830s–1880s*

Stefania Gallini

Introduction

The environmental history of nineteenth-century export commodities allows scholars to move away from the idea of environment as a backdrop and towards the study of how agro-ecosystems influenced export regimes and how export regimes influenced the environment. The historian David McCreery showed how 'from the 1850s, and at an increasing rate in the 1860s, the new export crop of coffee revolutionised the countryside of Guatemala'. What was the role of Guatemalan agro-ecosystems in designing the export regime, and how did the latter influence the former? The process called 'the coffee revolution' after McCreery's seminal and comprehensive work is re-examined here through the lens of the environment and the Maya–Mam community in south-western Guatemala where the revolution first took place. The essay should be seen as an exercise in what environmental history might bring to the robust Latin American coffee historiography, which has granted only marginal importance to the environment in shaping the very diverse local histories of coffee production.[1] When some ecological concerns are displayed, they often 'map the geographical extension of coffee cultivation' and predict timing and quantity of the required labour force.[2] A few paragraphs about the ecological requirements of *Coffea arabica* are also frequently included, as well as some words on its African origin. Nevertheless, this information tends to have a flavour of erudition, rather than being an analytical tool. Confined to a descriptive function, it is not clear how the few scattered environmental data contribute to the interpretation of coffee's history.

* The author is grateful to the Bogliasco Foundation for a residential fellowship which allowed her to work on the manuscript leading to this chapter. Sincere thanks also to René Reeves, Greg Grandin, Oscar Horst, Arturo Taracena, Chris Lutz, Ana Carla Ericastilla, Ana Tobar and Christian Brannstrom for their generous help at different stages of the research. I greatly benefited from the comments of the participants in the Workshop on Latin American Environmental History held in London in November 2001.

1 This concern is expressed in Topik's comprehensive review of coffee historiography in Latin America: 'historical coffee studies continue to be anthropocentric with little concern for coffee's ecological consequences' (Topik 2000, p. 254). Exceptions apply; see Dean (1995); Secreto (2000); Brannstrom (2000).

2 Williams (1994), p. 11.

William Roseberry, who gave a taste of an environmental history of coffee in a brief article,[3] addressed a number of potential paths to be explored in his co-edited book *Coffee, Society, and Power in Latin America*. However, since the focus of the book was on labour relations, state building and competing 'fields of power', environmentally rich themes such as 'the new (coffee) forests', changing land use and property and the frontier character of many coffee regions remained largely unexplored.[4] The same might be claimed for regional histories, although the scale of nuances of environmental disregard varies, ranging from a one-line reference in Palacios's classic book on Colombia to Yarrington's more concerned contribution on Venezuela.[5] Central America has pillars of more integral explorations of its coffee histories in Hall's historical geography of Costa Rica and Samper's attention to the history of agrarian science and coffee technology.[6] Nevertheless, the literature in Guatemala has hardly followed this promising path and the environment is generally considered only as much as it helps frame political, economic or socio-ethnic concerns.[7]

Environmental history might contribute to understanding the complexity of coffee as a milestone issue in modern Guatemala. The post-1870 Liberal regime and coffee expansion in the last third of the nineteenth century are usually considered historical watersheds for *ladinos*[8] and Indians alike. According to a conventional understanding, the Liberal government encouraged the expansion of coffee plantations and their economic and political reforms dragged the country into modernity. The financial system, urban development, banks, ports, roads, rationalism, secularisation and virtually every aspect of what was believed to represent modern life were the product of Liberal reforms and the chain of events stimulated by the coffee economy. These also produced a deep impact in indigenous peoples' lives. McCreery's work sets the standard view of this topic. He convincingly rejects as mythological oversimplification the common assumption that the Liberal Reform abolished village *ejidos*,[9] and that coffee was responsible for widespread losses of land by highland communities. He argues that the impact of coffee and the liberal reforms on land tenure was threefold: many *pueblos* increased their grip on common land they possessed and used near to the village. Other communities had to give

3   Roseberry (1991).
4   Roseberry (1995).
5   Palacios (1983), p. 178; Yarrington (1997), pp. 129–33.
6   Hall (1982); Samper (1994).
7   Besides McCreery's (1994) extensive work, classic references include Castellanos Cambranes (1996); Acuña Ortega (1994); Cardoso (1975); and Dominguez (1977).
8   *Ladino* is the Guatemalan term for *mestizo* in both biological and cultural senses.
9   *Ejido* is common land granted by law to any village. *Ejidos* included common agricultural plots, woodlands and pastures; they were inalienable and to be administered by the local Indian officials.

up broad and poorly defined claims to land and defend reduced — but clearly identified and titled — landholdings. Thirdly, highland villages suffered net land loss as a result of the shift to large-scale coffee production in the 1870s and 1880s, but even so, it was a more gradual and complex process than the term 'abolition of *ejidos*' suggests.[10]

Figure 1.1: The Agro-ecosystem of San Martín Sacatepéquez, South-western Guatemala, before the Coffee Boom

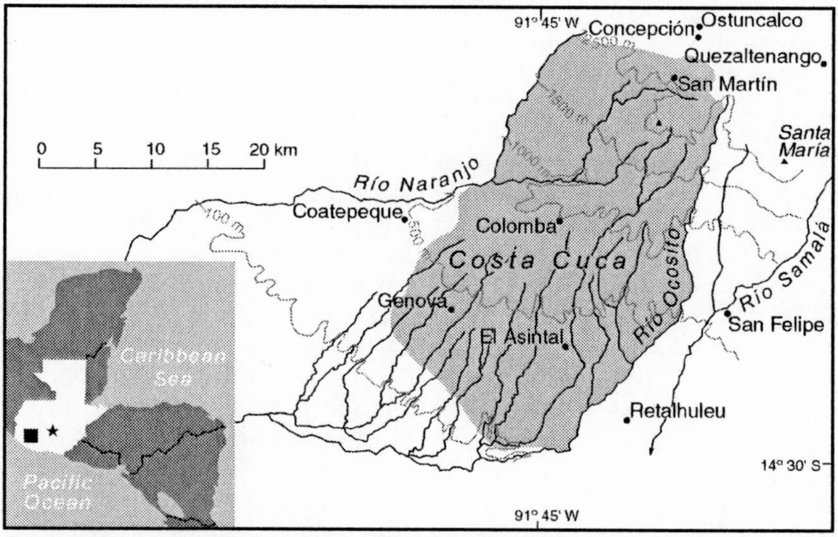

Base map from the Instituto Geográfico Nacional of Guatemala, Quezaltenango (map ND 15-7 series E503), original scale 1:250,000.

This chapter argues that looking for massive indigenous land loss at or around the beginning of the large-scale coffee plantation era (after 1873–74) is a misleading approach to appreciate the depletion of indigenous resource bases and the socio-ethnic impact of coffee. Land loss may be better understood as ecological marginalisation, which undermined the very basis of survival of the indigenous pueblos as autonomous and economically complex communities. Ecological displacement meant the loss of access to complementary patches of an indigenous agro-ecosystem. In this respect, the spread of coffee plantations along with liberal reforms consolidated a phenomenon that had started in the 1830s and accelerated after the mid-1850s rather than beginning in the 1870s. The phenomenon was the crumbling of economic complexity based on controlling south-western Guatemalan ecological heterogeneity. The time shift from the conventional emphasis on post 1871 —

10   McCreery (1994), pp. 243–53.

the beginning of the Liberal era — to the 1830s suggests that other dynamics will be stressed as relevant. The expansion of coffee made it impossible for Indian communities to overturn changes that had been underway for nearly 40 years.

These conclusions are suggested by studying the case of San Martín Sacatepéquez, a Maya-Mam village standing 2,670 metres above sea level, just above the edge between highland and lowland in the Department of Quezaltenango, south-western Guatemala (see Figure 1.1). This chapter will sketch the story of how the Costa Cuca, a portion of the Pacific piedmont which turned into the first and most successful coffee-producing region in the 1870s and 1880s, had been 'constructed' on the agro-ecosystem of San Martín since the 1830s.

The Agro-ecosystem of San Martín and its Legal Titles

Societies in landscapes with extreme elevation gradients often develop sophisticated and creative techniques to take advantage of ecological complexities.[11] The Mam village of San Martín Sacatepéquez relied on the resource complementarity granted by having access to both highland and the Pacific lowland environments (Figure 1.1). This interaction had two strategic goals. First, it was vital from an agro-economic perspective, as stated for highland Mayan *pueblos* in general by anthropologist Shelton Davis.[12] The resources obtained from lowlands included cacao, sugar cane, maize (*milpa de segunda*), fruit, flowers, seasonal pastures, chile, cotton, salt, straw and timber for construction. Such resource complementarity was the product of the ecological diversity of the Bocacosta (the piedmont belt between 100 and 1,500 metres), which also provided other advantages if well managed. Mayan peasants practised shifting cultivation, for which they required vast area. In tropical environments, dispersion worked as the best insurance against epidemics of pests and diseases, but it also allowed exploitation of a variety of microclimates and land with diverse soil composition.[13] By retaining control of many different microenvironments throughout the piedmont and the coast, indigenous peasants multiplied their chances to respond successfully to ecological hazards. At the base of such a prosper-

11   The Andean model of the vertical archipelago, first outlined by John Murra, is possibly the most outstanding example. Some scholars have attempted to apply Murra's model to Guatemalan history: see Zamora Acosta (1979; 1985, pp. 352–53); Carrasco (1979). In archaeology, the notion of highland-lowland interaction is widely accepted: see Miller (1983); Sabloff and Henderson (1993). For Cunill, the question of how Americans reacted to environmental and geographical constraints of the continent is an issue in environmental history (Cunil, 1999).

12   Davis (1970, p. 17) claims that highland villages would have been simply unable to secure their own survival without having access to the pool of resources in the lowland.

13   See Levi (1996), pp. 94–8.

ous land control was precise knowledge of the topography of the Pacific slopes, the patchwork-type soil composition, the seasonal climatic fluctuations and the uneven vulnerability of crops to pests and diseases.

The second reason to secure access to the lowlands was to exploit its role as ecological buffer. Demographic growth by the end of the seventeenth century was absorbed by recovering extinguished or much reduced villages in the lowland, as confirmed also by the lack of compelling evidence of significant demographic pressure on the highlands at least until the late nineteenth century. Besides offering a demographic escape, the lowlands were important as ecological shelter in case of exceptional natural disasters or ordinary agricultural losses. Devastating volcanic activity and earthquakes were (and are) permanent threats in south-western Guatemala. In 1902, for instance, a large explosive eruption of Santa María volcano, just south of Quezaltenango, spewed ten cubic kilometres of dacite in 36 hours and deposited debris of almost entirely pumice over a vast area north-west of the volcano.[14] To escape the immediate catastrophe and the painful material recovery afterwards, people from San Martín moved downward along their traditional path to the lowland, and resettled in Taltut (363 metres), one of the more distant places of the coastal frontier in Mam territory.[15]

Poor agricultural harvests were less extreme but more frequent. In these cases access to the lowlands proved vital to the survival of the highland economy as a whole. State and religious authorities were well aware of the crucial link. In 1861, after heavy and devastating rain in the Department of Quezaltenango, the *corregidor* ordered the Indian villages to:

> Begin planting communal lands in maize and other crops suited to hot regions [*terrenos cálidos*] where they will be able to cultivate, as it is not possible in cold climates [*climas fríos*], thus using September for a second cropping season, whose harvest will be transported when possible to cold regions [*lugares fríos*] to be stored and prevent shortages and want that may occur.[16]

Maize from the coast was especially important. Although it is not as nutritionally rich as highland maize, lowland maize had a shorter cycle that permitted two or even three harvests annually, becoming available when grain was becoming scarce in the highlands.[17]

Given these advantages, highland-lowland interaction was a rational choice for indigenous communities who relied on shifting cultivation and

---

14   Williams and Self (1983); for a historical account, see Horst (1995).
15   In 1920 Taltut became what is now known as Génova, a middle town of the Costa Cuca.
16   Archivo General de Centroamerica (hereafter AGCA) B leg. 28583 exp. 41.
17   McBryde (1969), vol. 1, pp. 83–90.

UNIVERSITY OF WINCHESTER
LIBRARY

small-scale trade, and were settled at the edge of the ecological border between the two macro-environmental zones. It is little surprise, then, that various primary sources indicate the existence of a large agro-ecosystem managed by the Mam people of San Martín, comprising the highland area — where the village was located — and a vast lowland area that the village controlled. A review of some of the archival and archaeological evidence will clarify this point.

Evidence of the long presence of a complex agricultural society in the Pacific lowland is provided by the reports of the Intercontinental Railway Commission, who crossed the region while surveying a line for the railway in 1891–93. They reported clay heads, big stone sculptures, signals of Mayan ancient cemeteries scattered along the Pacific coast, including sites in the Costa Cuca.[18] This suggests that the ecosystem of the Pacific slopes had been early transformed into an agro-ecosystem.[19] In addition, the *Título Mam*, a unique Mayan document of the time of the Conquest, proves that Mam people were to be responsible for such a transformation as they originally controlled the Bocacosta. The *Título Mam* is a claim written in 1583 by Mam elders from Ostuncalco, the *pueblo cabecera* of the Mam communities of the Department of Quezaltenango, and presented to the Spanish *audiencia* as evidence in a land dispute against the K'iché of Quezaltenango.[20] It provides a valuable description of political boundaries between the expansionist K'iché and the displaced Mam. The Mam claimed they once possessed the whole region intersected by the Samalá River, but were later reduced in their territorial holdings by the K'iché expansion toward the Pacific coast. The colonial authorities legalised the new situation, with the effect of crystallising it.[21] In fact, by 1572 Quezaltenango appeared to hold an important cacao colony in what had previously been Mam land.[22]

The *encomienda* system implemented by the Spaniards further contributed to immobilising both Mam resettlement and Mam–K'iché (dis)equilibrium of power. Ostuncalco and the nearby Mam town San Pedro Sacatepéquez (and the territory they controlled) were granted to Alvarado's relative

18 Intercontinental Railway Commission (1898), p. 404. The engineers did not investigate their findings, and by the time archaeologist and geographer Franz Termer studied the area some decades later, the reported pieces disappeared or had been destroyed or unavailable (Termer, 1939, p. 26).

19 This conclusion is driven also by the evidence provided by archaeological findings in Salinas La Blanca and La Victoria, closer to the Mexican border; see Coe and Flannery (1967).

20 First published by Crespo (1956), it was later named *Título Mam* by Carmack (1973, p. 68). The document is part of a longer one, which is in AGCA A1, leg. 5987, exp. 52660. The transcription is also published in Hostnig (1997, pp. 255–68), without noting that it contains the *Título Mam*.

21 Hostnig (1997), p. 256.

22 Feldman (1992) p. 52.

Francisco de la Cueva, who became the largest *encomendero* of the Audiencia de Guatemala. The wide and varied range of items paid as tribute by these two *pueblos* and the villages in their orbits, such as cocoa from the lowland in addition to maize and processed cotton, proves that the unity of the Mam agro-ecosystem had survived the colonial segmentation of ethnic territorialities. It also confirms that access to resource complementarity had remained a considerable feature of these communities.[23]

Later sources suggest that the Mam agro-ecosystem preserved its complexity until the early nineteenth century. A document dated 1816, produced by the official of the Department of Quezaltenango, not only stated the existence of such a unit, but possibly also drew a vivid portrait. It is an extended indigenous land survey that collected reports sent by each of the municipal and parochial authorities of each indigenous *pueblo* of the Department.[24] Energy and protein came from the *milpa* next to the village at 2,670 metres elevation and from potatoes cultivated possibly in the forested land climbing to the sacred Chicabal lagoon. At a short distance from the settlement, Mam peasants also grew wheat for trade in Quezaltenango and Ostuncalco. Fuel supply was half a *legua* distant (2.5 kilometres north-east), where San Martín's residents collected wood for cooking and timber and straw for construction. Sheep pastures were southward in the upper piedmont (around 1,500 metres) and two *leguas* (ten kilometres) from the village. This was the first link in a chain of a vigorous highland textile industry. In the mountains of the upper piedmont many of the 'sons of the village' used to hunt 'animals of the mountain' with traps or rifle. Meat was then carried to the regional markets in Quezaltenango and Ostuncalco. From the lowlands, at about 400 metres elevation, in a strip of land at eight leguas (40 kilometres) from San Martín between the former village of Magdalena and the river Nil, San Martín drew a large and nutritionally important basket of resources, such as fruits, lowland maize (*maíz de la costa*; also used to feed the few farm animals such as pigs or chickens), beans (rich in protein), herbs and chili (providing vitamin A and C, with formidable digestive content important to balance the amino acid-rich Mayan diet).

According to modern scholars of ecology and traditional agriculture, the picture above portrays a 'traditional indigenous agro-ecosystem' that represents the evolution of an ecosystem transformed by generations of peasants through the management of natural cycles, land and vegetation in

23 Feldman (1992), p. 1): Hostnig (1993–96), vol. 2, pp. 137–43). Tribute included 'Indian domestic labourers, cacao, textiles, salt, chickens, maize, honey, beans, eggs and Indian tributaries.'

24 AGCA–Sección de Tierras (hereafter ST) (Quezaltenango) 1/17, f. 87 for San Martín. The survey originated after the delegate of Quezaltenango to the Spanish Cortes proposed a general land redistribution according to the updated demography of the *pueblos*. For insightful readings of this episode in the history of political regionalism in Guatemala, see Taracena (1997, pp. 81–2).

such a way as to divert or expand flows of energy and goods with the objective of stimulating the production of useful products.[25] The agro-ecosystem comprises several species, exploits a variety of microenvironments which are diverse in soil composition, soil drainage, temperature, altitude, slope and fertility. Systematic intercropping generates positive results for pest control. The agro-ecosystem is not technology-intensive but highly intensive of human and animal power.

Ecology and Titling of the Mam Agro-ecosystem

The idea of a Mam agro-ecosystem situated in the Costa Cuca presented above stands on the presumption of extreme ecological complexity. But this is not the conventional representation of Guatemalan geography and climate. The Bocacosta is usually portrayed as homogeneous fertile land, with mild weather and no extreme temperatures, good drainage, rich volcanic soil and generally ideal conditions for commercial agriculture.[26]

According to this view, the expansion of coffee plantations throughout the Bocacosta since the 1870s satisfied the region's natural vocation for hosting agricultural development. More detailed scrutiny, however, reveals a more complex picture. An examination of the ecological features of the Mam agro-ecosystem described above will support the argument that losing control of sections of it undermined the entire system.

The change is abrupt from the highland to the lowland. Within the range of 16 to 20 kilometres one leaves the healthy and cool weather of the highland (*tierra fría*) at 2,500 metres to the hot and humid upper lowland (*tierra templada*) at 1,000 metres. It takes another 15 kilometres to reach the warmer land at 500 metres (*tierra caliente*). Local farmers had a surprisingly precise knowledge of the boundaries between zones, as proved by tracking plots as classed in archival documents on a modern map.[27] The abrupt topography assures marked variability in climatic conditions (temperature and rain) over short distances. Using data collected between 1894 and 1902, the German geographer Karl Sapper reported average annual

---

25 Altieri (1991); Wilken (1987); Harrison and Turner (1978); Whitmore and Turner (2002), pp. 49–71.
26 A survey of sources and a discussion of the representation of nature in Guatemala is in Gallini (2002), chapter 1.
27 For example, the coffee *finca* Matazano is classified in *tierra caliente* (Archivo de Gobernación de Quezaltenango [hereafter AGQ] 108/1874, Libro de matrículas de terrenos). The same *finca* appears in a 1888 map and again in the modern map drawn by the Instituto Geográfico Nacional (Hoja 1859 I, Guatemala 1960). Based on this cartographic information, I suggest the *finca* was approximately 700 metres, which is in fact *tierra caliente*. Using the same methodology and sources, San Diego Buena Vista would be in *tierra caliente* (850 metres) and San Isidro Buena Vista in *tierra templada* (1,400–1,500 metres).

rainfall in the Bocacosta (800–1,000 metres) between 3,000 and 4,250 millimetres, but falling to 900 millimetres in San Martín.[28]

Steep slopes have resulted from high rainfall on land uplifted recently and rapidly by volcanoes and earthquakes. Amidst this rough topography, rivers flow very rapidly and impetuously from their springs in the mountains and the volcanoes down to the Pacific Ocean. In their reach, deep canyons (*barrancos*) and narrow valleys created the distinctive surface configuration in the Department of Quezaltenango. Rough topography always made for very difficult transit from the highland towards the Pacific coast. Indigenous paths run horizontally along the volcanic axis and the Pacific coastline only below the elevation of 500–600 metres, where the slopes flatten. Above that frontier, communication developed basically along two vertical lines: the current road connecting Ostuncalco, San Martín, Colomba and Coatepeque, and the one from Quezaltenango following the River Samalá.

As to the soils of the Bocacosta, they are believed to be among the finest of the American tropics,[29] because they derived from deep accumulations of volcanic material and are friable and highly productive. However, behind the comprehensive classification, the only soil survey available (carried out in 1959 by an engineer of the US Department of Agriculture) shows that the soil map of the Department of Quezaltenango is a mosaic with a common feature: serious vulnerability to erosion and leaching action of heavy rainfall.[30] Although the cartographic scale of this map may mask an even more diverse and patchy soil composition within each grouping,[31] the broad point about the extreme soil variability of the Costa Cuca remains valid. Thus, if one examines the San Martín agro-ecosystem from a soil perspective, it is easy to appreciate the importance of gaining control of large productive spaces in the lowland.

San Martín's agro-ecosystem extended over three very different soil classes. The village itself and land in the vicinity occupied excessively drained and shallow sandy loams of volcanic mountains (Ostuncalco series) that were completely covered by ash from the 1902 San María volcanic eruption. Below a first layer of organic material (around 20 centimetres deep), and a second

28 Figures for the Bocacosta have been calculated from data collected in the *fincas* Las Mercedes, San Francisco Miramar, El Transito and Esmeralda, and published by Sapper in *Meterologische Zeitschrift* from vols. 13 to 23 (1896–1906). I took the station in Quezaltenango as representative for San Martín. For climate in Guatemala, see McBryde (1969), vol. 1, p. 44, mapa 6; Vivó Escoto (1964), pp. 210–3; Sapper (1897), cuadro 1; West and Augelli (1989), pp. 40–1.

29 Higbee (1947). In the US classification system they are Andisols; see Sanders and Murdy (1982), pp. 22–3.

30 Simmons, Tarano and Pinto (1959).

31 I am grateful to Christian Brannstrom for pointing my attention on this. It means that infertile soils may be found in fertile regions, and vice-versa.

layer of pumice deposited in the eruption (from 50 centimetres to more than one metre thick), the soil surveyors found older subsoil, darker and better drained. Even before the 1902 devastation, which depleted soil fertility even further, the problems with this highland section of the agro-ecosystem were steep topography and soil erosion.

Cultivation here never yielded satisfactory harvests. According to one document from 1836, 'it is necessary to begin soil preparation for cultivation one year in advance because these lands are sterile and slow in producing [*tardío*]'.[32] Green manure or, whenever possible, animal manure were crucial in improving land fertility.[33] Wheat could grow even without manure, but 'only those who possess manure can have' maize and other fundamental crops for the indigenous diet.[34] In 1880 a petition of San Martín complained that maize productivity in the upper piedmont was one-eighth that of the coast.[35] Therefore, the importance of this sub-region of the agro-ecosystem for the peoples of San Martín was not so much for crops, but wood and other resources extracted from the thick vegetation cover.[36]

Pacific coast soils occupied the rest of the agro-ecosystem. These are developed on volcanic ash, and display more favourable characteristics for agriculture. Both the middle (Alotenango and Palin series) and southern (Chuvá and Samayac series) sections have texture varying slightly from an even balance of sand, silt and clay, ideal for agricultural exploitation in terms of water retention ability, friability and fertility.[37] Susceptibility to erosion remains high, especially in the middle section, where slopes range from 12 to 60 per cent. Where the abrupt topography of the Bocacosta gets closer to the alluvial land of the coast, erosion is considerably reduced.

Access and control of these areas were crucial to complement the otherwise poor diet and economy of highland villages such as San Martín. Meat, fodder, water, maize and fruit were reportedly obtained from the Bocacosta. But other resources and food (including recently adopted exotics) crossed the region to reach Quezaltenango, Ostuncalco and other highland markets. Some commodities were well documented because they were taxable in colonial times and commercially valuable afterward. Cacao, the 'minas de la costa',

---

32   AGQ 1836/18.
33   The general practice is described in Stadelman (1940); McBryde (1969), pp. 76–7. Explicit reference to the need for manure is mentioned in AGCA–ST 1/17 f. 88–9. Green manure was certainly more common. For a description of it in the region of San Martín see Wilken (1987), p. 61.
34   AGCA–ST 1/17, Informe del Curato de Ostuncalco.
35   AGCA–ST (Quezaltenango) 29/7 in Hostnig (1997), p. 739.
36   The first national census of natural resources reported the following species in the *municipio* of San Martín: *cedro, pino, pinabete, canoj, roble, chichique, cedro blanco, encino, palo colorado, cipres, mora* (Guatemala, 1880).
37   Sanders and Murdy (1982), pp. 22–3.

was the most important. In the sixteenth century every indigenous community in the highland held coastal colonies (below 650 metres) to provide cacao for tribute. The colonial map of the *estancias cacaoteras* scattered in the lower Bocacosta[38] depicts six Mam *estancias* linked to Ostuncalco and Sacatepéquez.[39] With the demographic collapse of the late sixteenth and seventeenth century, distant colonies were abandoned, but the link between lowland colonies (*sujetos*) and highland villages (*cabeceras*) possibly never disappeared in the collective memory of highland communities.

Equally fundamental was salt coming from the coastal lagoons and the salt works in Champerico, Ixtan and Acapán, along the Pacific coast. Salt provided sodium to the almost exclusively vegetarian diet of indigenous peoples and was important for animals, food conservation, rituals and celebrations and medical properties.[40] In the nineteenth century salt-works in the coast were privately run by *ladinos*, but indigenous peoples controlled transport and trade especially during the less intense period of the *milpa*.[41] A range of less visible but equally important resources were moved from the piedmont and the coast to the highland and vice versa. Flowers played an important role in Maya cultural and ethnic reproduction, while lime had more practical functions. All of them together built the special symbiotic relation between the highland and the lowland which San Martín learned to manage and transform.

To secure the agro-ecosystem against alienation or usurpation, the eighteenth-century San Martín leadership standardised communal landholdings within the Spanish legal system. In 1714, nearly 150 years before coffee was introduced, 'los alcaldes y común' of the village and the authorities of the sister Mam community of Concepción paid 100 *tostones* and 20 *fanegas* of wheat to buy 6.5 *caballerías* (292.5 hectares) classified as 'cattle ranch' from a prominent *ladino* from Quezaltenango.[42] The area was located in the Llano de los Coyoles (and named Los Coyoles afterward), near present day Asintal on the Pacific lower piedmont, eight *leguas* (40 kilometres) from the village. In 1744 San Martín also succeeded in titling the *ejido*, a vast area of 346 *caballerías* (15,570 hectares) with poorly defined boundaries. After a fire in 1811 burnt all the papers, San Martín promoted a new, costly, risky and time-consuming titling of its land. The long process was stopped by the end of the colonial rule, wars of independence and subsequent political turmoil and social unrest. Only in 1837 did it come to con-

---

38   McBryde (1969), mapa 11.
39   Feldman (1992), pp. 18, 52, 60. The Tzutujil *cabecera* Santiago Atitlan and the K'iché Quezaltenango also held coastal *estancias*; see Carmack (1973), p. 380; Orellana (1995), pp. 29–30; McBryde (1969), pp. 113, 282–3; Zamora (1985), p. 333.
40   Andrews (1983), p. 1.
41   Watanabe (1996), pp. 233–43.
42   AGCA A.1, Leg. 5963, exp. 52305, also published in Hostnig (1997), p. 595.

clusion, when a new land title was granted by the Liberal president Mariano Gálvez. The title consisted of two folders beautifully decorated on the front page with two gold and coloured pictures of residents of San Martín in their typical dress.[43] One folder contained the title of Los Coyoles, the well-defined area held as private property. The other folder produced the formal title of the large *ejido* yet to be demarcated.

Two years later the state land surveyor measured the area properly according to the topographical description in the title. The measurement found that the *ejido* of San Martín actually covered an area of 1,085 *caballerías* (48,825 hectares), more than three times the declared extension.[44] Meanwhile, the legal situation of the *ejido* had not changed in isolation. The entire region was facing deep and far-reaching changes in land tenure and use, and in population distribution.

The Construction of the Costa Cuca by *Altense* Regionalism

By the early eighteenth century, demographic recovery had become noticeable throughout Guatemala. In the area analysed, Ostuncalco increased from 519 inhabitants in 1749 to 4,454 in 1821 and 5,189 in 1847. In the same period, the two dependencies of Ostuncalco, Concepción Chiquirichapa and San Martín Sacatepéquez registered similar trends. In 1749 Concepción had 250 residents, while San Martín numbered 500. By 1825 the population had grown to 1,731 and 3,252, respectively. By 1847 there were 2,164 registered residents in Concepción and 2,177 in San Martín.[45]

As already suggested, the demographic growth of Mam (but also K'iché) people in highland villages prompted attempts by *pueblos* to reclaim control of the Pacific lowlands. It was not just a recovery of ancient territoriality — especially the border with the K'iché of Quezaltenango — and traditional agro-ecosystem spaces. The movement towards the Pacific slopes corresponded also to the specific Mam political structure of dispersed and nuclear-type communities.[46] Settlements in the lowland that had been abandoned during colonial times of demographic and economic depression were repopulated in a process of 'domestic re-colonisation'.[47] Land conflicts sometimes arose between villages now suffering uneven land–population balance, but this does not necessarily suggest that environmental depletion was occurring in the highlands. As already argued,

43   AGCA–ST (Quezaltenango) 1/1.
44   AGCA–ST (Quezaltenango)10/6.
45   Demographic data on the Ostuncalco area come from Reeves (1999), Appendix 1.
46   Watanabe (1996), p. 233; Hostnig (1991), pp. 1–9; and Ebel (1969) note a highly dispersed community.
47   That was the case, for example, of Santa Catalina Retalhuleu and Santa Maria Magdalena, both coastal *estancias* of Ostuncalco. Reeves (1999, pp. 48–60) follows the process on basis of archival evidence.

the interrelation with the lowlands was an essential part of the indigenous highland settlements. Regaining ancient settlements, trading routes, bridges and resources were signs of the general recovery of Mam (and other Mayan) communities in the eighteenth and nineteenth centuries, rather than environmental stress in the highland.

Indigenous communities were not alone in their rush to the Pacific lowland. The *ladino* population also grew in the entire Quezaltenango region. By the end of the eighteenth century, Quezaltenango was the second largest city in the country, the centre of a vital textile industry and the biggest market of western Guatemala. During the next three decades, it also became the most interesting case of the dual nationhood of Guatemala. On the one hand, K'iché elites took advantage of the troubled times during the transition to Independence from Spain to strengthen their economic base and make Xelajú (the K'iché name for Quezaltenango) a laboratory of a new form of indigenous political power.[48] On the other hand, the same commercial growth of Quezaltenango stimulated the emergence of a network of local *ladino* and Spanish elites, expressing a strong political and economic regionalism. Their geopolitical project aimed to separate the region called Los Altos — ideally comprising the whole west including the coast — from Guatemala and participate in the Central American Federation as an independent state. The 'Estado de Los Altos' was eventually established in 1838–39, but soon was overwhelmed by a wave of violent indigenous revolts in the country against liberal reforms, land privatisation and other measures eroding indigenous autonomy and land access. The *mestizo* Rafael Carrera led the reaction, finally defeating the *Altense* experiment and establishing a conservative regime that lasted 30 years. A second attempt in 1848 also failed, ending the polity (but not the spirit) of the State of Los Altos.[49]

In spite of political defeat, *Altense* regionalism prospered and survived in different form. Since the late 1820s and 1830s *Altense* elites had increasingly expanded their economic interests towards the Pacific lowland, which corresponded also to a political step. The success of the political project of the State of Los Altos depended on gaining access to the Pacific Ocean ('access to the sea' or '*la salida al mar*'), as convincingly stated by Taracena.[50] Considering the geopolitical design behind the expansion to the lowland helps to explain the cohesiveness of the group of *ladinos* who actively occupied and titled land in the Bocacosta well before the coffee boom.

There were, of course, good economic reasons to push the frontier southward, as both elite and poor *ladinos* migrated there. Until the late

48   Grandin (2000), pp. 25–31; Taracena (1997), pp. 17–54.
49   For the political history of Los Altos, see Taracena (1997); González (1994). On Carrera, see Woodward (1993).
50   Taracena (1997), p. 21.

1850s, the instrument of *ladino* penetration into the Bocacosta was cattle ranching. The increasing number of land conflicts between indigenous individuals and communities and *ladino* ranchers suggests that the two systems of land use, indigenous agriculture and *ladino* cattle ranching, were hardly compatible.

The conflict proved to be fatal to indigenous peasants in the Mam agro-ecosystem. In 1841 the elders and people of the village accused some 30 *ladino* ranchers of owning 'cattle ... that damage our *milpas*, cotton fields and other crops'. According to the official in Quezaltenango, there in fact were more than 60 *ladinos* in the landholding of the community.[51] The majority of them were either from Quezaltenango or Ostuncalco, where they had settled as early as the beginning of the century.[52] In most cases land occupation had occurred in the 1810s and 1820s, but acquired legal visibility only with the first Liberal reforms in 1837.

At that time, the State of Los Altos was established. According to San Martín's people, the State of Los Altos 'only had one goal, that is, to put an end to the Indians. It authorised several [land] alienations (sales), plotting with the *alcalde* who was Pedro Vasquez, who only tried to harm us, despite [the fact that] he is an Indian as we are'.[53] This probably was an accurate picture of what happened in the whole Bocacosta. The vast *ejido* of San Martín was undergoing a radical reorganisation and the Costa Cuca was about to be born.

Unable to prevent *ladinos* from taking control of *ejido* land, and short of financial resources to sustain the retitling of the *ejido*, San Martín's authorities in 1837–38 inaugurated an unexpectedly damaging policy with enduring and dramatic consequences for the autonomy of the community. The policy consisted in agreeing to sell the right of leasing *ejido* land to *ladino* claimants in exchange for payment of annual rent or *censo enfitéutico* .[54] By right of annual rent, *ladinos* were granted the use of the land for cultivation (or ranching), but ownership remained inalienable in the hands of the community.[55] Between 1838 and 1841, contracts were signed with a number of *ladinos*, including some of the most prominent amongst the *Altense* elite. In retrospect, the *censo enfitéutico* was a transitional stage to the liberal legal system based on full private property.[56] To the Mam people involved

51   AGQ 1841/28.
52   This emerges by comparing their names with those of 50 men resident in Ostuncalco 'capable of holding the post of alcalde' in a 1806 municipal document (Hostnig, 1993–6, p. 533).
53   AGQ 1841/28.
54   The *censo enfitéutico* is known in English as emphyteusis, a long-term lease. McCreery (1994) defines the *censo* as 'long-term lease on community land.'
55   AGQ 1841/28, AGCA–ST (Quezaltenango) 10/6; and Rivas (1838), pp. 6–14.
56   On the *censo enfitéutico*, see Castellanos (1996), p. 54; and Gudmundson (1996).

it was probably the only viable strategy to face the emergency of *ladino* invasion while maintaining some control over their land. However, 30 years later the *censo enfitéutico* provided the legal base for the *ladinos* to claim full property rights to rented lands and start planting coffee.

The Coffee Revolution

In 1863, when coffee surpassed cochineal exports in revenue, the coffee revolution officially started. In fact, the process was not as abrupt as the term 'revolution' would suggest. After playing the role of economic engine of the country for several decades, cochineal decadence had become noticeable since the 1850, and irreversible since the appearance of a chemical substitute.[57] Coffee, sugar cane and cotton were increasingly seen as the most promising crops, similar to the cases of Costa Rica, Brazil and, later, Colombia and Venezuela. Thus, the replacement of cochineal with coffee had been prepared for at least some five years before 1863, which was also the time required to clear land, plant coffee and pick the first crop.

The timing of Guatemala's coffee boom was also the result of an important shift in the history of transport in Central America and the world.[58] In 1855 the first railway line was opened in Panama. The next year the Pacific Mail Steamship Company inaugurated a line connecting San Francisco in California to several Pacific ports in Central America, including San José in Guatemala. Goods and travellers could now travel by ship to Panama, then cross the isthmus by railway toward the Caribbean Sea. Markets across the Caribbean in the North Atlantic system became far closer, and reaching them was shorter and cheaper. As a result, the commercial axis of Guatemala shifted from Caribbean to Pacific, giving a crucial boost to the Pacific regions

Ladino expansion to the Pacific lowland of Quezaltenango could not have been more welcoming to such a development. Land first occupied to raise cattle or cultivate sugar-cane in the Bocacosta could now more profitably be planted with coffee shrubs without the cost and risk of land clearance.[59] Coffee rapidly colonised the whole volcanic axis. Guatemalan exports of the new crop grew from about 20,000 quintals in 1863 to over 131,000 in 1871 (Figure 1.2). In that same year, the Liberals, led by the powerful *Altense* coffee planter Justo Rufino Barrios, descended from the highlands to the Valley of Guatemala to defeat the Conservative regime of Rafael Carrera, with Rufino Barrios becoming the new president of the Republic. With Barrios, *Altense* elites now ruled not just Los Altos but the entire country.

57   For an economic history of these years, see Pompejano (1999).
58   Lindo Fuentes (1993), pp. 162–9.
59   On the relationship between coffee labour arrangements and forest clearance in a different context, see Brannstrom (2000).

Figure 1.2: Guatemalan Coffee Exports, 1853–1905

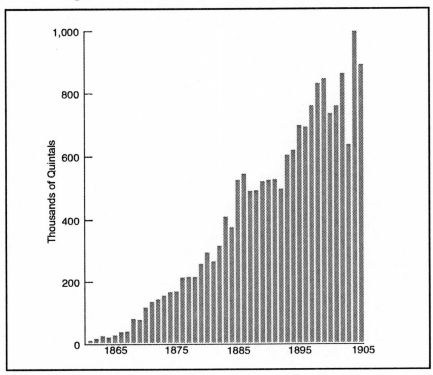

Source: Reeves (1999), p. 9; Mosk (1980); McCreery (1994), Appendix; Solis (1979); Jones (1940); Gosling (1893), p. 3; Castellanos (1996), p. 146.

The Barrios government proceeded to implement a programme of reforms aimed at fostering agrarian capitalism as the way to encourage development and progress. The Bocacosta of Quezaltenango was at the core of such a programme. Although the region was already at the leading edge of the coffee frontier, legal obstacles impeded full land exploitation by would-be agro-exporters. The main difficulty was purchasing land. Since the Costa Cuca was acknowledged as *ejido* of San Martín, legal access was possible only through the *censo enfitéutico*, which did not grant full private property. The easy solution came in 1873, when the Liberal reformers classified the entire Costa Cuca as uncleared state-held land ('*tierra baldía*') to be sold at auction.[60]

60　Guatemala (1890), p. 85, published 22 July 1873. See also McCreery (1994) pp. 181–6.

The Costa Cuca decree was neither part of a comprehensive and co-ordinated land policy[61] — a general land law was issued only some 20 years later — nor was it the result of any geographical or topographical survey of the national territory aimed to identify potential exporting regions.[62] In Guatemala City very little was known of the Costa Cuca, a region that the national state had never even named before the 1873 decree. The whole process of naming and materially transforming San Martín's land into the leading coffee producer of Costa Cuca was generated locally, not at the national level. In fact, the decree was issued as an answer to a specific request by the *jefe político* in Quezaltenango, who happened to be Francisco Sánchez, a highly prominent *Altense* leader who profited greatly from the change in land legislation and became one of the more successful coffee planters of the region.[63] Months earlier, he repeatedly asked the minister of government to simplify the procedures for purchasing land, to extend more formal polit-ical control over the coastal region and to allow those indigenous villages holding *ejidos* in the lowlands to rent partly through the *censo enfitéutico*.[64] These land policies were not a national strategy of internal colonisation, but rather an expression of regional expansionism. The story of the naming of the Costa Cuca corroborates the same conclusion. The area was referred to as 'Costa sur' until it appeared for the first time as 'Costa Cuca' in 1854–55 in municipal correspondence, and not named as such by a document of the central government until almost the 1873 decree.[65]

The importance of the decree liberalising land tenure in the Costa Cuca became even more manifest with a second decree, issued soon after, as a consequence of a request by the officer in Quezaltenango. The new regula-tion appointed the German topographer Herman Aú as land surveyor for the whole Costa Cuca. One indirect result of his work was the cartographic birth of the Costa Cuca. In fact, Aú published in Hamburg the first map of the country on which the region is clearly marked (Figure 1.3). More impor-tantly, the regulation stated that previously cultivated plots had to be sold at a much lower price. The topographer had the responsibility of distinguish-

---

61   Of course, a *post hoc* reading suggests that this and other acts were representative of Liberal agrarian policy and the agrarian paradigm of the reformers. The 1877 Decree No. 170 was especially clear in providing for the conversion of *censo enfitéutico* lands into individual private property. For an assessment, see McCreery (1994), pp. 185–6.

62   This was the case of Colombia's Comisión Corográfica, led by Augustin Codazzi. For a sophisticated analysis of the Commission and its function, see Restrepo (1984); Sánchez (1999).

63   I traced the story of Francisco Sánchez from dispersed archival evidence in AGQ and AGCA. See Gallini (2002), pp. 281–2.

64   AGCA B leg. 28634 exp. 317, leg. 28636 exp. 630; and Guatemala (1890), p. 85, art.1.

65   For Gall (1978) the Costa was named Cuca meaning pretty ('coqueta'). First mention to Costa Cuca is in 1854 according to Reeves (1999), p. 6; and in 1855 according to my finding in AGQ 1855/61.

ing between cultivated and uncultivated plots, but the decree established the basic criterion: 'The land surveyor will understand as cultivated plots only those plots where any of these plantations are found: coffee, sugar cane, forage and cacao.'[66] In other words, export crops were considered proper cultivated fields, while indigenous crops were classified as natural fruits.

Figure 1.3: The Cartographic Birth of the Costa Cuca, 1876

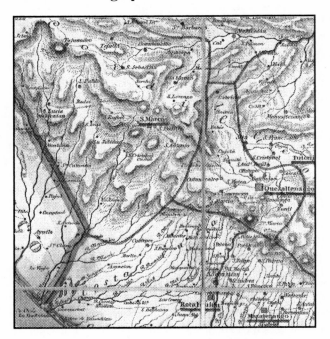

Source: Detail of the *Mapa de la República de Guatemala, levantado y publicado por orden del S.mo Gobierno por Hernan Aú, Ingo.* (Hamburg, L. Friederichsen y Co., 1876), British Library, Catalogue No. Map 78810 (4).

The decrees inspired a wave of requests for titling land in the Costa Cuca and 'helped turn that region into one of the republic's leading coffee zones'.[67] Previous studies have equated legal with material processes and therefore have stated that the Liberal decrees generated the coffee revolution in the Costa Cuca. However, land occupation and titling did not usually occur simultaneously. What happened after 1873 was more frequently the legalisation of land transformation that had occurred much earlier. Historian René Reeves

66   Guatemala (1890), p. 86, art. 5; and AGQ 1874/108.
67   McCreery (1994), p. 184.

calculated that perhaps 75 per cent of private landholdings registered after 1873 were in fact already secured in private hands.[68] Although the projection is rather speculative due to gaps and errors in the sources, land registers of Quezaltenango — on which it has been calculated — allow other assessments. In particular, they are enlightening on the origin of the *fincas* (coffee plantations). Because the owner was required to state when the landholding began, the registers disclose that at least 40 of the approximately 200 registered *fincas* of the Costa Cuca first occupied lands between 1837 and 1841, dating to the unfortunate pact of San Martín with the first *ladino* invaders.[69]

Coffee Plantations in the Agro-ecosystem of San Martín

To appreciate the relative importance of the dynamics of the Costa Cuca in the Guatemalan context it is important to understand the characteristics of its *fincas* and the weight of the Department of Quezaltenango in national coffee production. In the 1880s, when coffee plantations reached their mature age in the Costa Cuca, the Department of Quezaltenango was the leading producer of the country, with its harvest ranging from 20 to 28 per cent of national coffee production (Table 1.1). Alta Verapaz, later to become legendary for coffee quality and productivity when in the hands of mainly German planters, was just beginning to experience forest clearance to start the plantations.

The Costa Cuca was entirely responsible for the performance of the Department of Quezaltenango, as it was the only sector that was ecologically suitable to coffee shrubs. In 1886 there were 185 coffee plantations in the municipal district of Franklin (Colomba). Out of their collective production of 136,000 quintals dispersed in 13 *Cantones* (smaller administrative units), more than half came from three *Cantones*: Mercedes,[70] Las Delicias and Chuvá. In terms of plantations, over 27 per cent of the total was harvested in only four *fincas* (Table 1.2). Mercedes ranked first, with over eight per cent. Indeed, it was not completely hyperbolic to fête it as the largest and the best coffee plantation in Central America.[71] At the bottom, 130 *fincas* accounted for only three per cent of total production, with individual harvests amounting less than 0.5 per cent of the total production in the district.[72]

---

68 Reeves's (1999), p. 129; sources are the *Libros de matrículas* in AGQ 1874/111. Of 497 entries, 203 refer to the Costa Cuca.
69 I consulted the same AGQ 1874/111.
70 Mercedes refers to the *Cantón* dominated by the *finca* Las Mercedes.
71 German source quoted in Castellanos (1996), p. 146.
72 *Estado que manifiesta el número de quintales de café cosechados en cada una de las fincas de la comarca de Franklin, 1886*, in AGQ 1886/56 G. (A 'G' at the end of a reference means that the document was provided to me by G. Grandin. There is a discrepancy between the classification he quoted and the one I found some years later in the same archive.)

Table 1.1: Coffee Harvest (quintals) of Selected Guatemalan Departments, 1880s

Department	Coffee harvest (quintals)		
	1881	1882	1887
Alta Verapaz	n.a.	14,937	18,352
Amatitlán	52,244	36,024	27,329
Chimaltenango	n.a.	22,908	24,968
Escuintla	51,669	9,643	38,696
Quezaltenango	68,798	121,793	155,538
Retalhuleu	28,778	30,702	45,190
Sacatepéquez	49,284	47,849	38,051
San Marcos	25,863	44,357	133,480
Sololá	19,097	25,229	50,777
Suchitepéquez	39,124	47,609	89,357
Guatemala total	**343,283**	**434,293**	**655,073**

Sources: Rubio Sanchez (1953–54), p. 227; Guatemala (1883), p. 177; Reeves (1999), p. 86.

Table 1.2: Coffee Harvest in the District of Franklin, Costa Cuca, 1886

Cantón	Harvest	
	Quintals	% of total Franklin District Harvest
Mercedes	31,129	22.9
Las Delicias	23,189	17.1
Chuvá	18,003	13.2
Xolhuitz	17,109	12.6
Nopalera	13,369	9.8
Las Flores	13,355	9.8
Matazano	6,083	4.5
[illegible]	5,510	4.1
Morazán	3,651	2.6
Asintal	2,187	1.6
Other Franklin Cantones	2,416	1.8

Source: *Estado que manifiesta el número de quintales de café cosechados en cada una de las fincas de la comarca de Franklin, 1886*, in AGQ 1886/56 G

Note: Franklin is the name a town which existed as the capital of the district from 1881 to 1886. It occupied land of the finca Las Marías (and appeared with this name in Figure 1.4). In 1889 the municipality was transferred to a new land close to Franklin, and named Colomba Florida. Today it is known as Colomba (see entry for Colomba in Gall, 1978).

These figures lead to the conclusion that by late 1880s the piedmont had become a patchwork of plantations ranging in size, type of ownership, capital, number of machines in use and profitability. As to the nationality of the owners, German presence became pervasive in plantations, the coffee trade and finance only after the mid 1880s, although some prominent individuals invested in some agricultural enterprises in the Costa Cuca in the early 1870s. German success had to do with personal skills, access to capital and credit, strong political support by the Guatemalan government, favourable commercial conditions settled by diplomatic treaties between the two countries and ability to adapt to local political and social circumstances.[73] By 1892 British diplomats reported with concern that Germans were 'steadily acquiring the best and most productive coffee and sugar estates'.[74] A decade later, the Guatemalan delegate to the first meeting of coffee producing countries, which had gathered in New York to discuss causes and remedies of the overproduction crisis, stated that Germans monopolised Guatemalan coffee production.[75]

Thanks to a member of the cohesive and successful German community, a coffee planter named Schultz, we have an invaluable picture of how the Costa Cuca looked after the new export crop of coffee revolutionised the countryside (Figure 1.4). The map is especially useful because it dates from about the same years as the coffee harvest data (Table 1.2). The overlay of Schultz's map on the original San Martín's landholding shows the impact of the coffee revolution on this indigenous community. The new system of agriculture spread over the *ejido* and especially its most fertile core.

According to the 1886 agricultural census, Las Mercedes, San Francisco Miramar and La Libertad were the three most productive plantations in the Costa Cuca. The latter was owned by the president of Guatemala, Manuel Lisandro Barillas, who was probably the single largest landholder in Guatemala. His land fortune resulted from his previous post as official of the Department of Quezaltenango during the onset of coffee development in the region. He is probably the clearest example of how well-connected Liberals speculated in public land and land belonging to Indian communities either as *ejido* or private property.[76] In fact, Los Coyoles, the land upon which San Martín defended private property rights throughout the nineteenth century, shared a quite inconvenient border with La Libertad.

---

73 See Wagner (1996). For an interesting and critical insight of the German community in Guatemala in historical perspective, see Stelzner and Walther (1998).
74 Gosling (1893).
75 Lazo Arriaga (1903).
76 McCreery (1994), p. 184.

Figure 1.4: Coffee Districts in the Costa Cuca, 1888

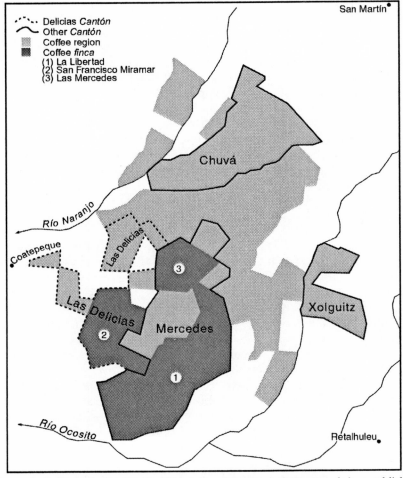

Source: Carlos Schultz, 'Coffee Producing Districts of Guatemala,' unpublished map, 1888, Library of Congress, Washington, DC. This map was reconstructed by O.H. Horst and is redrawn here with his permission.

Las Mercedes and San Francisco Miramar illustrate another point. They descended directly from the core of the land occupations led by high profile figures of the State of Los Altos and denounced by San Martín in 1841. San Francisco Miramar was rooted in a large landholding taken to the *ejido* of San Martín in 1841 and converted into pasture and ranching. Some 24 *caballerías* (1,080 hectares) were then alienated in 1859 to Manuel Fuentes Franco, one of the more prominent figures in the history of Los Altos.[77] Within the next six years he turned the *finca* into a model for any would-be planter of the Costa Cuca. When he sold it to the Swiss national Santiago Keller in 1868, he obtained 40,000 pesos, having purchased it for 325 pesos ten years earlier. After Keller, ownership went in 1877 to Otto Bleuler, a large-scale German planter and businessman, and later to his society Koch, Hagmann & Co., based in Hamburg.[78] When captain Macomb and the team of the Intercontinental Railway Commission stopped at the *finca* in 1891, they were impressed by the solid and comfortable house of the owners, and by the level of mechanisation and capital investment, including depulpers, dryers, separators and railway track for transporting coffee bags to the processing areas and manure to the plantations.[79]

Even more instructive of the onset and development of coffee in Guatemala is the case of Las Mercedes, possibly the most celebrated *finca* in Central America, and certainly the most frequently cited in Guatemalan historiography.[80] Las Mercedes originated from an extensive occupation of some 47 *caballerías* (2,115 hectares) by the prominent *Altense* captain Gertrudis Robles in 1837–38. When he died in defence of the State of Los Altos in 1848, his widow and heirs started to breed cattle and cultivate sugar cane. They also probably cleared land to plant coffee. In 1866, when the coffee revolution was already underway, they agreed to sell half of the large *finca* to Colombian partners, who included the conservative former president of the Republic of New Granada, Mariano Ospina Rodríguez, and his relatives, the Society Vasquez & Jaramillo. The group had chosen Guatemala in 1863 as land of political exile and for promising business ventures for a family conservative in politics but liberal in economics. The Colombians acquired Las Mercedes for 4,000 pesos in 1866 and sold it for 150,000 pesos in 1875 to a Costa Rican grower, who almost immediately resold it to German firm, Hockmeyer & Cia., based in Hamburg. It was the beginning of an enduring dynasty in Las Mercedes, which lasted in the hands of the Hockmeyer family for 67 years until the nationalisation of all German properties in 1944.[81]

---

77   See AGCA Protocolos (hereafter Prot.) Lucas Orellana, 1866, and Taracena (1997), p. 375.
78   See AGCA Prot. Lucas Orellana, 1868, AGQ 1874/111; AGCA–ST (Quezaltenango) 6/8; Wagner (1996), p. 146.
79   Intercontinental Railway Commission (1898), p. 398.
80   See Wagner (2001), pp. 64–7. It is often cited because the Scottish administrator during the golden era of Las Mercedes, William Everall (1912), provided a detailed account of how the *finca* started; possibly this is the only published first-hand report of the coffee revolution in Guatemala.
81   AGCA Prot. Narciso Muñoz 1876 t. 2; AGCA Prot. Antonio Valenzuela Abril 1877; AGCA Prot. Miguel Alvarez 1883; AGCA–ST (Quezalt.) 30/14; Wagner (1996), pp. 131, 145, 369–92; Rodríguez et al. (1986), pp. 6–7.

Much remains to be researched about the coffee *fincas* in Guatemala. For the purposes of this essay and under the limitations of the sources, the picture sketched of the better-known cases indicates how profitable the Costa Cuca — and especially its core — became for large-scale plantations held by high-profile figures of Guatemalan politics. Confronting their power and the enormity of their economic interests in the region — reinforced by how coffee generated revenues for the state — proved impossible for indigenous communities.

Conclusion

The analytical exercise of overlapping maps showing the coffee belt in late 1880s (Figure 1.4) and the extent of the agro-ecosystem of San Martín before the export boom (Figure 1.1) suggests that coffee *fincas* extended over the most productive soils and the land best suited to agriculture.

The same conclusion is also supported by archival documents tracing the long-running process of how the huge San Martín landholding (more than 48,825 hectares) was progressively reduced to the mere legal *ejido* (1,710 hectares). In society with the sister community of Concepción and other Mam villages, San Martín first tried to adopt the private property logic enforced by the new regime and buy the land in excess of the *ejido* on a private basis at a moderate price. The request was emphatically rejected by the departmental and national authorities as contradictory to the 'political and economic functions of the [liberal] government', which was precisely committed to take land out of indigenous control.[82] Then in 1880 it filed a new request for legal title to the *ejido* to purchase some 40 *caballerías* (1,800 hectares) around the sacred Chicabal lagoon.[83] After four years, San Martín succeeded in obtaining a new title for the *ejido*, but which had been reduced to the 38 *caballerías* (1,710 hectares) granted by law. As for the Chicabal area, the process ended only in 1889, when the title was eventually issued to the *pueblo*, but by request of the very authorities of San Martín it was later redistributed on an individual basis to a number of families possibly settled far away from the village.[84] This episode would suggest that a by-product of coffee-induced transformation was the reduction of the cohesiveness of the indigenous community and the possible cutting of links between *cabecera* and distant colonies.

---

82 AGCA–ST (Quezaltenango) 1/1; and AGQ 1874/108. The *jefe político* argued that 'The state of extreme ignorance and scepticism, in which the indigenous people find themselves, will deprive land of the most enterprising and intelligent people'.

83 AGCA–ST (Quezaltenango) 29/7, Hostnig (1997), p. 735.

84 AGCA–ST (Quezaltenango) 25/16 in Hostnig (1997), p. 687; and AGQ 1885/161.

Thus, San Martín's case indicates that indigenous communities with land access to the Pacific piedmont suffered dramatic land loss, as the literature had noted previously. Does this necessarily mean that San Martín had entered a path of economic and cultural decline? In other words, was the coffee revolution as destructive to indigenous peoples as traditionally claimed?

One could argue that in quantitative terms the Mam community succeeded in defending a considerable landholding, large in relation to the population of the *pueblo*.[85] However, it is debatable whether indigenous land loss simply implied the complete conversion of land to coffee plantations. It is indisputable that the Costa Cuca experienced a massive process of ecosystem simplification similar to other export monoculture production regions elsewhere in Latin America.[86] However, the *fincas* themselves were not monocultural; rather, they conserved patches of forest, *milpa*, pasture and other commercial crops (cacao, in the lower Costa Cuca) of variable size.[87] In the case of Las Mercedes, approximately one *caballería* (45 hectares) was reported as being still preserved as 'semicontrolled natural mature ecosystem' in 1986. Comparing this area with the landed property as it was in 1894 suggests that remnants of natural forest covered the area supplying water to the *fincas*, which probably explains such significant conservation.[88]

Finally, the occupation of the most productive section of San Martín's original agro-ecosystem by coffee *fincas* should not be interpreted as the complete and definitive end of the interaction with the lowlands. Highland communities supplied seasonal labour to the *fincas* of the Costa Cuca, and some of them might have also retained usufruct rights to land within the plantation for subsistence. To this extent, the coffee revolution would be just a chapter of the long-running story of the transforming relations between highland and lowland.[89]

Critical interrogation of the impact of the agro-export economies on Guatemalan indigenous communities is legitimate and necessary in a political and historiographic context that abandoned a long-lasting tendency to portray indigenous peoples as passive victims of capitalist expansion and national assimilation policies. More sophisticated inquiry found, for example, that indigenous class stratification played a strategic role in deepening

---

85 Reeves (1999, Appendix 1, San Martín column) reports 3,422 *vecinos* en 1877, 1,872 in 1880 and 941 in 1898.

86 See Funes Monzote (this volume) for the case of Camagüey in Cuba.

87 McCreery (1994, pp. 195–202) shows the distribution of land use for one *finca*, El Porvenir. Due to the nature of the sources available for this research and to the fact that access to private archives in the Costa Cuca proved infeasible, an analysis of land uses on *fincas* has been impossible. This is the most urgent task for a more sophisticated comprehension of complex economic and ecological dynamics.

88 Rodríguez et al. (1986), p. 48; and AGCA–ST (Quezaltenango) 14/30.

89 I thank Laura Rival for this argument.

ethnic identity while state power increased and the economy changed.[90] It must be clear, however, that to analyse indigenous society in gender and class terms and uncover that different groups acted differently in face of deep transformations is in no way intended to deny or minimise the brutal treatment indigenous peoples suffered throughout Guatemalan history or to obviate the overall exclusion they faced and still face.[91] In this regard, I have no intention of offering a revisionist version of Guatemalan history here. There is no revolutionary conclusion that the coffee revolution worked as economic or political dynamiser for San Martín and indigenous peoples. More modestly, this chapter reinforces the argument that coffee's spread throughout the Pacific piedmont created severe, permanent and irreversible economic and cultural depletion of Mam communities such as San Martín. The intention is not a reappraisal of the basic results of the coffee revolution, but rather of the ways in which it was produced. An environmentally-informed scrutiny of the first coffee-exporting region in Guatemala reveals that indigenous land loss *per se* is a misleading approach towards an appreciation of the effects of this transformation for the indigenous communities at the edge of the coffee belt.

The cartographic analysis suggests that the best *fincas* extended over a section of the Mam agro-ecosystem fundamental to resource complementarity. Loss of access to the lower section of the agro-ecosystem undermined the economic and ecological complexity upon which the community relied. Conditions of land use in the piedmont changed dramatically. Although it would be inappropriate to conclude that the access to the lowland was definitely closed to indigenous peasants, because of the role they assumed in the coffee economy (as providers of labour and food for the *fincas*), the fundamental shift of conditions of access cannot be disregarded. In the Costa Cuca the Mam community could no longer continue the same patterns of land use as it did in the 'Costa sur ejidos de San Martín'. The community as a united and cohesive group was forced to renounce resource complementarity as a cornerstone of identity and economic organisation. Ecologically marginalised to more fragile and less fertile zones, indigenous peoples reacted in different ways, ranging from tightening commercial links and market participation to acquire products from the lowlands to becoming forced labour supply in the *fincas*. Indigenous adaptive reaction to the coffee revolution is a complex topic beyond the

---

90   Grandin (2000). A central argument of the book is in fact 'that as a changing, increasingly commodified, economy disrupted communal relations, K'iché elites came to rely to an ever increasing extent on the state to maintain their caste power and privilege'. From this follows the apparently contradictory effect of deeper ethnic identity in a stronger state (Grandin, 2000, p. 54).

91   See the official statement of the Commission for Historical Clarification (1999).

scope of this chapter. Further research could unveil the subtle ways in which San Martín and other Mam communities reconstructed spaces of economic and cultural reproduction in such a changed landscape. Ecological marginalisation to patches of the upper piedmont and highlands may have accelerated dynamics of environmental overexploitation in accessible areas. Indigenous agronomic practices were projections of an oral tradition based on the knowledge of resource complementarity. Once that was no longer available, Mam agronomy also must have reacted, but, with little time to respond, indigenous peasants possibly shortened the intervals of shifting cultivation, cleared forest and cultivated soils of low agricultural suitability. If this hypothesis proves to be true, the coffee revolution would be responsible for not only the ecological simplification in the Bocacosta, but also the forced degradation of the highland.

CHAPTER 2

The Geographical Imagination, Resource Economies and Nicaraguan Incorporation of the Mosquitia, 1838–1909*

Karl H. Offen

How Nicaragua reincorporated its Atlantic Coast. The Mosquitia, from colonial times until its definitive reincorporation. The Nicaraguan struggle with England for its territorial sovereignty. The actions of Nicaraguan patriots to achieve the triumph of the Republic. Nicaragua defeats Great Britain with weapons of law. (1944 Nicaraguan book title)[1]

Giant forests rich in precious hardwoods, immense savannas of amazing fertility, broad rivers apt for navigation, incalculable lodes of valuable minerals, inexhaustible quantities of shellfish and many other treasures that have enriched foreigners without leaving any benefits for Nicaraguans, have been rediscovered. [...] Separated by Geography and History, our peoples are getting to know each other and, hand in hand, they embrace a united nationalist effort to achieve the aggrandisement of the Patria. (1976 government report)[2]

Introduction

Inspired by the proposed interoceanic canal through the Río San Juan and the certainty of European immigration, French geographer Paul Lévy undertook an expedition to Nicaragua in 1868 to improve knowledge of the country. According to Lévy, extant scholarship on Nicaragua sacrificed 'scientific precision for a form of literary vanity'. We can get a sense of how Lévy corrected this oversight if we follow the narrative along his trek from the Mosquitia coast to Nicaragua's central cordillera. At the coast Lévy met 'only a few scattered families of Zambos-Mosquitos, who live by hunting and fishing'. The areas behind the coast were 'almost unpopulated, with the only sounds of civilisation ... being those of the mahogany cutters and rubber tappers'. Inland savannas, he wrote, could 'feed an unlimited number of cattle'. Behind the savannas,

*   The author would like to thank participants of the Workshop on Latin American Environmental History, and especially Laura Rival, for their perceptive remarks. Christian Brannstrom made invaluable comments that significantly improved the present chapter, and he painstakingly redrew several maps.
1   Vega Bolaños (1944).
2   Nicaragua (1976), p. 8.

Lévy encountered the 'virgin forest' and 'the settlements of the uncivilised Indians'. Like their coastal cousins, these Indians subsisted only by 'hunting and fishing' and from 'the spontaneous fruits of the forest'. Gazing eastward from the vantage point of the central cordillera, Lévy let out an 'involuntary yelp of admiration' and envisioned a future Mosquitia:

> [Here,] one encounters intermittent creeks and churning streams with each step. Their sands contain not only gold but other precious metals, indicating that the giant trees that surround the traveler sink their roots in a veritable *El Dorado* ... These forests should cede their place to large rural enterprises; happy country homes should spring forth among the foothills; hundreds of steamers should fill lake horizons. It is inevitable that such an unbelievable and advantageous geography, so exceptionally favourable, will soon attract the two things that Nicaragua lacks: people and capital.[3]

For Lévy, uncivilised Indians who failed to improve upon nature's bounty must give way to the progressive designs of civilised man. Accompanied by a map, Lévy's 500-page tome became an influential compendium of geographic information for European investors and Nicaraguan statesmen alike. As with other 'scientific' treatises produced by similar visitors to Latin America in the second half of the nineteenth century, Lévy's geographical imagination helped enact the social and environmental change it envisioned.

Influential world views help create the world in their own image. How such views go about 'doing' this has interested environmental historians and geographers for some time.[4] Political ecologists in particular have insisted that society-nature relations — and hence environmental change — cannot be properly understood without considering how dominant groups seek to establish regional environmental truths 'most conducive to their interests'.[5] For Richard Peet and Michael Watts, two influential geographers taking this post-structuralist approach, 'regional discursive formations [contain] certain modes of thought, logics, themes, styles of expression' that favour certain values and positions while simultaneously obscuring others.[6] These kinds of discursive articulations underpin and promote a geographical imagination that advocates for a specific kind of 'truth' about how a given society–nature relationship *is* and how it should be. For example, even in the short excerpts above, Lévy managed to inform his readers of several fallacies about the Mosquitia: that it had no history; that 'unpopulated lands' were unused lands; that nature provided no constraints

3   Lévy (1873), pp. vii, 133–36, 208.
4   See McEvoy (1986); Worster (1993).
5   Jarosz (1996), p. 150; Offen (2004).
6   Peet and Watts (1996), p. 16; see also Peluso (1992).

to human endeavours; that progress meant resource extraction, requiring new people and capital; that the Nicaraguan state was sovereign; that indigenous peoples had no rights to the land they traditionally occupied.

In the first half of the nineteenth century new Latin American states often relied on a constellation of interlocking discursive formations such as Lévy's to both justify and project their authority over the national territory. In general, the weaker the state, the stronger the need to construct discursively a territorial whole, and Nicaragua's relationship to the Mosquitia exemplifies this general rule. By the second half of the nineteenth century, Nicaraguan elites viewed the Mosquitia as a place of unlimited natural resources that, not coincidentally, lay adjacent to the leading trans-isthmian route. Not surprisingly, Nicaragua moved to establish its authority over the region in direct proportion to the route's international attention. Since discursive constructions preceded an actual state presence, this chapter considers the role of the former in directing the processes of the latter. I argue that everyday elite narratives about the Mosquitia and its proper place in the Nicaraguan 'nation' significantly influenced the kind of human-directed environmental change that occurred there. To demonstrate this assertion, I examine how ideas of territory, nature and race — what I call the geographical imagination —provided a discursive foundation for governmental policies, and how this platform influenced economic investment, political stability and natural resource economies in the Mosquitia. Unfortunately, a detailed analysis of the environmental impacts of the processes I describe is beyond the scope of this chapter. In this sense, the environmental history described herein concerns the history of an evolving society–nature relationship.

The chapter is divided into two parts. The first part examines the political, geographical and discursive context of Nicaragua–Mosquitia relations up to its annexation of the so-called Mosquito Reserve in 1894 under the watershed presidency of José Zelaya Santos (1893–1909). The second part deals with resource use and control patterns in the Mosquitia as a reflection of the prevailing political conditions grounded in the geographical imagination set out in part one. I do this by focusing on the four resource economies that had the greatest social and environmental impact in the Mosquitia by the end of Zelaya's presidency: mahogany, rubber, bananas and gold.

Three issues need clarification before developing the argument. First, Nicaragua had no meaningful relationship with the Mosquitia before Independence in 1838. The region was principally controlled by the Miskitu Indians and British officials and, after emancipation in 1842, Afro-Caribbean Creoles. Thus, the need to construct the Mosquitia discursively as an integral part of the Nicaraguan nation was immense during the period discussed in this chapter. Second, it is certainly not suggested that foreign or Nicaraguan geographical imaginations actually assisted state incorporation of the Mosquitia. Indeed, I suggest the opposite. Pervasive myths about Indians and nature continually obscured more sobering lessons about Mosquitia reality. Third, although environmental perceptions and dominant discourses influence land use, the link between ideas and specific environmental outcomes remains arguable. This is particularly true in the sparsely populated Mosquitia, where human-induced environmental change — directed mainly by three centuries of foreign-induced resource extraction — is difficult to trace or measure. Indeed, present-day Mosquitia landscapes reveal little of the history that created them, giving the region 'an amnesic quality'.[7]

Part I: Nicaragua-Mosquitia Relations

The Mosquitia before the Nineteenth Century

The Mosquitia is a lowland tropical region that extends roughly from Cape Camerón in present-day Honduras to Monkey Point in Nicaragua (Figure 2.1). The region is a complex patchwork of interlocking ecosystems conditioned by seasonal climatic variations. Near the coast, behind sand berm ridges, salt-water tolerant *Raphia* palm in the south and mangrove swamps in the north extend inland for several kilometres. Within the flood plain, one finds clay banks covered with course cutting-grasses and towering *guadua* canes. In the north-east, the coastal plain is characterised by a 10,200 kilometre square pine savanna, likely a human-created but edaphically conditioned biome.[8] West of the savannas, between 50 and 145 kilometres from the coast, is the rainforest, actually a mosaic of interlocking riparian and ridge forests whose compositions change in proportion to sunlight, rainfall, drainage and human activities.

Before and after contact with Europeans the indigenous peoples of the region developed varied cultural ecologies associated with watersheds and regional economies. In general, the Kukra, Rama, Pech, Tungla and Miskitu Indians lived closer to the coast, relied more substantially on marine resources and tuber cultivation than did the Mayangna (Ulwa, Twahka and Panamahka) and Matagalpa Indians, who relied more on maize and long-distance regional trade. Linda Newson has estimated a pre-Hispanic Mosquitia population of 100,000 people, but for the purposes of assessing human impact on the environment, absolute numbers are probably less significant than the fact that indigenous peoples have modified the Mosquitia through a mix of silviculture, horticulture, transplanting, swidden and riverine agriculture, hunting, fishing, gathering and burning for at least a thousand years before Europeans arrived.[9]

7   Dozier (1985), p. 235.
8   Parsons (1955).
9   Newson (1986; 1987).

Figure 2.1: Nicaragua in the 1880s

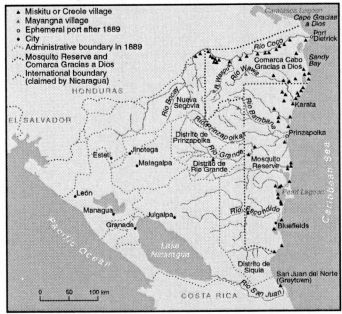

Nicaraguan departmental boundaries from the map, International Bureau of the American Republics, 'Nicaragua,' USNA, War Department Collection, RG-77, Nicaragua 16-A (1903).

Although the Spanish never established permanent settlements in the Mosquitia, northern Europeans formed friendly relations with some Mosquitia indigenes. Beginning in 1629 English colonists settled on Providence Island (240 kilometres east of Mosquitia in the Caribbean Sea), and developed significant trade relations with the Miskitu Indians. The Spanish took the island in 1641, sending escaping African slaves to the Mosquitia where they intermarried with select Miskitu families. Eventually, two geographically distinct Miskitu groups emerged: the Sambo in the north and the Tawira in the south.[10] By the mid eighteenth century, some 500 British settlers and their 1,700 African slaves introduced citrus, mangos and rice, raised livestock, cut mahogany, hunted hawksbill turtle and gathered sarsaparilla between Black River and Bluefields under a political institution known as the British Superintendency for the Mosquito Shore.[11]

10   Offen (2002b).
11   The belief that Englishmen also cut logwood in the Mosquitia is false; see Offen (2000).

Separate from, but related to, the Superintendency was the Miskitu Kingdom, a Miskitu polity formed when settlers took the son of a local chief to England in 1631. During the eighteenth century the kingdom flourished, as settlers needed the Miskitu more than the other way around. Intra-ethnic Miskitu cleavages among the Sambo and the Tawira, however, divided the kingdom into four territorial districts overseen by a general, king, governor and admiral. Each of these districts, in turn, had a slightly different relationship to the environment. The Tawira of the admiral's district near the Río Grande concentrated on hawksbill turtling and the Indian slave trade, and relied more heavily on European trade goods. In contrast, the Tawira of the governor's district around the savanna lands of Yulu and Twappi were known as agriculturalists. The Sambo Miskitu in the north managed large herds of cattle and horses on the savannas and traded with neighbouring Indians and Europeans.[12] Although the environmental impacts of these colonial-period enterprises are poorly known, they provide an important correction to the foreign and Nicaraguan discourses of 'virgin' and 'unused' lands presented below. Indeed, the Mosquitia was a very humanised place by the second half of the nineteenth century.

Nicaraguan Nationalism and the Mosquitia in the Nineteenth Century

The idea of a unified national territory that would link natural resources of the Mosquitia with the modernisation project of Pacific Nicaragua is arguably *the* central element of Nicaraguan nationalism. During his presidential address in 1945, Anastacio Somoza (Tacho) hailed the first road linking the Mosquitia to Pacific Nicaragua as central to the 'moral life of the country' because it would open up the 'rich mining, timber and agricultural lands [of the] unexplored' Mosquitia.[13] His younger son, Tachito, vowed to continue the morally redemptive project, stating 'I will not rest until I see the Atlantic Coast integrally incorporated into the economic, social and cultural life of my country'.[14] Such rhetorical flourishes were not invented by the Somozas, but rather represent the continuity of an earlier discourse that continues to this day.

The Mosquitia's importance to Nicaraguan territorial integrity reflects a significant history of territorial disputes. While still a province of the Central American Federation (1823–38), Nicaragua's southern Guanacaste region seceded and was annexed by Costa Rica, a territorial loss known

12   Frank Cockburn, Government House, Belize, 7 February 1830, Public Record Office (hereafter cited as PRO), Colonial Office (hereafter cited as CO) 123/41; F. Edward Grunewald and Gustav Feurig, 'Voyage to Cabo Gracias a Dios in 1859,' published in von Oertzen, Rossbach and Wünderrich (1989), p. 141; Offen (1999; 2002a).
13   Nicaragua (1955), p. 30.
14   Nicaragua (1976), p. 2.

today in Nicaragua as the *guanacastración*.[15] By the 1860s Nicaragua and Honduras initiated a series of disputes concerning their border in the Mosquitia. First demarcated in 1870, significant border disputes erupted again in 1894 and 1906, remaining unsettled until the World Court located the border along the Río Coco in 1960 (Figure 2.1). Still, Nicaragua's most important territorial dispute in the nineteenth century concerned British and Miskitu claims to the Mosquitia.

Nicaragua's secession from the United Provinces of Central America in 1837 coincided with the rise of Victorian England and a formal return of the British to the Mosquitia. Although British settlers initially left the region following the 1786 Treaty of Versailles, Belizean mahogany cutters and Jamaican merchants began to renew activities in the region after the 1824 crowning of the Miskitu King Robert Charles Frederic in Belize. Contemporaneous stereotypes of the drunken and malleable Miskitu kings made popular by E.G. Squier and others reflect the unique behaviour of this man.[16] Eventually, King Frederic granted British speculators unprecedented land concessions, allegedly in lieu of debt accrued by the king's subjects (Figure 2.2).[17] By 1838 the British consul to Central America announced that the lands of the 'Mosquito nation' extended from Cape Honduras to Bocas del Toro, Panama, and formed part of a British Protectorate.[18] After the Miskitu General Robinson ceded his northern-most district to Honduras in 1843, the British sought to re-establish more direct control of the region and appointed Patrick Walker as the British agent and consul general to the Mosquito Shore in 1844.[19] Considered in conjunction with colonial-period pirate attacks and Anglo–Spanish disputes in the western Caribbean, the Protectorate became the proverbial thorn in Nicaragua's nationalist side.

Following Independence in 1838 Nicaragua's political leaders focused much of their attention on acquiring international financing for a trans-isthmus canal route through the Río San Juan.[20] However, after gold was discovered in California in 1848, Nicaraguan plans were eclipsed by US ambitions and power. In 1852, without Nicaraguan or Miskitu input, the USA and Britain signed the Webster–Crampton Agreement formalising an Anglo–Mosquitia territory that extended to the Río Coco but gave Nicaragua

15　Chamorro (1991), p. 1.
16　See Olien (1985; 1983).
17　Naylor (1967).
18　Rodriguez (1964), p. 128; Naylor (1989), p. 133.
19　Based at Bluefields, Walker created a new political structure known as the Mosquito Council. Although headed by the Miskitu king, Council activities increasingly reflected a growing Afro-Caribbean or Creole influence — long the majority population in the Bluefields area (Olien, 1988).
20　Brannstrom (1995). As early as 1841, 75% of Nicaragua's meagre exports shipped from San Juan del Norte (Burns, 1991, pp. 54, 57).

control over the Río San Juan. Not consulted in the matter, Miskitu King
George Augustus Frederic sent off an angry missive to Queen Victoria:

> the sacrifices of Mosquito territory ... constitute what I must be permit-
> ted to state, a totally uncalled for cession of far the larger portion of the
> territory of the Kingdom —inhabited by a majority of its population — to
> the unfriendly, if not hostile states of Nicaragua and Honduras. The pres-
> ent frontiers of this Kingdom — well known and long established —
> include the entire territories of all the associated tribes who have ever
> formed its population ... But the frontiers proposed in the aforementioned
> 'Project of Settlement' would have the disastrous effect of cutting through
> the territories of every one of the few tribes left within my dominion.[21]

**Figure 2.2: Map of British Protectorate and Private Land
Concessions, 1845**

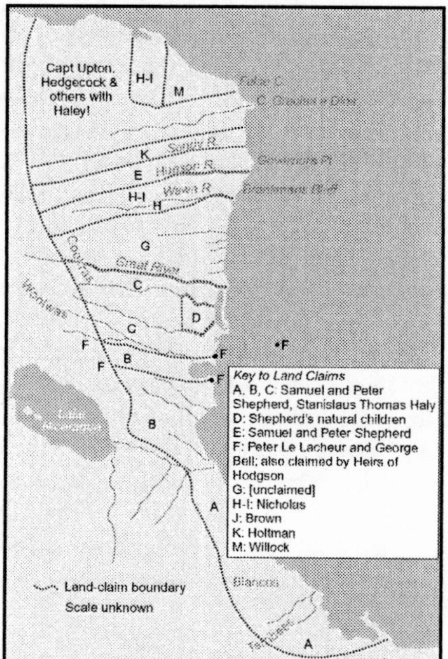

Redrawn from Map of British Protectorate and Private Land Concessions (1845),
PRO, FO 53/44, p.78.

---

21   King George Augustus Frederick to Queen Victoria, Blewfields–Mosquito, 25 August
      1852, PRO, Foreign Office (hereafter cited as FO) 53/29, ff. 108–9.

The king's note contradicts the assumptions of Nicaraguan contemporaries and others who have always considered the Miskitu king a British puppet, thus readily dismissing Miskitu territorial claims. In general, Nicaraguans have viewed the Miskitu as 'zambos', or inauthentic Indians and British stooges, a discourse inseparable from Nicaraguan nationalism, territorial integrity and myths of *mestizaje*, or a mixed race identity.[22]

Two years after the 1852 Webster–Crampton Agreement disputes between officials of Cornelius Vanderbilt's Accessory Transit company and British–Mosquitia representatives inspired the USA to bomb and destroy Greytown at the mouth of the Río San Juan.[23] Turmoil beset Nicaragua as resentful Liberals contracted William Walker and a band of mercenaries to re-establish their authority. Walker eventually rose to national power, uniting Liberals and Conservatives in opposition. After the National War (1855–57) that ousted Walker, the Conservative Tomás Martínez was named president in 1858, and his government initiated the so-called 'Golden Age' in which Conservatives ruled Nicaragua until 1893.[24] Under Martínez, Nicaragua and Great Britain signed the Treaty of Managua in 1860, whereby Britain agreed to relinquish claims to the Mosquitia in return for Miskitu autonomy within a new territorial entity called the Mosquito Reserve (Figure 2.1).

Interpretations about how Nicaraguan sovereignty would be exercised vis-à-vis those of the Reserve quickly ensued. Eventually, both sides agreed to arbitration by the Emperor of Austria in 1881.[25] The emperor's ruling upheld Nicaraguan sovereignty but sided with Anglo–Miskitu interpretations concerning mundane Miskitu powers to regulate natural resources, port duties and the like within the Reserve itself.[26] As we will see, the emperor's ruling, and the veneer of political stability that it provided, were a necessary condition to attract North American capital to the Reserve. From the Nicaraguan perspective, however, the ruling made a military solution the only viable option to exercise its territorial sovereignty. After the 1893 election of the Liberal José Santos Zelaya, Nicaragua occupied the Reserve by force and exiled the Miskitu king. As this chapter's first epigraph suggests, this action marked the 'definitive reincorporation' of the entire Mosquitia for Nicaragua — although the second epigraph suggests the project would remain ongoing.

22   On mestizaje in Nicaragua, see Gould (1998).
23   Dana (1999).
24   Konrad (1995).
25   As early as 1864, Nicaragua passed a law requiring that all goods entering the Reserve had to pass first through Nicaraguan ports; 'Decreto de 4 de Octubre de 1864, Estableciendo que la Introducción de Efectos Extranjeros al Territorio de Mosquitos debe Hacerse por los Mismos Puertos y Bajo las Mismas Reglas e Impuestos que la que Se Hace en el Resto de la República,' published in Nicaragua (1920, tomo 2, anexo 8, pp. 415–6).
26   Kahle and Potthast (1983).

The Geographical Imagination: Mapping Race, Nature and Progress

In nineteenth-century Nicaragua elite discourses of progress, race and nature were inseparable from one another and the political process of Mosquitia incorporation. Within these discourses the perceived 'naturalness' of nature was used as an index to measure the quality of the inhabiting 'race' and the advancement of 'civilisation'. Civilisation, in turn, was measured by outward manifestations of progress, material things such as roads, rails, steamers, telegraphs and industry. These ideas reflect contemporary notions of societal evolution espoused by the English philosopher Herbert Spencer, and the scientific positivism of Auguste Comte, two European thinkers widely read in nineteenth-century Latin America.[27] Race, for statesmen, politicians and scientists — and particularly the retarded development of the Indian, black and mixed race elements of the population — was seen as a fundamental barrier to progress and a central 'problem' in need of 'solution'. Men of science, often commissioned by the state and with a financial interest in fostering investment, articulated this problem in a series of studies that described and mapped the Mosquitia. The scale of these geographical imaginations increased towards the end of the nineteenth century and were assumed to act as both a precursor and indicator of actual progress.

Geographical imaginations juxtaposing backward Indians with unlimited natural resources became a powerful norm for the nineteenth and early twentieth centuries. Consider the 1853 journey down the Río Coco by the Nicaraguan Juan Francisco Irias. Irias found the lower Río Coco was 'well adapted to raising black cattle and horses, as also for the introduction of [European] colonies, which in a few years, could attain to prosperity and riches upon its virgin soil'. Mentioning the resident Miskitu, Irias found it lamentable that such a beautiful region had 'no other population than a few worthless Moscos, unable, from want of education, as unfitted by disposition, to make any improvement in the future'.[28] When such discourses were accompanied by a map showing the Mosquitia as an integral part of Nicaragua they helped generate a particular kind of inevitability.

In 1859 the German-born scientist Maximiliano Sonnenstern drew upon his four years of exploration to produce Nicaragua's first 'national map'. His Map of the Republic of Nicaragua initially contained only western Nicaragua and did little to convey the territorial unity nationalists sought. Sonnenstern revised this map in 1863. The new version ignored the Reserve, but its rivers and topographic features were apparently drawn at random. Nevertheless, his second map is often credited with being the

27 See Burns (1980), pp. 18–34.
28 Irias (1853), pp. 162, 163–4.

country's first depicting Nicaragua as a territorial whole.[29] In 1869
Sonnenstern carried out reconnaissance down the Río Coco and wrote
about the region's cultural geography:

> The majority of the Indians are in their initial condition; they are lazy
> and extreme enemies of work, and they could only be civilised by
> means of immigration, creating economic desires and imparting moral-
> ity with Christianity. In contrast, without this approach, they will
> remain indefinitely in their condition of savagery.[30]

The famed Nicaraguan historian Pérez-Valle affirmed the nation's debt to
Sonnenstern in 1995: 'He carried out extraordinary heroic deeds, always
inspired by scientific curiosity and the best utilisation of natural resources:
those resources hidden behind exuberant vegetation in the heart of the
wilderness or in a bend of a river, awaiting their discovery to serve the benefits of progress and the happiness of the nation.'[31]

Shortly after the creation of the Mosquito Reserve in 1860, the
Englishman Bedford Pim received a Nicaraguan concession to build a railway line connecting Lake Nicaragua to the Caribbean across the southern
edge of the Mosquito Reserve (Figure 2.3). Pim's proposed route received
a great deal of attention. Miners were already shipping gold from new
fields in Chontales in west-central Nicaragua and rubber had just been discovered in the Mosquitia. At a London tavern in 1867, in the presence of
Nicaraguan President Martínez, Pim had called together a group of 'gen-
tlemen interested in Mosquito Land Securities', who included Pim's partner Berthold Seeman, the engineer John Collinson and John Fielding. Pim
claimed to have been 'deputed by the Mosquitians to look after their interests', and Martínez was dealing with him on this basis. The tavern's cigar
smoke was probably thick when Fielding noted that 'there was incon-
testable evidence that [the Mosquitia's] mineral wealth was practically inexhaustible'. But it was Collinson's presentation that captured the geographical imagination of the evening. Having been the first to hack his way from
lake to sea through 'primeval forest', Collinson sought to:

> ... bear the strongest evidence to the innate fertility of the soil: its nat-
> ural productiveness is, perhaps, unrivalled; its virgin woods, hitherto
> veiled to the eye of man, reveal such wealth as must astound the least
> observant on beholding. Picture to yourselves forests of rubber ...

29   Bolívar Juárez (1995). Although E.G. Squier had produced a map titled 'Map of
     Nicaragua' in 1851 to accompany his book (Squier, 1852), it is not considered
     Nicaragua's first because it was not produced in the country.
30   Sonnenstern (1938 [1870]), pp. 232, 242. Sonnenstern became a naturalised
     Nicaraguan and was named Civil Engineer of the State in 1869.
31   Pérez-Valle (1995), p. 17.

groves of stately mahoganies, and cedars of the largest growth; dye-
woods ... producing colours of dazzling brilliancy; hard woods in quality on par, if not superior, to any yet introduced into the English market; vanilla and sarsaparilla clinging to the trees ... you can imagine,
without even bringing to your aid its vast mineral resources.[32]

Figure 2.3: Detail from Map of Pim's Interoceanic Rail Line, 1869

Source: Pim and Seeman (1869).

Contemporary narratives conveying the inexhaustible abundance of
Mosquitia nature described as much about the indigenous inhabitants as
anything else. For most period writers steeped in the social Darwinism of
the day, nature's abundance actually delayed social development. The
English mining engineer and amateur naturalist Thomas Belt explained
Indian backwardness thus: 'there has been no such process of natural

32 Mosquito Land Securities, the Mining Journal, London, 12 October 1867, PRO, FO
    56/22, ff. 127–9; Memorandum of an Interview with General Martinez, London, 15
    October 1867, PRO, FO 56/22, ff. 130–3; see also Collinson (1868).

selection in operation amongst the Indians [because] even the most indo-
lent can obtain enough food'.[33] What was the solution to such a problem?
The eminent naturalist Walter Bates provided the same answer as Lévy,
Irias and Sonnenstern:

> The obstacle to the full development of [Nicaragua's] vast natural
> resources lies not so much in any difficulties connected with the culti-
> vation of the land, as in the very exuberance with which Nature has
> here lavished her gifts on man. As soon as he discovers that he can live
> at ease with minimum of labour, man is ever prone to shirk all vigor-
> ous action, and to continually retrench all superfluous wants of luxu-
> ries, in order to have the greater leisure for leading a life of idleness ...
> The grievous impediment to the progress of civilisation might be per-
> haps to some extent be balanced by a large accession of immigrants,
> developing a spirit of competition on the one hand, and on the other
> maintaining a higher standard of social culture, with all its accompany-
> ing wants, such as can be supplied by work alone.[34]

In general, foreign writers felt that colonisation by 'a new race' was
inevitable. Belt claimed that 'When the destiny of Mexico is fulfilled, with
one stride the Anglo-American will bound to the Isthmus of Panama, and
Central America will be filled with cattle estates, and with coffee, sugar,
indigo, cotton and cacao plantations.'[35] Berthold Seeman, Pim's business
partner, claimed that Nicaraguans recognised:

> [that foreign whites are a] different species of *Homo* ... and that a day
> must come when the greater part of Spanish America will be cleared of
> its present occupants ... our millions will pour into this long-neglected
> region, and found thriving colonies and happy homes along the magnifi-
> cent mountain-ranges and on the splendid table-lands, while busy steam-
> ers will ascend the mighty rivers, railroads break in upon the stillness of
> the virgin forests, and silent telegraphs flash along the intelligence ...[36]

In short, nineteenth-century geographical imaginations of the Mosquitia
blended notions of progress, race, and nature into a commonplace, mat-
ter-of-fact narrative that justified and guided the incorporationist strategies
that affected the scope and directionality of environmental change.

33   Belt (1985 [1874]), p. 171.
34   Bates (1882), p. 135.
35   Belt (1985), p. 387.
36   Pim and Seeman (1869), pp. 58–9.

Enacting the Geographical Imagination: 1860–94

Following the creation of the Mosquito Reserve in 1860 Nicaragua finally began to integrate its estranged national territory. Although the Nicaraguan Mosquitia — even without the Reserve —was as large a region as Nicaragua proper, we can estimate that its population comprised only about two per cent of Nicaragua's estimated 400,000 in 1860. By 1897 the entire Nicaraguan Mosquitia — some 60 per cent of the national territory — contained only 25,000 people.[37] With such 'virgin' and 'empty' territory suddenly at its discretion, Nicaragua set out to enact its geographical imagination. Based on visions of a unified national territory, the unlimited potential of tropical nature and the shortcomings of resident 'races', the state sought to do three things: establish its civil and military authority over the new space; unite natural resources with progressive industry; and civilise and assimilate Mosquitia indigenes.[38] Policies enacted to meet these aims, however, were neither discrete nor simultaneous, but rather adhered to the singular goal of integration and were often modified in response to resource demands and political objectives.

After 1860 the government authorised the ministry of finance to spend whatever was necessary to explore the new territory and to improve river ports and roads linking the Pacific to the Mosquitia.[39] It also authorised Catholic missionaries to evangelise among indigenous residents; and it commissioned two superintendents to oversee the new national territory.[40] In

---

37 'Informe del Gobernador é Intendente del Departmento de Zelaya, Juan Pablo Reyes', published in Nicaragua (1897), pp. 68–75. Unfortunately, without defining the territorial extent of 'the Mosquitia' such data are unreliable. A promotional pamphlet published in Rome with Nicaraguan authorisation in 1898, for example, estimated that the Mosquitia population was 39,000, or 12% of Nicaragua's total (Graziosi, 1898, p. 71).

38 See Alegret (1985).

39 Governmental decree created 'a port that drains to the Atlantic to register imports and exports' in the Department of Nueva Segovia, a classic example of Nicaraguan legislation before exploration; 'Decreto de 28 de Diciembre de 1840, Habilitando el Puerto de Coco, en el Departmento de Segovia', published in Nicaragua (1920), pp. 392–3. These plans involved signing a treaty with representatives of the Miskitu government in 1847. This elaborate and forgotten treaty granted the Miskitu a fair amount of autonomy but asked them to 'recognise that from now on this territory formed a department of the sovereign state of Nicaragua'; see 'Convenio Celebrado entre el Comissionado del Estado Soberano de Nicaragua y el Jefe Principal de la Costa de Mosquitos en 1847,' published in Nicaragua (1920), pp. 396–400.

40 'Decreto de 24 de Marzo de 1861, Autorizando al Gobierno para Hacer los Gastos Necesarios a Efecto de Poner en Estrechos Relacciones con el Interior de la República a los Habitantes de la Mosquitia,' published in Nicaragua (1920), tomo 2, anexo 5, p. 405; 'Decreto de 13 de Marzo de 1861, Autorizando al Gobierno … al Envío de Misioneros a las Costas del Norte,' published in Nicaragua (1920), tomo 2, anexo 4, p. 404; 'Acuerdo de 20 de Marzo de 1862 Nombrando al Señor Don Pío Castellón, Superintendente de la Costa Norte del Departmento de Nueva Segovia,' published in Nicaragua (1920), tomo 2, anexo 6, p. 406; 'Acuerdo de 1 de Abril de

1863 the new Comarca of Cabo Gracias a Dios was established (Figure 2.1) and, in the following year, the state authorised Superintendent Manuel Gross to 'make contracts for the cutting and exportation of timber and whatever other natural resources are available in [the Comarca], and in whatever location he judged to be convenient'.[41] Nicaragua's new 'national lands' were also opened to foreign immigrants. With only a passport and a promise to become a citizen, a family from 'the United States or whatever nationality' could receive between 25 and 60 *manzanas* (18-42 hectares) of 'unused land' if they agreed to put at least half of it under the plough.[42] As was typical given its agenda, limited knowledge and scarce resources, things rarely developed as planned. As I show in more detail in Part II, monopoly concessions in timber and rubber combined with uncooperative indigenes and border disputes to produce a political climate that subverted incorporationist objectives.

In response to political needs, an authoritative approach toward the Mosquitia gave way to *laissez faire* over the course of two decades. Immediately following Sonnenstern's expedition down the Río Coco in 1869, Nicaragua established a municipal government in the new Comarca with a military inspector and judge at Cabo Gracias (Cabo Viejo). Under the new municipal ordinances, anyone extracting natural resources from national lands had to first receive a permit in Cabo Gracias. To raise revenue, the ordinances also specified elaborate extraction and export duties.[43] These new laws, however, did not sit well with the indigenous population, and so the government became more vigilant in its assimilationist efforts. With the expected revenue increase from imposed rents, the government instructed municipal authorities to establish primary schools in Miskitu communities, to be more attentive to Catholic and Spanish-language instruction and to 'instil enthusiasm [amongst the indigenous populations], and love for the institutions and laws of Nicaragua [as well as] a

---

1862, Nombrando al Señor Coronel Don Manuel Gross, Superintendente en la Costa Norte en el Departmento de Matagalpa,' published in Nicaragua (1920), tomo 2, anexo 6, p. 406.

41   'Acuerdo de 7 de Febrero de 1863, Establecimiento una Prefectura en el Cabo de Gracias a Dios,' published in Nicaragua (1920), tomo 2, anexo 6, p. 409; 'Acuerdo de 2 de Noviembre de 1864, Comisionado al Señor Don Manuel Gross, para Reconozca la Costa Norte de la República,' published in Nicaragua (1920), tomo 2, anexo 6, p. 416.

42   'Decreto que Faculta al Gobierno para Dar Tierras Nacionales a los Inmigrantes,' *La Gaceta*, 16 March 1865. Even before this law, President Martínez had granted a concession to the Englishman James Welsh to bring Germans to colonise the Río Coco, but the few who came ended up settling along the Rio Grande in the Mosquito Reserve; Houwald (1975), p. 135; see also Potthast–Jutkeit (1994).

43   'Acuerdo del 18 de Septiembre de 1869 Aprobando la Ordenanza Municipal del Puerto del Cabo de Gracias a Dios,' published in Nicaragua (1920), tomo 2, pp. 421–6.

respect for the government and its authorities, and the knowledge that they form part of the Nicaraguan nation'.[44] In 1877, as revenues fell below expectations, Nicaragua abandoned the Miskitu and reversed its approach to natural resources. New laws now opened up national forests to 'free exploitation' and declared Cabo Gracias a free port for the exportation of all natural resources, reduced import duties and ended monopoly sales.[45]

This reversal needs to be viewed in the context of the geographical imagination. Following Sonnenstern's reconnaissance in 1869, Nicaragua officially recognised — but promptly ignored — its Mosquitia border with Honduras along the Río Coco. By 1887, Nicaraguan laws for denouncing unused national lands covered areas up to the Río Patuca and national maps had extended Nicaragua's territorial boundary to this limit (Figure 2.1).[46] To understand why this came about, we need to go back to 1865 when Nicaragua granted the Englishman William Vaughan, Jr., exclusive rights to cut timber along the Río Coco 'and its tributaries for six miles back', some of which were in Honduras. In addition, Vaughan was awarded the exclusive right to use the 1.3 square-kilometre Cayo Martínez at the mouth of the Río Coco. By 1869 Cayo Martínez possessed 82 workshops and living quarters. In 1870 Nicaragua sold Vaughan the island 'for important services that he has contributed to the nation'.[47] But Honduras claimed Cayo Martínez. To make its case, Nicaragua employed a circular logic, arguing that granting concessions 'could be considered a right of possession ... [and anyway] Nicaraguan authorities have always extended their jurisdiction to the Rio Patuca ... as stated in authentic documents, and ancient maps'.[48] The forest liberalisation laws of 1877 were designed to attract foreign investment and colonists as a way to buttress Nicaraguan authority over a contested region.

44   'Acuerdo del 28 de Septiembre de 1872, Adicionando la Ordenanza Municipal del Cabo Gracias a Dios y Costa Mosquitia de la República de Nicaragua,' published in Nicaragua (1920), tomo 2, anexo 11, pp. 439–41.

45   'Acuerdo de 21 de Septiembre de 1877, Declarando Libre la Explotación de Maderas en la Comarca de Cabo de Gracias a Dios,' published in Nicaragua (1920), tomo 2, p. 454.

46   'Decreto de 21 de Agosto de 1887, por el que se Dan Reglas al Inspector General del Cabo de Gracias a Dios, para la Distribución y Adjudicación de Terrenos,' published in Nicaragua (1920), tomo 2, p. 450; Ireland (1971 [1941]), p. 13.

47   'Concesión a William Vaughan Jr., 2 October 1866,' published in Nicaragua (1920), pp. 428–33; Consul Green to Lord Stanley, Greytown, 26 November 1866, PRO, FO, Confidential Prints (hereafter cited as CP) no. 4013 (1860–73), no. 30, ff. 64–66; Sonnenstern (1938 [1870]), p. 238; 'Venta de la Islita de la Barra en Cabo Gracias a Sr. Vaughan,' published in Nicaragua (1920), tomo 2, p. 435.

48   Tomás Ayon to Ministro de Relaciones Exteriores de Honduras, Managua, 12 October 1875, published in Nicaragua (1920), tomo 2, anexo 12, pp. 457–58; see also Zuñiga (1938). This border dispute first emerged in 1868 and prompted Sonnenstern's trip down the Rio Coco in 1869, as well as a subsequent trip headed by

Just as Nicaragua used Vaughan as a foil to contest its boundary with Honduras, it used him to test British resolve to protect to the Mosquito Reserve. In 1870 Nicaragua granted Vaughan cutting rights in the upper Ríos Wawa and Grande, apparently east of the 84⁰ 15' Mosquito Reserve boundary established by the Treaty of Managua. Fearing a hostile takeover of the Reserve by Nicaragua with Vaughan's assistance, Miskitu Indians from Wounta Haulover seized one of Vaughan's ships. In a subsequent letter explaining their actions, 475 'residents of the Reserve' stated that the 'Indians are prepared to resist' Nicaraguan incorporation.[49] Although tensions temporarily subsided, Nicaragua repeated this tactic just before annexation in 1894. According to British Captain Curzon-Howe, 'as soon as any industry was introduced' into the Mosquito Reserve, Nicaragua's idea of the 'frontier immediately advanced so as to take it in'.[50] Not surprisingly, territorial disputes in the Nicaraguan Mosquitia helped create a climate of political uncertainty that hampered efforts to attract investment and foreign colonists.

Following the Emperor of Austria's 1881 decision against Nicaragua concerning the Mosquito Reserve, the Nicaraguan government became more proactive in its attempts to attract settlers. Amongst other political initiatives in 1881, the government passed a new Agricultural Law which intended to alienate Indians further from their collective lands and, in western Nicaragua, effectively forced them to provide compulsory labour. Combined actions of the state and Indian resistance produced the Matagalpino Indian Rebellion of 1881 in which hundreds of Matagalpa Indians were killed.[51] Although the Agricultural Law intended to subsidise foreign coffee production in the high-

the Ministro de Hacienda, Ramón Sáez; see 'Acuerdo Aprobando un Plan de Arbitrios en el Cabo, 30 Julio 1870,' published in Nicaragua (1920), tomo 2, anexo 11, pp. 436–7; 'Tratado de Límites entre Nicaragua y Honduras, Celebrado en Esta Ciudad el 1 de Septiembre del Año de 1870,' published in Nicaragua (1920), tomo 2, p. 412; 'Acuerdo del 28 de Septiembre de 1872, Adicionando la Ordenanza Municipal del Cabo Gracias a Dios y Costa Mosquitia de la República de Nicaragua,' published in Nicaragua (1920), tomo 2, anexo 11, pp. 439–41.

49   Petition of the Indians and Other Residents of Mosquito Reservation, February 1870, PRO, FO 56/22, ff. 247–48; Consul Gollan to Earl of Derby, Greytown, 1 September 1875, PRO, FO, CP no. 4014 (1875–1877), f. 14; Wm. Vaughan to Consul Green, Wanks River, 8 February 1870, PRO, FO 56/22, ff. 252–3.

50   When Reserve Chief Clarence protested, Nicaragua responded that 'since his government was not party to the Treaty of Managua, he had no right to interpret the western boundary'; Capt. Curzon-Howe to Vice Admiral J. Hopkins, Blewfields, 18 March 1894, published in Oertzen, Rossbach and Wünderrich (1989), p. 373; [Nicaraguan] Commissioner Urtecho to Chief Clarence, Bluefields, 21 September 1891, PRO, FO, CP no. 6486, p. 12; Chief Clarence to Commissioner Urtecho, Bluefields, 2 October 1891, PRO, FO, CP no. 6486, p. 12; Commissioner Urtecho to Chief Clarence, Bluefields, 31 October 1891, PRO, FO, CP no. 6486, p. 13.

51   'Ley de la Agricultura,' *La Gaceta*, 24 March 1881, pp. 93–6; Gould (1998).

lands, it also sought to spark new immigrant schemes in the Mosquitia. In 1884, the government granted Toribio Tijerino the right to bring 15,000 'American or European' colonists to the Río Coco, which would have doubled the existing population. Each man between 21–50 years old would receive 30 hectares of unoccupied land (*terreno baldío*), not extending for more than 200 metres along the river.[52] Like all such arrangements intimately tied to the discursive justifications producing them, the government never feigned to recognise the rights or existence of the numerous Miskitu communities in the region.[53] Failed immigration schemes continued throughout Zelaya's presidency and even into the 1950s.[54]

Part II: Resource Economies

While Part I examined the discursive, legislative and political context of Nicaraguan plans to incorporate the Mosquitia, I have not systematically examined the resource economies that such geographical imaginations instigated and affected.

---

52 As compensation, Tijerino would receive 345 acres of land for every 100 colonists he brought: 'These lands would be separated from but adjacent to those of the colonists in 175 acre lots, each only extending for 500 yards along the river and alternating with equal-sized lots reserved for the Government'; see 'Contrato Firmado por el Señor Ministro de Fomento ... y Toribio Tijerino, para Colonización del Río Coco, 10 de Junio de 1884,' published in Nicaragua (1920), tomo 2, pp. 447–50. Alegret (1985, p. 84) suggests that Tijerino managed to attract only a few Nicaraguans disguised as foreigners.

53 The 'Indian problem' and the planning of an immigrant 'solution' were also being advanced in the Mosquito Reserve. Speaking publicly at the Mosquito Council, the Englishman Bedford Pim argued that 'it was universally admitted that population was all that was required to make Mosquito [Reserve] prosperous and happy'. Pim suggested that the Reserve look to the United States, 'to receive the coloured people of the South'. This, he argued, would make friends on all sides. The USA 'would be delighted to see a fruitful source of discord removed from their midst ... [and such immigrants] would find themselves amongst a people speaking the same language, professing the same religion .... as in the country they had left'. Put to a vote at the Council, Pim's proposal 'was carried unanimously, every hand being held up for it'; Notes of Public Meeting, King's House, Bluefields, 1 May 1867, PRO, FO 56/22, f. 14.

54 By 1896 Nicaragua planned to establish 'poles of development' that would attract colonists; O'Hara, Dispatch 126, 8 January 1896, Dispatches from US Consuls in San Juan Del Norte, Nicaragua, United States National Archives (hereafter USNA), RG 59, Microfilm roll T–348, roll 12. In 1897, Edward Spellman received a concession of 5,000 hectares in the Comarca of Cabo Gracias to 'promote immigration of useful people of the European race to the territory'; see 'Contrato, con Eduardo W. Perry, para Augmentar la Población de la Comarca del Cabo Gracias,' in *La Gaceta*, 7 March 1897. Schemes to improve the 'race' of 'unoccupied lands' continued until the 1950s; see 'Contrato con la Tropical Colonies Inc.,' published in *La Gaceta*, 26 October 1951, pp. 2163–5.

Mahogany

Early British political pretensions to the Mosquitia did not conflict with Nicaraguan efforts to retain and attract British capital. By the 1840s Nicaragua understood that incorporation would mean taking in and oversee-ing the Mosquitia's existing commercial ventures, which before 1858 meant mahogany. Mahogany was the primary British interest in the Mosquitia in the early nineteenth century and, by the 1840s, British citizens held land rights to most of the region (Figure 2.2). Early nineteenth-century terms for mahogany concessions were very liberal. In 1836, for example, the Miskitu king granted Bryan Vaughan the right to work any part of the Río Wawa 'which he thinks proper to occupy for the purpose of cutting mahogany or any other woods ... during the space of three years inclusive from the com-mencement of cutting'. In return, the king agreed to insure Vaughan's 'peace-able possession without molestation ... for an annual sum of two hundred dollars'.[55] A one-time sum, an undelineated cutting area and the right to work without 'molestation' were typical terms for the times. The reference to molestation was a conventional trope implying Miskitu sabotage. Without question the Miskitu often made such concessions difficult if they felt their interests were infringed upon or neglected. Unlike the eighteenth century, when individual district officers of the kingdom worked through village head-man in granting concessions and distributing their benefits, deals struck by a distant Miskitu king and British officials with absentee concessionaires ignored local Miskitu interests, often with serious consequences.

Political stability increasingly became the most important factor influ-encing where mahogany cutters operated. Although British capital sus-tained nineteenth-century mahogany operations, political loyalties were less important than an acting government's ability to guarantee property. After the Miskitu General Robinson ceded his district to Honduras in 1843, both Honduran and British-Mosquito officials vied to regulate mahogany enterprises in areas north of the Río Coco. Apparently, British investors felt that Honduras, not the British-Mosquito government, could better protect their interests. British Consul Christie complained in 1849 that he sought to collect mahogany dues for the entire 'Mosquito territo-ry', but that north coast receipts had gone to Honduras:

> The mahogany dues are £4 for a license to cut mahogany which always extends over four miles river-frontage and eight miles back, and 8 shillings for every tree fallen. The dispersion of the mahogany cutters and the difficulty of communicating with different parts of their coun-try render the government almost entirely dependent on the cutters for the trouble of their actions. I see no trace in the records of any money

55   Grant from King Frederic to Bryan Vaughan, Belize, 22 June 1836, PRO, FO 53/44, ff. 310–11.

having been yet received for trees cut north of Cape Gracias á Dios [where] cutting is chiefly carried on.

British receipts for mahogany cutting in 1848 only reached £52, suggesting that political uncertainty hindered reported mahogany cutting south of the Río Coco.[56]

Figure 2.4: 'Gang' and Non-Gang Mahogany Cutting, 1850s. Information on 'Gang' Cutting Sites

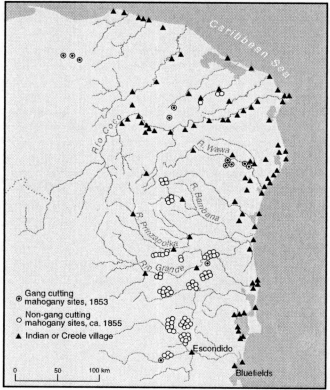

Source: taken from: Lieut. A.D. Jolly, [Map of] Mahogany Trade on the Mosquito Coast between Blewfields and Limas, Jamaica, 1 April 1853, PRO, FO 53/31, p. 126. Non-gang cutting sites taken from Bell (1862), pp. 240–1.

---

56   Christie to Palmerston, Grey Town, 17 May 1849, PRO, FO 53/19, ff. 82–92; see also Mahogany Cutters to Consul of State at Bluefields, Mosquito Coast, 31 October 1848, PRO, FO 53/19, ff. 95–98; Christie to Palmerston, Grey Town, 15 May 1849, PRO, FO 53/19, ff. 1–10; Christie to Haly, Jamaica, 5 January 1849, PRO, FO 53/19, f. 101.

Investor confidence in the Mosquito Territory increased after the 1852 Anglo-American Webster-Crampton Treaty. In a detailed 1853 report Lieutenant A.D. Jolly mapped 12 British 'gangs' of mahogany cutters, seven of which operated south of the Río Coco (Figure 2.4). Jolly's report, the most detailed account of mahogany cutting for any period in the nineteenth century, is worth citing at length:

> First the speculator sends his 'hunters' with a few weeks provisions up the river where he intends applying for grants, should these hunters prove successful in finding wood, on their return, if they report a sufficient number of trees, a grant is applied for and of course given. This grant costs one hundred dollars and expires in five years after its date; its extent is four miles of river frontage and eight miles back, unless a navigable River or Creek intervenes. Besides the one hundred dollars for the grant, a payment of three dollars is exacted for every sound tree that is felled. If the patch of timbers is near the main river or creek, say within a mile, it is termed rolling wood, i.e. when it is felled it is rolled into the river or creek by men with handspikes; if it is further off it is then called trucking wood, being taken to the water in trucks drawn by oxen — seven pair of oxen to one truck, six pair drawing and one spare. The logs can only be extracted during the dry season (March, April and May) as it is only then the ground is sufficiently firm. On the logs being floated down to the mouth of the river they are again hauled up and manufactured, that is squared, they are then ready for shipment.

> The trade is not at present in a flourishing condition in this territory, specifically I believe on account of the unsettled question of the boundaries. It is thought that if the boundaries were finally arranged there would be much more speculation . . .

> There has existed a sort of superstition among the natives, causing them to try to conceal from the mahogany cutters the position of the wood; this superstition the King is exerting himself successfully to overcome ...

> To engage in mahogany operations with any prospect of success requires the individual, or company, to have ... considerable capital in the first instance, as large quantities of provisions and goods have to be provided for food and payment of the hands employed, who are always paid half in cash and half in goods, besides a great outlay in purchasing oxen and implements. It is said that unless employment can be found for at least five or six gangs the returns will be inconsiderable. These gangs consist of about twenty four men each, and cost in pay-

ment, food etc. from two thousand to two thousand five hundred pounds annually each …

It appears that there is no particular season for shipping the wood, and there is no harbour or road head whatever on the Coast, but the vessels simply anchor off the mouth of the river where the wood is and raft it off when the weather and the state of the bar permits. They have often during the season of the Northers to slip and go to sea and many have been wrecked in consequence of holding on too long.[57]

The report also noted that Garifuna labourers from Honduras and Belize were preferred over the local Miskitu, suggesting that labour avoidance was another aspect of Miskitu 'superstition'. Jolly's report suggested that high start up costs, poor security, an uncertain border agreement and labour force, a limited cutting season and an problematic loading climate combined to limit capital investment in the Mosquitia. Such reports provide a corrective to the geographical imaginations presented in the last section. Yet, cautious reports such as Jolly's did not influence Nicaraguan thought, as national myths obscured a more complex reality.

What can we say about the environmental impacts of period mahogany operations? Jolly's report implies widespread environmental impacts associated with gang operations. A contemporaneous sketch map of such bifurcating networks from the northern Mosquitia suggests significant environmental change associated with mahogany cutting and extraction (Figure 2.5). For example, as one of the small-scale (non-gang) operators shown in Figure 2.4 and overlooked by Jolly, Charles Bell's descriptions indicate potential for significant environmental change. His men rolled trunk sections a 'reasonable distance' from the river on sledges along 'truck-passes' that were 'grand avenues 30 feet wide, which extend for miles through the forest, having all the creeks and ravines bridged with trough logs, overlaid with fascines and covered with earth'.[58] In addition to modifying forest dynamics in innumerable ways, both large and small-scale activities multiplied the natural effects of erosion. By destabilising river banks and increasing river loads, mahogany cutting raised river banks, diverted stream channels, modified lagoon outlets and raised coastal bars. As an indication of increasing sediment loads, soundings of the Greytown bar recorded depths of 'many fathoms' in 1850, but only four metres in 1860 and merely two metres in 1867.[59]

57   [Lieut. A. D. Jolly], Report on the Mahogany Trade on the Mosquito Coast between Blewfields and Limas, Jamaica, 1 April 1853, PRO, FO 53/31, ff. 118–22.
58   Bell (1989 [1899]), pp. 189–96.
59   Bedford Pim, 'The Chontales Mining District, Nicaragua,' Paper read at Dundee on 7 September 1867, PRO, FO 56/22, f. 623.

UNIVERSITY OF WINCHESTER
LIBRARY

Figure 2.5: Sketch Map of British Logging on the Río Aguán near Quebrada de Arenas, Late 1840s

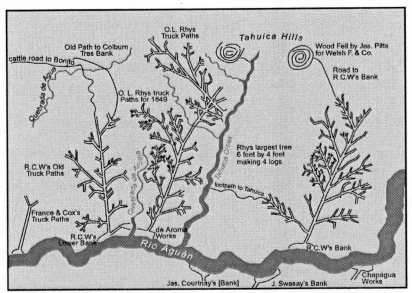

Redrawn from PRO, MP 1523. I thank Bill Davidson for providing me with a copy of this map.

Granting resource concessions in a disputed area served to enact Nicaragua's geographical imagination and, from a governmental position, promoted 'territorial integration'. James Sheldon, mentioned by Jolly, acquired Nicaragua's first Mosquitia concession in 1862. Sheldon received the exclusive rights to cut mahogany along the margins of the Río Coco up to 300 metres back for three years. When Sheldon's contract ended in 1865, William Vaughan, Jr., enjoyed even more generous terms: he paid no import or export taxes, only an annual fee of 2,000 pesos. As was implied in the last section, Vaughan was the largest commercial operator in the Mosquitia until the mid-1880s. His operations relied almost exclusively on Belizean labourers. Although we do not have any quantitative data on Vaughan's operations, we know his impacts were immense because the demographics of the Río Coco changed significantly over the 1865–85 period, as Black communities appeared in the record for the first time and Miskitu communities surged as far west as the Río Bocay.[60]

60　Consul Green to Lord Stanley, Greytown, 26 November 1866, PRO, FO, CP no. 4013 (1860–73), no. 30, ff. 64–66; Sonnenstern (1938 [1870]), p. 238; see also footnote 44.

By the mid-1880s a new lumberman began to displace Vaughan as the mahogany king of the Mosquitia. In 1884 George Emery of Boston received a monopoly concession from the government of the Mosquito Reserve to log mahogany on the Río Grande and its tributaries. A decade later Emery's Río Grande operation employed 500 men, established some 19 kilometres of light rails (the first in the Mosquitia) and was exporting about 2,000 logs per month: 'The overseers are white men, and the labourers are natives, Indians, and a few Jamaican and Caymans men'.[61] By 1890 Emery also had pine and mahogany camps on the Río Wawa where he operated 'the only saw-mill between Panamá and the city of Truxillo in Honduras'.[62] Initially on good terms with President Zelaya, Emery also received the exclusive rights to 'all the Atlantic coast exclusive of the Mosquito Reserve' before 1894. Following the annexation of the Reserve, Emery consolidated both his concessions into a single monopoly for the entire Mosquitia in 1898. The terms of this agreement were typical of later concessions. Emery paid two pesos silver for each trunk exported regardless of its size, an additional peso gold for each trunk of mahogany, cedar, granadillo and iban trees. He had the exclusive right to log 'in uncultivated national territory' in the Mosquitia; he was required to plant two trees for every one cut; he was also required to carry out 'improvement projects' or his contract would expire; he had the right to establish pastures for his livestock; and he had the right to duty-free import of needed goods and equipment. Infrastructural investment was also part of the deal: if 80 miles of rail lines were not built by 1912, Emery would be fined a half million pesos.[63] By 1907 Emery had worn out his welcome in Nicaragua. Although his company had paid the government US$44,500 annually since 1898, Nicaragua argued that Emery had annulled his contract by reselling goods he had been allowed to import duty-free. Zelaya's exact motivations for doing this are unclear, but many contemporary competitors viewed Emery's monopoly as detrimental to their own interests.[64]

---

61 Vice-Consul Harrison to the Marquis of Salisbury, Bluefields, 8 October 1896, published in Oertzen, Rossbach and Wünderrich (1989), p. 425; Callejas (1896), p. 523; Vice-Consul Herbert Harrison to the Earl of Kimberly, Bluefields, 26 February 1895, published in Oertzen, Rossbach and Wünderrich (1989), p. 405.
62 Kalb (1893), p. 259; Anon. (1892), p. 639.
63 'Se aprueba contrato con Herbert Clark Emery,' *La Gaceta*, 7 August 1894; 'Extender el contrato de Emery,' *La Gaceta*, 22 March 1898; 'Se aprueba modificación del contrato de Emery,' *La Gaceta*, 21 August 1900; Spellman to Merry, Managua, 21 November 1906, published in Nicaragua (1907), p. 228. Twenty five miles of track had been laid by 1907 when Nicaragua annulled Emery's contract.
64 Emery representatives were very upset and predictably asked for US intervention; Spellman to Merry, Managua, 21 November 1906, published in Nicaragua (1907), p. 227; Gismondi and Mouat (2002), p. 859.

Rubber

Nicaragua was among the first countries to provide rubber to the world market. Although the Miskitu and Mayangna had been trading natural gums and India-rubber to merchants since the early nineteenth century, the rubber trade took off only after 1858.[65] Unlike *Hevea* rubber native to Amazonia, the Central American rubber tree (*Castilla elastica*) can safely be tapped only once a year, preferably in the rainy season. With unlimited demand and an early start, rubber quickly became a significant portion of all Nicaraguan exports, reaching 19 per cent by 1871.[66] With the spectre of extraction abuses threatening the rubber trade, the government made itself the owner of all rubber trees in 1860, even those on private lands, and established stiff fines for those who 'destroyed the rubber tree'.[67] By 1868, however, Belt reported that 'The government attempts no supervision of the forests: any one may cut the trees, and great destruction is going on amongst them through the young ones being tapped as well as the full-grown ones.'[68]

From its beginnings in the forests of the Río San Juan, the rubber industry spread quickly to the north-east. In 1866 Nicaragua granted R.H. Stonehesser the exclusive rights to extract rubber along the Río Coco 'and its tributaries' for five years.[69] With new opportunities in rubber, the first significant migration of Nicaraguan *mestizos* into the Mosquitia began in the 1870s. In 1884 the inspector general at Cabo Gracias noted that along the Ríos Waspuk and Bocay 'great establishments [of mestizos] have been founded for the sole purpose of extracting rubber'.[70] The influx transformed Mayangna

---

65   Offen (1998), p. 60.

66   And these figures do not include exports from the Mosquito Reserve; Lévy (1873), p. 507. Rubber accounted for 9% of Nicaraguan exports in 1864 (Burns, 1991, p. 57). By 1891, export duties on rubber were one-half cent a pound, generating port revenues of about US$5–10,000 annually (De Kalb, 1893, p. 260).

67   'Acuerdo Imponiendo Multa á los que para Extraer la Leche Destruyen el Árbol de Hule,' *La Gaceta*, 21 July 1860; 'Decreto por el Cual Puede el Gobierno Conceder el Derecho Esclusivo para la Extración del Hule de los Bosques Nacionales,' *La Gaceta*, 14 July 1860; 'Decreto Declarando Ramo de la Hacienda Pública la Leche de Hule de los Terrenos Nacionales,' *La Gaceta*, 27 October 1860.

68   Belt (1985 [1874]), p. 34.

69   'Acuerdo de 23 de Octubre de 1866, por el cual se Aprueba el Convenio Celebrado entre el Comisionado Don Manuel Gross y Don R.H. Stonehesser, Concediéndole el Privilegio Exclusivo de Extraer de Los Bosques Nacionales de las Márgenes del Río Wanks o Coco, la Leche de Hule por Tiempo Determinado,' published in Nicaragua (1920), tomo 2, pp. 430–31.

70   'Informe de Inspector General del Cabo Gracias a Dios, M. Brioso, 1 de Junio de 1884,' published in Nicaragua (1885), anexo A, 10, 11. Cabo Gracias had 812 residents in 1873 but only 112 in 1885, the reason for this change was 'the lack of rubber'; see 'Informe de Gobernador Intendente de San Juan del Norte, Isidro Urtecho, 1885,' published in Nicaragua (1885), anexo A, 14.

lifeways in these regions, and oral traditions denote the rubber era as a significant break between their traditional and modern history.[71]

Figure 2.6: Nicaraguan Rubber Exports and Value per Pound, 1867–1920

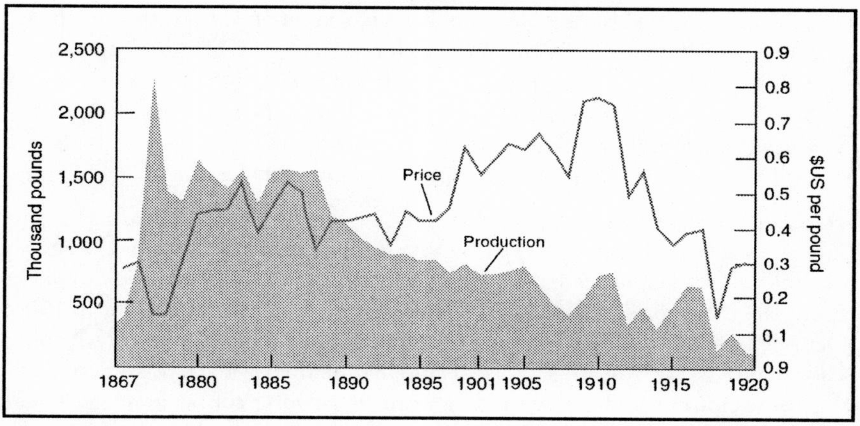

Note: data excludes rubber shipped from the Mosquito Reserve (1860–94). Data for 1885–1910 reflect July-June accounting and only measure rubber shipped to the United States. The July year was used.

Sources: Consul H.H. Leavitt to Assistant Secretary of State, 'Report on Agriculture, Manufacturers, and Commerce,' Managua, December 1884, USNA, RG 59, T–634, roll 1, dispatch 10; *India Rubber World* 1896–1921; Nicaragua (Oficina del Recaudador General de Aduanas), *Memoria del Recaudador General de Aduanas y Alta Comisión* (Managua: [Gobierno de Nicaragua], 1913–21); Burns (1991), p. 57; Belt (1985 [1874]), p. 33.

Nicaraguan rubber production declined steadily after 1890, even as world market prices increased (Figure 2.6).[72] These figures suggest that the state was unable to regulate rubber cutting and that local cutters had little incentive to ensure long-term production. One visitor in 1895 wrote that 'wanton destruction' was everywhere: 'even with the most careful treatment, [trees] will stand but a few years of tapping. [Worse still,] trees were generally felled and drained.'[73] By 1886 Nicaragua attempted to improve rubber production by attacking labour abuses. For a period, officials inspect-

71   Lino, Erans and Davis (1994).
72   During the years 1891–94, the Reserve's rubber exports amounted to approximately half of Nicaragua's. Available shipping data are as follows: 1891: 606,955 lbs; 1892: 408,054 lbs.; 1893: 425,777 lbs.; 1894: 573,842 lbs.; *India Rubber World* (1897) vol. 15.
73   Colquhoun (1895), pp. 246, 248.

ed payment books and outlawed the hereditary transfer of debt.[74] Until the cash economy fully developed in the 1920s, debt-peonage characterised indigenous social relations with foreign enterprises.[75] Indeed, for the most part Indians *only* agreed to work if goods were provided to them in advance. According to De Kalb:

> ... long-continued labor is almost unknown, and service of any sort is usually rendered only as a favour into which one must wheedle the people by infinite cajolery. It is not appearance merely, but in fact, that the money consideration is the less powerful inducement. Imagination can easily picture the indolence and shiftlessness following naturally from this state of things. ... Deceit and falsehood are among their commonest vices.[76]

To offset unreliable labour and fickle trees, North Americans in the Mosquito Reserve started cultivating *Castilla* rubber in plantations behind Pearl Lagoon by 1890. By the early 1900s the Reserve had numerous plantations totalling some 400,000 *Castilla* rubber trees. During a visit to these plantations in 1904, Henry Pearson noted that the only problem with cultivation was the Morning Glory vine: 'as soon as the land is cleared and planted it takes possession, and if it were not cut down constantly around the young rubber trees, it would most effectively smother them'. Although a constant problem in the tropics, weeds never seemed to attract much attention in the geographical imagination. At the end of his cheery report, full of embellished potential of profit per hectare, Pearson also noted the prevalence of a leaf and stem disease and a 'wood borer' that laid its larvae in the tree's wounds — the well-known problem that had plagued wild *Castilla* trees for the last 60 years.[77] Still,

74   'Decreto, Criando un Produrador en el Cabo de Gracias a Dios, y Reglamentado el Arriendo de Servicios en Aquella Jurisdicción,' *La Gaceta*, 5 December 1885; 'Informe de Gobernador Intendente de San Juan Del Norte, Isidro Urtecho, 1885,' Nicaragua (1885), anexo A, 14; Alegret (1985), p. 74.

75   But under conditions of labour shortage and debt-peonage also gave extractors some room to manipulate the system to their own advantage; see Palmer (1945), p. 24; Offen (1998).

76   De Kalb (1893), p. 264.

77   Treatments of tar, kerosene, sulphur and black oil would treat the larvae, while 'whale oil soap' was prescribed for the disease, but both remedies proved too expensive; see Pearson (1905), pp. 330, 333; Anon. (1906), p. 63; 'Se Denuncia Terreno Baldío en Laguna de Perlas,' *La Gaceta*, 6 January 1899, p. 3; Dozier (1985), p. 158; Consul Report on Commerce and Industries, Cape Gracias a Dios, 15 February 1909, vol. 5, Consular Posts, USNA, RG 84, p. 3. The recognition of environmental problems associated with plantations did not constrain regional admiration for them. For example, the Nicaraguan engineer José Vitta admired the coconut plantation of the German resident Gustav Schultz at Wounta, which was allegedly four miles long and a mile wide. Although Vitta noted that the plantation was being attacked by a worm that gnaws at the heart of new shoots and kills the tree, he upheld this kind of land use as the ideal, and contrasted it with the 'primitive' land use systems of native peoples; see Vitta (1946), p. 42.

Pearson assured his readers that the future looked promising. Yet, even before the South-east Asian *Hevea* rubber plantations would flood the world market and decimate interest in *Castilla* rubber, back-to-back hurricanes of 1906 and 1908 flattened the majority of Nicaragua's rubber plantations.[78] What nature did not demolish world markets did, and interest in Nicaragua rubber faded away until a temporary resuscitation during the Second World War.[79]

Bananas

Following the emperor of Austria's decision of 1881, a new sense of political stability enticed investors to the Mosquito Reserve. US capital flowed in, and within a year US companies were exporting the first banana bunches from the region. The low alluvial flats of the Río Escondido or the Bluefields River became the early centre of Nicaraguan banana production. By 1892 the Río Escondido contained 180 kilometres of plantations, extending two to four hectares deep. These plantations, however, generally remained in the hands of individual producers, with US citizens owning only about 35 per cent. In general, North American and Caribbean labourers were imported because indigenous peoples proved 'unreliable'. By 1890 monthly production totals reached about 180,000 bunches, yielding an annual profit of $213 per hectare.[80] Still, in contrast to the way that banana production developed in Honduras and Costa Rica, major companies did not start establish their own plantations. In 1899, however, the United Fruit Company formed and received a transportation monopoly in the Bluefields area. In retrospect, this had broad implications for the future of Mosquitia banana operations. Using its transportation monopoly, United Fruit squeezed out its large rivals and upset local growers. This produced a notable political instability that allowed United Fruit to accumulate, but not plant, 78,000 hectares of land.

Nicaragua's annual banana production rarely exceeded two million bunches a year before 1920. The country emerged — after a promising start — as an insignificant producer on the world market. Hurricanes combined with labour shortages and political instability effectively to deter large company investment in Nicaragua's Mosquitia bananas. Nevertheless, banana production remained a significant local economic activity on the Ríos Escondido and Grande into the 1930s.[81] Attempts to grow bananas

78   Anon (1907b), p. 113; Anon (1907a), pp. 87–9.

79   Douglas Allen, 'Report on the Operations of the Rubber Development Corporation, 1944,' Records of the Reconstruction Finance Corporation Rubber Company, USNA, RG 234; Offen (1998).

80   Consul Braida to Assistant Secretary of State, San Juan del Norte, 28 June 1892, USNA, RG 59, T–348, roll 10; Dozier (1985), pp. 142–8.

81   Adams (1914), pp. 62–72, 217–8; Karnes (1978), p. 120; Vice-Consul Herbert Harrison to the Earl of Kimberly, Bluefields, 26 February 1895, published in Oertzen, Rossbach and Wünderrich (1989), p. 405; Miner (1915), p. 32.

commercially on the Ríos Prinzapolka, Bambana and Coco came later and succumbed to Sigatoka disease, but the powerful hurricanes of 1935 and 1941 proved the *coup de grâce* and, today, in marked contrast to the Honduran and Costa Rican Caribbean coasts, there are no commercial banana plantations in eastern Nicaragua.

Gold

There is little question that the discovery of gold in the Mosquitia transformed the region overnight. In 1889 gold had been found in the Cuicuina area of the upper Río Prinzapolka, setting off a prospecting frenzy (Figure 2.7). By October 1889 Nicaragua produced legislation to oversee placer mining — new to the country — and the expected flood of immigration. Terms specified that anyone could denounce a wash of 100 square metres for 50 pesos in advance (a fee lowered to 30 pesos by 1891), and maintain exclusive rights by paying 20 pesos annually thereafter. To investigate what was actually happening in its territory, Nicaragua sent the German-born state geologist, Bruno Mierisch, to survey the region in 1892. Mierisch described a very prosperous future for the region, but only if the government extended its authority over the entire Mosquitia.[82] In early 1894 the Italian-born Nicaraguan state engineer, José Vitta, assured his readers that the new mining region would become 'a second California'.[83]

With the discovery of gold the state redoubled its efforts to establish a presence in the Mosquitia. In 1889 Nicaragua created two new districts to the west of the Mosquito Reserve (Figure 2.1).[84] Within a year all major rivers leading to and from the gold district, but within Nicaragua proper, had police and customs houses.[85] Prior to the gold rush, these lands had been occupied exclusively by Mayangna Indians. With the prospector invasion, the Mayangna Indians began seeking out Moravian missionaries at coastal Quamwatla and elsewhere. The Moravians eventually responded by settling the Mayangna in nucleated villages, a significant change from their previous lifeways and a direct result of the gold rush.[86]

---

82   On the resident Indians, Mierisch affirmed the belief that 'the Indian needs very little [as] nature gives him everything he needs ... thus it is difficult to get him to work'; see Mierisch (1893), p. 31; Mierisch (1895), pp. 57–66.

83   Vitta (1946), p. 2.

84   Consul Brown to Assistant Secretary of State, San Juan del Norte, 5 January 1890, USNA, RG 59, T–348, roll 9; 'Se Marcan unos Límites entre los Distritos,' *La Gaceta*, 3 December 1902.

85   Lerch (1896), p. 183; 'Informe del Gobernador é Intendente del Departmento de Zelaya, Juan Pablo Reyes,' published in Nicaragua (1897), p. 70; 'Se Aprueba un Acuerdo para Adjudicar Lotes en Distrito de Prinzapolka,' *La Gaceta*, 26 November 1897.

86   The Moravians were apparently unaware of the connection between gold and Mayangna efforts to learn the gospel; Sieboerger (1891a; 1891b).

Figure 2.7: Map showing Mosquitia Mining Locations, 1889–1920

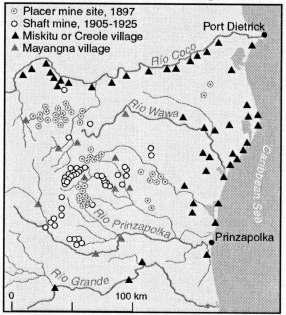

Sources: placer mine locations from map accompanying Nicol (1898); shaft mine locations from Garbrecht (1920); base information from US Marine Corps, 'Marine Corps Map of Nicaragua (Quadrangles)' (1934), USNA, RG-127, 1:150,000.

The Miskitu resisted Nicaraguan attempts to establish police and customs houses amongst communities in the Comarca of Cabo Gracias. In 1891 Moravian missionaries claimed the Indians at Sandy Bay were 'greatly excited … over the erection of a customs house and military post at [nearby] Para'. The word 'excited' was a common Moravian term meaning everything from 'upset' to 'in rebellion'. The Nicaraguan commander confirmed this view by discussing the 'state of insurrection that one finds in the [ten] villages comprising Sandy Bay'. He added that until recently '8 policemen had been sufficient to keep order but since March 6th they cannot command the respect of authority'. At one point in 1892 over 100 Miskitu 'rose up' and held the Nicaraguan governor of the district for ransom.[87]

Although the gold washes were in Nicaragua proper, the Reserve towns of Bluefields and Prinzapolka became the embarkation points for miners and the transhipment points for gold. Although the port town of

87 Anon. (1892), p. 639; 'Informe del Inspector del Cabo Gracias a Dios, Ramón Romero, 31 Octubre de 1892,' published in Nicaragua (1893), p. 79.

Prinzapolka did not exist before 1890, its population stood at 1,500 in 1896 — compare with the Mosquitia's largest town of Bluefields, which had a population of 2,500 *circa* 1894. In 1892 US Consul Braida reported that, 'The export of gold dust has considerably increased; the miners, mostly Americans, in the Districts of Prinzapolka, Wawa River, Wanks [Coco] River and Piqui on the Great River, are very satisfied.'[88] In 1892 only La Constancia mine worked quartz veins, or shaft mines. All other gold works were placer digs.[89] In the following year, Consul Braid stated that US$9,000 in gold left Bluefields every three months. He reckoned the greatest limitation to production was the law limiting claim sizes. He suggested to Governor Daniel Sacasa that 'were a more liberal allowance made to each miner, as is the case in the United States, that it would be an added inducement for American miners to prospect for gold and make claims'. Sacasa agreed. He asked for a copy of the US laws and promised to have the Nicaraguan laws 'altered to conform to those of the United States'.[90]

By the first decade of the nineteenth century placer mines began to give way to shaft mines operated by North American companies. By the end of Zelaya's presidency in 1909 at least eight shaft mines were in operation in the Pispis River region, and by the mid-1920s several shaft mines had been established (Figure 2.7).[91] By 1905 the cyanide process of gold extraction had become the norm, and exports were often labelled as 'cyanide gold' and 'other gold' (Figure 2.8). Available export statistics suggest increasing production after cyanide was introduced. Dumped into rivers without treatment, cyanide, along with lime and other waste products, transformed downstream flora and fauna and forced several Indian villages to relocate.[92] In areas around the mines, unprecedented environmental transformation occurred, as tramways, rails, mine shafts, buildings, dynamite blasting, forest clearing, industrial waste and mule and cattle pastures filled foothill and valley regions where only the Mayangna Indians had lived a few years earlier. Moravian missionary Grossman visited the region in 1908 and, on a trip from the Constancia to the Siempre Viva Mine, he described the landscape this way:

88 Vice-Consul Harrison to the Marquis of Salisbury, Bluefields, 8 October 1896, NMHD, p. 427; Consul Braida to Assistant Secretary of State, San Juan del Norte, 28 June 1892, USNA, RG 59, T–348, roll 10.

89 He estimated 500 men working placer digs. The output for 1891 was 5,000 oz. gold (US$85,000), and that January–October 1892 produced 8,000 oz. (De Kalb, 1893, p. 260).

90 Consul Braida to Assistant Secretary of State, San Juan del Norte, 10 January 1893, USNA, RG 59, T–348, roll 10.

91 The first eight mines read like a who's who of placenames of this part of present-day Nicaragua: Bonanza, Siempre Viva, Panama, Concordia, Lone Star, Morning Star, Eden and Mars.

92 A recently deceased Mayangna elder recalled that 'The river became completely contaminated. ... The gringos, who were now throwing more materials into the river, did not think about the people who had to drink this water ... The pure waters had been converted into evil waters' (Green, 1984, p. 20).

What an enchanting picture presented itself here in this wilderness; from the mountain top I could see over mountain after mountain right away to the Wani district; and opposite on the cleared mountain-side lay in a pretty group the neat buildings of the Siempre-viva mine, all painted white. The mine comprises five hills, into which shafts have been sunk and tunnels driven, through which the cars, running on rails, bring the ore to light. From these it is carried to the mill, to be stamped and cleaned, and the gold separated by the cyanide process. The pure gold is melted into the shape of a brick and thus exported to the United States — per month on an average $10,000 worth, US currency.[93]

Figure 2.8: 'Mill and Cyanide Plant, Eden Mine' (Bonanza), 1919

Source: Garbrecht (1920), p. 796.

The Mosquitia under Zelaya 1893–1909

The discovery of gold in the Nicaraguan Mosquitia in 1889 changed the way the Nicaraguan state and foreign investors perceived the region in general and the status of the Mosquito Reserve in particular. US residents of the Reserve — previously hostile to the Nicaraguan government—began

---

93 Grossmann (1909), p. 261. Throughout the early 1900s the more successful mines produced upwards of US$50,000 annually (Gismondi and Mouat, 2002, p. 856).

to question their allegiance to 'a Black state' supported by a 30-year old British treaty. With the election of the Liberal José Zelaya Santos in 1893 the Nicaraguan government also began to see US residents of the Reserve as partners in Mosquitia exploitation. The combination of these factors changed political perceptions and made Nicaragua's annexation of the Mosquitia inevitable. This alliance is a major irony of Nicaraguan history. Although Nicaraguan governments routinely blamed foreigners for enriching themselves on Mosquitia resources at the expense of Nicaraguans — a valid discourse that is part of the nationalist narrative — Nicaraguan governments before the Sandinistas always entertained a vision for the Mosquitia that privileged foreign capital. This paradoxical tension between a nationalist stance and foreign dependence played out in the relationship between governmental policy and the activities of foreign investors under Zelaya. This opposition, combined with changing environmental conditions, border disputes and indigenous struggles, underscores how human activities directed the Mosquitia's environmental history.

If Nicaragua's history is circumscribed by US–Nicaraguan relations, then the Mosquitia's history is a story of US–Nicaraguan relations before and after the discovery of gold. Foreign investment in the Mosquitia before 1889 paled before the investment that followed, and this changed US–Nicaraguan relations. Indeed, it was not Nicaraguans who initiated the actual military annexation of the Mosquito Reserve, but the Reserve's US residents.[94] By 1893 US investment in the Reserve surpassed US$10 million, a large sum at a time when the total Reserve population was about 10,000.[95] This created friction between US merchants and Reserve officials. US Consul Brown described white resident's changing attitude before and after gold was discovered, and how this related to race and the perceived tyranny of a Black state.

> [T]here was a decided change of sentiment being manifested by the foreign residents toward the Government of Nicaragua, and towards the authorities of the Reservation. There was generally expressed serious apprehensions of peril to life and property of the whites in the Reserve resulting from the ignorance and prejudice of colour, which the negro officials of the Reserve, it is claimed, manifest in their conduct. In that time, in February and March, the residents in general were very much excited and alarmed by the arbitrary action of the magistrates in the Forrest Case [a British subject arrested and imprisoned for killing a black man in Bluefields], some of the Americans announcing

---

94   Sujo (1986), pp. 17–22; see also Vice-Consul Herbert Harrison to the Earl of Kimberly, Bluefields, 5 February 1895, published in Oertzen, Rossbach and Wünderrich (1989), pp. 402–4; Gismondi and Mouat (2002).

95   Nelson (1894), p. 1210.

themselves in favour of requesting the Government of Nicaragua to send her troops into the Reservation to protect the interests of foreigners from the danger to life and property to which they were exposed under the existing government administered by negroes.[96]

For their part, Miskitu leaders complained that North Americans had began acting as representatives of the Nicaraguan government immediately after gold was discovered.[97]

For Zelaya bringing modernisation to the Mosquitia meant swapping Mosquitia concessions for North American capital. Although Zelaya is often referred to as Nicaragua's first true nationalist president, his image of the Mosquitia was heavily steeped in the geographical imagination of his times.[98] With the entire Mosquitia now under Nicaraguan control for the first time, the government moved to develop an infrastructure that connected the more populous Pacific, the coffee highlands and the new mining districts with Mosquitia ports. Nicaraguan 'imagineers' planned new rail schemes and resurrected older ones. Planners worked to establish a line from Momotombo to the Río Grande and one to connect Matagalpa with the Río Wawa.[99] Even Bedford Pim's defunct rail line from Monkey Point to San Miguelito (Figure 2.3) received attention.[100] Still, the most ambitious of these modernisation schemes was Zelaya's concession to the newly formed United States and Nicaragua Company operated by James Dietrick.

In 1903 Nicaragua granted Dietrick the right to build and operate a wharf at Cape Gracias a Dios. By 1905 a customs house and wharf had been built 16 kilometres north of the municipal seat of Cabo Viejo, and by 1908 the new town was renamed 'Port Dietrick'. During its short existence (1903–11) merchants exported hides, rubber, green turtles, hawksbill turtle shell, coconuts,

---

96 Consul Brown to Assistant Secretary of State, San Juan del Norte, 7 April 1889, USNA, RG 59, T–348, roll 9, no. 220; see also Petition to Chief Clarence from Persons in the Mosquito Reserve, Pearl Lagoon, 15 March 1900, PRO, FO, CP no. 7493, p. 11.

97 'Complaint of the Headmen of the Indians and Inhabitants of the Mosquito Reservation to the President of Nicaragua, Blewfields, 21 September 1889,' PRO, FO, CP no. 5929, pp. 46–7.

98 President Zelaya is a complex historical figure and this study is not the place for a thorough consideration of his role. For further details see Stansifer (1977), pp. 468–85; Wünderich (1996), pp. 9–44; Gismondi and Mouat (2002).

99 None of these schemes ever materialised; 'Decreto por el que Se Convoca al Congreso de la República a Sesiones Extraordinarias,' *La Gaceta*, 12 September 1891; 'Decreto por el que Se Aprueba Otro del Señor Comisario de la Reserva Mosquitia,' *La Gaceta*, 22 August 1891; 'Se Aprueba Modificación del Contrato de Emery,' *La Gaceta*, 21 August 1900.

100 In 1909, the 116-mile Atlantic Railroad project secured a US$5.75 million loan to pay debts but the project died quickly thereafter; Anon. (1909), p. 221.

mahogany, gold and cattle in reasonable quantities.[101] But, as with Emery, politics eventually affected Dietrick's position in Nicaragua, and Zelaya voided his concession. While North Americans blamed Zelaya's impertinence in the matter, and Nicaraguan historians blamed Dietrick for trying to make a profit from the extravagant concession Zelaya gave him, a more complex explanation of Dietrick's fall revolves around the mutually constitutive relationship between political processes and environmental change, what we would call today political ecology. Zelaya's Mosquitia concessions created political conflict on three intersecting levels. First, wharfage and other infrastructural concessions made the fate of some concessionaires dependent on the goodwill of others. Second, concessions were specific to natural resources and not geographically defined. And, third, concessions included lands north of the Río Coco, a situation that involved military troops from Nicaragua and Honduras. Once again, international arbitration would not favour Nicaragua.

In 1905 Nicaragua granted Lomax Anderson the exclusive right to cut timber on the Mosquitia's pine savanna for 50 years. Milling pine that originated in what is today Honduras, Anderson's two mills produced some 300,000 cubic meters of pine annually by 1910 — all of it for internal consumption at the mines. Yet, the Lomax concession, along with that of Dietrick, overlapped in space with Emery's monopoly concession for hardwoods discussed above.[102] Although tensions had always been part of this arrangement, serious conflicts only grew after the King of Spain announced his border arbitration decision in favour of Honduras in December 1906. Although a discussion of this latest border incident is beyond the scope of this chapter, the king's decision established the border (once again but not yet for the last time) along the Río Coco. This cut off Nicaraguan concessionaires from the richer timber grounds to the north. Concessionaire unease with this decision was aggravated by Zelaya's solutions. Just as Emery had his contract annulled in 1907 at the request of his competitors, merchant and mining interests did the same with Dietrick's port and Río Coco transport monopolies. According to US Consul Trimmer, 'Merchants at [Port Dietrick] and the Pis Pis miners claim that the Dietrick concessions have caused great damage to their interests, and in my opinion they are using every effort to have them annulled.' Despite having invested about US$1 million since 1904, Dietrick's contract was annulled before Zelaya left office under extreme US pressure in 1909.[103]

101　Some 25,000 head of cattle roamed the Comarca by 1910; Dispatch Book, 1903–09, Consular Posts, Cape Gracias a Dios, USNA, RG 84, vol. 11. On Dietrick see Gismondi and Mouat (2002), pp. 859–60.

102　Zelaya also granted concessions for rubber and the tree saps balsam and liquidambar; 'Contrato Acerca de los Bosques Nacionales,' *La Gaceta*, 17 October 1901.

103　Trimmer to Hon. Merry, 25 November 1907, Dispatch Book, 1903–09, Consular Posts, Cape Gracias a Dios, Nicaragua, USNA, RG 84, vol. 11, p. 119; Trimmer to Hon. Merry, 16 April 1908, USNA, RG 84, vol. 11, p. 139; Trimmer to Assistant Secretary of State, 29 May 1908, USNA, RG 84, vol. 11, p. 149.

Two kinds of environmental problems underscored the region's political apprehensions. First, forest clearing significantly increased river silt loads. Second, unusually strong and frequent hurricanes augmented the effects of human-induced environmental change. In short, these two environmental effects combined to raise the costs of doing business in the Mosquitia. They also laid bare the lack of public or private improvements and, ultimately, influenced the turmoil that forced Zelaya from office. At the mines, for example, supply and transport costs outstripped most others. Incoming foodstuffs and industrial supplies for the mines had to be poled up sinuous rivers by crews of Miskitu men in 15-metre canoes (Figure 2.9). High coastal sand bars, harbour siltation, seasonal river changes, river sand bars and rocky rapids greatly limited the utility of steamers. At Port Dietrick, steamers had to be unloaded at sea. Their goods were ferried across high sand bars, reloaded at the dock and then transported in dugout canoes dozens of kilometres up river before they could be placed aboard a Dietrick steamer that only went half way to the mines. While hurricanes altered the functioning of port facilities and flattened banana and rubber plantations, they also limited the local availability of food supplies. An 1892 hurricane destroyed the Cape region and all surrounding indigenous plantations; even six months later no local provisions could be purchased.[104] One US consul summarised environmental constraints to production costs in monetary terms: 'feeding men in the mining districts costs more on average than the wages paid'.[105]

Figure 2.9: Miskitu Men Poling Goods to Goldmines circa 1920

Courtesy of Archives of Moravian Church, Bethlehem, PA.

104 Mierisch (1895), p. 66.
105 Trimmer to Assistant Secretary of State, 1 October 1908, Dispatch Book, 1903–09, Consular Posts, vol. 11, USNA, RG 84, p. 159;

Despite the clear link between extractive economies and environmental change, scholars have never examined the role of the latter in influencing the former in the Mosquitia. This is surprising because several astute period authors noted that, if not addressed, environmental problems would constrain the expansion of the regional economy. Immediately following annexation in 1894, Nicaragua's special commissioner for the Mosquitia claimed that the government would have to dredge all coastal bars to insure that commerce did not suffer. In 1898 the mining engineer John Nicol noted that the Río Grande bar was very bad: 'the enormous quantity of *débris* brought down by the river, and the constantly shifting sandbanks at its mouth, would always cause great expense, if an attempt were made to keep open a good harbour here'. Río Coco silt loads were so great that the Moravian missionary Guido Grossmann found that the cape had extended seaward two kilometres during his 20 years in the Mosquitia.[106] Meanwhile, Nicaraguan understanding of the relationship between forest clearing and river siltation prompted a series of new forest laws in 1905 that prohibited tree cutting on steep slopes, along water margins and near mountain summits. Slash-and-burn farming was also prohibited. In effect, the government assumed the power to regulate all forest use in an attempt to deal with the problems of erosion.[107]

Political and environmental problems also coincided with an upsurge in Miskitu mobilisation. By the early 1900s, many Miskitu chafed under Nicaraguan occupation. Accustomed to writing off indigenous complaints as insignificant, Moravian meddling or the work of 'foreign' agitators, Nicaragua was forced to act militarily for more or less the first time. General indigenous resistance to Nicaraguan authority combined long-standing Sambo-Tawira divisions to produce the so-called Sam Pitts rebellion in 1907. A Tawira Miskitu from Yulu, Pitts had refused to recognise the Nicaraguan-crafted ascension of the Río Coco Chief Andrew Hendy. Pitts also resented Hendy's capitulation to Nicaragua during the signing of the Mosquito Convention in 1895, in which Miskitu delegates recognised Nicaraguan sovereignty. Pitts actively sought out British support in Jamaica but after none materialised he decided to instigate a rebellion on his own. Contemporaneous reports from Moravian missionaries suggest that Pitts had a significant number of Tawira supporters from several savanna communities that had been in the Mosquito Reserve. The missionaries repeat-

---

106 Callejas (1896), p. 524; Nicol (1898), p. 659; 'Informe de Inspector General del Cabo Gracias a Dios, R.B. Montcrieffe, 1897,' *La Gaceta*, 7 December 1897; Grossmann (1988 [1940]), p. 17.
107 There is no evidence that such legislation was ever enforced in the Mosquitia; see Nicaragua (1905), 'Sobre El Impuesto Forestal de 8 de Mayo de 1912,' *Boletín Judicial*, 31 May 1920, p. 2927.

edly used their trope of village 'excitement' to refer to Pitts's mobilisation and subsequent Nicaraguan efforts to put it down. Though Pitts was killed by Nicaraguan troops in 1907, his activities represent the beginning of more visible and coordinated Miskitu mobilisation against Nicaraguan authority.[108] When considered alongside the more prosaic acts reported throughout this chapter — superstition, deceit, excitement, uprisings, unwillingness to work, false compliance and letter writing — Miskitu political practices affected how the state and foreign investors viewed and acted upon the Mosquitia.

Conclusion

Dominant and interwoven perceptions of territory, race and nature — what I have termed the geographical imagination — guided state strategies that attempted to incorporate the Mosquitia, a contested frontier region. The enactment of these incorporationist strategies produced specific kinds of political posturing and social responses that interacted with the ecological conditions of natural resource economies. I have argued that the totality of this conjuncture influenced the scope and directionality of environmental change in the Mosquitia, and that no environmental history of the region can ignore the cultural and political forces that produced it.

Examining the complex interaction among state expansion, the geographical imagination and environmental outcomes in the Nicaragua–Mosquitia context suggests five conceptual generalisations that could apply to environmental history elsewhere in Latin America. Firstly, the weaker the state within its self-defined national territory, the greater was the need to construct a geographical imagination that naturalised the right and inevitability of state expansion. Stated differently, the more an alienated region was deemed 'integral' to the nation, the more discursive must be the geographical imagination justifying incorporation. Secondly, the more that the prevailing geographical imagination deviated from the experiences or reality of local residents, neighbouring states, foreign investors and foreign guarantors, the less likely that state policies achieved their intended objectives, such as native assimilation, expanding natural resource economies or establishing legitimate political control.

Another generalisation from this study of the Mosquita is that the more that the prevailing geographical imagination overlooked environmental constraints as a significant factor affecting the viability of human endeavours, the more probable that environmental constraints accentuated social or political conflicts, which further limited the viability of those

---

108 Anon. (1908); 'Sam Pitts, 1908,' published in Oertzen, Rossbach and Wünderrich (1989), pp. 271–4; Rossbach (1985).

endeavours. Fourthly, weak states had a deep reliance on foreign capital to carry out the incorporationist agenda. Weak states often had to grant monopoly concessions for infrastructure and sought foreign concessions to attract 'racially appropriate' colonists as a means to justify claims to a contested territory. But, foreign concessionaires often had very different objectives than the state. The resulting paradox may have hindered the incorporationist objectives of the state and the profit ambitions of concessionaires. Finally, territorial ambitions of the state were as much about controlling and benefiting from natural resource economies as they were about fulfilling nationalist-territorial discourses.

Nicaragua's nationalist narrative, from the regimes of Martínez and Zelaya to Somoza and the Sandinistas, has remained grounded in a discourse of a foreign-thwarted territorial integrity. The attending nationalist narrative casts the state in the role of the hero in unifying the national territory, and thus making the natural resources of the Mosquitia available for 'national' development. The two epigraphs at the beginning of this chapter endeavour to illustrate these points. But what does any of this have to do with an environmental history of the Mosquitia? I have argued that a nationalist narrative and the environmental history it helped enact should not be separated; that the directionality and scope of Mosquitia environmental change through the nineteenth century is coterminous with Nicaragua's geographical imagination, which was itself anchored in the national narrative. By perpetually conceptualising Nicaragua's geography as a national problem to be solved and as the moral duty of the state to overcome, imagineers of public discourse built 'progressive' and seemingly self-evident solutions into their explication of the problem. In the process they circumscribed how Nicaragua beheld and acted upon the Mosquitia: they conditioned the social and political context in which the environment was perceived and used; they sowed the seeds of local dissent and subversion; and they insured that knowledge of environmental constraints would be obfuscated.

What makes this story so compelling to me is that by leaving few 'visible' imprints on the landscape, the nineteenth-century geographical imagination and the environmental histories it orchestrated do not influence current Mosquitia environmental debates. New geographic imaginations emanating from state institutions in Managua — notably grounded in those of the nineteenth century — seek to inscribe their legislative and technical visions on a set of deeply historical problems. Still, prevailing Nicaraguan geographical imaginations of the Mosquitia have always reflected those of foreigners. A few years after Port Dietrick collapsed, William Miner of the USA sailed by the defunct landscape and described it as a 'monument' to all harebrained schemes that go forward without requisite knowledge. After voicing this note of caution, Miner ignored his own insights and declared that 'once exploited and its resources investigated, [the Mosquitia] will become the garden spot of the earth and a source of wealth to those who are in a position to accept its bounty ... [thus it is] only a matter of time when the world will awaken to this *El Dorado* which lies at the very door of [the United States]'.[109]

109   Miner (1915), pp. 19, 51, 58.

CHAPTER 3

From Lakeshore Village to Oil Boom Town: Lagunillas under Venezuelan Dictator Juan Vicente Gómez, 1908–1935[*]

Nikolas Kozloff

Between 1914 and 1922 subsidiaries of the British oil company Shell, including Venezuela Oil Concessions (VOC) and the Caribbean Petroleum Company (CPC) entered the Lake Maracaibo Basin, located in western Venezuela in the provincial state of Zulia. The oil companies' move into Zulia was swift, as the law favoured oil companies seeking to expropriate local lands, and residents could not count on expert lawyers to defend their interests. During the oil boom, local people around Lake Maracaibo paid the price for the government's lack of technical oversight over the oil industry. Once the oil companies took control of the land, many of the same environmental problems associated with previous oil development, for example in Mexico, were repeated in Venezuela, including blow-outs, defective oil storage, oil waste from refineries and oil transport on land and sea.

The oil presence in Zulia also gave rise to environmental problems not strictly associated with oil contamination, such as swamp drainage to combat malaria and water diversion for oil operations. Oil extraction gave rise to great urban and rural changes, transforming sleepy agricultural or fishing villages into bustling and populous oil boomtowns. Oil companies imported West Indian labourers who joined Venezuelans in the sprawling settlements. Despite racial discrimination, some West Indians managed to make a modest living in the oil boomtowns. On the fringes of the boomtowns, oil companies grabbed up *ejidos* or common lands belonging to municipalities.[1] However, urban residents and local authorities were poorly equipped to deal with the emergence of the oil industry and its social,

[*] I would like to acknowledge Alan Knight, Professor of the History of Latin America at St Antony's College, Oxford University Latin American Centre, who oversaw work on my dissertation, entitled 'Maracaibo Black Gold: Venezuelan Oil and Environment during the Juan Vicente Gómez Period, 1908–1935'. Much of the work in this chapter is based on research for that dissertation. I should also like to thank Christian Brannstrom for his welcome assistance editing this chapter.

[1] *Ejidos* refer to lands held by municipalities to cover municipal needs. The terms *ejido* and municipal land were used interchangeably in the early 1900s; see McBeth (1983), pp. 146–7; Ovidio Quirós (1960), p. 21.

environmental and public health consequences. It was only after 1922, when US oil companies rushed to join their British counterparts in Lake Maracaibo, that the state, presided over by the dictator Juan Vicente Gómez, provided technical oversight, and even then this was insufficient.

In many ways Gómez resembled Latin American military caudillos of the nineteenth century. A military general and native of the Andean state of Táchira, Gómez seized power in 1908 in a US-backed coup. Over the next 25 years he maintained tyrannical control over Venezuela by establishing family members, fellow *tachirenses* and army officers in key political positions. During his rule Gómez was able to amass an astounding personal fortune through ranching and became the largest landowner in the country.[2] Momentously, however, growing oil wealth after 1922 transformed the Gómez state and allowed the government to expand its bureaucracy. As Ewell has written: 'The Gómez system built a political bridge between the personalistic caudillo system of the past and the modern bureaucratic state of the future.'[3] With the money from oil development, the government was able to finance road building and public works programmes. Maintaining growing technical and military bureaucracies in place to oversee such projects, however, would prove costly. In Ellner's view, 'Gómez's success in centralising political and military structures depended on his deriving enough revenue from the oil industry to finance the expanded bureaucracy and new projects.'[4] Accordingly, within the growing development ('fomento') ministry, which was in charge of promoting and overseeing industrial development, officials sought to exert greater control over oil revenue by monitoring the oil industry and oil production. Simultaneously, as the oil presence in Zulia grew during the 1920s and 1930s, an expanding local bureaucracy of inspectors working within the development ministry called on higher authorities in Caracas to become more actively involved in protecting workers and local residents from oil company abuses. Such sentiments were echoed by Vincencio Pérez Soto, who was appointed Zulia state president by Gómez in 1926. A tough and energetic bureaucrat, Pérez Soto had previously served as state president of the Andean state of Trujillo.[5] Pérez Soto replaced Isilio Febres Cordero, a reportedly very weak and irresolute state president.[6] The new state president quickly revised state laws, discouraged petty graft and

2   Lieuwen (1965), p. 46.
3   Ewell (1984), p. 59.
4   Ellner (1995), p. 98.
5   National Archives, Washington, DC [hereafter NA], 891.00/1299, Alexander Sloan to Secretary of State, Maracaibo, 5 June 1926.
6   NA, 891.00/1299, Alexander Sloan to Secretary of State, Maracaibo, 5 June 1926; 831.00/1315, Alexander Sloan to Secretary of State, Maracaibo, 26 November 1926.

reorganised the school system.[7] A frequent critic of the oil companies, Pérez Soto wrote personally to Gómez concerning the oil companies' environmental and safety abuses.

Lagunillas and the Onset of Petroleum Extraction

During the 1920s Lake Maracaibo was still surrounded by villages located on the banks of the lake. In this chapter, I focus on one lakeshore village, Lagunillas, which was located directly within the most important oil zone in Venezuela during this time (Figure 3.1). Lagunillas residents lived from fishing and hunting of wild ducks.[8] In 1929, according to the *Guía General de Venezuela*, indigenous peoples still lived in the lake villages in order to avoid plagues of mosquitoes on the banks of Lake Maracaibo.[9] Lakeside residents apparently derived much of their diet from fishing and from 'curma', an abundant wild root that grew in the swamps along the banks of Lake Maracaibo. *Curma* was considered at least as good as potato, but was 'eliminated by petroleum'. The water used by local residents for domestic uses came from the lake itself, and according to one local resident there was little risk of getting sick from the water as it was clean, such that one could even see the head of a coin or a needle in the water. With the arrival of the oil companies however, the water became dirty.[10] Lagunillas, whose Indian inhabitants plied the town in canoes, and who also made grass mats during the late nineteenth century, took their water from the lake. Houses were constructed in the midst of a beautiful inlet called Lagunilla.[11] The grass mats were produced from the extensive cattails that grew between vast bogs and stagnant water.[12] The *Guía General de Venezuela* stated that Lagunillas was constructed of houses, built on stilts, which were set into the lakebed itself.[13] The great swamp of Lagunillas occupied 15 square kilometres, covered in mangroves and other aquatic vegetation.[14] During the oil boom the Lagunillas area was still a swamp, home to abundant wildlife. One ornithologist, for example, remarked that 'on the large cienaga at Lagunillas there were thousands of tree ducks...While not allowing a close approach when resting on the water, these ducks when flying seemed to have little fear of a boat.'[15] In the late 1920s, Lagunillas had 1,478 total residents (792 men and 686 women),

7   NA, 891.00/1304, Alexander Sloan to Secretary of State, Maracaibo, 5 August 1926.
8   Depons (1889), p. 71.
9   Benet (1929), p. 645.
10   Interview with Sra. Antonia Rall published in Bello et al. (1980), pp. 7, 8, 12.
11   No author (1875), p. 111.
12   *Tópicos Shell*, 'Drenaje de Lagunillas,' March 1940, p. 2.
13   Benet (1929), p. 700.
14   *Ibid.*, p. 642.
15   Osgood and Conover (1922), pp. 45–6.

occupying 341 houses.[16] It is not clear how many fishermen were employed in Lagunillas and there is no written record that they complained about oil pollution to the companies or to the authorities.[17]

Figure 3.1: Lagunillas and the Lake Maracaibo Petroleum Region

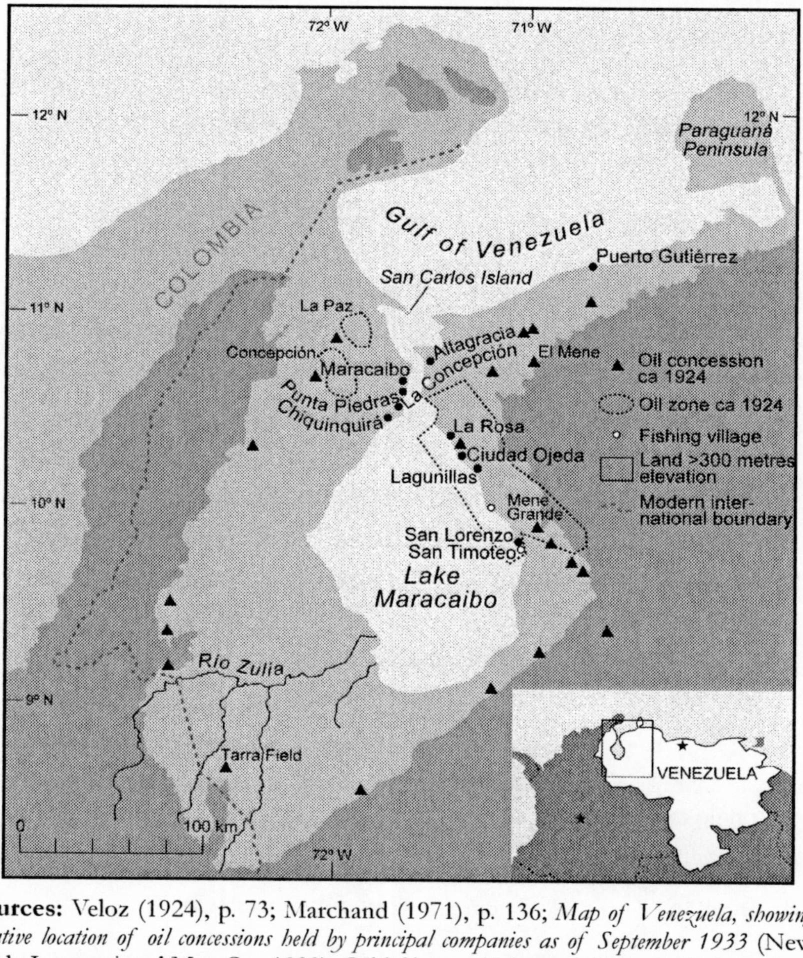

Sources: Veloz (1924), p. 73; Marchand (1971), p. 136; *Map of Venezuela, showing relative location of oil concessions held by principal companies as of September 1933* (New York: International Map Co., 1933); *Oil field map of Maracaibo Basin, Venezuela, showing holdings of various companies-shipping fields-oil pools, etc.* (New York: International Surveyors, 1921); base map from National Imagery and Mapping Agency, ONC K-26 (1:1,000,000), revised 1988.

16   Benet (1929), p. 675.
17   Oldenburg (n.d.), p. 264.

In 1925 Venezuela Gulf Oil Company started drilling in Lagunillas, and in 1926 Lago Petroleum Corporation (LPC) and VOC began operations.[18] By 1927 the Lagunillas field had produced more than 25 million barrels in a drilled area not exceeding 273 hectares.[19] This principal producing area in Venezuela quickly came to be known as La Rosa-Lagunillas, a narrow strip about 40 kilometres long stretching along the east bank of Lake Maracaibo.[20] By April 1927 there were more than 230 wells completed along this 'Golden Lane', producing more than 100,000 barrels daily.[21] In the late 1920s and early 1930s production in Lagunillas soared, and the field would become one of the most prolific in Venezuela (see Table 3.1) with 616 wells drilled between 1926 and 1932.[22] By the late 1920s Lagunillas production dwarfed that of other fields in the Maracaibo Basin (Table 3.2).

Table 3.1: Oil production in Lagunillas, 1926–31

Year	Production (barrels)
1926	1,207,913
1927	28,825,578
1928	61,451,468
1929	78,493,631
1930	75,376,078
1931	65,844,197

Source: McDermond (1932), p. 123.

Opening up the Lagunillas field required back-breaking work. At one point workers had to open a road between Lagunillas and La Salina, a distance of 45 kilometres. Two teams working at either end began in 1926 and met in mid-January 1927. Men worked 14 hours daily cutting down dense jungle, trees and weeds with machetes.[23] For the oil companies, unhealthy swamps and jungle created problems not just for workers opening up roads, but also for workers stationed in the new oil installations. In 1926 Gulf had 180 workers at Lagunillas. In an effort to rid itself of swampland, Gulf spread oil over marshland and flattened gullies and depressions.[24]

18   Quintero (1991), p. 65.
19   The Lamp (1927), p. 7.
20   Megargel Publications (1927), p. 11.
21   *Ibid.*, p. 12.
22   McDermond (1932), p. 121.
23   Baptista (1964), p. 7.
24   R. Faría Nones, Altagracia, 15 December 1926, published in Venezuela (Ministro de Relaciones Interiores) (1928), p. 308.

Table 3.2: Venezuelan Petroleum Production by Principal Fields, 1926–30 in Barrels

Field	1926	1927	1928
La Paz	734,280	228,910	16,692
Benitez	133,684	1,146,278	1,406,658
El Mene	2,316,690	2,475,084	1,806,538
La Concepción	832,501	633,782	1,195
Tarra	49,513	107,188	135,485
Mene Grande	8,443,418	9,818,296	13,287,776
Ambrosio	1,729,817	272,325	1,954,324
La Rosa	21,215,300	19,309,649	25,106,650
Lagunillas	1,207,913	28,825,576	61,452,468

Source: US Department of Commerce (1931), p. 29.

A central question relating to oil company drainage and dyke projects, in addition to the campaign to eliminate swamplands, was whether these measures spelled disaster for the vegetation and cattails from which local residents built grass mats. If this artisan craft vanished, and if local people protested, there is no mention in government reports. Another concern was the effect of the dykes and drainage upon local ranchers who relied on watering holes for cattle. In 1923 there were 5,760 cattle in the Lagunillas municipality.[25] There is some indication that the oil industry and its infrastructure displaced ranching, although documentation does not specify the exact chronology. During the Second World War ranchers wrote to President Medina Angarita that they had been displaced by oil development around Lagunillas, and that their cattle had had no water to drink. As a result, ranchers had had to emigrate to nearby savannas.[26]

Who were the oil workers who came to Lagunillas? There is little evidence that US or British staff lived in Lagunillas, although oilmen might have frequented houses of prostitution. It is more likely that Anglos lived on shore in the choicest housing, which was freer from risk of industrial accident. In Lagunillas West Indians mingled with other immigrants and with Venezuelans during the 1920s and 1930s. In 1933 there were 35 'antillanos', or people from the Dutch, French and British Caribbean possessions, and 12 Chinese working for LPC in Lagunillas, out of a total of 573

25 *Boletín de La Cámara de Comercio de Caracas* [hereafter *BCCC*], 1 January 1923, no 110, p 1851.
26 Archivo Histórico de Miraflores [hereafter AHM], 1–1–3, Criaderos de Lagunillas, Rolendio Bracho, Simon Cruel, Ismael Sánchez, others, to Medina, undated.

workers.[27] At Lagunillas *antillanos* and Chinese working for LPC and paid on a monthly company scheme represented nine per cent of the workforce (seven individuals) as opposed to six per cent in the case of Venezuelans (five individuals). Even jobs that could have been filled by Venezuelan women, such as waiters or servants, were filled by black Trinidadians.[28] It would seem that, in addition to the Chinese working within the oil companies, a number of other Chinese had set up as independent businessmen: as early as 1933 there is mention of Chinese traders in Lagunillas.[29] Another ethnic group within Lagunillas were Middle Eastern merchants, including Syrians and Lebanese.[30] Presumably, some foreign and Venezuelan women would have been working in prostitution, but there is scant documentary reference to such houses, perhaps because the *gomecista* authorities themselves were involved.[31] As in other oilfields, complicated racial and social hierarchies within Lagunillas would have made community organising more difficult.

For West Indian migrants, Lagunillas was not the most promising of destinations. New arrivals had to contend with appalling standards of public hygiene, including dysentery, malaria and industrial accidents. According to one doctor, Lagunillas was one of the worst malaria zones in the oil belt, and even as late as 1928 exhibited severe cases.[32] There were other public health problems. According to government documentation William Goneda, a married Barbadian painter, died of dysentery on the LPC oilfield in Lagunillas. The oil company provided medical assistance, but to no avail.[33] Marcello J. Benjasmin, native of Grenada and five-year resident of Lagunillas, died of gastroenteritis at the age of 40. Benjasmin had worked as a carpenter and had married, but at time of death did not possess 'goods of fortune'.[34] Though local authorities did not state how the West Indians fell ill with dysentery and gastroenteritis, lack of pure drinking water must have been a problem. Furthermore, the water around Lagunillas was contaminated with oil.

27 Archivo Histórico Ministerio Energía y Minas (Caracas) [hereafter AHMEM], 1932–33, Inspectoría Técnica de Hidrocarburos [ITH], Asunto: Correspondencia e Informes, G. Gabaldon P. to ITH, Lagunillas, 12 March 1933.

28 AHMEM, 1932–33, ITH, Asunto: Correspondencia e Informes, Carlos Pérez de la Cova to ITH, Mene Grande, 8 March 1933.

29 Public Records Office [hereafter PRO], FO 369/2340, K 12726, 8 November 1933, MacGregor to Secretary of State for Foreign Affairs, London. Letter dated 27 September 1933.

30 Archivo Histórico Estado Zulia [hereafter AHZ], unmarked folder 1934, 'Novedades ocurridas en el cuartel de policía durante el día de ayer, 3–5–34 and 2–5–34'.

31 Bergquist (1986), p. 228.

32 Nieto Caicedo (1946), p. 105.

33 Registro Publico, Maracaibo [hereafter RP], Defunciones Lagunillas 1927, Lagunillas, 17 March 1927.

34 AHZ, unmarked folder 1934, Telegramas Jefes Civiles Distritos Foráneos, July 1934, La Rita, 18 July 1934, Mario Maya to Secretario General Estado Zulia.

Oil Infrastructure and Industrial Accidents

By the 1920s oil ports and infrastructure had greatly expanded. Oil was loaded onto shallow draught tankers at San Lorenzo, Lagunillas, La Rosa, Altagracia and Punta Piedras and shipped to the deep water ports of Las Piedras and Salinas on the Paraguaná Peninsula, and to refineries on Aruba and Curaçao.[35] Moving crude out of Lake Maracaibo proved challenging, and the Venezuelan authorities, including Pérez Soto, sought to exert greater control over burgeoning marine operations, tugboats and shipping. The new Zulia state president promptly addressed the issue of heavier maritime traffic, which had made navigation more difficult within Lake Maracaibo. Oil derricks, platforms, tugboats and other infrastructure were stationed at great distance from the banks of the lake. However, this infrastructure carried no system of lighting or signals. Accordingly, Pérez Soto ordered the companies involved in offshore drilling or oil infrastructure in the lake to construct a line of red lights delineating the maximum distance of the infrastructure from the lakeshore. The same companies also had to construct a system of green and white lights indicating the route that tankers would follow to public docks to avoid colliding with oil infrastructure. *Jefes civiles*, who oversaw the organisation of the police at the district and municipal levels, and who were personally appointed by Pérez Soto, were to ensure that the companies complied with the law.[36] However, their reports are silent on the issue of maritime traffic and safety, so it is difficult to know the extent to which the law was applied. The legal moves came none too soon. Tankers, each carrying between 14,500 and 25,000 barrels, could make up to ten round trips per month between Lake Maracaibo and refineries on Curaçao and Aruba. In addition to tankers, oil barges were used for transporting fuel oil between the various lake ports.[37]

Even after Pérez Soto and other government officials sought to make lake transport safer, there were still serious accidents. For example, in January 1931 the schooner *Fortuna*, bringing gasoline to CPC and LPC at Puerto Gutiérrez, was lost in the entrance to Lake Maracaibo, causing unknown damage.[38] During the 1930s there was also grave danger of oil spill due to collisions or sinking boats in Maracaibo Lake. For example, in November 1935 Vincencio Pérez Soto reported personally to President Gómez that in Lagunillas a gas cylinder had burst into flames creating an explosion on board a LPC tugboat. One worker was killed and another two

---

35   Megargel Publications (1927), p. 13.

36   Bohórquez (1994), pp. 86–7; AHZ, vol. 3 (1928), Compañías Petroleras. Decree, Vincencio Pérez Soto, Maracaibo, 7 August 1928.

37   McDermond (1932), p. 167.

38   *BCCC*, 1 February 1931, no 207, 'Información de Maracaibo,' dispatch from Maracaibo, 15 January.

burned.[39] If the ship leaked oil into the lake, Pérez Soto did not mention it, nor did he dwell on the potential safety or environmental risks involved in the transport of crude over the lake. As late as the Second World War, in fact, one newspaper reported that in Lagunillas tugboats lacked fire extinguishers and life-jackets.[40]

Additionally, off-shore oil operations were vulnerable to fire, as boiler stations with boardwalks connected the oil wells. Each well was in turn flanked by other kinds of oil infrastructure, including platforms holding pumps, mud tanks, pipe racks, manifolds, flow stations and separator or transformer tanks.[41] Obviously, such oil infrastructure and derricks in Lake Maracaibo posed an enormous environmental threat. Oil blow-outs, having wreaked havoc on land, now continued to cause havoc on the water. For example, LPC's well no. L44 blew out on 6 December 1927 with such force that the drilling tower was ripped from its supports. According to one undated newspaper clipping, probably the English-language *Tropical Sun* from Maracaibo,[42] the blow-out was almost 'another Dos Bocas', a reference to the famous Mexican gusher of 1910. According to the clipping, at least 20,000 barrels were spread over the lake as a result of the accident.[43]

Lagunillas: Politics of Risk and Relocation

Venezuelan authorities were aware of the industrial risks at Lagunillas, and wrote to Caracas of the danger of incidents. Zulia state president Pérez Soto had originally warned Venezuela Gulf in 1926 that the company should do its utmost to protect human life and prevent industrial accidents.[44] At around the same time Pérez Soto wrote to President Gómez about Lagunillas, attaching a set of photographs and a map. By now, the LPC and Gulf had oil concessions in Lagunillas, and oil production looked to be as promising as the La Rosa field. However, Pérez Soto thought Lagunillas was a worrisome situation, as drilling was occurring in close proximity to human habitation. Pérez Soto warned that serious accident was inevitable, as oil and

39   AHZ, unmarked folder 1935, Telegramas Copiadores 1935, Vincencio Pérez Soto to Juan Vicente Gómez, Maracaibo, 1 November 1935.

40   'Información de Lagunillas, jefes despotas y falta de seguridad industrial,' *Aquí Está*, 28 February 1945, p. 6.

41   'Lake Exploration Extends Seven Miles From Shore,' *Oil and Gas Journal*, 25 December 1941, p. 152.

42   The article refers not to well 44, mentioned in *El Farol*, but to well 444. It is probable that both publications were referring to the same accident.

43   American Heritage Center, University Wyoming Laramie [hereafter AHC], John Douglas Collection, Box 1 #6017, undated newspaper clipping, 'Lago's 444, Far Out In Lake, Blows In Unexpectedly —— Well Craters —— Sand Saves Calamity'.

44   'Empresas extranjeras,' Vincencio Pérez Soto to Chester Crebbs, Maracaibo, 17 August 1926, published in Venezuela (1928), p. 153.

gas leaks presented an industrial risk for the local people.[45] For Pérez Soto, the challenge was to relocate Lagunillas residents to a new site in a safer zone, and to indemnify the inhabitants for the cost of the move. Pérez Soto thought the oil companies could easily cover relocation costs. Moreover, the town's inhabitants had few resources, as municipal lands or *ejidos* had been occupied by the oil companies, depriving local people of the means to produce grass mats. The original Lagunillas inhabitants, therefore, were in direct environmental conflict with the oil companies in this case.

Pérez Soto believed that the companies were resistant to any amicable resolution of the Lagunillas dispute and simply wanted to proceed with drilling. He added that he had instructed the local authorities to prohibit further construction in Lagunillas so long as the companies refused to pay any indemnities. The Zulia president asked Gómez if this seemed like a viable solution to the problem.[46] Pérez Soto also apprised the minister of the interior of the situation, expressing concern that expropriation would be unfair and out of touch with the 'patriotic norms of our dearest Chief'. A better solution, Pérez Soto suggested, would be for the companies to pay an indemnity to local residents for the removal of their houses to a new site, or alternatively buy houses for a 'fair price' from locals who did not want to move their houses.[47]

By late 1926 Pérez Soto thought he had found a solution to the Lagunillas problem when the VOC agreed to pay annual rent between one and two bolívares per hectare on common land. Under the agreement, the company reserved the right to determine where new houses were built, and retained rights over the land. This meant that the company could oblige a homeowner to move after the VOC agreed to pay suitable compensation. Pérez Soto informed President Gómez that he was satisfied with the arrangement, remarking that because of the poor quality of the land the 'municipalities will never secure a better tenant than the company'. Afterwards, the company agreed to compensate the residents of Lagunillas with 5,000 hectares personally selected by Pérez Soto to form the town's new communal lands. However, the trouble with the oil companies did not end with this arrangement, as the question of the relocation of residents still remained.[48] As Pérez Soto noted in a letter to Gómez, when the conflict first arose between Venezuela Gulf, LPC and the town

45   *Boletín del Archivo Histórico de Miraflores* [hereafter BAHM], 'Pérez Soto y Las Compañías Petroleras 1926,' Pérez Soto to Gómez, Memo, Maracaibo, 18 August 1926, p. 339.
46   *Ibid.*
47   'Empresas extrangeras,' Vincencio Pérez Soto to Ministro de Relaciones Interiores, 17 August 1926, published in Venezuela (1928), p. 150.
48   McBeth (1983), p. 148. VOC's annual rent of 1–2 Bolívares per hectare was approximately US$0.20–0.40.

of Lagunillas, the government had notified the oil companies that they should not continue construction. The town residents, in turn, were advised to halt construction until a settlement could be reached. Pérez Soto and the state authorities refrained from taking any position, while the companies were advised that they could plead their case before the ministry of development and the judiciary. Pérez Soto, meanwhile, advised the town residents not to sell their holdings and to ask for a lot of money. Pérez Soto told town residents confidentially that they could continue to build, thus blocking the advance of the oil companies, while Gómez decided what would be the most 'convenient' option.[49]

Apparently, Pérez Soto and Gómez both had different solutions to the thorny problem of Lagunillas. On the one hand, Pérez Soto wanted the village moved to a healthier site, and for the same communal lands to be granted with the companies paying the costs of the move. Under this plan, the local residents could continue the manufacture and sale of grass mats and be given better resources. In fact, Pérez Soto had ordered Pedro Pinto, the *jefe civil* of Bolívar District, to halt all further construction at Lagunillas. However, Gómez and the minister of the interior (Arcaya) advised Pérez Soto not to intervene, stating that the companies' request to have the village moved had been turned down and that all work near Lagunillas should be indefinitely suspended. Gómez's motivations in the Lagunillas case are murky. Could he personally, or his followers, have had real estate interests in Lagunillas? The proposal allowing the companies to settle their claim before the ministry of development and the judiciary would be nothing more than Gómez's ruse to bide time. Ostensibly, this delaying tactic was to obtain a better deal for the locals of Lagunillas, who could get higher prices for their homes. Meanwhile, Lagunillas residents continued to construct more houses on the surface of the lake.[50]

At the same time, LPC asked that the national government remove the town of Lagunillas altogether to make way for its oil exploration in the area. The ministry of the interior had replied that there was no legal precedent for moving towns.[51] By 1927 LPC was arguing that oil spillages around Lagunillas and surrounding waters were 'inevitable' and that inflammable gas posed a significant danger to locals. LPC had suspended its operations in the area even though the owners of buildings on the lake lacked property deeds and were constructing over territorial waters.[52] In a

---

49   AHM, 584–C, Secretario Cartas, 1–30 November 1926, Pérez Soto to Juan Vicente Gómez, 1 November 1926.
50   McBeth (1983), p. 149.
51   'Construcción en Lagunillas', Antonio Alamo to A.A. Sobalvorro, Caracas, 7 January 1927, published in Venezuela (1929b), p. 123.
52   A.A. Sobalvorro to Ministro de Relaciones Interiores, n.d., published in Venezuela (1929b), p. 125.

communication to the minister of the interior, Ebert Boylan of Gulf claimed that it was the residents of Lagunillas, and not the oil companies, who were to blame for the ever-worsening risk of an industrial accident. According to Boylan, when Gulf first started to drill at Lagunillas the locals' houses were almost 140 metres away; however, by June 1927 houses were being built at a distance of less than 80 metres from the oil drills. Additionally, there was the problem of oil tubing. Along the coast of the lake, at a distance of approximately 160 metres, the oil companies built tubing above the water. Originally, this tubing had been situated 20 metres from the town's houses; however recently built housing had been situated above the lines.[53] Pedro Arcaya, the minister of the interior, issued a government resolution stating that Lagunillas would stay in the same spot but no new construction would take place.[54] Pérez Soto subsequently drew up a new map delineating the town's borders and instructed residents to build only within the new boundaries.[55]

In practice, however, oil continued to collect in the waters surrounding Lagunillas. Even if all oil activity had been halted around the town there still would have been previous oil contamination, and no state official, Pérez Soto included, seemed willing to attempt a genuine clean up. Another solution would have been for the authorities, including Pérez Soto, to press for much tougher guidelines for the oil industry, instead of blindly accepting the industry's claim that spills were 'inevitable'. It may be that Pérez Soto felt the issue of oil contamination was effectively outside his political jurisdiction as state president. In October 1927 he alerted President Gómez to oil contamination in Lake Maracaibo, without naming any particular companies or, for that matter, analysing the matter in any great detail. Pérez Soto raised the pollution issue as though it were an irritant or inconvenience for his boss, stating that he was merely an honest and conscientious servant obliged to report these problems. He remarked that much had been written and published about the issue, suggesting that pollution was by now a public concern. Pérez Soto included in his letter to Gómez some press clippings about pollution. He recalled that he had spoken to the minister of development concerning the issue as early as November 1926. The Zulia state president sought Gómez's 'authorisation' to continue to send press clippings about the matter to the ministry of development, even though pollution did not fall strictly within his responsibilities as state president.[56]

---

53 Pedro Arcaya to Vicencio Pérez Soto, Caracas 15 June 1927, published in Venezuela (1929b), p. 131.
54 McBeth (1983), p. 150.
55 'Construcción en Lagunillas', Secretario General Estado Zulia, 15 July 1927, published in Venezuela (1929b), p. 134.
56 AHM, 607 C, 1–15 October 1927, Pérez Soto to Juan Vicente Gómez, 7 October 1927.

Three weeks later an uninterested Gómez responded simply that Pérez Soto had authorisation to send press clippings to the minister of development. The exchange of letters suggests that Pérez Soto was honestly concerned about pollution, but his cautious tone indicates the care he took to preserve his position within the Gómez hierarchy. Pérez Soto hinted that sufficient progress was not being made to control oil spills and that the culprit was the ministry of development, which he had alerted to the pollution but was not doing enough.[57]

Meanwhile, Lake Maracaibo's habitat was coming under greater threat with increased oil exploration. One US diplomat in the late 1920s wrote that

> The waters are covered with oil which is carried up to shore by the waves and blackens all vegetation which it touches. Along the shore are rows of palm trees whose leaves are so covered with oil that they droop to the ground. Oil is spattered everywhere on the vegetation and the houses. It is carried into the offices and dwellings on the shoes or the clothes of those who enter.[58]

The water around the town of Lagunillas was now a real fire hazard and a danger to the community. When vital interests were at stake, local inhabitants were not slow in complaining to the authorities. In May 1928, for example, local Lagunillas merchants complained to the Bolívar *jefe civil* that commercial traffic had slowed in and around the Lagunillas swamp because of Venezuela Gulf's drainage projects, which had resulted in oil pollution and sanding up of these coastal areas.[59] News of the obstructed and contaminated waters was forwarded to the Zulia secretary of government on 20 May[60] and by 12 June the company, prodded by local authorities, had constructed a canal that enabled river commerce and canoes to pass freely.[61] The authorities, then, were appraised of the contaminated waters in Lagunillas for quite some time, but seemed more concerned with commercial interests and freedom of navigation than with the pollution problem. Local merchants, for their part, complained of oil pollution, but only insofar as it harmed business.

---

57   AHM, Co 301, Correspondencia de Juan Vicente Gómez, 14 July 1927/14 December 1927. Juan Vicente Gómez to Pérez Soto, Maracaibo, 22 October 1927.
58   Quoted in Land (1957), p. 48.
59   'Obstucción del caño de Lagunillas,' H. Rodríguez O., Pineda and Alonzo, and others, to Jefe Civil del Distrito Bolívar, Lagunillas, 16 May 1928, published in Venezuela (1930), pp. 93–4.
60   Pedro Pinto S. to Secretario General de Gobierno, Santa Rita 20 May 1928, published in Venezuela (1923), pp. 92–3.
61   C.M. Crebbs to Secretario General de Gobierno, 12 June 1928, published in Venezuela (1930), pp. 95–6.

The Lagunillas Explosion

Shortly after the exchange of complaints from Lagunillas, in June 1928, the entire community paid the price for Gulf and LPC's pollution when a major fire occurred, destroying hundreds of houses and engulfing the town in flames. Pérez Soto informed President Gómez that the fire had been started by a spark from one of the open-hearth fires that ignited oil spilled by a leaky drill near the town.[62] Pedro Pinto, the *jefe civil* in Bolívar District, claimed that the fire destroyed more than 80 per cent of the town, claiming no lives but making more than 100 families homeless.[63] In a separate communication to the authorities in Maracaibo, he also remarked that the fire lasted for more than two hours and left only 125 of 700 houses standing.[64] One scholar has remarked that 'the rest of the town did not suffer because of the prevailing winds, which stopped the fire from spreading, and because of the rapid intervention of the authorities', as well as the oil companies, which leapt into action as soon as their infrastructure was threatened.[65]

In the wake of the fire, local authorities and the oil companies united in an effort to help by attending to the homeless. One local official admitted, however, that the oil companies were slow to help with the rescue operation.[66] As with previous oil-related accidents, President Gómez apparently showed little interest in the Lagunillas fire and the destruction unleashed on the lakeside town. On 16 June 1928 he tersely replied to Pedro Pinto: 'I very sincerely deplore the fire which occurred in that town; and I take into account that in spite of the catastrophe perfect order has been restored.'[67] The following day, Leonte Olivo, the Zulia secretary of government, reported to Gómez that only 20 houses had survived and the other 800 had been completely destroyed.[68] Some civilians had been burned and were being attended at oil company hospitals.[69] The VOC, 'following a minute investigation' into the matter, denied any responsibility for the catastrophe.[70]

---

62 McBeth (1983), p. 154.
63 AHM, 1048 T, Telegramas 15–25 June 1928, Lagunillas, 16 June 1928, Pedro Pinto S. to Juan Vicente Gómez.
64 AHZ, vol. 4, 1928, Calamidades Públicas, Incendio de Lagunillas, Pedro Pinto S. to Secretario General de Gobierno, Santa Rita, 18 June 1928.
65 McBeth (1983), p. 153.
66 AHZ, vol. 4, 1928, Calamidades Públicas Incendio de Lagunillas, Pedro Pinto S. to Secretario General de Gobierno, Santa Rita 18 June 1928.
67 AHM, Borrador no 384 B, Telegramas 1–19 June 1928, Juan Vicente Gómez to Pedro Pinto S., Maracay y Trujillo.
68 AHM, 1048 T, Telegramas 15–25 June 1928, Maracaibo? 16 June 1928, Leonte Olivo to Juan Vicente Gómez; see also Perozo (1993), p. 67, who reports only 319 houses destroyed.
69 AHM, 1048 T, Telegramas June 15–25 1928, Maracaibo? 16 June 1928, Leonte Olivo to Juan Vicente Gómez.
70 AHZ, vol 4 1928, Calamidades Públicas, Incendio de Lagunillas, VOC (signature illegible) to Presidente Estado Zulia, Maracaibo 18 June 1928.

One Maracaibo paper, *Occidente*, provided full coverage of the events of 1928. According to one article, the Lagunillas fire was of such magnitude that it had no historical precedent in the state of Zulia. *Occidente* claimed that oil slicks helped spread the fire; however, the paper reported that the fire had started at the Chang and Ling Laundry and ripped through the town at an alarming rate because the 'the planks which served as streets were covered in a fresh layer of oil, which contained a high level of gas'. The material losses were considerable, but none of the oil companies suffered any damages, as their offices and installations were located on land at a secure distance from the water.[71] Ramón Díaz Sánchez, an acclaimed contemporary Venezuelan novelist, pointed out how the oil industry victimised and sacrificed 'inferior races'. Industrial science, argued Sánchez, was firmly in the hands of Anglo-Saxons who cared little if inferior races died in furthering technological progress.[72]

Reconstruction and Pollution Control

Although the inhabitants of Lagunillas wanted to commence reconstruction of their town, both Gulf and LPC seized the opportunity to try to relocate the town far from the oilfield on which Lagunillas was located. Meanwhile, Pérez Soto rigorously enforced the resolution, which defined the city limits of Lagunillas, that he had enacted in the previous year. The Municipal Council of Bolívar District, meanwhile, passed another resolution calling for the town's reconstruction in the same location.[73] Gómez, however, was still reluctant to move the population. In late June 1928 Gómez sent a coded message to Pérez Soto, stating that 'it is convenient for the interests of the national government that the current Lagunillas situation stays the same, in other words that the population is not moved, as I have reports that there [the present location Lagunillas] lies a true fortune.'[74] Again, it is unclear what Gómez's motives were. It seems unlikely that he would altruistically seek to help Lagunillas residents, who would benefit as real estate prices soared. Was he trying to defend 'national' interests, as he put it? Did he have other, private interests? One historian has written that Gómez sympathisers were running brothels in Lagunillas.[75] Could the dictator have had a financial stake himself?

    In summing up the Lagunillas tragedy, it seems quite apparent that the oil companies were the chief culprits. However, if President Gómez had

71   'El Gran Incendio de Lagunillas', *Occidente*, 20 June 1928, no. 9, p. 4.
72   Ramón Díaz Sánchez, 'Ramonerías oportunistas despúes del incendio,' *Occidente*, 23 June 1928, no. 91, p. 3 .
73   McBeth (1983), p. 154.
74   Quoted in Perozo (1993), p. 64.
75   Bergquist (1986), p. 228.

taken firmer steps to move the inhabitants, as Pérez Soto tried to do, the tragedy could have been averted. Moving the town would have been difficult, although not impossible; the coastal area of Lagunillas was composed of mangrove, marshes and lagoons, which were unhealthy and full of insects,[76] and a move to land would have required swamp drainage. In the wake of the fire, local government officials corresponded with Pérez Soto about possible future moves to avoid similar accidents. One local official stated that a VOC superintendent had suggested placing an iron wall around the town of Lagunillas, at a depth of 30 centimetres below and 60 centimetres above the water level. The wall, claimed the superintendent, would not allow oil mixed with gas to arrive within close proximity of Lagunillas, since the oil would not go beneath the surface of the water. When the oil sank deeper in the water, it would be free of volatile and inflammable material, which did not represent a threat to Lagunillas.[77] There is no evidence, however, that oil companies suggested this option prior to the fire or that Pérez Soto personally lobbied for such a protecting wall before or after the 1928 fire.

In July 1928 a group of local Lagunillas residents appealed to President Gómez personally concerning the fire and damage to their homes and businesses. Addressing the dictator very respectfully, the residents argued that the fire was 'owing no doubt' to abundant oil spills in Lake Maracaibo. The residents informed Gómez that they were preparing legal action against LPC and Gulf.[78] Privately, Pérez Soto commented to President Gómez that he had had to calm feelings because otherwise the population would have attacked the 'foreigners and their drilling rigs, presenting us with a serious dispute'.[79] Pérez Soto's suggestion of vandalism in this case is significant. It is a rare instance in which a high government official hinted of violent threats to the oil companies. However, if Gómez was alarmed by such threats, he gave no indication. In a non-committal telegram, Gómez responded personally to the Lagunillas residents, curtly remarking that, 'I believe that you should work through the State President's Council in regard to that matter'.[80] Thus Gómez, characteristically, sought to wash his hands of controversial political issues by delegating such matters to his subordinates.

Undeterred, in August 1928 Lagunillas residents asked Pérez Soto for advice on how to proceed with legal action against the companies. The res-

---

76   AHZ, vol 4, 1928, Calamidades Públicas, Incendio de Lagunillas. Vincencio Pérez Soto to Juan Vicente Gómez, Maracaibo, 8 July 1928.
77   *Ibid.*, Pedro Pinto S. to Vincencio Pérez Soto, Maracaibo,12 July 1928.
78   *Ibid.*, Gerardo Salvatierra, Simon Paris, J. Hadad, etc. to Juan Vicente Gómez, Maracaibo, 12 July 1928.
79   McBeth (1983), p. 154.
80   AHZ, vol. 4, 1928, Calamidades Públicas, Incendio de Lagunillas. Maracay, 13 July, Juan Vicente Gómez to Faria Hnos, Francisco Castellanos and others.

idents hired lawyers and actively sought a judicial claim against LPC and Gulf for damages suffered in the fire.[81] Pérez Soto seemed wary of the residents' proposals. He reasoned that, in accordance with Gómez's wishes and the dictator's communication of 13 July, the residents should desist from their motion, and seek a 'friendly' solution to the issue. He also stressed that all the mechanisms of the state would be available to residents should they resort to the legal process, including the judiciary.[82] Pérez Soto's response is not surprising given the political reality at hand. If the Zulia state president had pressed residents' claims further, the companies might have lobbied Gómez to remove Pérez Soto from office. Furthermore, in his correspondence with Gómez regarding pressing social issues, Pérez Soto was always informative but very careful to maintain a humble and obsequious tone.

The residents might have responded to Pérez Soto, arguing that recently passed measures could have been interpreted in their favour in this case, but there is no evidence that they did. A few weeks after the Lagunillas fire, the state passed a Law of Hydrocarbons. Under Article 73 companies now faced fines of between 1,000 and 5,000 bolívares if they did not comply with laws passed by the state protecting the 'life and health' of workers and employees.[83] Again, however, this vaguely worded clause could be subject to different interpretations. In the case of Lagunillas, the companies could always deny that they had started a fire. Alternatively, they might argue that a given accident was the fault of local people and their own irresponsibility. In any case, if Pérez Soto was aware of the provisions of the new law, he did not suggest that residents press them in a potential lawsuit. By November, there were four suits pending by Lagunillas residents seeking damages from the fire. LPC had not been cited.[84] In the wake of the disaster, Dr Angel Francisco Brice, an LPC lawyer, recommended that the company act to occupy areas of the burnt town, as there were no longer any houses in that part of Lagunillas and the company was not subject to any operational restrictions under the law in these areas.[85]

There is little to indicate that the company heeded Brice's advice concerning Lagunillas construction, and problems afflicting the town would not end with the 1928 fire. At four a.m. on 16 April 1929 a fire broke out

81   'Incendio de Lagunillas', *Occidente*, 4 August 1928, no. 103, p. 6.
82   *Ibid.*, p 6.
83   Venezuela (1937), p. 199. Earlier oil laws had been passed in 1922 and 1925 (Lieuwen, 1954, p. 49).
84   Archivo Histórico Pdvsa [hereafter AHPDVSA], Creole Petroleum Corporation, Dr Angel Francisco Brice, Opiniones nos 1–167, 1921–29, Dr Angel Francisco Brice to Howland Bancroft, 'Juicios Pendientes Hasta el 15 de Noviembre 1928,' 19 November 1928.
85   *Ibid.*, Angel Francisco Brice to J.D. Burnett, 26 July 1928.

once again. The blaze quickly spread to the main street of Lagunillas, where it destroyed 52 houses but took no reported casualties.[86] Pérez Soto, in a telegram to Gómez, mentioned only that the fire had been extinguished without elaborating.[87] As in 1928 Gómez expressed satisfaction that the matter had been resolved without pursuing it further.[88] In June 1929 another fire (the third) was reported when a blow-out occurred near the banks of Lake Maracaibo, destroying pier infrastructure and 25 lake-borne houses.[89] In Lagunillas, the VOC and Gulf finally managed to extinguish the fire.[90]

It is indeed perplexing why these frequent fires could be allowed to continue, even after the major conflagration of 1928. There is nothing in the historical record to suggest that Pérez Soto, who liked to portray himself as an activist state president who fought to get the companies under control, took any legal action against the oil corporations for their fires and accidents. Following the first fire, companies such as LPC and Gulf continued to pressure the Maracaibo authorities to halt reconstruction of the town so the area could be opened up to unimpeded offshore oil production.[91] If local people were aware of the oil companies' plans and attempted to halt further expansion, there is no mention of activism in government reports. Meanwhile, it seems that Gómez and Pérez Soto decided that they would continue with the earlier policy of keeping Lagunillas in situ. Meanwhile, the authorities would claim publicly that they were trying to keep oil operations at some distance from the town. Shortly after the fire of 1928 Pérez Soto reminded Gómez that the ministry of the interior and the ministry of development, as well as Gómez himself, had agreed as far back as 1927 that Lagunillas would have to stay in its current site. The town had been demarcated with iron posts, and inhabitants were ordered not to build over these limits, while oil companies could not build within the town perimeter.[92] Gómez, for his part, had already agreed with Pérez Soto, complementing his subordinate on his reasoning and thoughtfulness, and agreeing that Lagunillas should not move.[93]

86 'Última hora, incendio en el pueblo de Lagunillas,' *Occidente*, 17 Abril 1929, p. 1; 'Más sobre el incendio,' *Occidente*, 18 April 1929, p. 4.

87 AHM, 1073 T, 1–9 Abril, 1929, Vincencio Pérez Soto to Juan Vicente Gómez, 16 April, Maracaibo.

88 AHM, 410 B, 13–22 Abril 1929, Juan Vicente Gómez to Vincencio Pérez Soto, 17 April Maracay.

89 BCCC, 1 July 1929, no. 188, p. 4461, 'Información de Maracaibo,' dispatch dated 14 June.

90 *Ibid.*, p. 4462.

91 AHZ, vol. 4, 1928, Calamidades Públicas, Incendio de Lagunillas. Howland Bancroft, K. Winship to Secretario General de Gobierno, Maracaibo, 27 June 1928.

92 AHZ, vol. 4, 1928, Calamidades Públicas, Incendio de Lagunillas. Vincencio Pérez Soto to Juan Vicente Gómez, Maracaibo 8 July 1928.

93 AHZ, vol. 4, 1928, Calamidades Públicas, Incendio de Lagunillas. Juan Vicente Gómez to Vincencio Pérez Soto, Maracay, 6 July 1928.

Residents wrote not only to Pérez Soto, but also to higher officials. In September 1927 various residents of Urdaneta District, in the Municipality of La Concepción, located on the west bank of Lake Maracaibo, complained to the Federal Executive of oil slicks on Lake Maracaibo. The oil spills, they argued, poisoned the water, killed fish and prejudiced the fishing industry. Moreover, oil slicks made water unusable for daily use and for irrigation of sown fields in coastal areas.[94] The residents' complaint was formally lodged with the ministry of development on 24 October 1927.[95] It is unclear from where these particular oil slicks emanated, whether the oil zone on the east bank of Lake Maracaibo or somewhere closer on the west bank. Could it have been a ruptured VOC pipeline? One possibility is that oil seeped into coastal waters from blow-outs, accidents or deficient storage at La Paz and Concepción, for example. Another possibility might have been that oil contamination from across Lake Maracaibo and the oil belt had made its way to the opposite bank. If Gómez was aware of the problem, his telegrams to subordinates through September make no mention. Far from expressing curiosity or concern about oil contamination or social conditions within the Maracaibo Basin, Gómez preferred to discuss other matters with his lieutenant, Pérez Soto, in Maracaibo. For example, Gómez expressed avid interest in new political appointees in the state, robberies in Maracaibo and expulsion of foreigners from Zulia.[96] Gómez addressed oil contamination neither with Pérez Soto nor with Zulia residents with whom he was in contact during that time.

In a striking reversal, however, President Gómez personally ordered the ministry of development and ministry of the interior to constitute a technical commission, composed of an engineer (Siro Vázquez), a doctor (Toledo Rojas) and a lawyer (Diego Bautista Urbaneja) that would study the causes and effects of oil contamination in Lake Maracaibo. Just how or why Gómez

---

94　Venezuela (1929a), p. xviii, Exposición.

95　*Ibid.*, 410.

96　AHM, 364 B, September 1–20 1927, Juan Vicente Gómez to Pérez Soto, Maracay September 20 1927; 365 B, 21–30 September 1927, Juan Vicente Gómez to Pérez Soto, Maracay 22 September 1927, Juan Vicente Gómez to Pérez Soto, Maracay 22 September.

97　It is tempting to say that local residents made the key difference in spurring the government to act. The commission made a point of interviewing local residents about the pollution, so it would seem that the welfare of local people was a primary consideration. If Gómez was genuinely moved to act because he was concerned about pollution, however, there is no indication which group might have proven most influential. Unfortunately, the commission's report does not give us any real clues as to why Gómez acted when he did. It is possible the government simply desired more information about the location of spills and wanted to know which companies were guilty to better control oil production. A third possibility might have been that Gómez was concerned about possible secessionist sentiment in Zulia and the need to shore up public opinion.

acted is shrouded in mystery.[97] Although historical documents do not suggest that oil and the environment were a major concern, complaints may have accumulated to such a degree that he was forced to deal with the issue. Gómez had been receiving reports about industrial accidents and contamination from the likes of Pérez Soto for several years. Gómez's commission eventually would recommend measures for the termination of oil contamination.[98] The Caracas newspaper *Mundial* praised the creation of the commission as 'a transcendental government initiative [*medida*]'.[99]

Subsequently, the commission embarked for Maracaibo, visited the east bank of Lake Maracaibo and met with 15 local residents within the municipality of Chiquinquirá (Urdaneta District). Some residents and signatories of the petition were state employees. The commission also met with residents in the municipalities of El Carmelo, La Concepción and settlements of La Ensenada and Palmarejo. These people complained too of the contaminated water. One of the principal causes of the pollution, according to the commission's report, was the existence of oil wells at the bottom of the lake. The authors of the report added that the companies were not adopting satisfactory measures to avoid oil spills within Lake Maracaibo. When the oil left the well, it was transported to tanks or deposits. After the sand had fallen to the bottom, the petroleum was transported to other tanks and the sand dumped in the lake. This sand, impregnated with oil, polluted the water. Embarkation of oil also led to many oil slicks. Oil slicks recurred when the oil pipeline's flexible tube was disconnected from the tanker's tubing during the loading process.

Another common cause of marine pollution in Lake Maracaibo was overflowing tanks. According to the commission's report, an oil worker mistakenly might allow a deposit tank to overflow as oil escaped from the upper opening. Generally, the report added, the tanks had a capacity of between 300 and 500 barrels, depending on the production of the individual well. Unfortunately, drill connections could not withstand the force of the oil that rose together with gas in the main tubing, and the workers in charge of renewing these connections let the oil run into the lake. Workers at drill sites were not the only culprits, however. Pollution was also caused by oil tankers and the loading process. Typically, tankers would unload oil at refineries in Aruba and Curaçao and then fill their tanks with sea water as ballast. On their return to Venezuela, tankers would discharge

---

98   Venezuela (1929a), p. xviii. The commission was appointed in December 1927; its final report was submitted in February 1928 as 'Informe de la comisisión nombrada para estudiar los derrames de petróleo en las aguas del Lago de Maracaibo' (Venezuela, 1929a, p. 418).

99   'El petróleo en el Lago de Maracaibo, una trascendencia medida gubernativa,' *Mundial*, 3 December, p. 1.

the ballast in the vicinity of the island of San Carlos, at the entrance to Lake Maracaibo, or even within the lake itself. This water was mixed with oil and highly contaminated.

Remarkably, the commission's report also displayed an awareness of the dangers posed by oil to animal life. As the report noted, oil was harmful to fish and birds, as well as domesticated animals that ingested contaminated water. Contaminated water, furthermore, destroyed fish eggs and as a result threatened the fishing industry. Oil on the lake was so prevalent that slicks on the water could be seen as far as Maracaibo District and in the port itself, as oil stuck to virtually every boat navigating the lake. The oil contamination was so bad, reportedly, that bathers at lake beaches had to wash with gasoline to get the stains off their bodies. Oil contamination was ubiquitous on both the east and west bank of the lake.[100]

Having drawn this grim picture of daily life on Lake Maracaibo, the commission went on to make some positive recommendations. First, the oil companies should recover sediment from deposit tanks in appropriate tugboats designed to transport the material to land. Later, the sand and residual material could be used for highway construction. Second, before disconnecting the tanker's connection plate, the companies should install a receptacle of sufficient capacity that could receive oil left in the tube. Third, the companies should advise the Fiscal Inspector when a well was two-thirds done. The inspector would then visit the site and make certain that the company had adopted precautionary measures designed to avoid oil spills in the lake area. Fourth, company tankers returning from Aruba and Curaçao would be obliged to dump their ballast in the open sea before passing close to San Carlos island at the mouth of Lake Maracaibo. Apparently, the commission had no idea of what to do with this ballast and recommended that it be dumped on the high seas when the tide was receding, so that oily wastes would be washed out to sea. Fifth, companies should supply each deposit tank with an indicator device that would signal when the level of oil had reached its maximum. Sixth, companies should replace connections that could not withstand oil and gas pressure emanating from the master tubing. Seventh, each oil camp and oil tanker should be monitored by supervisors who would carry out these recommendations. The report noted that though oil contamination was serious in the lake, there was still hope; the Commission suggested that the government sign onto an international oil contamination convention, which had been established at a 1926 international oil contamination conference in Washington DC, and to pass its own legislation based on the convention's recommendations.[101]

100 Venezuela (1929a), p. 409–11.
101 *Ibid.*, p. 411.

Interestingly, the report made no mention of the risk of oil tankers or other boats sinking in the lake. Similarly ignored was the issue of oil separators, and the commission apparently had little notion of what to do with oil wastes, ultimately favouring their elimination on the high seas. Some observers were not terribly impressed with the findings. Alexander Sloan, the US consul in Maracaibo, considered that the report had been 'very mild in its statements as to the effects of the presence of oil in the waters of Lake Maracaibo'. The waters of the lake, remarked Sloan, were 'so brackish, except in the southern section, that irrigation ditches through which lake waters are forced are covered with a salt deposit'.[102]

What result did the investigating commission achieve? Shortly after the arrival of the Gómez Commission, residents could welcome the passage of the Supervisory Law to Impede Water Pollution by Petroleum. If there were debates on the floor of the Senate or House of Deputies concerning the new law, these have not survived, perhaps because of the rubber-stamp status of the legislature under dictatorship. The law included several provisions. People or companies engaged in coastal oil exploration or transport were informed that oil slicks constituted a serious danger to health, the economy and 'public comfort'. Companies had to collect oily wastes on board tankers and transport them to land on tugboats, which would later be deposited in coastal sites. Each deposit tank had to be supplied with a monitoring device indicating when the maximum level of petroleum had been reached. Companies had to consult the Fiscal Inspector of Hydrocarbons each time a new drilling was to commence, thus initiating an inspection of the new site as soon as possible to ensure that drilling would not contaminate waters with oil. Companies arriving in Lake Maracaibo had to ensure that their tankers would dump waste in 'appropriate sites', apparently the high seas, and not within the lake itself; companies had to immediately renew worn-out drill connections which could not withstand oil and gas pressure. Companies had to admit ministry of interior personnel on board their tankers at the ministry's convenience. No oil tanker was permitted to dump crude oil, combustible, diesel oil or mixed waters containing oil in Venezuelan territorial waters. Finally, violation of the terms or provisions would be punished with a fine of between 100 and 5,000 Bs, according to the gravity of the infraction, and subject to approval by the Federal Executive and ministry of interior. Following three discussions in the Senate, the law was approved.[103] Apparently, the bill also passed in the Chamber of Deputies, and the new law was announced in the government's *Gaceta Oficial* dated 19 July 1928.[104]

---

102 Quoted in McBeth (1983), p. 173.

103 Archivo Histórico Cámara de Diputados, *Estados Unidos de Venezuela, Cámara del Senado, Ley de Vigilancia Para Impedir La Contaminación de las Aguas Por el Petróleo*, Caracas, 10 July 1928.

104 Barberii (1997), p. 110.

In a greater effort to get Zulia oil companies under control, Venezuelan authorities passed a 1930 *Reglamento* that established stricter technical guidelines for the oil industry. As part of the new legislation, the government created the Oficina Técnica de Hidrocarburos (OTH). During the Depression, OTH oil inspectors were able to fulfil an important economic purpose: closer monitoring of oil production and greater extraction of state revenue. Creation of the OTH also led to greater environmental controls, as oil inspectors sought to keep track of oil losses to Venezuela. OTH inspectors also made inspections of working conditions and oil operations within boom towns, and their reports often touched on environmental and public health issues within the Maracaibo Basin. Though the OTH had inadequate staff and resources to carry out the monitoring of oil fields, and apparently never fined the oil companies for their spills, inspectors nevertheless now undertook careful tabulation of oil production. Monitoring of the foreign oil companies was weak. Oil inspectors wrote reports, and some even pressured oil managers to comply with the law, but they did not press their superiors to fine oil companies for spills. Oil money accounted for 30 per cent of government revenue during the Depression, a time when Gómez needed oil revenue more than the oil companies needed the oil. Furthermore, even had the authorities sought to apply the law vigorously, the companies were in a more advantageous position than the government as they were better organised technically and managerially. With all of these institutional and macroeconomic barriers obstructing successful enforcement, the OTH did not face very promising conditions.

Conclusion

The beginning of offshore oil development brought big changes for traditional lake villages. Major losers under the new terms of economic expansion were fishermen and Indians living in villages built on water, not to mention the surrounding marine and land based wildlife. The delicate lakeshore ecosystem, including the mangroves, already under stress following blow-outs based on land which also contaminated Lake Maracaibo, was now placed under even greater threat. One town which survived the onslaught of oil was Lagunillas, where the original Venezuelan inhabitants were joined by more recent immigrants. In government reports the most visible lobbying group pressing its demands in the Lake Maracaibo region seems to have been local residents of boom towns, who organised amongst themselves and worked through established legal and political channels. In a sense, this is not surprising. Local residents, unlike oil workers, were not vulnerable to dismissal. During the 1920s the Gómez regime undertook investigations, reports and even legislation designed to protect workers, residents and the environment from oil spills and oil pollution.

Venezuela, a largely agricultural country, was poorly equipped to deal with the influx of large multinational companies from Britain and the United States and lacked much of the technical expertise necessary to oversee the industry. Even though Gómez and his subordinates were corrupted by oil and land deals, it is still undeniable that the Gómez authorities eventually made an effort to curb abuses, which is somewhat surprising given the dictatorial nature of the regime. The commission appointed by Gómez to report on oil pollution, which led to a 1928 anti-contamination law, was an important development that signalled to the companies that the government was prepared to undertake some oversight. The problem, however, was that laws were very often inadequate, and policing and political muscle were frequently deficient. Meanwhile, Gómez was unwilling to consider the option of moving Lagunillas to a land-based site with compensation, a plan the authorities finally were forced to make following an even more devastating Lagunillas fire in 1939. In hindsight, Gómez's reckless response of encouraging more house construction, rather than seeking to limit it, was mistaken. Pérez Soto seems to have taken a more level-headed view about Lagunillas, but there was little he could do against Gómez's authority.

Postscript

In 1935 Gómez died and his successor, General Eleazar López Contreras, under increasing pressure from more combative and militant oil labour unions, granted workers the right to rally, organise and strike.[105] What were the environmental impacts of momentous political and social changes? What were the implications for lakeshore towns like Lagunillas? Even if provisions of the 1930 *Reglamento* were not always enforced, such legislation formed an effective framework for supervision of the industry. Once set up, the institutional framework and bureaucracy enabled inspectors to fine oil companies for their pollution and blow-outs during the López Contreras administration of 1936–41. However, even under this more nationalist regime, economic concerns commonly outstripped environmental regulation. Enforcement proved lax as Venezuela moved to become one of the world's foremost oil producers.

Following the death of Gómez, reports continued to reach authorities in Caracas about pollution and the dire situation in Lagunillas. Nestor Luis Pérez, the new minister of development in 1936, a critic of the oil companies' contamination, was concerned that the waters around Lagunillas were completely polluted and that the town's wooden houses were covered in oil.[106] By order of President López Contreras, who was concerned

---

105 Bergquist (1986), p. 236.
106 Monet (1986), p. 333.

about Lagunillas housing and its vulnerability to fire hazard, local people were to be moved to a nearby inland site called Ciudad Ojeda. The authorities declared that Ciudad Ojeda would be supplied with potable water, a sewer system, gas for domestic uses, electric lighting, paved roads, a market, schools, church, hospital and sufficient housing. One million bolívares would be allocated for the new move and costs,[107] which would be overseen by the ministry of public works.[108]

In 1936–37 a major oil strike crippled the oil industry in Lake Maracaibo. Demanding union recognition and improvements in pay and working conditions, workers challenged the hegemony of some of the largest oil companies in the world for an unprecedented 42 days.[109] Even worse, from the point of view of the oil executives, Communist organisers had come to influence oil workers by founding a newspaper.[110] Reacting with contempt, the companies refused to negotiate with any unions during the strike or to accept any of the workers' demands.[111] Officially, the government adopted a public posture of neutrality whilst harassing and jailing strikers on the oil fields. In January 1937 López Contreras decreed an end to the strike and workers were ordered back on the job. In a small concession, the government ordered a slight rise in wages for the poorest paid oil workers. The workers interpreted the end result of their titanic effort as a failure.[112]

Lagunillas played an important role within this volatile political environment. The lakeshore town was rapidly becoming an eyesore, both from an environmental and a political perspective. Lagunillas was home to a vigorous oil labour union in 1936.[113] Furthermore, since the death of Gómez, Lagunillas had been a 'focal point of lawless elements', according to the US chargé d'affaires. The official added that the population of Lagunillas, approximately 1,500,

> ...lives in decrepit buildings, some of which are on stilts in the waters of the lake, others behind a wooden dyke ten feet or more in height, flimsy houses, disease and lack of sanitation or protection from the heat have contributed to the reputation of Lagunillas as a breeding spot for petty crimes, radicalism and attacks on the oil companies.

107 AHZ, expediente Incendio de Lagunillas 1939, telegram Caracas 19 January 1937, Regulo Olivares to Presidente Estado Zulia, transcript of decree published in *Gaceta Oficial*. In 1935–36, the average monthly salary in Zulia oil camps was 344 bolívares and Venezuela's net oil income was 45.7 million bolívares (McBeth, 1983, pp. 127, 188).

108 NA, RG 59, 831.5045/44, Henry S. Villard to Secretary of State, Caracas, 22 January 1937.

109 Bergquist (1986), p. 230.

110 *Ibid.*, p. 233.

111 *Ibid.*, p. 239.

112 *Ibid.*, p. 240.

113 *Ibid.*, p. 236.

According to the US official, the oil companies were very pleased with government initiatives to move Lagunillas, as such a measure would 'materially assist in the solution of the present strike problem'. Moving the population would also relieve oil company managers, who were worried that agitators might dynamite a dyke in the vicinity.[114]

Unfortunately for the oil companies, the inhabitants of Lagunillas showed little desire to leave the town, despite the fact that many oil wells were still located close to the town, with the nearest derrick some 200 metres distant, and Ojeda had a much healthier location on higher land with good drainage. In 1939 the residents of Lagunillas again suffered when yet another fire damaged the town (Figures 3.2 and 3.3). According to the US chargé d'affaires, the fire was caused by an accidental explosion of a gasoline or kerosene lamp in a bar room located on the main boardwalk of the town. 'With the help of the wind', added the US official,

> ... the fire swept rapidly throughout the town, burning down all but twelve shacks at one end of the rectangle. The bridge connecting to land was burnt down at the outset, and a large portion of the inhabitants were cut off from shore. Since the walled dike prevented inhabitants from swimming to shore, most of these residents were rescued in boats. Some, however, drowned or burned to death. Some thirty corpses were later found.[115]

Figure 3.2: Lagunillas, 18 June 1937

Source: 'La tragedia de Lagunillas de Agua (1939),' *Boletín del Archivo Histórico de Miraflores*, no. 147–9 (January 1996–June 1997).

114 NA, RG 59, 831.5045/44, Henry S. Villard to Secretary of State, Caracas 22 January 1937.
115 NA, RG 84/848, Archer Woodford to John Bernhard, Maracaibo, 23 December 1939.

Figure 3.3: Lagunillas, 15 November 1939

Source: 'La tragedia de Lagunillas de Agua (1939),' *Boletín del Archivo Histórico de Miraflores*, no. 147–9 (January 1996–June 1997).

Lake Maracaibo was covered with a patchy scum of petroleum, but the chargé personally doubted that this surface oil, which had lost its volatility, could have caused the fire, as such slicks had to be subjected to intense heat before they would burn.[116] This time, unlike previous fires, the accident claimed a substantial number of victims. The state president reported that 1,240 houses had been destroyed, and more than four million bolívares in damages sustained.[117] By the time the fire was extinguished, 24 people had died and the town was left in ashes.[118] In the wake of the fire, Standard Oil published an account of the Lagunillas fire in its official magazine, *El Farol*. In its account the oil magazine did not seek to address the causes of the fire, preferring instead to dwell on measures which LPC had taken to extinguish the fire, to provide financial assistance for displaced residents and to improve the sewer system and other infrastructure within the new settlement of Ciudad Ojeda.[119]

Once Lagunillas was destroyed, residents were forced at long last to emigrate to Ciudad Ojeda. However, the new settlement was hardly ideal for the newcomers, and in 1942 residents who had been displaced from Lagunillas submitted a list of grievances to President Isaias Medina Angarita when he arrived on an official state visit. Residents requested a medical dispensary, access to promised funding for the displaced, creation of a girl's school and water for rural homes and agriculture. Residents had

116 *Ibid.*
117 BAHM, nos 147–9, Jan 1996–June 1997, Manuel Maldonado to López Contreras, Lagunillas 14 November 1939, pp. 232–3. In 1940, salaries for welders, riveters and other oil labourers did not exceed 450 bolívares ('Earnings of foreign employees of oil companies in Maracaibo, Venezuela, 1945,' *Monthly Labor Review* (July 1945).
118 BAHM, nos 147–9, January 1996–June 1997, 'La Tragedia de Lagunillas de Agua (1939)', telegraph, Manuel Maldonado to López Contreras, 7–8 November 1939, p. 223.
119 'El lamentable siniestro de Lagunillas', *El Farol*, November 1939, p. 8.

not received state, federal, or municipal monies to pay for supplies, firemen or repairmen. Residents also claimed that they were exposed to malaria despite improved drainage. Another problem was that Ciudad Ojeda was not located on municipal or federal lands, but on VOC property. As a result, no one had the right to build within the urban fabric of the town. Residents wrote to Medina that they had petitioned municipal, state and even national authorities, but their needs had not been addressed.[120] Ranchers, who had been displaced by oil development in the vicinity of Lagunillas and had relocated to the Ojeda area, also petitioned Medina. They remarked that their cattle had no water to drink and requested improved highway networks.[121]

120 AHM, 1–1–3, 'Informe Sobre Situacion I Necesidades de Ciudad Ojeda,' Junta Pro Mejoras de Ciudad Ojeda, Alberto Nuñez, Eugenio Zamarripa, Carlos R. Prieto, to Medina Ciudad Ojeda, 16 November 1942.
121 AHM, 1–1–3, Criaderos de Lagunillas, Rolendio Bracho, Simon Cruel, Ismael Sánchez, others, to Medina, n.d.

PART II

Commodities: Export Booms and the Environment

CHAPTER 4

Transforming the Central Mexican Waterscape:
Lake Drainage and its Consequences during the *Porfiriato* (1877–1911)*

Alejandro Tortolero Villaseñor

Introduction

The accomplishments and contradictions of the long Porfirian period (1877–1911) have long impressed scholars. The biggest contradiction is the spectacular growth of the economy and strong political stability during the *Porfiriato*, in contrast with its fall by violent agrarian revolution during the second decade of the twentieth century. Here, I do not wish to analyse the fall of the Porfirian regime; rather, I am interested in the Porfirian modernisation project, which was not only central to its overall legacy, but also was key to its downfall. The Porfirian regime adopted a French development model — based on modern, cosmopolitan and urban nationalism — that aimed at a homogenous and Westernised nation oriented toward international markets, and which would be scientifically regulated and organised. White immigration and foreign investment were also key components of this idea of development and modernity.[1] Several aspects of this modernisation model, including politics, education, society, economy and technology, have received scholarly attention.[2] In this chapter I analyse the ways in which modernisation affected central Mexico's waterscapes. I assume that Porfirian modernisation had the following imperatives: to expand irrigation as a means to boost agricultural productivity and to drain lakes for health and economic reasons.

If the Porfirian regime relied on an urban model for modernisation, then the countryside would be responsible for supplying the city with its surpluses and necessary inputs such as fresh, cheap food. Nevertheless, the subordination of countryside to city was not only an economic relationship, but it also was spatial and cultural. Urban space, with its ideals of symmetry and functionality, was seen from the positivist perspective as a human body, which consumed inputs and expelled wastes. To this end,

* I would like to thank the Guggenheim Foundation for supporting the research that underpins this chapter. This chapter was translated by Christian Brannstrom.
1 Tenorio (1998).
2 See Tortolero (2002); Tenorio (1998); Guerra (1988); Martínez Moctezuma (2001); Coatsworth (1990); Haber (1992).

sewage systems were built to remove wastes. In addition, a hygienist ideology would support the idea that any water not in circulation was the origin of miasmas and the basis of illness and disease.

With the adoption of positivism as the scientific ideology of the Porfirian regime, it was possible to argue that society was analogous to the human body and thus it was possible to apply concepts of health and illness to society in general. It followed that the most civilised cities had better health, requiring daily bathing to remove bodily wastes and the construction of complex systems for supplying water and removing urban wastes. Cities should possess waste-removal systems that would remove putrefying material, using water as the means to remove excrement. Thus, following this logic of spatial subordination, the countryside was synonymous with the removal site of urban wastewater, while its lakes would become the sites for drainage of stagnant water, which in turn would make former lakebeds the locations of productive agriculture needed for urban food supply.[3]

The subordination of countryside to cities and urban functions is visible in the deeply rooted idea, ever since Mexico's colonial period, of a water hierarchy. The best waters were thought to be crystalline, of neutral odour and colour, pure and, preferably, from generous mountain springs. Turbid, cloudy, stagnant and foul-smelling waters, often found in shallow lakes, were considered the poorest.[4] Supporters of lake drainage, such as entrepreneurs, physicians, engineers and the *Porfiriato*'s technocrats, often referred to the lakes as swamps and marshes. By contrast, residents near the lakes, such as poets and artists, would refer to the wonders of lake water. For example, pro-drainage engineer Nicolás Ramírez de Arellano, a member of a government commission charged with studying the viability of draining the Lago de Chalco, argued in 1895 that the lake's 'existence was unfavourable to health, because the lake does not communicate with the ocean and its waters are not in movement, becoming a true swamp'. By contrast, Juan Ramírez, an engineer on the same commission, but an opponent of drainage, argued that 'the lake should not be considered a swamp, because it is maintained by a freshwater spring and its waters are in circulation'.[5]

The *Porfiriato*'s water ideology supported an increase in irrigated agriculture for the production of food surpluses and an attack on central Mexico's lakes. The latter phenomenon also represents a new business model that assumed that making the countryside an efficient supplier of cities would end underdevelopment. Shallow lakes, considered unhealthy under the

3   Woude (1987), pp. 381–4.
4   Musset (1992).
5   See Tortolero (2000b); quotes from 'Dictamen del Consejo Superior de Salubridad respecto a la desecación de la parte de Lago de Chalco en terrenos de R. Noriega y Hno.,' Archivo General de la Nación (México, DF), Secretaría de Comunicaciones y Obras Públicas (hereafter AGN, SCOP), 546/4, pp. 27–8. The commission's final report favoured draining the Lago de Chalco.

regime's hygienist ideology, should be substituted by productive agriculture. This is the topic to which I will turn, while leaving aside, until the final section, an evaluation of the spatial, economic and ecological implications of a model bent on the destruction of central Mexico's waterscapes.

Draining the Waterscape: Ideologies and Policies

Two different periods of Mexican water management characterise the nineteenth century. Both follow from the country's general situation and two general factors influenced change. The first is Mexico's political and economic situation. At the time of Independence from Spain in the early nineteenth century Mexico was fragmented into local and regional power centres. While colonial rule was based on the hegemony of the core of Spain and Mexico City over colonies and regions, central administration in Mexico was inverted during the War for Independence. Between 1821 and 1876 the lack of strong central control encouraged the consolidation of power among regional elites and oligarchs. With relation to water the situation was no different; water was controlled by local and regional authorities until at least 1888 when a law on communication routes granted centralised control to federal authorities over water resources. A weak Mexican state created possibilities for elites to expand business activities. During the Porfirian regime, this situation was inverted, as the state recovered its controlling and hegemonic functions, and Mexico City regained its former political, administrative and commercial hegemony.

Intimately connected to the issue of water centralisation is a second factor, regarding the representation of water during the nineteenth century. Since the Enlightenment, water had been associated with hygiene and cleanliness, which was part of notions of respectability. But in the nineteenth century hygienist ideas would be established definitively. For physicians, air and water would be contaminated if in contact with any putrefying substance. Filth was synonymous with excrement and putrefaction. In theory, filthy air and poisonous miasmas were the focus of attention. For the nineteenth-century circulationists, who adhered to Harvey's theory of blood circulation, both the human body and the city as organism had to consume and excrete, thus requiring construction of drains and pipelines. Illnesses resulted from the accumulation of filth and the poor use of water.

These two factors were decisive in Mexico's nineteenth-century water politics. Between 1821 and 1888 the lack of a strong state allowed water to be controlled by local and regional authorities. Afterwards, the state recovered its centralising functions and simultaneously motivated Mexico's economic development and the representation of water and hygiene that would force the adoption of new policies. The issue of property rights to water appears with regard to legal disputes over water between competing interests. In a landmark legal case, argued by the famous Mexican lawyer Luis Cabrera, water rights of one party were asserted on the basis of 'a sort of administrative inertia' of water possession dating from the time of the 1888 Water Law. According to Cabrera, the 1888 law marked the beginning of centralisation over water access and rights.[6]

By 1880 the Porfirian state had begun to create the institutional conditions for a new economic stage. It achieved political stability after a convulsive period of internal and external disputes that cost Mexico the loss of more than half its territory to the USA. Railroads, which linked central Mexico's internal market to overseas sites, also connected internal regions. Industries were transformed; in 1880 Mexico's main industries were transformative, such as mills for grain, sugarcane, textiles and tobacco. Giant industrial complexes, such as breweries, foundries and paper mills, would soon appear.[7] The innovative commercial agricultural sector, spurred by population growth and market increases, developed sugarcane, cotton, henequen, coffee and wheat sectors. Agriculture with irrigation potential would transform regions such as the Yaqui, Mexico and Atlixco Valleys, and sugarcane regions in Morelos, amongst other regions. For these reasons, scholars have asserted that the Mexican economy crossed a watershed during the *Porfiriato*. Before the *Porfiriato*, the Mexican economy did not have a basic transport or communications systems, nor did it have banks, capital, technology and training. Economic organisation suffered from inefficiency; property rights were poorly established and infrequently secured, while fiscal policies caused more harm than good, usually stifling private initiative, fragmenting markets and encouraging unproductive initiatives. By contrast, in 1910 it was no longer accurate to assert that Mexico was a backward country.

Water resources management was the responsibility of the development ('fomento') ministry.[8] This ministry and other bureaucracies spread

6   Cabrera (1972), p. 361. Andrés Molina Enríquez (1981, p. 252), another prominent twentieth-century intellectual and friend of Cabrera's, agreed with the argument that centralisation began with the 1888 law. The Cabrera–Molina thesis on water centralisation has been discussed by Kroeber (1994); Tortolero (1995); and Aboites (1998). However, similar to other ideas attributed to Molina Enríquez, recent studies have shown that centralising policies were not achieved until after the Mexican Revolution; see the case of Chalco and Zacupu in this chapter and Sánchez (2001).

7   See Coatsworth (1984; 1990) and Haber (1992). Coatsworth noted that even though social saving attributed to passengers in 1910 was low, approximately 1.3% of GDP, the savings attributed to cargo were nearly 11% of GDP (Coatsworth, 1984, p. 138). This stimulated the export to GDP ratio, which increased from 4.6% in 1860 to 17.5% in 1910. Railroads and large industrial plants were supported by foreign investors, which injected approximately US$2 billion into the Porfirian economy (Bortz and Haber, 2002, p. 16).

8   In 1897 the ministry of development was divided into six divisions; the personnel responsible for managing water concessions and confiscation were in the fifth division, which was divided into three commissions: the Nazas River Inspectorate, the Research and Regulation Inspectorate and the Rivers and Concessions Inspectorate.

contemporary medical opinions indicating that water contamination caused illness, especially the idea that cholera followed the course of rivers and reached the population through drinking water. These innovative ideas spread rapidly: in July 1884 Robert Koch gave a seminar on cholera in Berlin, and in 1885 his text was published in Mexico. Water came into direct contact with fruits and vegetables, helping spread the bacterium *Vibrio cholerae* into the intestinal tract, where infection caused severe vomiting and diarrhoea, often causing death. The 1829–30 cholera epidemic in Europe killed one million people. By the end of the nineteenth century few doubted cholera's waterborne origins. The cholera-inspired terror motivated the construction of infrastructure to supply safe drinking water and improve hygienic conditions. As one scholar noted, 'Europe's sanitary organisation is a child of cholera'.[9]

It is not surprising that cholera was noticed in Mexico, nor that in 1885 the Mexican government pursued hygienic policies such as lake drainage, construction of drainage systems, supply of potable water and monitoring of aqueducts, public wells and other water reservoirs.[10] Medical opinion, which held that the health of a population depended on the good quality and supply of drinking water, was to be constructed physically by distribution systems that hid filth. Uncovered canals, which had existed for more than three centuries in Mexico City, had served as much for water supply as for waste disposal, but now were viewed disparagingly. Aqueducts, signs of an ancient civilisation and a visual symbol of architectural pride, were replaced by invisible systems of hidden tubes. Water scarcity or abundance, visible in an aqueduct-based system, was a public concern, but an underground tubular system put these concerns out of sight. Dirty, malodorous and contaminated canals could not compete with the modern image of railroads and street trams. Modern engineers spread the image of water control through tubular systems and grandiose drainage projects in Mexico and surrounding lakes. As Alexander von Humboldt noted in the early nineteenth century, water in the lakes was seen as an enemy against which defence was necessary.[11]

Thus began the *Porfiriato*'s offensive against the Mexican waterscape, which became indicative of the supremacy of city over countryside. Besides health considerations and the city–countryside relationship, the modernising project made agriculture an agent in the transformation of nature. Unlike pre-Hispanic *chinampa* raised-field agriculture of the Basin of Mexico, in which agriculture modified soil–water relations but did not demand the full destruction of aquatic ecosystems,[12] the new farming

9   Pedoya (1990), pp. 93–4.
10   Birrichaga (1998).
11   Humboldt (1997), p. 250.
12   Whitmore and Turner (2002), pp. 213–24.

UNIVERSITY OF WINCHESTER
LIBRARY

model required complete drainage of lakes in the interest of obtaining the maximum output from land. The irrigation projects and drainage schemes of the Lagos de Mexico, Chalco and Texcoco, in addition to lakes in the Chalpa, Lerma and Zacapu basins, are examples of this ideal.

Land and Water in the Basin of Mexico

The Basin of Mexico is an interior-drainage basin comprised of three elevation-defined zones: a lower zone below 2,250 meters, a hilly region between 2,250 and 2,400 meters and a mountainous zone above 2,400 meters (see Figures 4.1 and 4.2). Volcanic sierras surround the Basin, with the Sierra Nevada to the east and the Ajusco to the south; high volcanic peaks such as Popocatepetl (5,465 metres) and Ixtaccihuatl (5,230 metres) are outside the Basin. Irrigated agriculture was practised in the lower zone, while hilly and mountainous regions remained an obstacle for irrigation, but had considerable agricultural terracing before 1500.[13] The landscapes of the Basin were varied, ranging from pine and oak forests to alpine grasslands and snow-capped volcanic mountains.[14] Vegetation at lake margins included cattail reeds (tule or *Typha dominguensis*) at the shoreline and, in the water, plants such as water lily (*Nymphaea* family), pondweed (*Potamogeton* genus), riccia (*Ricciocarpus* genus), duckweed (*lentejas de agua* or *Lemna* genus), water hyacinth and a variety of other hydrophilic floating and submerged plants.

The hydraulic system of the Basin was comprised of three sub-basins: Zumpango in the north, Texcoco in the centre and Chalco-Xochimilco in the south. In the sixteenth century, the Basin covered approximately 8,000 square kilometres, of which one-eighth was a shallow lake environment with depths rarely exceeding two metres. Thus, a conservative estimate is that this waterscape amounted to approximately 1,000 square kilometres surrounding Mexico City.[15] The extent and shallow depth of the lakes are significant. Deep bodies of water are not very ecologically productive, as photosynthesis occurs only at the surface levels, which makes the volume of water essentially inert. By contrast, water in extensive and shallow lakes is populated by plants and algae, which sustain abundant aquatic life. The lake is even more productive ecologically if organic matter drains in. And,

13   Whitmore and Turner (2002); Ezcurra (1990).
14   Vegetation zones were defined by elevation, such as fir (*oyamel*) forests (between 2,700 and 3,500 metres); pine forests (2,350 to 4,000 metres); juniper (*enebro*) forests (2,450 to 2,800 metres); oak forests (2,350 to 3,100 metres); grasslands (2,250 to 4,300 metres); and dry woodlands (2,250 to 2,700 metres). Approximately 2,000 phanerogams and 250 non-vascular plants were present; see Espinosa (1996); Niederberger (1987).
15   Palerm (1990), p. 189. Musset (1992, p. 61) estimates that the basin covered 9,600 square kilometres; Ezcurra (1990, p. 577) cites the figure of 7,000 square kilometres, of which the lakes in 1500 covered 1,500 square kilometres.

at tropical latitudes, where solar radiation is greater than at higher latitudes, productivity increases further. Hence, the shallow tropical lakes of the Basin of Mexico were among the most productive of the Earth's ecosystems. Organisms that avidly took in solar radiation and found sufficient nutrients in the water were able to synthesise high amounts of organic matter; immense armies of insects, larvae, and fish and aquatic birds consumed this aquatic plant life. Various fish species and turtles, salamanders (*axolotl*), snakes and birds were present in the lakes.

Figure 4.1: Central Mexico and the Río Lerma

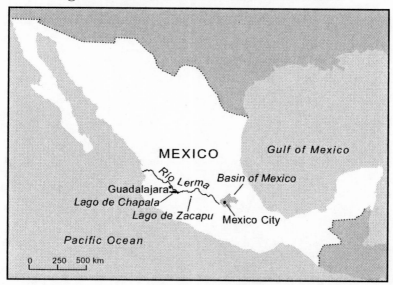

The Basin's waterscape was supplied by three sources: rainfall, river runoff and springs. The geography of these sources made the Chalco-Xochimilco and Zumpango freshwater lakes, while Lago de Texcoco was salty and briny and the Xaltocan was brackish.[16] The sources of water to the Basin include more than twenty springs in the south and rivers descending from surrounding mountains, although the latter do not discharge large volumes. The main supply of water to the Basin's lakes was not from peren-

---

16 Salinity is caused by the fact that stream runoff acquires salts from the substrate, which is introduced into the lakes, accumulating and increasing in concentration over time as lake water evaporates. Freshwater lakes drain into the lower lakes, and thus the lowest-elevation lake, Texcoco, accumulated the highest concentration of salts (Espinosa, 1996, p. 59).

nial streams, but rather from rainfall supplying streams descending from the mountains and numerous springs.[17] Rainfall in the Basin of Mexico is concentrated between May and October, with highest precipitation in the mountains and humidity concentrated in the south. The dry season lasts approximately between November and April. Mean annual rainfall is approximately 500 millimetres, and moving south toward the Ajusco region rainfall reaches 600 to 700 millimetres annually. Mean annual precipitation reaches 800, 1,000 and 1,200 while climbing Chichinautzin and approximately 1,500 near the Ajusco peak.

Figure 4.2: The Central Mexican Waterscape, c. 1500

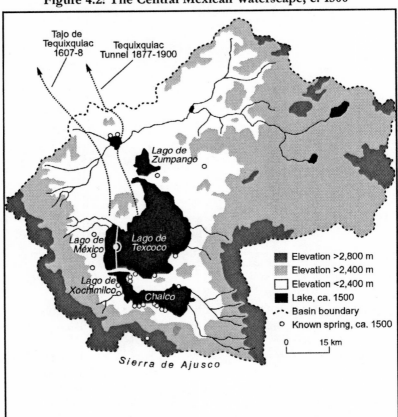

Source: Musset (1992).

17　*Ibid.*, p. 63.

Mexico City

Seasonal water excess in the Basin of Mexico explains the constant flooding of Mexico City. To combat flooding during the colonial period, huge drainage works were carried out, such as the Nochistongo Cut (1607–08). Flood-control measures were continued during the *Porfiriato*, resulting in schemes such as the Tequixquiac Tunnel (1877–1900) and the Great Drainage Canal ('Gran Canal del Desagüe') (1886–1900). Around the time that Porfirio Díaz began draining the area around Mexico City with the Tequixquiac Tunnel, the city had a population of 250,000 and the urbanised area was 14 square kilometres. By 1910 the city's population had reached 721,000 and the urbanised area had increased to 40 square kilometres.[18] At this time the Tequixquiac and the Gran Canal had reduced the area of the former lucustrine environment, which had covered Zumpango in the north, Texcoco in the centre and Chalco-Xochimilco in the south, reducing surface water primarily to the salty Lago de Texcoco.

Causes of this considerable reduction of the lake surface area include health policies, the hierarchical relationship between city and countryside and agricultural modernisation. In Mexico City, flooding regularly caused serious damage, and as a result the Drainage Office, with a salaried director, was created in 1826. The Gran Canal del Desagüe had been proposed to capitalise on the Nochistongo 'Cut', but in fact officials continued to study Humboldt's idea to create a direct canal from Texcoco. To carry out this project, M.L. Smith, a military engineer from the invading US Army, proposed to completely and gradually drain the entire valley by draining the Lago de Texcoco, through various canals and a tunnel that would drain to the Tequixquiac. Francisco de Garay, a Mexican engineer who had studied in Paris and London, proposed a different scheme. An uncovered canal would leave from the San Lázaro Gate and cross Lagos de Texcoco, San Cristóbal and Zumpango, capturing water from all contributing streams along the way. In addition, a tunnel and secondary canals would drain the Lagos de Chalco and Xochimilco and would be used for both irrigation and lake drainage. With the 1853 creation of the development ministry, Garay's project was approved, but progress was slow because of political turbulence. In spite of French intervention and the ensuing civil wars, Garay was the general director of the drainage project from the 1850s until 1881. The following year, Luis Espinosa, an engineer, substituted Garay and benefited from new institutional conditions to carry forth the drainage project.

18 Ezcurra's (1990, p. 580) area and population estimates for 1800 are 10.8 square kilometres and 137,000, similar to those of Boyer and Davies (1973, p. 42). For 1900, however, Boyer and Davies (1973, p. 42) provide estimates of 345,000 and Bataillon (1968, p. 173) estimates a population of 344,000, whilst Ezcurra (1990, p. 580) gives 541,000 with an area of 27.5 square kilometres. For 1910 population estimates vary from 400,000 (Academia de la Investigación Científica, 1995, p. 68) to 720,000 (Bataillon, 1971, p. 84).

These institutional conditions helped Mexico receive international credit, in the form of US$2.4 million, with the option for an additional US$1 million for the drainage project. The financial problem was resolved, as was the political problem, with Porfirio Díaz, who, in spite of heavy rainfall in 1888, gave the project highest priority. His objectives had extraordinary resonance with medical opinion, leaving him only with the technological and practical problem of building the works. Officials believed that the best solution was to hire foreign firms, whose technologies and labour control would be able to complete the work successfully. Actors and methods changed, as during the colonial period the drainage project was carried out under state tutelage and relied on forced labour, such as the *repartimiento*, inmates and soldiers; in the future, private entrepreneurs would use different labour relations. The problem of an underdeveloped construction industry would be attributed to a lack of technology, mediocre technicians or poor technical capacity. Under the gaze of young scientists, technical training only could be obtained abroad. The contractor selected from four bidders was an Englishman, Weetman Dickinson Pearson, who, thanks to contracts with the Porfirian regime, would become one of the most important contractors of the time, and would build an enormous personal fortune.[19]

The economic interest in carrying out lake-drainage projects is clear if we look at Pearson's profits and the other drainage projects in the Basin's lakes. Francisco de Garay's project, which would capitalise on water for irrigation, navigation and industrial power, while avoiding stagnant water, would be buried when Luis Espinosa was named in 1882 to direct the drainage project. Mier and Celis's 1881 project was for drainage in exchange for title to land, irrigation and transport routes, but these were not granted.[20] By contrast, in 1889 officials approved Pearson's project, which sought an annual income of two million pesos over three years of the project's duration, without expecting title to land or full use of water from the lakes. Although Pearson did not obtain this amount, he recovered 1.3 million pesos annually over six years of the project's duration; only a small portion of this amount was invested in Mexico. The contract was lucrative for Pearson, permitting him to extend his activities in other areas of Mexico, such as port construction in Veracruz, Coatzacoalcos and Salina Cruz, and the reconstruction of the Tehuantepec railroad, among other projects.

Lago de Chalco

To drain Lago de Chalco, the Porfirian regime awarded the contract to a group of Spanish businessmen, the Noriega brothers.[21] These Asturian

19   Conolly (1987).
20   *Ibid.*, p. 228.
21   Martínez Moctezuma (1996).

immigrants would be in charge of transforming a 10,000-hectare lake supplied by streams descending from the Sierra Nevada, which had a reputation for abundant and crystalline water that was considered excellent for drinking. Lago de Chalco, which was described by proponents of the drainage scheme as a marsh and by opponents as lake, had variable depth depending on rainfall fluctuations. Draining the lake required hydrological study, which produced widely variable estimates, ranging from 81 million cubic metres to 233.7 million cubic metres. Imprecision became a weapon in the arsenal of entrepreneurs. Engineering works would negatively affect only villages, while the Noriega brothers' firm, Negociación Agrícola, would be protected from flooding. Excess rainfall that could not be accommodated by the narrow canal projects would be permitted to overflow banks or floodgates would be shut to flood opposing villages.[22]

The Noriega brothers established a conflictive relationship with villages neighbouring the works, as imprecision of lake volume allowed them to control the lake waters, which varied according to rainfall and water demand. Lakeshore villages had become accustomed to planting on the shore after its peak had been reached. Nevertheless, in 1889 the Noriegas built a canalisation scheme in the southern region of the lake, near the villages of Huitzilzingo, Ayotzingo, Mixquic, Tezompa, Ixtayopan and Tulyehualco. These villages opposed the project, but the Noriega brothers flooded protesting villages by building that would encourage the lake's flood waters to spill on to village land. In 1904 the Noriega brothers closed floodgates, thus flooding the village of Huitzilzingo. The village's representative claimed that 'Noriega diverted the waters for its own ends, taking great pleasure in flooding all the villages that were bold enough to not let their lands be stolen'.[23]

Water was not only useful for coercion of villages, but also to support one of Mexico's most prosperous agricultural regions, from which one maize variety, the Chalquense, has survived to the present.[24] In addition, the region's large industries, such as the San Rafael paper mill and the Miraflores textile mill, had located near the lake to take advantage of water supply. The San Rafael paper mill, for example, obtained water from the springs and snowmelt of the Sierra Nevada, but its use of water caused tensions between the industry and surrounding communities. The villages and the *ayuntamiento* continued fighting until the mill promised to pay a higher amount for water and, at its own cost, to install a pipeline to supply the village of Tlalmanalco.[25]

22   See Tortolero (1997).
23   AGN, SCOP, 546–9–f. 3.
24   Tortolero (1996).
25   Huerta (1993).

Canoe traffic on the lake was quite lucrative. Eighteenth-century Mexico City received approximately 5,000 *fanegas* or 277,500 litres of maize weekly in canoes.[26] By the nineteenth century, approximately 50,000 canoes from Lago de Chalco supplied the city yearly.[27] To put this into context, there were 5.7 million litres of maize sold in Mexico City's public granary (*alhóndiga*) in 1741 and 3.8 million litres sold in 1786. In good agricultural years, rarely were more than 2.2 million litres sold from the granary. Mexico City's annual eighteenth-century maize consumption was not greater than 11.1 million litres, while farms in the Chalco region produced 13.9 million litres annually.[28] By the mid nineteenth century, the commercial fleet plying the Chalco–La Viga trade brought approximately 50,000 pesos annually, while first- and second-class passenger traffic was worth approximately 21,000 pesos. Commodities entering the San Lázaro Gate, excepting overseas imports, were worth 5,000 pesos, according to a conservative estimate, thus adding up to 76,000 pesos. This amount may be better appreciated if compared to passenger traffic in 1890, when the Chalco-Tlamanalco railroad line was constructed. Between 1890 and 1895, annual receipts from passenger traffic were 74,000 pesos and an additional 9,000 pesos came from commodities, thus suggesting the relative importance of waterborne canal transport.[29]

José Reyes and his partners, a gang of robbers, knew the lucrative water trade quite well. In 1846 they had come before the judicial system for robbing passengers on the Chalco canoes. The same was true of José Feliciano and Espiridión Lucio.[30] Were they predecessors of the renowned Bandidos del Río Frío, who were so well portrayed by Manuel Payno in his eponymous nineteenth-century novel, in which the lake and its canals become two of the most important protagonists? Certainly, the Chalco's canals are one of the main features of nineteenth-century Mexican novels, and there is no doubt that the presence of water was reflected in all aspects of regional life, as it was fundamental for spatial relations, productive activities, myths and customs. Nearly all the nineteenth-century travellers in Mexico wrote colourful accounts of the lakes and canals. Travellers emphasised festivals, songs, dances, daily life and many other characteristics. The lakes and canals became sites for obligatory visits captured in G. Prieto's poetry (1842), A. García's oil paintings and the artwork of J.M. Rugendas, E. Landesio, Luis Coto and many others.[31]

26   See Tortolero (2002).
27   Tortolero (1996).
28   Florescano (1986), p. 219; Tortolero (2003b).
29   See Martínez and Tortolero (2000).
30   Archivo del Tribunal Superior de Justicia del D.F., México, Canoas, Paquete 2.
31   Manuel Payno, *Los bandidos de Río Frío* (1889–1891). On travellers, see Glantz (1982), p. 680; see García's 'La mejicana' (1857); Rugendas's 'Viernes de Dolores en el Canal de la Viga en la fiesta de Santa Anita' (1832), Landesio's 'La garita de la Viga' (1856) and Coto's 'La garita de la Viga' (1860).

The importance of the Chalco's waterborne economy was seriously underestimated in the government's nineteenth-century statistical reports. According to these reports, the poor residents of Zumpango relied on duck hunting and fishing in the village lake. The author of the report, Pascual González, governor of the state of Mexico in 1849, noted that 'these resources were quite insignificant: it would be much more lucrative for the needy classes and for public finances to drain the lake, which would be easy, and this would result in large agricultural harvests'.[32] The governor mentioned that fishing in the Lagos de Chalco and Texcoco was only a 'secondary resource' for the subsistence of the inhabitants, while agriculture was the primary livelihood of the villages. This situation appeared clearly in the three general population censuses carried out under the Porfirian administration. In Chalco, for example, the census counted 41 fishermen in 1895, none in 1900 and only five in 1910. In Zumpango, the census found 390 fishermen in 1895, but only 67 in 1910. In Texcoco, the census counted four fishermen in 1900 and 118 in 1910 (Table 4.1).

Table 4.1: Fishermen in the State of Mexico, 1895–1910

District	Year		
	1895	**1900**	**1910**
Chalco	41	0	5
Zumpango	390	17	67
Texcoco	—	4	118
Lerma	2	11	58
Tenango	5	96	10
Others	—	—	24
State Total	**458**	**128**	**282**

Source: México (1920) for 1910 data and the Censo General de Población for 1895 and 1900.

Government statistics better reflected cultural biases, which I discussed in the introduction, than the actual economic and environmental situation. Spaniards and Indians perceived water differently; the former did not appreciate lake water: from the sixteenth-century chronicles of Tomas López Medel, who claimed that lake water contributed to the bad odour of the Basin of Mexico during drought, to the reports of nineteenth-century

32   González (1849), p. 17.

travellers, such as Humboldt or Jules Leclercq, who wrote of the poor health caused by the basin's waters and how in drought periods the dead fish would foul the air with their smell.[33]

Nor did the elites appreciate aquatic fish and other fauna of the lakes. The Spaniards, for example, preferred to eat fish brought from the coast. In the early seventeenth century, Priest Cobo wrote that the lake fish of the Central Valley had a disagreeable smell because of their muddy habitat. Later, in 1885, the president of the Royal Belgian Geographical Society, Jules Leclercq, described the lake fish as repugnant.[34]

The same classification of lake water and fauna appears amongst those actors mentioned previously as supporters of using 'marsh' to describe the lakes. In 1895 a government health council, while considering a drainage request, carried out a study of hygienic conditions in the southern lake. They established that the lakes in the southern Basin of Mexico emitted sulphurous hydrogen miasmas that were felt on the streets of Mexico City whenever southern winds were blowing. In their words, 'this is why this country has unhealthy wind. The Aztecs' hieroglyphs even represented this with the image of a skull'.[35] The Second Mexican Congress, convened in 1878 by the development secretary for the purpose of reducing the stench in the capital, also characterised the lakes as true swamps with 'stagnant water that becomes more unhealthy every day'.[36] From the chroniclers to the physicians, engineers and hygienists, the conception of lakes — swamps, more than lakes — as a dirty and disagreeable space that should disappear would confront the village world of Indians, who surmised that lake water circulated underground. Far from being stagnant and a source of disease, lake water was a central element in village and household subsistence.[37]

The Noriega brothers attempted to capitalise on the situation in which expert opinion, the idea of a lake water hierarchy and official statistics were in their favour. It was difficult for the filth of a large city like Mexico City to

---

33   Musset (1992), pp. 44–7.

34   *Ibid.*

35   AGN, SCOP, vol. 564–4, f. 41. The skull was used to identify cartographically the village of Mixquic, located in the centre of the Lago de Chalco–Xochimilco, where worship of the dead has important meaning at present. In spite of the hygienist reading, it is something else entirely to associate it with decomposing organic matter from the lakes.

36   'Memoria de los trabajos ejecutados por el Consejo Superior de salubridad en el año de 1878,' Archivo Histórico de la Secretaría de Salubridad y Asistencia (México, DF), C. 5, Exp. 12.

37   Indigenous peoples believed that the mountains were inverted water pitchers that drained liquid in wet seasons and stored them in dry seasons. The theory of underground circulation of water was not dismissed until the eighteenth century in Europe, when it would be replaced by the atmospheric circulation model, which would arrive too late for indigenous peoples to switch. See Musset (1992); Tortolero (2000a).

yield to a world occupied by 41 fishermen in 1895. Thus in 1894 the Noriega brothers petitioned the Mexican government to drain Lago de Chalco. In 1894 Iñigo Noriega, a prominent landowner in the region, requested permission from the secretary of state and the Communication and Public Works Departments to open a canal that would divert waters from the Lagos de Chalco and Texcoco, thus effectively requesting their drainage.

The Noriega entrepreneurs justified their request with three claims: change in land use would increase arable surface area; an increase in agricultural production would create employment; water would be redirected to flush Mexico City's sewers. Their project rested on the principle of dominion over the lake, which was held by their Hacienda de Xico. They also mentioned similar, but experimental, lake drainage schemes they had conducted on another of their farms, the Hacienda de la Compañía. There, they discovered that drainage had converted reclaimed land into 'fields so fertile and productive that only in exceptional conditions could similar ones be found'.[38] Thus, they proposed to convert a low-productivity environment, with meagre fishing and grazing of low-quality aquatic grasses, into fields where one-third could be used as summer pasture and the remaining two-thirds could be planted in maize. The figures they suggested for maize production indicated the fertility of the drained area: annual production of 200,000 grain *cargas*. By contrast, the Chalco's most productive haciendas at the time produced 6,000 annual *cargas*. Chalco drainage would make the Noriega hacienda amongst the most productive in Mexico.

The logic of expanded employment, improved hygiene and increased agricultural productivity justified the construction of 203 kilometres of canals. One canal, a 16-kilometre stretch, was devoted to taking water from Lago de Chalco to Lago de Texcoco. Another canal, 18 kilometres long and 12 metres wide, would take spring water from the south of the former Lago de Chalco to the region of Lago de Xochimilco, and take water from the Sierra Nevada during the wet season. Another canal, 14 kilometres long and eight metres wide, located north of the Noriega brothers' Hacienda de Xico, would pass through the villages of San Lucas, Tlapocayan, Ayotla and Tlapisahua, and would collect rainy-season runoff from mountainous regions to be sent to Lago de Texcoco. The rest of the canals, adding up to 154 kilometres, would drain and irrigate the fields, while providing transport routes to milling centres.[39] Thus, an essential element of the landscape, a longue durée actor, disappeared in favour of new actors, capitalists and entrepreneurs in charge of lake drainage.

---

38   AGN, SCOP, vol. 546.
39   *Gaceta de Gobierno*, vol. XV, no. 59, 21 January 1903.

The shareholders of the Negociación Agrícola de Xico S.A. were part of the Porfirian elite;[40] some went on to carry out lake-drainage schemes in other countries. The firm's capital and works were intended to end thousands of years of the human–environment relationship in the lake region, and to begin an era of large hydraulic works that would signal a century of ecological punishment and battles against nature that would privilege economic rationality over ecology. Reports written by a member of the administrative board of the Mexican Industrial Finance Society, which had made sizeable loans to Xico, indicated that the Negociación sold 38,000 pesos of milk, 14,000 of pulque, 130,000 of wheat and alfalfa and 1.2 million of maize for a total of 1.4 million pesos in 1908.[41] The Noriega Negociación had an annual turnover of 1.5 million pesos, the same amount as the Banco del Estado de México claimed as its capitalisation.[42]

Thus, the firm had been converted into a model farm with production levels exceeding all other haciendas in the country. The firm also brought a Spanish professor of fructiculture from Zaragoza, Mariano Gajón, who was named technical director of crops and orchards of the Noriega enterprises. Gajón introduced 100,000 fruit-bearing tees, all of which were imported from Europe (especially Spain and France), forage grasses and vegetables. He also introduced new resinous trees, which supplied the raw material for paint, varnish and solvent, for which the firm imported Spanish workers from the Avila region. All in all, at the turn of the century, the Noriega Negociación had become a laboratory for agricultural revolution that moved from shipping wharves to railroads, from manual labour with hand implements to mechanisation, from ancient to modern hydraulic structures, from extensive to intensive cultivation. The integration between cattle ranching and agriculture became more important, as did the organisation and administration of traditional work to new forms of labour organisation, with the arrival of Spanish workers and directors, and from small-scale to large-scale and market-oriented production.[43]

This transformation of the Mexican waterscape would not have been possible without favourable treatment from public officials helping the interests of the Noriega brothers. The policy of federal concessions per-

40   Members included Thomas Braniff (US industrialist); José Sánchez Ramos (Spanish industrialist); Henry Waters (English banker); Faustino Martínez (Spanish merchant); A. Richard (Spanish merchant); A. Hackmack (Austrian merchant); José Breir (Austrian merchant); Valentín Elcoro (Spanish merchant); Luis Barroso (Mexican merchant); and D. Dorantes (Mexican merchant).
41   Genin (1910).
42   Pérez (1998). The Banco del Estado de México was not a small bank; founded in 1897, it had headquarters in Toluca and several offices in Mexico, the USA and Europe.
43   Tortolero (2000a).

mitted entrepreneurs to benefit from a series of advantages that made investment attractive: tax exemptions, land purchases and duty-free import of equipment. These factors, and the overall economic and cultural context, facilitated the work of entrepreneurs. This pattern would be repeated in the case of Lago de Texcoco.

Lago de Texcoco

Described as a marsh covered by 'black and greenish foul-smelling mud' that gave physician José María Guyosa headaches during his 1892 visit, Lago de Texcoco discharged approximately 3,800 litres per second from the Basin of Mexico. The engineer Luis Espinosa had been designated in 1886 as director of drainage works for Texcoco, which would be done by means of a canal, tunnel and drainage cut or *tajo*. Studies estimated the depth of the lake at not less than 3.5 metres between 1881 and 1890; during the rainy season depth exceeded five metres.[44]

A series of factors distinguished the draining of Lago de Texcoco from the draining of the Lago de Chalco. First, the project was carried out by a company that was completely controlled by the federal government's secretary of communication and public works, through the Hydrological Commission for the Valley of Mexico, which had direct responsibility for draining Texcoco.[45] The first surveys of water and surrounding land had been carried out much earlier by the federal government. Chalco drainage was undertaken by a private firm, while Texcoco's larger area comprised private property such as villages, but also federal property. Another difference is that the drainage of both lakes responded to different traditions. Although both drainage schemes, in principle, meant to obtain land for large-scale agricultural production, the Lago de Texcoco project was at a disadvantage: the soils of its drained lakebed would be saline, and thus unsuitable for agriculture, while drainage of the Chalco exposed highly fertile soils to agriculture.

A private group was responsible for carrying out experiments to determine the type of crops most suitable for the drained lands and thus to pay, with interest, the project's expenses. The Sociedad Financiera para el Fomento de la Irrigación established an experimental station in Santa Clara, which was run by Miguel A. de Quevedo. Previously, Quevedo had been chief of the Forest Department, during which time he had responded to a questionnaire from the secretary of agriculture inquiring as to the possibility of farming in lacustrine environments. His answers suggested that he had been able to generate botanical knowledge that would have

44 Guyosa (1892), p. 29.
45 Approximately 2,300 pesos in public funds had been secured from the Caja de Préstamos para Obras de Irrigación y Fomento a la Agricultura.

been impossible to acquire without lake drainage. His activities as station chief led him to conclude that the most appropriate plants for frost-prone saline environments were halophytic (salt-tolerant) shrubs and plants of the chenopodiaceae family. Amongst shrubs, Quevedo favoured reeds, and, amongst tree species, Quevedo reckoned that the most resistant were tamarisk (*Tamarix gallica* and *T. africana*), *Casuarina* and *Eucalyptus* (*E. robusta, E. rostrata, E. resinifera* and *E. tereticornis*).[46]

Quevedo suggested planting reeds, which would serve as raw material for the production of paper pulp for Mexico's paper industry, which otherwise would have to import raw material. He viewed favourably the cultivation of sugar beets as forage and as a source of sugar. Sugar beets could help not only the Morelos industries that were having difficulty planting sugar cane, but also were considered to be a transitional crop that would help the halophytic chenopods remove excess salt from the soil. His experience with commercial use of recently-drained lake environments would encourage Quevedo to differentiate three separate environments according to salt content, presence of other elements, degree of soil humidity and soil texture. He emphasised that his suggestions were unique to the particular soil environment of the drained lake, and not applicable to all drained areas. He proposed that in the first years after drainage, only forest plantations should be attempted to improve the soil; later, land uses could include production of vegetables and other crops. But Quevedo also noted that at least one-third of the drained area should be planted in trees, which would preserve a climatic equilibrium that would benefit agricultural fields and Mexico City.[47]

Obviously, Quevedo's advice was not followed precisely. Government resources were short and the federal government would not recover all the funds invested because its intention had not been to exploit the land itself. Hence, the forestry dimensions of the project were cut drastically. The land dedicated to forests was not between 30 and 50 hectares, but rather only 6.8 hectares, and was staffed only by one person.

Differences were substantial between the quality of land in the Chalco, which was very fertile, and the Texcoco, which required investment of capital and material that only the federal government could have made. The differences also show the great faith placed in human action, through regenerating crops, flushing and the use of fertilisers, could triumph over the challenges presented by the nature of the drained lands. Although it was not known how long it would take for lands to be made suitable for agriculture, Quevedo alleged that it would only be a short time before they were productive.

46   Huerta (1999).
47   *Ibid.*

Quevedo's suggestions guided the selection of plants and, above all, the project that would be developed in the drained lands of Lago de Texcoco. He especially encouraged afforestation of drained lands with acacias (*Acacia melanoxylon*), casuarina (*Casuarina cunninghaniana*), pirús (*Schinus molle*), mezquites or huisaches (*Prosopis juliflora*) and tamarisk (*Tamarix parviflora*) to create windbreaks, control soil erosion and improve soil fertility. Afforestation would reduce the noxious effect of strong dust storms known as *tolvaneras*, which were thought to transport dirt, miasmas and pollutants to Mexico City. According to contemporary observers, the *tolvaneras* caused gastrointestinal and respiratory illnesses to a large number of Mexico City's residents. Afforestation also would reduce soil erosion, as root growth would secure soil, and the leguminous acacia would fix atmospheric nitrogen in the soil, thus fertilising the soil for other plants.

Quevedo also proposed the cultivation of commercial crops, especially forage such as alfalfa, four-wing saltbush (*Atriplex canescens*), oats, barley, turnips and holm oak. Thus, Quevedo elevated the development of commercial agriculture above all else. With the exception of maize, the main subsistence crop, Quevedo's reports do not mention any other crop with direct usefulness to the lake's inhabitants.

If high soil salinity was a formidable agricultural problem, then for some entrepreneurs salt was a resource to be exploited commercially. Several firms solicited concessions to exploit the salt flats. The requests specified access not only to which salt flats in the drained region, but also access to stream runoff, which was also rich in salts.

Not only did salt arouse the initiative and greed of investors, but so did irrigation farming of the drained lakebed. An agricultural firm requested information on the extent of the drainage carried out by Secretaría de Comunicaciones y Obras Públicas in the interest of acquiring a vast area of land. The company's plans were to drain and irrigate the fields by immersion. The irrigated fields would contain tree crops and forage, such as sugar beets, which would resist soil salinity, thus compensating the investment of capital. This firm had already acquired lands in Santa Clara and Los Reyes, where experimentation was underway. The firm's owners proposed to purchase lands considered to be federal property, alleging that their project would contribute to resolving the health problems that affected the capital and other regions around Mexico City.[48]

Demographic pressure became an important factor in converting uncultivated lands into agricultural emporia, as the Noriega brothers had done, that would supply food to Mexico City's growing population and clay bricks sold as construction material. Agricultural enterprises near the city modernised to keep pace with population growth. The Noriega broth-

48   AGN, SCOP, exp. 544/13.

ers are an example of how formerly non-arable spaces were made productive in former lake beds that were converted to commercial agriculture.
However, urban population increases also occurred elsewhere in Porfirian
Mexico. Guadalajara, which was Mexico's fifth-largest city at the start of
the nineteenth century, became the country's second-largest city, with
more than 100,000 inhabitants, by the late nineteenth century.[49]
Demographic pressure exerted pressure on agriculture to exploit the lakes
of Guadalajara, where lake-drainage projects were directed to the case of
Lago de Chapala, as we shall see in the next section.

Lago de Chapala

Since 1867 Ignacio Castellanos had requested from the Jalisco state government the authorisation to transform the Río Santiago, the main tribu-
tary of Lake Chapala, by removing rocks and silt and expanding the chan-
nel. In exchange, Castellanos asked for 'all of the lands that will become
dry' and payment from landowners on the former shorelines whose properties would be improved as a result of the project. The government
ordered a sounding of the project, finding general opposition amongst
landowners and villagers on the shore, who alleged that they would lose
irrigation water, fauna, the beauty of the lake and employment. Only in
1903 would Manuel Cuesta Gallardo secure a contract to exploit irrigation
water from the Chapala, acquiring the holdings of all federal shoreline
areas, which would be made available with the reduction of the lake's water
level. Cuesta, a hacienda owner, presented a project that intended to identify and sell irrigated lands, generate hydroelectricity and irrigate lands.
Once again, power relations are important: Manuel Cuesta Gallardo,
besides being a rich landowner, had established political relations that
would take him to the state governor's office in 1911. [50]

The Cuesta Gallardo group formed in May 1900 to canalise the Lago
de Magdalena, opening new possibilities to exploit the Chapala's water.[51]
Later, on 13 July 1909, they created the Compañía Hidroeléctrica e
Irrigadora de las Aguas de Chapala, with capital of 12 million pesos and
30,000 preferred and 90,000 common shares, all valued at 100 pesos each.
Amongst the Company's objectives were drainage of the unutilised marsh,
dredging of the Río Santiagio, irrigation of 20,000 hectares and generation
of electricity. The drained lands in this scheme were at the centre of the

49   Guadalajara's population grew from approximately 19,500 in 1803 to 70,000 in 1862
      and 101,208 in 1900 (Boyer and Davies, 1973, p. 37).
50   Bohem (1994); Archivo Histórico del Agua (México, D.F.), Exp. 8,935, Caja 617 and
      Exp. 55,698, Caja 4073.
51   The group's associates included José Somellera, Genero Arce, José López Portillo y
      Rojas, Alfonso Jones and Lorenzo Elízaga.

Compañía Agrícola de Chapala created in 1910. In 1917 the hydroelectricity branch would merge with the Compañía de Tranvías (street trams), which appointed to its administrative council National Bank officials (André Guieu, Agustín Legorreta and Miguel Macedo) and Central Bank officials (Marroquín y Rivera and Alexis Dubernard). Thus, the association of bankers and, in particular, the Sociedad Financiera para la Industria en México, created a clear modernising profile in these companies, which could be exemplified further by total income, from street trams and electricity produced for Guadalajara or other regions. During 1908–10 the company reported profits of approximately 450,000 pesos annually; profits rose to 500,000 pesos by 1910–14 and reached 1.2 million pesos by 1920.[52] Overall, the Cuesta Gallardo group was highly profitable and profited even during 1915–16, when the Mexican Revolution forced the printing of paper money, forcing profits down. The Compañía de Chapala was the most important of its class in Mexico, ahead of the Compañía de la Luz de Pachuca and the Guanajuato Power Company.[53]

Laguna de Lerma

Despite various drainage projects that began after 1857 when the governor of the state, Gumesindo Enríquez, took strong interest in drainage, it was only with the growth of Mexico City's population that initiatives began to reduce the area of the Laguna de Lerma. With an area of 740 square kilometres, the Lerma was considerably smaller than the Basin of México's 8,000 square kilometres, but still played a significant role in the region's economy until the advent of industrialisation. Human use of the lake's flora and fauna was intense and diverse, as the Lerma contributed in multiple ways to the development of other economic activities, such as livestock raising, production of artisan goods and commerce, in addition to agricultural production in general, which depended on a lake environment.[54] Around the lake, several activities were well developed, such as fishing, hunting, gathering, production of handicrafts, needles, canoes, paddles, scythes and other work implements associated with woodworking and metalworking.[55] This lake was subjected to two drainage projects during the period in which stagnant water was considered to be a cause of disease because it emanated miasmas and microorganisms. In this view, conservation of the lake environment would not bring any economic benefits and drainage would result in improved health and generation of wealth.

---

52 Archivo Histórico de Paribas (France), Carton 445, 'Memorandum sur la Compagnie "Hidroelectrica e Irrigadora de Chapala",' 10 July 1924.
53 Tortolero (2002).
54 Albores (1995), p. 413.
55 *Ibid*, p. 423.

The first project, led by Gumesindo Enríquez in 1906, attempted to obtain land by draining the lake. However, the project faced the serious problem of the depth of the lake not being known. Enríquez had been the state's governor, and was also a farmer and politician, but he was not an engineer. His concession was transferred to the Compañía Agrícola del Lago de Lerma (Lerma Agricultural Company), represented by Luis Zaldívar, who changed the idea of lake water exploitation. Earlier, projects had been restricted to specific regions; with Zaldívar they became gigantic projects that would affect the entire lake catchment.[56] The project's aims of generating electricity and irrigation water by draining the lake reveal the new scale of hydraulic intervention. The project called for an eight-kilometre tunnel and a 20-kilometre canal that would link the waters of the lake and facilitate drainage. The cost was approximately two million pesos, while equipment was estimated at four million pesos. Electricity was destined to Mexico City, to the mining towns of Zacualpan and Sultepec, Cuernavaca and to the Morelos sugarcane plantations.[57] Although the Revolution would interrupt these projects, the overall vision for hydraulic transformation represented the continued subordination of the countryside to the needs of cities. After the Revolution was over, the federal government would take over the project and the Lerma's hydraulic resources to supply water to Mexico City.

Lago de Zacapu

In the state of Michoacán, Morelia and Zamora were surrounded by lakes, while the Lagos de Cuitzeo and Zacapu were further north.[58] Engineers who saw these lacustrine environments noticed that the lake bottoms had high productive potential for agriculture, but, without intervention, they would remain sterile, poor and unhealthy.[59] Again, scientific arguments for lake drainage supported the entrepreneurs' claims for drainage. In Zacapu, the projects began to appear in 1864, when the governor of Michoacán, Felipe B. Berriozábal, signed a decree declaring that draining the lakes would benefit the health of the population. But it was not until the increase in the economic scale of projects in the 1880s that entrepreneurs would associate with hydroelectricity and irrigation firms to carry out projects. Thus, the 1886 drainage project of Antonio P. Carranza and Manuel Vallejo was replaced by the Noriega brothers, who took over Zacapu drainage by the end of the nineteenth century.

56   Camacho (1998), p. 268.
57   *Ibid.*, p. 270.
58   Morelia had a population of 24,000 in 1884, increasing to 37,278 in 1900 (Boyer and Davies, 1973, p. 45).
59   Reyes (1991), p. 27.

Brothers Eduardo and Alfredo Noriega were nephews of Iñigo Noriega. Uncle Noriega's experience in Chalco encouraged the secretary of development, colonisation and industry to approve his nephews' Zacapu drainage project in 1899. The drainage project ended in 1902 and irrigation was completed in 1907, setting the stage for the 1908 inauguration of the modern Cantabria hacienda. Arguments for drainage were similar to the ones used for the Chalco: to make new lands productive; to create employment; to make the region healthy; and to become owners of one-third of the drained lands. In 1902 the E. & A. Noriega Collective (Sociedad Colectiva) obtained a 400,000 peso loan from the Mexican Crédit Foncier, supplemented by a 1908 loan from the Caja de Préstamos for 1.4 million pesos.

The Noriega organisational structure and capital permitted the creation of an agricultural enterprise that covered 12,261 hectares in the Zacapu region, where it linked agricultural production to Cantabria's granary and to the railroad line, expanding the scale of farm's operations. The railroad link allowed the export of 99 per cent of production in 1912 and only 68 tonnes of maize were sold on the hacienda.[60]

Considering the thousands of hectares of fertile soils reached by irrigation, the farm equipment and machinery, a large workforce and the rail transport network, it is not surprising that profits were very high. During its first four years of operation, the Cantabria Hacienda had made 833,825 pesos, averaging 208,456 pesos annually. Initially, this was on the basis of maize production primarily, which in 1909 was 4,200 tonnes and in 1912 7,700 tonnes. By contrast, wheat and chickpea production were only 420 and 120 tonnes, respectively.[61]

These profits were the source of the high salaries of qualified personnel, ranging from 500 pesos annually received by the person in charge of the granary to 15,478 pesos received by the general manager. The middle sectors of the hacienda were made up of sharecroppers or tenants, approximately 400 heads of households, who received land, housing and cash for their labour. Finally, unskilled labourers, approximately 1,431 heads of households, 77 per cent of Cantabria's population in 1915, worked two months annually on the farm, one during planting and the other two during the harvest. In spite of the farm's modernity, with its machinery and organisational structure, the income from farm stores under the notorious *rayas y fletes* system was 114,11 pesos in 1909 but only 75,413 pesos in 1912. With salaries paid only two months per year to a population displaced by mechanisation, the price abuses of these hacienda stores are proverbial.

60   *Ibid.*, p. 40.
61   *Ibid.*, p. 32.

Notwithstanding the *rayas y fletes* stores, the agrarian revolution had successfully entered the productive logic and in 1914 the Noriega brothers, worried by the victory of the Constitutionalists, separated 13,000 hectares from Cantabria and Copándaro, transforming its sharecroppers and tenant farmers into small landowners. This was a condition imposed by the Caja de Préstamos, which required the subdivision of land in cases of outstanding debts. The next period of subdivision would occur between 1921 and 1927 with the granting of *ejido* status in Trinadaro, Naranja and Tarajero.

Conclusion: Economic and Ecological Effects of Lake Drainage

Thus far we have seen how the modernising Porfirian regime's attitude to water resources was based on two arguments. On the one hand, increased rural productivity was necessary to feed cities, requiring policies for irrigation and lake drainage. On the other hand, the hygienist argument held that the lakes were unhealthy marshes; drainage would cause infection to be reduced. However, the imperative to feed growing populations and attend to perceived public-health dangers had enormous social and ecological costs. In the Basin of Mexico, for example, the social costs created inequalities that explain the armed revolt of 1911 leading to the Mexican Revolution. Modern lake-drainage schemes concentrated wealth; Mexico's economy grew during the *Porfiriato*, but with substantial social costs, primarily the loss of subsistence means amongst large segments of the population, especially lakeshore communities. Most lakeshore towns in the Chalco complained that lake drainage had ended their access to traditional resources.[62] Before draining the Lerma 'the lake was a spring' and 'canoes returned so full of fish that they nearly sank', but drainage left the lakeshore towns without access to resources.[63] Active peasant participation in subdividing haciendas in Chalco, Lerma and Zacapu indicates the high social costs of an agricultural system that consumed resources to the detriment of village and peasant economies. On the eve of the Revolution, haciendas occupied 97 per cent of Mexico's farm land, but there were only 847 owners, or three per cent of the population.[64] Such inequality was addressed by the Revolution, which by 1935 had distributed 10.8 million hectares to 545,000 families; between 1934 and 1940 another 17 million hectares would be distributed.[65] These social costs have been evaluated in terms of land concentration and peasant expulsions.[66] However, the eco-

62   Tortolero (1999), p. 222.
63   Albores (1995).
64   Rojas (1990), p. 218; Bellingeri (1981), p. 324; García de León (1988), p. 79. For a critique of these estimates, see Guerra (1998) and Tortolero (2003a)
65   Tortolero (2003a).
66   Tortolero (1997; 1999).

logical costs were significant, as Porfirian modernisation caused an eco-logical revolution in the Basin of Mexico as dramatic as the early sixteenth-century 'plague of sheep' that transformed central Mexico's pre-European social and environmental relations.[67]

The pre-European Basin of Mexico was a mixture of approximately 521,600 hectares of forest, 175,360 hectares of thornscrub (*matorral*), 161,140 hectares of grassland and 102,000 hectares of surface water. Forests occupied 54 per cent of the Basin and were comprised of pine, firs (*oyamel*), live oak (*encino*) and oaks, providing habitat for several species of animal.[68] The lake water contained 68 million cubic meters of plant growth, 11 species of fish and 109 species of aquatic birds. By the late nineteenth century, the lakes had virtually disappeared and the forest zone had become a degraded and denuded hilly landscape, which reduced spring volume, encouraged flash flooding in the descending streams and caused sedimentation of rivers.[69] By 1994 approximately 80 per cent of forest area and 99 per cent of the lake surface had disappeared; 71 per cent of the soils were in an advanced state of degradation.[70]

This was the ecological cost of the modernising projects that empha-sised the economic aspects of nature and for which a new model, which differed dramatically from the former individual-led projects of M.L. Smith, I. Castellanos, Manuel Cuesta Gallardo or Felipe Berriozábal, had been created. The new model intended to extract the greatest profit from the transformation of nature; it was based on high investment of capital, the formation of corporations supported by entrepreneurs, sought economies of scale and used cutting-edge technologies. These points are summarised below.

Lake drainage required considerable capital investment. Pearson obtained a loan of £2.4 million to drain the Lago de México. In Chalco, the Noriega brothers borrowed five million French francs from the Sociedad Financiera para la Industria en México, which was based in Paris and Switzerland. In Texcoco, the Caja de Préstamos para Obras e Irrigación e Industria granted a loan of 2.3 million pesos for lake drainage. In Chapala, the same Sociedad Financiera extended a loan of four million pesos, an amount to which loans from Mexican banks would contribute. In Lerma, capital investment was approximately six million pesos. In Zacapu, the Crédit Foncier and the Caja de Préstamos invested 1.4 million pesos.

The millions of pesos in investment attracted to lake drainage were administered not by family enterprises, but by corporations. Pearson &

67　Melville (1994).
68　Canabal (1997), p. 29.
69　Forest area had been reduced to 106,392 hectares by the beginning of the nineteenth century; there are estimates of 37,924 hectares for 1910; see México (1911).
70　Tortolero (2000b), p. 128.

Son would be in charge of drainage in Mexico, the Negociación Agrícola de Xico S.A. carried out drainage in Chalco, the Sociedad Financiera para el Fomento de la Irrigación drained Texcoco and the Compañía Agrícola de Chapala, which would join with the Hidroeléctrica, drained the Chapala. In Lerma, the Compañía Agrícola de Lerma would carry out the project and in Zacapu the E. y A. Noriega Sociedad Colectiva was responsible. Within a few years, the business model changed from one of individuals to corporations. The individual-based firm relied on a family network that combined family fortunes from relatives and friends, while the corporation would gather invited entrepreneurs and investors. These important stockholders would not hesitate to sell stock in their corporation to entice foreign investment. Thus, Iñigo y Remigio Noriega Hermanos became the Negociación Agrícola de Xico S.A., Manuel Cuesta Gallardo became the Compañía Hidroeléctrica de Chapala and Gumesindo Enríquez became the Compañía Agrícola de Lerma.

Corporations sought out economies of scale as they drained lakes. In Lerma and Chapala electricity generated supplied cities and mines. The drained lakes of Zacapu and Chalco supplied agricultural products to urban centres via railroads. Production was no longer aimed at local markets but rather targeted large-scale urban centres and higher profits. Investors developed regional and national economic projects; the Noriega brothers, for example, integrated economies of scale in agriculture, banking, industries and urban land speculation to create a huge fortune.[71] Estimates of profits corroborate the corporate, capital-intensive nature of lake drainage. The Negociación Agrícola de Xico reported annual profits of 1.4 million pesos, while Pearson & Son earned 1.3 million pesos annually. In Cantabria, annual income was 200,000 pesos. In Jalisco, more than 400,000 pesos annually arrived in the Hidroeléctrica de Chapala's coffers.

Advanced technologies were crucial for highly capitalised corporations to carry out drainage projects successfully. Dredges, excavators and other necessary equipment constructed the image of modernity and the human domination of nature. In 1900 at the inauguration of the drainage project in the Basin of Mexico, Porfirio Díaz gave the order to raise the San Lázaro gates, thus concluding a project that was intended to control water in the Basin and end a perennial source of problems. Photographs of this project graced the calendars of the period. The project's bridges, gates and tunnels built to drain the Basin rivalled the image of modernity created by the factories, broad avenues, theatres, statues and gardens. The ancient monumentality of churches was now shared by an architectural image in which the drainage works had become part of the image of modernity.

71 Martínez Moctezuma (2001).

The results of lake drainage were contradictory, as spectacular profits for firms were made in exchange for high social and ecological costs.[72] It is no coincidence that the first opposition to lake drainage began in Chalco, Lerma and Cantabria in the form of agrarian protest that resulted in the Mexican Revolution and subsequent land redistribution. In Chalco, villagers eloquently explained their reasons for participating in the Revolution. Tlapacoya's villagers complained of being evicted from their resources during lake drainage. In Tlapizahua, the villagers had hunted and fished in what had been Lake Chalco. In Ayotla, residents claimed that the village, founded on the lake shore, where its residents had lived for several generations, relied on cultivating small plots of land, hunting and fishing, as well as livestock feeding on aquatic plants removed from the lake. Villagers from Tezompa cultivated raised fields or *chinampas*, where they produced several types of beans, peas, chiles and maize, yielding 150 to 200 annually per planted seed. Representatives of lake shore villages such as Chalco, San Juan Ixtayopan, Huitzilzingo and Mixquic alleged that they had relied on fishing and *chinampa* agriculture located on lands watered by the lake.[73] Much of the villages' food supply depended on the lake system; when the lake disappeared, villagers became receptive to revolutionary ideas.

In conclusion, hydraulic manipulation became an important part of an economy that, before 1880, lacked adequate transport, communication, banks, capital, technologies and education. The achievement of the *Porfiriato* in these areas was substantial, but also partial and contradictory. The Porfirian modernising project generated inequality, which explains the armed uprising of 1911–17, and caused profound ecological change that disarticulated entire communities as they lost access to traditional communal resources, such as water and forests, and were left with no option other than joining the Revolution.[74]

---

72   Tortolero (2002).
73   Archivo Histórico del Estado de México, México, DF; for: Tlapacoya (AHEMCAM, 1917–1931, Exp. III, G.4, 92fs); Tlapizahua (*ibid.*, vol. 160, Exp.III, G.6, f. 29); Ayotla (*ibid.*, vol. 159, Exp. III, G.5, 113fs); Tezompa (*ibid.*, vol. 162, f. 12); Chalco, San Juan, Huitzilzingo and Mixquic (*ibid.*, vol. 161. Exp. III, 215fs); also see Tortolero (1997; 1999).
74   Porfirian modernity was not that distinct from the modernising project of industrialising Britain, where self-interest and economic logic had higher priority than social and communal interests, and higher than ecological rationality. But in the UK modernity initiated the Industrial Revolution and its spectacular economic growth, while in Mexico modernity generated a social revolution; see Wrigley (1988), p. 98–105.

CHAPTER 5

Deforestation and Sugar in Cuba's Centre-East:
The Case of Camagüey, 1898–1926[*]

Reinaldo Funes Monzote

Introduction

Although Cuba had a sugar industry since the early seventeenth century, Cuban sugar became important globally only after the late-eighteenth-century slave revolt in Haiti. Early on, sugarcane was planted in forested lands. Wood provided construction material and fuel for mills and, after biomass was burnt, abundant organic material encouraged high agricultural yields. When wood fuel reserves or soil organic material declined, planters sought new forests, repeating the cycle of deforestation. From the middle of the nineteenth century, increasing fuel wood shortages encouraged technological innovations for using bagasse (sugarcane stalks after crushing) and coal as fuel, avoiding the fatal decline of the sugar industry from lack of fuel. Nevertheless, the promise of extensive forested regions on the sugar frontier was much more powerful than warnings against future problems for Cuba resulting from continued cultivation practices. This mobile and predatory practise depended on short-term soil fertility, which resulted in high sugarcane yields at the expense of burnt forest biomass. Neither the frequently cited cautionary example of deforestation elsewhere in the Caribbean nor the case of the Havana region, which had suffered the same process in the late eighteenth century, was sufficient to counter nomadic sugarcane production in search of the quick return promised by clearing forest. Sugarcane lands continued expanding as long as flat or gently rolling forested land was available. Cuba's centre-east, or the Camagüey region (Figure 5.1) as I shall refer to it here, represents the most extreme example of twentieth-century deforestation for sugarcane in Cuba.[1]

[*]   An earlier version of this chapter was prepared for the panel 'Export/Plantation Agriculture and Environmental Change' at the September 2001 Latin American Studies Association meeting in Washington, DC. This chapter was translated by Christian Brannstrom. The author's thanks also go to José A. Piqueras, John Soluri, Allen Wells and José F. Buscaglia.
[1]   The region generally coincides with the present provinces of Camagüey and Ciego de Avila. During the late nineteenth century, the region was the Puerto Príncipe province, which in 1903 was renamed Camagüey.

Figure 5.1: Sugar Latifundia and *Centrales* (Large Sugarcane Mills) in Camagüey, 1898–1926

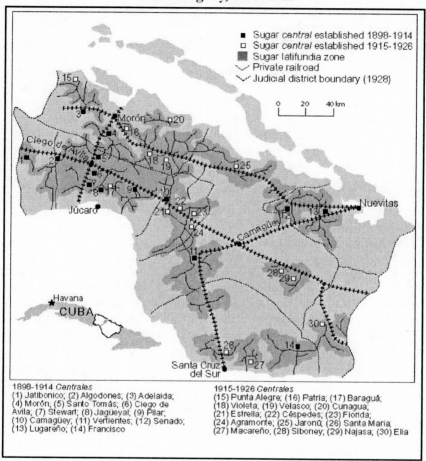

Inset map shows present-day provinces of Camagüey and Ciego de Avila; the study region extends east of the border depicted.

Source: Torre and Aguayo (1928).

Most scholars of the Cuban sugar industry have noted the expansion of sugar at the expense of forest, but usually only briefly and within much broader intellectual projects. Classic studies, such as Moreno Fraginal's *El ingenio* and Leví Marrero's *Cuba, economía y sociedad*, make several references to this issue; however, their works do not analyse in detail the different historical moments or the specific places and ecosystems affected, nor the environmental consequences or its relation to economic and social aspects.[2] Similarly, the works of Roland T. Ely and Laird Bergad, on the impact of monoculture on Cuban society and economy, do not discuss fully the environmental aspects of sugar's expansion in Cuba.[3] More recent scholarship pays even less attention to the effects of sugarcane on Cuba's centre-east environment during the late nineteenth and early twentieth centuries.[4] Frequently, the presence of forests has been eclipsed by terms such as 'virgin', 'fertile' or 'available' lands, which discourage analysis of the condition of environments before and after the sugar revolution. Studies on the history of Cuba's forest policies and Cuban natural history have encouraged interest in environmental conditioning factors in sugarcane expansion and the environmental impacts of the sugar economy.[5] Studies of scientists since the nineteenth century, who warned of the consequences of rapid deforestation of Cuba,[6] and geographers and historians, such as Juan Pérez de la Riva and Antonio Nuñez Jiménez, have also been important in encouraging this new research emphasis.

Environmental history and ecological history have begun to inform studies on the environmental impact of sugar production in Cuba and elsewhere in the Caribbean. David Watts's study, for example, warns that very little is known about the effects of deforestation on the environment, which probably were considerable.[7] Richard Tucker argues that Cuba became the first place in which the US 'ecological empire' became established; however, he also notes that not enough data are available for in-depth analysis of the environmental costs of Cuban sugar production.[8] In an earlier study, Mark Smith uses the case of the Manatí sugar mill, located in the Cuban centre-east, to illustrate how the intensity of natural resources use was connected directly to the political economy of domination and dependency initiated during the US military occupation of Cuba between 1898 and 1902.[9]

2   Moreno Fraginals (1978); Marrero (1974–84).
3   Ely (1963); Bergad (1992).
4   Iglesias (1998); Dye (1998); Santamaría (1996; 2000); Ayala (1999).
5   Martín (1944); Matos (c. 1970); Pruna (1956); Casals (1989); Aranda (1995); Opatrný (1996).
6   The most relevant examples are Rodríguez Ferrer (1876) and Sagra (1862).
7   Watts (1987).
8   Tucker (2000). This chapter offers new evidence on the environmental cost of sugar in Cuba during the late nineteenth and early twentieth centuries.
9   Smith (1995) is an excellent pioneering study based on documents relating to the Manatí Sugar Company held in the Braga Brothers Collection of the University of Florida. Smith's objective was to show how global forces and the imperialist presence of the USA in Cuba caused environmental impacts in the Manatí region of northern Oriente province. The imperialist political economy allowed Manatí to control a large area for export agriculture, which provoked large ecological transformations.

One of the aims of this chapter is to explain the impact of sugar estates on the forests and the environment of Cuba's centre-east during the early twentieth century. Camagüey is the most representative of the post-1898 expansion of the sugar economy that ended with the 1926 prohibition of sugarcane planting on forested lands in an attempt to restrict Cuban sugar production. This chapter is part of broader research on the historical relations between increasing sugar production and the reduction of Cuban forests. The environmental implications of this relationship, in Cuba and other Caribbean islands, are comparable to other events, such as the disappearance of indigenous populations and use of African slavery as labour for plantations oriented to world markets.

No other region of Cuba suffered such a rapid and intense change in natural environment as Camagüey. Environmental transformations from sugar production that had taken centuries, or at least several decades, in other Cuban regions happened within a few years in Cuba's centre-east during the early twentieth century. Although other factors, before 1898, affected changes to Camagüey's soil and vegetation, that phenomena in no way approximated the impacts of increased sugar production.

Camagüey before Sugar: from the Sixteenth Century to 1898

The late nineteenth and early twentieth-century expansion of sugarcane was not the first significant environmental change in Cuba's centre-east. Europeans exploring Camagüey in the 1520s probably encountered a forested environment that recent scholars have divided into three categories. Semideciduous forests of interior plains were developed on well-drained soils where average annual rainfall is between 1,200 and 1,600 millimetres. This forest probably had an upper stratum between 20 and 25 metres in height. A lower semideciduous forest had a single stratum approximately 15 metres in height, and would have been found on the region's coastal plains, where soils are exceedingly wet during the April–October rainy season and lack water during the November–March dry season; overall, average annual rainfall in this forest is approximately 1,000 to 1,200 millimetres. These two types of semideciduous forest, in which deciduous species comprised between 40 and 65 per cent of tree species, covered nearly 90 per cent of Camagüey. The remaining ten per cent probably was covered by a dominantly evergreen forest developed on wet soils in coastal and interior areas.[10] Indigenous peoples

10   Academia de Ciencias de Cuba (1989); Risco Rodríguez (1995). The mean annual temperature in Cuba's centre-east is between 24 and 26°C. Soils in the northern and southern plains are considered fertile, but they have drainage problems. The central plains are moderately fertile, sandy and erodible. The best soils are in the Júcaro-Morón plain, in western Camagüey, which are considered fertile and deep. Official estimates of present forest cover in Camagüey province, including neighbouring cays, are less than 17% (Ministerio de Ciencia, Tecnología y Medioambiente, Delegación Provincial Camagüey: www.cmw.inf.cu/citma/delegacion/index.htm)

who practised agriculture may have encouraged the formation of savannas within forested environments.[11]

During the late 1500s a livestock-based economy developed around Santa María del Puerto del Príncipe (future Camagüey city), founded in 1528 as the provincial administrative centre. Colonial land grants testify to the presence of forest and savannas in the region. References to land grants made for hogs or sheep usually referred to completely forested areas, while larger land grants, for cattle, usually included savannas that were cleared or burnt periodically to create grazing land.[12] Gradually, land-grant haciendas in Camagüey specialised in cattle. By the early 1800s the Puerto Príncipe district was home to some 276,000 bulls and cows, but only 77,500 hogs.[13] A later census indicated that Puerto Príncipe was Cuba's leading breeder of bulls, cows, yearlings, draught horses, stallions and mares.[14] The cattle economy encouraged the creation of savannas as pasture; forests on cattle ranches, however, generally were not converted to pasture, but nevertheless improved cattle nutrition by offering essential forage and browsing during the dry season.

The nineteenth-century wood-products trade also affected Camagüey's forests. No significant wood trade existed until 1815, with two exceptions: minor royal concessions authorising the shipping of timber to Havana and the clandestine cutting of trees on the southern coast for contraband trade with Jamaica. In 1815 Cuban landowners were permitted to clear forests that previously had been subject to control of the Spanish Royal Navy.[15] Later, individuals and firms dedicated to logging located in Camagüey. During his long residence in Puerto Príncipe, the Spanish naturalist Miguel Rodríguez Ferrer 'met many foreigners who lived there as agents of several foreign merchant houses and companies, whose job it was to buy *caballerías* [one *caballería* = 13.4 hectares] of forest for clearing and utilisation'.[16]

The port cities of Nuevitas and Santa Cruz del Sur were centres of the wood trade, although coves at Júcaro and Vertientes on the southern coast were also used (Figure 5.1). Loggers selectively felled the best trees with the most valuable wood for construction, taking advantage of rising rivers to float logs to either coast. Amongst the final destinations were London, New York, Bremen, Rotterdam, Philadelphia and Boston. Wood shipped

11   Domínguez, Febles and Rives (1994). The term 'savanna' probably originated from an indigenous word for flat and treeless land. Savannas are often confused with plains. Whether savannas are natural or anthropogenic is still an open question; see Herrera (1984).
12   Rouset (1918).
13   Dionisio Vives (1829).
14   Centro de Estadísticas (1864).
15   Funes (1998).
16   Rodríguez Ferrer (1876), p. 700.

via Santa Cruz usually went to international markets, while Nuevitas was more connected through intercoastal shipping with Havana.

Areas surrounding Nuevitas and Puerto Príncipe were the main locations of Camagüey's modest sugar production. In 1860 the region had 102 *ingenios* (small sugar mills) of which 36 used steam power. This represented 35 per cent of Camagüey's farms; by contrast, *ingenios* were found on 78 per cent of farms in Cuba's Occidental Department, the main slaveholding plantation region in central Cuba. While 43 per cent of Occidente's sugar-producing farms were in sugarcane, the rate was only ten per cent amongst sugar-producing farms of Puerto Príncipe and Nuevitas.[17] The remaining lands were mainly covered with forests. An astute observer, visiting the modern Oriente sugar mill in the 1860s,[18] reported that forests were important to *ingenios* for 'partially substituting old sugarcane fields left fallow', in addition to offering 'shelter to cattle on cold nights, during storms and from the rigours of the sun'. Without forests, *ingenios* would 'lack construction timber and fuel essential to making sugar during the harvest, in spite of the sugarcane pulp being a good fuel'.[19]

In 1851 completion of the Puerto Príncipe-Nuevitas railway, extending 72 kilometres, added to the modest impact of sugar in Camagüey. The project, owing more to the dedication of its promoter, Gaspar Betancourt Cisneros, than to objective economic criteria, encouraged the transport of forest products and consumed wood fuel, charcoal and sleepers.[20] During the Ten Years War (1868–78), Camagüey's sugar farms and cattle ranches suffered greatly, as the region was one of the main theatres of conflict. In addition, Camagüey was the site of one of Cuba's most famous *trochas*, fortified wooden barriers built by Spaniards to impede the insurrection from spreading west. The 56-kilometre military road between Morón and Ciego de Avila consumed a 500-metre swath of forest so that forts could be built within sight of each other.[21]

Reconstruction after the war centred on the first large sugar mills (*ingenios centrales*) in the newly created province of Puerto Príncipe, later to become Camagüey.[22] With the abolition of slavery in 1886, the sugar industry began to separate agricultural and industrial processes. This was achieved by the concentration of industry (milling) and decentralisation of

17　Rebello (1860). The *ingenios* of Puerto Príncipe had an average area of 530.6 hectares, but only 47.4 hectares of sugarcane. In Nuevitas, where 12 of 19 *ingenios* used steam power, the mean was 786.6 hectares total area and 84.4 hectares in sugarcane.

18　*Ibid.* The Oriente *ingenio* of Puerto Príncipe had 1,608 hectares and 134 hectares planted in sugarcane.

19　Perpiña (1889), pp. 90–1.

20　A nine-kilometre railway was inaugurated in 1863 to link San Miguel and Bagá, which was close to the bay at Nuevitas (Moyano, 1991).

21　Rodríguez Ferrer (1876), pp. 701–2.

22　Balboa Navarro (2000).

sugarcane supply.[23] In regions with a longer presence of sugar mills, many farms abandoned the industrial process and specialised in growing sugarcane to supply mills that had been able to upgrade technologically. These sugarcane growers were known as *colonos*, and the mills they supplied were *centrales*. In Cuba's centre-east, this process was characterised instead by the establishment of sugar mills in regions not previously occupied, or in regions abandoned during the war. Such was the case of the Redención mill, located in 1881 in the Tínima region near Puerto Príncipe. Nearby, 21 former sugarcane farmers enthusiastically supported the mill and began growing cane again. All of these farms had abundant forested land and wood fuel supplies.[24] In 1883 sugarcane fields supplying the mill amounted to 1,112 hectares, but this would increase to 1,608 in 1884 and then to 2,010 hectares the following year.[25] Overall, the establishment of sugar *centrales* in the Cuban centre-east encouraged an increase in production, from 1,241 tonnes in 1880 to 8,633 tonnes in 1889. Redención, Congreso, Senado and Lugareño (in 1891) mills maintained large areas of forest as key factors in the mill's success. The founders of the Congreso mill, for example, established seven-year contracts through which *colonos* would receive specified areas of forest for planting sugarcane.[26] This practice guaranteed high agricultural yields. The wood trade supported the sugar industry financially by providing quick returns to landowners, *colonos* and shareholders.[27]

The outbreak of a new war in 1895 again caused economic ruin to Cuba's centre-east, but by the end of the century, the following portrait of Camagüey may be drawn. Farms averaged 345.7 hectares, of which 41.2 per cent was 'high forest' and 19.6 per cent 'low forest'. Thus, nearly 61 per cent of the 8,237 square kilometres of land in farms was in forest. On a national scale, forests on Camagüey's farms accounted for nearly 35 per cent of Cuba's remaining forests.[28] Even though the census reported that only 30 per cent of Puerto Príncipe's (Camagüey) total area was in farmland, relatively little land was under public ownership. Landholdings not counted by the census probably had even higher forest-cover rates. Camagüey was still primarily hardwood forests, with areas of savanna and

23 Iglesias (1998).
24 Reed et al. (1880).
25 'Ingenios centrales,' *La Nueva Era*, El Roque (January 1883), p. 70.
26 *Colonos* were farmers responsible for supplying sugarcane to sugar mills. *Colonos* could include former owners of *ingenios*, newly arrived immigrants and ex-slaves. They tended to become more dependent over time to the sugar mills they supplied; see Santamaría and García (1998); Ayala (1999).
27 Reed et al. (1880); 'El *ingenio* central La Santa Cruz,' *La Nueva Era*, Roque (9 April 1883), p. 111.
28 Anon. (1900). 'High' and 'low' forests are not defined in this census; they may denote, however, a distinction between primary and secondary forests and between hardwood trees and fruit-bearing trees.

parkland vegetation, either natural or derived from fire, in the centre of the region (Figure 5.2). Such admirable wealth in forest resources would not be overlooked in Cuba's new political economy.

Figure 5.2: Early Twentieth-Century Vegetation in Camagüey

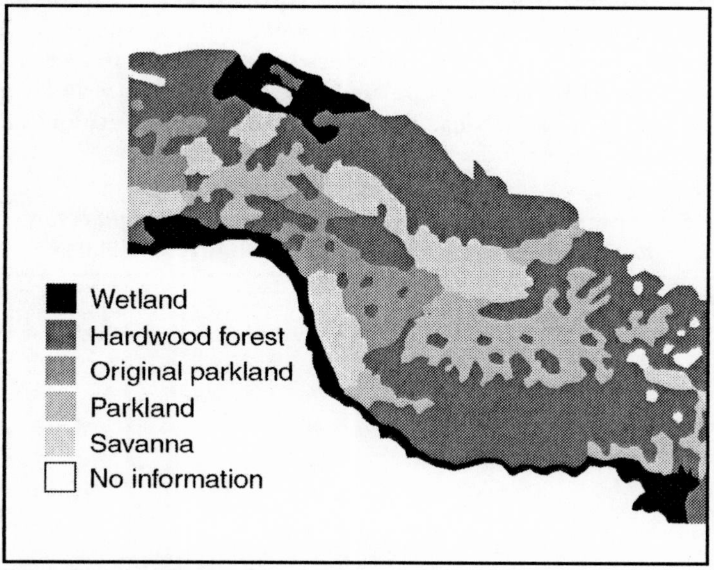

Source: Waibel (1984 [1943]).

From Cattle and Forest to Sugar, 1898–1914

US intervention in the Cuban War of Independence in 1898 wrestled Cuba from Spanish control and established a government of military occupation lasting more than three years. US occupation also enforced a new political economy that formed the basis for Camagüey's rapid economic, social and environmental transformations. The Republic of Cuba was inaugurated on 20 May 1902 with limited sovereignty under the Platt Amendment, which regulated relations with the USA and gave that country the right to intervene in Cuba to protect 'life, property and individual freedom'.[29] This guaranteed peace and stability for investors; in addition, the eradication of yellow fever encouraged travel to Cuba. The reciprocity treaty, which reduced US tariffs on various Cuban goods, including sugar, to 20 per cent, strongly encouraged expansion of the Cuban sugar industry.[30]

29 Pérez (1983), pp. 315–29.
30 By contrast, US goods received a reduction from 25 to 40% (Zanetti, 1998, pp. 229–76).

Favourable legislation for private railroads and reforms of landed property in Cuba's centre-east were also undertaken during military occupation. For example, Military Decree 62 called for the demarcation of communally owned haciendas. The extraordinary conditions granted for the influx of foreign capital resulted in opening Cuba to unimpeded action of capitalist firms that were free from the restrictions currently in place in the United States.[31] Capital invested in Cuba, encouraged by the state of relations between Cuba and the USA, found special conditions in the centre-east: extensive, untouched and unpopulated lands in Camagüey and Oriente were unavailable in La Habana, Matanzas and Santa Clara, regions already transformed by sugar production.

Figure 5.3. Forest-Product Transfer Authorisations (*guías forestales*) for Three Land Categories in Cuba, 1899–1900

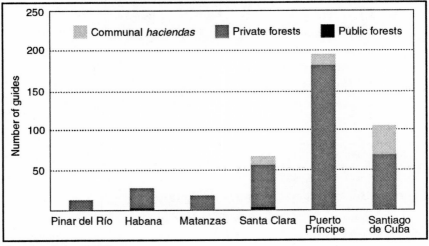

Source: Cuba (1900).

Following the end of the war, logging in Camagüey's forests received a new stimulus. Camagüey became Cuba's leading logging region throughout the early twentieth century. Puerto Príncipe, for example, appears as the top region in forest-product transfer authorisations (*guías forestales*) issued by the Forest and Mines Department between 1899 and 1900 (Figure 5.3). This trend would be sustained for several years. The supremacy of Puerto Príncipe's logging industry is also evidenced by data on the use of forest

31   For example, Guerra (1935, pp. 98–103) mentions the Sherman Anti-Trust laws and
     'an entire group of regulations devoted to maintain a healthy equilibrium between the
     diverse forces of industrial, financial and commercial development.'

products extracted (Table 5.1). Overall in Camagüey, flat topography and numerous rivers and creeks draining the region offered excellent conditions for large-scale clearings, in contrast to the more mountainous Oriente province. In fact, the forests of the centre-east became an obligatory example in publications aimed at the US public and, in particular, US investors. There were few differences between Cuban and US attempts to attract investment.[32] For example, in his article 'Cuba's natural resources and perspectives for American capital', Ramiro Cabrera argued that logging was Cuba's most attractive sector, as there was 'magnificent timber for construction' abundant in the island's 'centuries-old forests'.[33]

Table 5.1: Forest-Product Transfer Authorisations (*guías forestales*), 1899–1900

Province	Construction timber	Timber, fuel wood and charcoal	Fuel wood and charcoal	Total
Habana	8	11	9	28
Pinar del Río	3	4	5	12
Matanzas	3	5	10	18
Santa Clara	21	25	21	67
Puerto Príncipe	179	2	14	195
Santiago de Cuba	95	9	2	106
Total	**309**	**56**	**61**	**426**

Source: Cuba (1900), p. 137.

A more accurate assessment of Camagüey's forest riches in this period may be obtained from the 1919 census. The average estimate of useful logs per *caballería* (13.4 hectares) in high coastal forests was 300 mahogany (*caoba*), 50 cedar (*cedro*), 50 *yaba*, 100 *ocuje*, 100 *baria*, 200 *júcaro*, 50 *sabicú*, 100 *jiquí* and 50 other species.[34] In sum, 13.4 hectares could yield 1,000 useable logs, each measuring between 0.47 and 1.18 cubic metres. For interior forests, estimates

32   Norton (1900); Hill (1898); Clark (1898); Porter (1899).
33   Cabrera's (1897, pp. 2–4) article exaggerated Cuba's forests: 'Four-fifths of Cuba's territory is virgin, untouched during 400 years of Spanish colonisation, and inviting to American workers and capitalists with tempting prospects for secure reproduction'.
34   Caoba is *Swietenia mahogany;* cedro, *Cedrela mexicana;* yaba, *Andira jamaicensis;* ocuje, *Calophyllum antillanum;* baria (or varia), *Cordia gerascanthus;* júcaro, *Bucida buceras;* sabicú, *Lysiloma latisiqua;* jiquí, *Pera bumelifolia* (Roig, 1965).

were for 900 useful logs per 13.4 hectares.[35] Waibel's work on Cuba's original vegetation, noting the large quantities of hardwoods in Camagüey between 1906 and 1908, confirms these data (Figure 5.2).[36]

Santa Cruz del Sur and Nuevitas continued to be the most important ports for export of Camagüey's timber. Intercoastal trade was carried out in Júcaro to the south and San Fernando to the north, on the ends of the old military route and railroad between Júcaro and Morón. The USA, Germany and Britain were the main destinations of exported timber, although by 1920 Germany and Belgium became prominent importers.[37] Santa Cruz del Sur was especially important in the timber trade, being perhaps Cuba's most important timber port. During the dry season, at least three medium-tonnage sailing ships at anchor were commonly seen to be loading timber, in addition to smaller vessels engaged in coastal shipping. Forests covered approximately half of the municipality's 243,000 hectares and supplied timber for cabinet making and construction for European and US markets. Sixty of the municipality's 238 farms were dedicated to logging, while 'very well structured' sawmills were salient amongst local industries.[38] Other descriptions also attest to the importance of timber to Camagüey. According to one account, 'three-fourths of [Camagüey] are covered with trees', and numerous wood depots were situated along the Central Railway. In places close to the railroad, timber from forest clearings commonly was destined for local use in construction and railroad sleepers in addition to export.[39]

The idea of a railway connecting Cuba's east and west had been fostered since the end of the 1878 war. The events of 1898 revived the idea and in 1902 the railroad was inaugurated as one of the first and most important symbols of the new era, heralded as essential to obtaining resources from Cuba's inaccessible eastern regions.[40] Railroad construction stimulated the wood trade and contributed to the revived cattle industry. Nevertheless, its main influence was to encourage sugarcane expansion, although investors initially preferred to build large *centrales* in coastal regions, where they could use private port facilities.

Two distinct periods, separated by the outbreak of the First World War, characterise the transformation of Camagüey's landscapes by sugar. The

35   Cuba (1919), pp. 65–71. These estimates amount to between 35 and 88 cubic metres per hectare in the case of coastal forests, and between 32 and 85 cubic metres per hectare for interior forests.

36   Waibel (1984 [1943]).

37   Cuba (1925), pp. 510–5.

38   Pera y Peralta (1913).

39   Berchon (1910), pp. 145–54.

40   The builder of the Canadian Pacific, Sir William Van Horne, was in charge of the project (Zanetti and García, 1987), pp. 209–32.

fundamental factors of change, however, were in place as a result of the new political economy created by US hegemony over Cuba. Scholars such as Dye and Santamaría have described an 'institutional framework' that attracted heavy North American investments in the sugar industry and unleashed the maximum productive potential of the Cuban sugar sector. These authors explain the fact that investment flows preferred Camagüey and Oriente provinces because of greater economic incentives. Access to large areas of land was easier to obtain, private railroads were easier to build and control over sugarcane growers was easier to enforce.[41] For example, in 1904 one *caballería* (13.4 hectares) of land in Camagüey was sold at 100 to 800 pesos, but if large areas were purchased, the price would fall to less than 100 pesos. In other provinces, the *caballería* sale price was not less than 300 to 400 pesos.[42] However, insufficient emphasis has been placed on the key fact that sugarcane expansion took place in densely forested regions. In this sense, sugarcane expansion in the centre-east followed an older logic that governed sugarcane advance in Cuba's centre-west.

Early twentieth-century studies of Cuba's agriculture and soils are a good illustration of the workings of an agricultural system that depended on the occupation of forested regions. In 1905 the North American director of Cuba's Estación Agronómica, F.S. Earle, wrote that 'the planting of sugarcane in deforested regions is a well known issue in Cuba and always produces satisfactory results. These lands, when they are properly planted and cultivated, continue to produce for more than ten years, and up to 20 years, depending on their nature and fertility.'[43] Another North American director of the Estación Agronómica, J.T. Crawley, argued in 1917 that as a general rule virgin lands were densely forested. If there was valuable timber, and if deforested regions were close to a railroad, wood would be sold for fence posts, railroad sleepers or other uses, 'but in no case is there an effort to conserve wood, which is burned all together with small trees, branches and leaves'. After expounding on the cultivation methods that had been followed since the sixteenth century, Crawley admitted that 'to those unfamiliar with these issues, it will appear to be a very unsophisticated cultivation method'; however, 'if land is fertile the first harvest will yield 80,000 to 100,000 *arrobas* of sugarcane per *caballería* [68.7 and 85.9 tonnes per hectare, respectively]' and harvests would continue 'for ten to 20 years'.[44] Furthermore, there were big differences between Cuba's western and eastern regions. In Camagüey and Oriente, 'virgin lands could produce sugarcane for 15 years or more, with-

---

41 Dye (1998); Santamaría (1996; 2000).
42 Cuba (1904), pp. 34–7. Prices for one *caballería* in La Habana province were estimated between 400 and 2,000 pesos. In Matanzas and Santa Clara the price varied between 300 and 800 pesos.
43 Earle (1905), p. 7.
44 Crawley (1917), p. 4.

out ploughing and replanting', while in Santa Clara, Matanzas and La Habana, 'only five or fewer harvests are possible' before necessary replanting.[45]

Studies such as these tried to call attention to the long-term problems caused by planting in newly cleared forested areas, while searching for improved cultivation methods adapted to Cuba's soil characteristics. This concern had been expressed in the middle of the nineteenth century by Alvaro Reynoso, whose famous *Ensayo sobre el cultivo de la caña de azúcar*, first published in 1862, sought to implement a permanent and scientific agriculture, using irrigation and fertilisation, in place of traditional ways of planting in deforested sites. Similarly, the early-twentieth-century Zayas system sought to improve sugarcane cultivation by rejecting the traditional practice of abandoning *tierras cansadas* or 'worn-out lands'.[46] As Earle indicated in the early 1900s, almost all of Cuba's old sugarcane mills 'were surrounded by thousands of acres' of worn-out lands that 'remained useless while every day mills had to haul from more distant locations'.[47]

A new phase in sugar production began in 1899, when Manuel Rionda, an Hispanic-North American experienced in Cuba's sugar industry, purchased nearly 270 square kilometres in south-eastern Camagüey. The Francisco *central* began operations two years later (Figure 5.1). Within a few years, Francisco was endowed with a 100-kilometre railroad network that linked the *colonias* to the mill, and the mill to the Romero wharf, which exported the mill's sugar products. More than 5,000 hectares of sugarcane were under cultivation by 1914. In addition, 1,340 hectares were dedicated to pasture, while 6,700 remained forested and 7,200 hectares were unspecified. Two other mills established in the last decades of the 1800s, Senado and Lugareño, also had large forest reserves.[48]

Before the First World War, the nucleus for the expansion of sugarcane in Camagüey was the old military railroad line from Júcaro to Morón (Figure 5.1). South of Ciego de Avila, two mills were established, Jagüeyal in 1904 and Stewart in 1906. Jagüeyal had 4,757 hectares devoted to sugarcane, nearly 6,000 hectares in pasture and 5,360 hectares in forest. In 1912–14 its average yield was 64 tonnes per hectare. The Stewart *central* had 10,130 hectares planted in sugarcane, only 540 hectares in pasture and 4,200 hectares of forested land. Between 1912 and 1914 two other sugar mills, Ciego de Avila and Morón, located in the region.[49]

45 *Ibid.*, p. 48.
46 Zayas (1904)
47 Earle (1905), p. 19.
48 Senado, established in 1881, had 67,000 hectares in 1912–14, but only 3,430 hectares were planted in sugarcane. Lugareño, built in 1891, had 10,720 hectares, of which 2,948 were in sugarcane, 3,752 in pasture and 4,020 in forests (Cuba, 1914).
49 The Ciego de Avila *central* was unique in that it only owned lands where the mill was located. Sugarcane was produced by independent *colonos* on 1,876 hectares bordering the Júcaro–Morón railroad (Cuba, 1914).

In the central plains of Camagüey, which the Central Railway crossed, only two *centrales* were established, and part of the sugarcane lands of another mill were located in the neighbouring Oriente province. The Jatibonico mill, established by the Central Railroad, located in 1905 near the Santa Clara province and, in 1912–14, had 7,050 hectares of sugarcane. The fertility of recently cleared forest soils sustained yields of 64 tonnes per hectare. The Jobabo *central*, also established by the Central Railway, resulted from the purchase of 40,374 hectares and began its first harvest in 1911. Its industrial unit was located in Oriente, but many of its *colonos* were in Camagüey. One traveller described the hundreds of *caballerías* of sugarcane grown by *colonos* in Jobabo, Tana and Miraflores and 'extensive first-class virgin lands' that were divided amongst farmers.[50]

The Camagüey *central* was also contiguous with the Central Railway. Founded in 1914, the mill had 4,355 hectares of land, 1,072 hectares of which was devoted to sugarcane, 3,216 in forest and 67 in pasture. Overall, during 1912–14, Camagüey's mills reached 58 tonnes per hectare, much higher than Oriente's *centrales* (49 tonnes per hectare), and Cuba's other provinces, which usually did not surpass 42 tonnes per hectare. The effects of sugarcane on Camagüey's forests were not limited to sugarcane planting. Sugar mills demanded massive quantities of wood as supplementary fuel (Table 5.2). For example, during the 1913 harvest, the Francisco *central* burned 18,065 tonnes of fuel, while the Stewart *central* consumed 18,750 tonnes and Jagüeyal fired 13,400 tonnes. Approximately 134 hectares of forest could have been consumed as fuel wood in a single year for Camagüey's mills.[51]

Table 5.2: Annual Use of Wood Fuel in Sugar Mills, c. 1914

Province	Consumption (tonnes)	Mills (number)	Mean (tonnes)
Pinar del Río	11,538	7	1,648
Habana	29,753	19	1,565
Matanzas	80,883	41	1,972
Santa Clara	104,009	69	1,507
Camagüey	69,139	8	8,648.4
Oriente	105,319	31	3,397

Source: Cuba (1914).

50 Martí (1915), pp. 131–2. For the case of Manatí, see Smith (1995).
51 The average volume of fuel wood per hectare of forest in Camagüey was approximately 2,705 cubic metres.

Until 1914 the expansion of sugar into Camagüey was relatively slow. Camagüey produced 2.6 per cent of Cuba's sugar in 1902, increasing to ten per cent in 1915. The area of sugar-producing farms had increased more than ten times since 1899, but the total area of farmland, including sugarcane, pasture and forest, was only 7.3 per cent of Camagüey's overall territory. Camagüey was still a region of cattle and forests, although, with the help of the Central Railway, the sugar industry was expanding steadily. Ironically, Camagüey's official iconography still displayed faith in timber, cattle and sugar. This was about to end spectacularly.

Sugar Conquers Camagüey, 1915–26

The fall in world sugar production resulting from the First World War caused Cuban sugar production to boom.[52] The Cuban harvest increased from 2.2 million tonnes in 1914 to 4.1 million tonnes in 1919, and 5.2 million tonnes in 1925. The zenith of the sugar boom, between 1918 and 1920, is known as the 'dance of the millions'. The speculative orgy during the first few years after the First World War was in no place more intense than in Cuba.[53] Between 1915 and 1919 34 sugar mills were established in Cuba; another 16 were inaugurated between 1920 and 1926. These 50 mills amount to double the number of mills built between 1900 and 1915.

High sugar prices during the War and the immediate post-war period, and the need to rapidly increase sugar production, attracted the attention of North American investors to Cuba as never before. In 1903 investment in Cuba amounted to 98 million pesos, of which 25 million were dedicated to the sugar sector. In 1928 the sugar sector accounted for 800 million of the 1.5 billion pesos of total US investments in Cuba.[54] This huge financial investment was directed as much to the construction of new factories and expanding existing plants as to the creation of large landholdings and extending private railroad lines that would guarantee the supply of sugarcane to satisfy the maximum milling potential. Thus, foreign control of the sugar industry was consolidated over the extensive lands of Camagüey and Oriente provinces, the economic and social consequences of which would be denounced so eloquently in works such as Ramiro Guerra's *Azúcar y población en las Antillas*.[55]

The case of Camagüey provides the best example of changes in Cuba's sugar industry resulting from the First World War. In 1914 Camagüey had nine mills. 14 mills were established between 1914 and 1920–21, and another six were inaugurated between 1921 and 1926, resulting in

---

52   World sugar production fell from 8.6 million tonnes in 1913 to 3.6 million tonnes in 1919.
53   Jenks (1966), p. 199.
54   Pinto Santos (1973), p. 31.
55   Guerra (1970 [1927]).

Camagüey's six-fold increase in sugar production relative to 1915, when Camagüey was the fifth leading Cuban province, producing 263,300 tonnes of sugar. In 1923 Camagüey was in first place amongst Cuban provinces, producing 30.9 per cent of Cuba's sugar, followed by Oriente (25.9 per cent) and Santa Clara (20.6 per cent). Camagüey's 1.11 million tonnes in 1923 would continue rising until the record 1.56 million tonnes produced in the 1928-29 harvest.[56]

The significant increase in Camagüey sugar production resulted from the establishment of new *centrales* and the increase in the productive capacity of exiting mills. The nine mills existing before 1914 had been increasing daily capacity from 2,167 to nearly 5,000 tonnes. The most significant case was the Morón *central*, whose capacity increased from nearly 1,500 tonnes to 8,630 tonnes. The 14 mills in operation from 1915 to 1921 could achieve an average of 3,691 tonnes per day; the highest averages were Cunagua (6,905 tonnes per day) and Baraguá (5,745 tonnes per day). Among the six mills built between 1921 and 1926, the Vertientes *central* increased capacity from 1,841 tonnes per day in 1921 to 8,631 tonnes per day in 1925. The Jaronú central increased initial capacity from 7,480 to 11,507 tonnes per day.[57] Thus, Camagüey's *centrales* had the largest capacity in the country, milling an average of 4,472 tonnes of sugar per day, followed distantly by Oriente with 2,955 tonnes per day.[58]

Investment in sugar during and after the First World War created the so-called 'sugar colossuses', a term invented in 1940 to describe Camagüey's 15 and Oriente's 12 *centrales*.[59] The increase in productive capacity was accompanied by the tendency amongst sugar interests, including both new and old mills, to strengthen control over their large landholdings. Throughout Camagüey, the land controlled by sugar mills increased from approximately 1,500 square kilometres in 1914 to 8,000 square kilometres three decades later.[60] The increase in productive capacity and landholdings would translate into an unprecedented expansion of land planted in sugarcane.[61] Table 5.3 summarises the territorial extent of the landownings of sugar mills in Camagüey between 1928 and 1944. Most of this area was controlled by

56   Abad (1945), pp. 397–401.
57   Cuba (1914); Gilmore (1928).
58   Gilmore (1928). Average daily capacity per mill was dramatically lower in other Cuban provinces: La Habana (2,481 tonnes); Matanzas (2,187 tonnes); Santa Clara (1,997 tonnes); and Pinar del Río (1,866 tonnes).
59   The term '*ingenios* colosos' was used by Abad (1945), pp. 391–428.
60   The Morón *central*, inaugurated in 1914 with 2,854 hectares of land, had amassed 64,263 hectares by 1928. Cunagua and Jaronú, owned by the same company, claimed more than 134,000 hectares. The Vertientes *central* reached 100,781 hectares, the largest area controlled by a single sugar mill in Cuba.
61   For example, the sugarcane area of the Francisco *central* increased from 5,347 hectares in 1914 to 17,714 hectares in 1928.

North American capital, restructured as a few public-stock corporations. By 1926 North Americans or Cuban-North Americans owned 21 *centrales*.[62] Most of these mills were controlled by relatively few holding companies. In 1928 Camagüey's 24 *centrales* were owned by eight companies.[63]

Table 5.3: Territory Controlled by Camagüey Sugar Mills, 1928

Judicial district	Area (km²)	Mills (number)	Mill area (km²)	Mill area as % of judicial district area
Camagüey	4,000	4	1,547	38.7
Florida	1,500	5	1,016	67.7
Guaimaro	1,152	1	377	32.7
Santa Cruz	2,270	3	997	43.9
Nuevitas	4,000	2	807	20.2
Ciego de Avila	1,757	6	1,590	90.5
Morón	4,244	7	3,709	87.4
Jatibonico	1,200	1	356	29.7
Total	**20,122**	**29**	**10,399**	**51.7**

Sources: Torre and Aguayo (1928); Censo azucarero de la República de Cuba (1936).
Notes: Judicial district boundaries taken from 1928 data; mill area percentage is not exact because mills could have been located in more than one judicial district; of the 51.7 per cent of Camagüey under control of centrales, 61 per cent was under mill ownership and 39 per cent was under lease.

The increasing scale of sugar landholdings stimulated the expansion of the railroad network. During the First World War work began on a railroad that would cross the northern region of Camagüey. Directed by the magnate and politician José Miguel Tarafa, the North Cuba Railway (Ferrocarril del Norte de Cuba) serviced the areas around Nuevitas, where Cuba's largest sugar port was built, renamed as Puerto Tarifa.[64] This line

62   Jenks (1966), pp. 258–9.
63   The corporations were: the Cuban Cane Sugar Co. (Jagueyal, Lugareño, Morón, Stewart, Velasco and Violeta); the General Sugar Co. (Agramonte, Camagüey, Estrella, Vertientes and Pilar); the Punta Alegre Sugar Co. (Baraguá, Punta Alegre and Florida); the Sugar Plantation Operating Co. (Algodonales, Ciego de Avila and Macareño); Intereses Rionda (Francisco and Elia); the American Sugar Refining Co. (Cunagua and Jaronú); Compañía Azucarera Najasa (Najasa and Camagüey); Compañía Cubana (Jatibonico and Jobabo) (Gilmore, 1928); see also Ayala (1999).
64   Zanetti and García (1987), pp. 259–63. The project was completed in 1930, with Santa Clara as the extreme western terminus.

served several *centrales* that had been established during the War and early 1920s (Cunagua, Velasco, Violeta and Jaronú), as well as older mills (Morón, Lugareño and Senado). A new spur linked Esmeralda, between Morón and Nuevitas, with the city of Florida, where the line would connect to the Central Railroad. Another rail line inaugurated during the 1920s linked the city of Camagüey to the port of Santa Cruz del Sur, which would serve *centrales* such as Santa Marta and Vertientes. In all of these cases the regions still had extensive forests. The arrival of railroads, thus, heralded the beginning of the final destruction of forests, which would be completed with the construction of private railroads.

The rapid expansion of sugarcane to satisfy market demand caused the most intense period of deforestation in Cuban history. The 1907 census claimed that 'nearly all territories of the north and south of the province [Camagüey] are not populated yet', but they contained 'large areas of excellent arable land that are abandoned for lack of fast transport networks necessary for the innumerable products that could be harvested there'.[65] It is impossible at present to estimate the forested area of Camagüey's landholdings, but Waibel's vegetation map allows comparison with the location of the province's new sugar mills, leading to the conclusion that the mills were located in the regions that had been noted as hardwood forest and parkland (Figure 5.2).

None of Camagüey's natural regions was exempt from the violent invasion of sugarcane during this period. The Júcaro–Morón Plain, site of the largest number of *centrales* before 1914, witnessed the establishment of colossuses such as Punta Alegre (or Puerto Alegre) near the Baraguá, Violeta, Patria and Velasco mills. *Centrales* Cunagua, Jaronú, Velasco and Violeta completed the occupation of the Camagüey–Maniabón Plains. The late-nineteenth-century expansion of sugar mills, which had begun with Senado and Lugareño *centrales*, continued in the early 1900s with the colossal Chaparra, Delicias and Manatí mills. These five mills and Cunagua and Jaronú *centrales* controlled approximately 4,476 square kilometres within a region of nearly 5,000 square kilometres. Similar phenomena may be observed in Camagüey's southern plains. Before 1914 the only mill was Francisco; later, the new *centrales* of Santa Marta, Elia and Macareño, as well as much of the supply fields of Vertientes, became established. The municipality of Santa Cruz, which in 1900 had forest cover on 83 per cent of the total area of its landholdings, had only 4.5 per cent forest cover on landholdings by 1945.[66]

---

65   Report of Rogerio Zayas Bazán, official for Camagüey province, dated 30 November 1907, published in Anon. (1907), p. 691.
66   Anon. (1900); Cuba (1951).

In addition to the advantages of occupying virgin lands to supply sugarcane to mills, the felling of thousands of hectares of forest during the War and post-war period was related to the old tradition of planting in freshly cleared forest areas. The temptation of quick returns amidst unique market opportunities removed any large-scale attempt to focus efforts on improving cultivation techniques in lands already deforested. As a writer for *National Geographic Magazine* noted in 1920, Cuba's advantage over other sugarcane growers was that replanting was necessary only every seven to 12 years, while in other countries cane had to planted every one or two years.[67]

Nevertheless, many of Camagüey's regions deforested during this unique period would prove to be poorly suited for sugarcane, or at least unable to maintain former high yields. By 1928 Camagüey had Cuba's highest yields, reaching an average of 46 tonnes per hectare, a marked decline from the 58 tonnes per hectare achieved in 1913. The first soil survey of Cuba, carried out in 1928 by North Americans, indicated that sugarcane plantings were satisfactory when made on virgin lands of the southern Camagüey interior plain, but in places such as the northern and southern coastal plains, soil salinity and poor soil drainage offered unfavourable results. These difficulties and the high degree of weed invasions would become serious problems to agricultural success in future years.[68]

The impact of the growing sugar industry on Cuba's forests also concerned Cuban scientists. After two field trips to Camagüey and Oriente in 1918, the prominent botanist Juan Tomás Roig was appalled by the 'extremely rapid disappearance of those magnificent forests that previously could be seen in all directions, today substituted by sugarcane and pasture'.[69] Two years later, when the crisis caused by the abrupt fall of sugar prices was plainly evident, an editorial in the secretary of agriculture's publication criticised the intense deforestation of previous years:

> Our forest reserve suffered a huge decline with the considerable increase in area devoted to sugarcane. In less than four years, the destructive axe has felled miles and miles of Cuba's best forests, of the scarce forests that had remained, and in short time there may not be even a single shade tree, for sake of ephemeral sugarcane ... And now, our dessert is to see the fatal result of our poor planning and our fever to convert all of Cuba into a vast sugarcane field. We have not even been able to secure an adequate present at the expense of the future.[70]

---

67 Showalter (1920), p. 24.
68 Bennett and Allison (1962 [1928]), pp. 181–224.
69 Roig (1918), pp. 168–75.
70 'Notas editoriales,' *Revista de Agricultura, Comercio y Trabajo*, November 1920, p. 1.

Certainly, the fertility of forest soils would continue to be an irresistible attraction to sugar interests. An observer of Cuba's forest dilemma wrote in 1929 that a 'super destructive event' had occurred, which was 'favourable only to sugarcane interests and greedy buyers of land momentarily fertilised by the ashes of hundred-year-old forests'.[71] This was the reason that Camagüey, in spite of the reduction in yield with respect to 1914, could continue to have Cuba's best sugarcane yields in the late 1920s, followed by Oriente; the yields of both was 8.6 tonnes per hectare greater than other provinces.[72] Other evidence is equally telling, as when an observer of the Jaronú *central* in 1928 wrote that 'due to the large quantity of tree trunks, few *caballerías* have been prepared for planting'.[73]

Facing the rapid disappearance of what remained of Cuba's forest resources, legislation for controlling deforestation began to appear. The culminating moment was Decree 495, signed by President Gerardo Machado on 13 April 1926 for 'The absolute prohibition of clearing public or private high forests'. Part of the decree argued that

> It is accepted doctrine amongst experts of every country that no less than one-third of total area should be conserved, but at present in Cuba forests do not cover even ten per cent of its territory, because the period of high sugar prices and sugarcane planting, from 1922 to the present, threatened to destroy the scarce forests that still remain, which demands that the state should intervene in private forest stands by placing justified limitations in the public interest.[74]

This decree prohibited clearing of high forests for sugarcane fields and was extended yearly until becoming law. But it was too late to save the forests, as large landowners had already cleared enormous tracts to plant sugarcane, which later had failed. A 1935 report had concluded that 'millions of pesos were lost in the useless increase of sugarcane fields' during the period of high sugar prices that followed the First World War. Examples abounded of *centrales* built near lands later discovered to be unsuitable for sugarcane.[75]

Cuba's national agricultural census of 1946 suggested the scale of the great transformation of Camagüey's natural landscapes.[76] In 1946

---

71   Frasquieri (1933), pp. 3–8.
72   The average yields for the provinces were as follows: Camagüey, 46 tonnes per hectare; Oriente, 45 tonnes per hectare; Santa Clara, 36; Pinar del Río, 36; Matanzas, 33; La Habana, 29 (Gilmore, 1928).
73   *Ibid.*, p. 159.
74   Corral Alemán (1936), pp. 173–5.
75   Foreign Policy Association (1935), pp. 501–19. Several *centrales* operated for short periods: Camagüey (1913–30); Ciego de Ávila (1913–30); Jagüeyal (1907–30); Pilar (1918–31); Santo Tomás (1916–23); and Velasco (1924–30).
76   Cuba (1951).

Camagüey's reported farms occupied 21,700 square kilometres, more than three times the area in farms in 1899 and 83 per cent of the province's total area. By comparison with 1899 forested area on farms had fallen from between 50 and 60 per cent to 11 per cent.[77] Other land uses included cultivated area (16 per cent), pasture (46 per cent) and 'other' (21 per cent), which included urban, roads and unproductive land. Camagüey was the national leader in land devoted to pasture, and was second in cultivated area and *marabú*, an exotic shrub that covered three per cent of total area (Figure 5.4). Camagüey was no longer the region of forests it had once been.

Figure 5.4: Land Use in Camagüey, 1899–1945

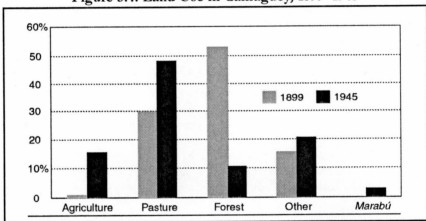

Sources: Anon. (1900), Cuba (1951).

The inclusion of *marabú* in land-use statistics is indicative of the transformations taking place in parallel with deforestation. *Marabú* (*Dichrostachys cinerea* or *D. nutans*), was Cuba's main invasive plant during the twentieth century and targeted Camagüey's plains as one of its main habitats. Originally from sub-Saharan Africa, the leguminous and compact shrub was introduced into Cuba in the late nineteenth century, presumably as an ornamental plant. It thrived and was disseminated by cattle. When sugarcane fields were abandoned during hard economic times or because of poor soil fertility, the land was converted to pasture, which encouraged weed invasions over vast stretches of land. *Marabú* thickets, which had become a worrisome issue already in the 1910s, became one of the main

---

77   Camagüey's farmland in forests was 19 per cent of the Cuban total, lagging only behind Oriente (34 per cent), but Camagüey also was the second leading province in total area and area in farms.

enemies of agriculture and cattle raising in Cuba, and Camagüey in particular, during the twentieth century.[78]

Conclusion

The new political economy implanted after 1898 caused enormous
changes in Camagüey province. In just two decades its lands were traversed
by public and private railways that substantially improved communication
with the rest of Cuba. Camagüey's old cities were modernised with the
construction of residential subdivisions and newly opened branches of
Cuba's most important banks. New cities, such as Florida, Céspedes and
Gaspar, were established simultaneously as large, modern *centrales* began
crushing cane nearby. Although Camagüey remained Cuba's least populous
province, it grew much faster than others. From 88,000 inhabitants in
1899, Camagüey reached 230,000 in 1919, representing more than double
the rate of increase of Cuba's total population. In sum, the expansion of
sugar in Camagüey had moved it on the route toward progress, as defined
by dominant contemporary views.

The economic growth and material progress that sugar inspired, however, had negative consequences that should not be ignored. The establishment
of sugar latifundia, controlled by powerful North American corporations,
brought serious political, economic and social consequences locally and
nationally. Several scholars, such as Jenks and Guerra, have analysed these
implications, which include, amongst others, reduction of national sovereignty, enrichment of absentee landowners, strangulation of local
economies, destruction of small- and medium-scale landholders and decline
of public railways. Nonetheless, few questions have been raised regarding
the environmental impact of sugar *centrales* and latifundia in Camagüey and
Oriente, apart from brief mention of the destruction of thousands of
forested lands to plant sugarcane and in recent environmental histories. To
put this in perspective, several sugar latifundia in Camagüey were larger than
entire sugar-producing islands in the Caribbean.

Several social and economic effects of sugar latifundia had poorly
explored environmental implications, such as the fact that sugarcane
monoculture supplied huge amounts of caloric energy to millions of people outside Cuba, exacerbating shortages of basic food supply within
Cuba. Related to this paradox is the fact that the extension of sugar latifundia caused the most intense period of deforestation in Cuban history.
As this chapter has shown, forests remained the favoured territory for the
new sugar expansion toward Cuba's eastern regions, largely because of the
traditional practices of obtaining high agricultural yields from forest soils

78   See Funes Monzote (1999).

immediately after deforestation. Within a few years, Camagüey had lost its celebrated forests, which had been converted mainly to ashes that would fertilise ever-increasing sugarcane fields and pasture for draught animals.

A series of environmental consequences followed the removal of Camagüey's forests. Rapid deforestation reduced Cuba's biodiversity, as habitat for the island's endemic and exotic flora and fauna was decimated to make room for sugarcane. The decline in bird populations attracted the attention of José Isaac del Corral, the director of Cuba's Department of Forest and Mines, who decried the 'complete disappearance or scarcity of many wild birds that previously were enchanting and useful in our countryside'.[79] The expansion of sugar latifundia and cattle ranches is also largely responsible for the marked soil degradation in the region, which today is considered to be one of the region's most serious environmental problems. Estimates for Camagüey at present indicate that erosion affects 75 per cent of its soils while 39 per cent of soils are considered very shallow.[80] Agricultural yields never returned to those of sugar's golden years in Camagüey, in spite of the use of inputs such as chemical fertilisers, pesticides and mechanisation. Other environmental effects include the polemic question of whether deforestation has caused a reduction in rainfall in Camagüey.[81] However, none of these environmental impacts may be separated from the economic and social effects. In the end, the destruction of natural environments by the sugar boom will affect generations of Cubans, who will receive nothing from the thousand-year-old forests that were turned to ashes for the primary benefit of a few corporations and their shareholders outside Cuba.

79   José Isaac del Corral Alemán, 'La devastación forestal y daños que ocasiona,' speech delivered 19 May 1928, Expediente de Académico de Número, Archivo del Museo Nacional de Historia de las Ciencias, La Habana, Cuba. Cuba's president was in the audience when the speech was delivered.

80   Soil degradation, of course, only began with large-scale deforestation of the early twentieth century. In later decades other powerful factors were involved, such as the increasing mechanisation of soil preparation and sugarcane harvest; see Díaz and Pérez (2000).

81   Abad (1945) indicated that during the 1940s sugarcane yields in Cuba were lower than nearly all other sugarcane-producing countries. Amongst the causes mentioned is the lack of rainfall and the particularly severe decline in Camagüey and Oriente resulting from deforestation during the early twentieth century.

CHAPTER 6

Talking to Sediments: Reading Environmental History from Post-Settlement Alluvium in Western São Paulo, Brazil[*]

Christian Brannstrom

Introduction

C
an environmental historians 'talk' to sediments in the same way that they engage with historical documents, such as judicial proceedings, diaries, company account books or propaganda maps? Does evidence of vegetation change inspire more meaningful dialogue between historians and evidence? Are environmental histories of forests, grasslands or savannas more perceptive, compelling and interesting than environmental histories of soil erosion and sediments? Do sediments and vegetation promote different understandings of past relationships between humans and the environment? In this chapter I wish to explore vegetation and sediments as two types of evidence for environmental history. I will be especially interested in how different choices of evidence and geographical scale affect environmental narratives, with potential implications for informing public policy debates. These issues will be examined with reference to environmental histories of twentieth-century south-eastern Brazil. Two specific examples will illustrate how divergent narratives may emerge from environmental histories based on soil and sediments, in contrast with vegetation, with possible significance for environmental public policies.

Vegetation and Sediments: Evidence for Environmental History

Environmental histories often address the changes to vegetation or soils over time, stressing human and natural causes. As suggested by key works, such as Worster's analysis of the Dust Bowl, Cronon's study of the early colonial transformation of the New England landscape and Dean's treatment of the destruction of the Brazilian Atlantic Forest, environmental historians presume that change has occurred in the environment.[1] In fact,

[*]   Research for this chapter was funded by the Organization of American States, the National Science Foundation, Sigma XI, The Scientific Research Society, the University of Wisconsin-Madison Graduate School and a grant by The William and Flora Hewlett Foundation to the Institute of Latin American Studies. The author's thanks also go to John Soluri, Bob Wilcox, Stephen Bell and Wendy Jepson.
1   Worster (1979); Cronon (1983); Dean (1995).

much (but not all) environmental history requires indicators or measures of environmental change that may be analytically and causally connected to socioeconomic or cultural factors (political economy, institutions, technology, perceptions, etc.) as well as 'natural' causes (precipitation, tectonic activity, fire, etc.).[2] In short, environmental history presumes that some aspect of the environment has changed, and, to some degree, that it has been caused by people. Teasing out the precise linkages between states, individuals, technology, economics, ideologies and beliefs, among other factors, is precisely what makes environmental history so compelling.

Vegetation and sedimentation are closely linked in several environmental processes. Vegetation is critical to protect soil from direct raindrop impact and to increase the infiltration of water in soil. In addition to slope, precipitation, physical and chemical soil characteristics, vegetation helps determine soil erosion rates, which vary dramatically under different types of land cover. When controlling for slope, precipitation and soil factors, several studies indicate that forest and grassland cause the least soil erosion, while sites of bare soil, such as agricultural fields ready for conventional planting, are scenes of the highest rates of erosion.[3]

However, in environmental history, vegetation and sediments, as variables or indicators of environmental change, are often separated analytically. There are heavy logistical and financial demands of carrying out vegetation and soil-sediment analyses together. Doing both is possible only with large grants to cover high administrative and logistical costs. Reliable baseline data are also necessary, but often lacking. Indeed, it is difficult to obtain proper training to do extensive documentary research and fieldwork in either vegetation or sediments. Perhaps for this reason, so much environmental history is based almost exclusively on written documents, often on topics crafted so that gathering field evidence is unnecessary to address the research question.

Here I want to raise epistemological questions about how we measure the environment, leading to the ontological question of what we mean by 'environment' and 'environmental change'. I am not arguing that all environmental historians should become soil scientists or fluvial geomorphologists; that would be to trivialise the point and also denigrate the fascinating research done in environmental history with only documentary evidence, such as those included as chapters in this book. Nor is my argument for a 'total' environmental history. Rather, I am interested in exploring the type of environmental history that begins with evidence of environmental change in a specific time and place, then creates a causal argument to explain the observed changes in the environment, by searching for (but not limited to) economic, political and social factors.

2   Worster (1988).
3   Pimentel et al. (1997), pp. 43–51; Dunne and Leopold (1978), pp. 518–42.

What are the problems and benefits of using either vegetation or sediments as measures of environmental change in environmental history? Which approach leads to more compelling narratives and more rigorous explanations? Are both dependent on the geographical scale of the research problem? Do environmental ideologies guide our selection of evidence? Overall, these questions are relevant to environmental history because they raise epistemological and ontological issues.

Vegetation in Environmental History

Vegetation is a common variable in environmental history. Large-scale changes in vegetation or land cover, in many cases forests, are often used to measure land use, land cover and environmental change more generally. Analysis of aerial photographs (after 1930) and satellite remote sensing data (after 1970) are two common methods addressing environmental history problems relating to vegetation.[4] Field study of present vegetation to infer past uses[5] and analysis of past descriptions of vegetation, often by land surveyors, are also commonly used,[6] usually for relatively small areas. Other studies have taken on much larger areas of vegetation, covering hundreds of thousands of square kilometres, such as large areas of the USA or Brazil.[7]

The use of vegetation as a category of analysis in environmental history faces several problems, especially the inherent dynamics and disturbances that must be considered in the creation of baseline information. These problems are most well exposed in the case of African forests and savannas[8] and, in the Americas, regarding the impact of indigenous peoples on vegetation, especially with agriculture and fire, before the sixteenth century.[9] Furthermore, the 'New Ecologists' argue that that vegetation formations, independently of human intervention, were not in 'equilibrium', nor were they particularly 'stable' or 'pristine'. In fact, scholars have begun to emphasise 'disequilibria, instability, and even chaotic fluctuations in biophysical environments' in contrast to premises of homeostasis and equilibrium.[10] All of this makes it problematic to determine a baseline, which in turn complicates the understanding of how humans altered vegetation because the environment itself was in constant change before humans intervened.

---

4   Bassett and Zuéli (2000); Fairhead and Leach (1998).
5   Rackham (1996); Russell (1997); Whitney (1994).
6   Melville (1994); Butzer and Butzer (1997); Brannstrom (2002).
7   Bahre (1991); Dean (1995); Whitney (1994); Williams (1989).
8   Bassett and Zuéli (2000); Fairhead and Leach (1998); Scoones (1999).
9   Denevan (2001); Vale (2002).
10 Zimmerer (1994), p. 108; Zimmerer and Young (1998), pp. 11–19; Scoones (1999).

Sediments in Environmental History

Trees are 'sexier' than dirt; stories about trees and forests are often more appealing than stories about sediments. Indeed, analysis of sediments in stream valleys or alluvial fans is uncommon in environmental history. However, sediments often serve as proxy data for measuring soil erosion and evaluating past land uses.[11] Spectacular records of sedimentation resulting from nineteenth- and twentieth-century land uses, mainly the introduction of agriculture and frontier settlement, have been reported in North America and Australia.[12] In Latin America, scholars have analysed sediments to study past pre-European land uses and Quaternary climates.[13]

Post-settlement alluvium (PSA) describes sediment eroded from catchment slopes during periods of destructive land uses associated with agricultural settlement. Several scholars have noted that PSA has buried a pre-settlement soil (paleosol), often termed a 'benchmark' soil horizon, and may be found as stream-valley deposits and on alluvial fans. The pre-settlement soil horizon (A) becomes a benchmark that, once described, is easily recognised in other field settings because of its distinct colour and texture, while its chemical properties are determined in laboratory analyses.[14]

The study of past environments and land uses based on analyses of sedimentation or PSA relies on a well-established postulate: relatively small amounts of the total eroded sediment leave source drainage basins, meaning that most eroded soil is deposited on new or existing alluvial fans. According to one expert, 'only a fraction, and perhaps a rather small fraction, of the sediment eroded within a drainage basin will find its way to the drainage outlet'; most eroded sediment is deposited and stored temporarily in the base of slopes, alluvial fans, floodplains or stream channels.[15] In the Upper Mississippi Valley, for example, 75 per cent of 'historically eroded sediment [after 1800] remains within their respective watersheds'.[16]

Analysis of post-settlement alluvium relies on laboratory and field methods, identification of benchmark soil horizons and localised topographical surveys. Several techniques that permit study of sedimentation are relevant to environmental historians. For example, the ideal baseline data would be a topographic survey of the stream valley under study. More realistically, researchers may find 'mobile cultural debris' such as fragments of leather, bottles, tyres, plastic and sawn wood in PSA. The age of wood

---

11   Oldfield and Clark (1990); Dearing (1994).
12   Brooks and Brierley (1997); Fryirs and Brierly (1999); Knox (2002).
13   Behling (1998); Ledru, Salgado-Labouriau and Lorscheitter (1998); McAuliffe et al. (2001); O'Hara et al. (1993).
14   Knox (2002).
15   Walling (1983), p. 210.
16   Knox (2002), p. 487.

and other plant material found in PSA may be estimated through radio-carbon analyses. Other forms of evidence come from bridges built near a single site, suggesting the width and depth of the former stream, and construction plans for bridges that often include topographical surveys. Sediment may bury dams and mills on floodplains. Roads and causeways may be used to measure lateral movement of streams as well as vertical accretion. Ground and aerial photography also may be useful. Finally, radionuclides, such as caesium-137, and heavy metals, such as zinc, chromium or lead, found in sediments downstream of mining sites or tanneries, or resulting from nuclear testing and lead in the atmosphere, have been used to measure and date sedimentation.[17]

Studies of sediments face their own equilibrium nemesis in establishing a baseline. Because sediment loss seldom equals sediment gain, it follows that sediment yield is a poor measure of soil erosion in catchments. There is no steady-state or equilibrium in streams; rather, disequilibria, either net storage or net loss, best characterises catchments.[18] Sediment may be stored as vertical accretion (sediment on stream banks), alluvial fans from small tributaries and colluvial deposits. A non-equilibrium model suggests a period of vertical accretion, then subsequent periods of vertical and lateral erosion. Slopes during an initial period produce sediment 'beyond the transport capacity of the stream', caused by either climatic changes or poor land management. 'Mobile cultural material' might be buried during this phase. Net loss of sediment occurs during a subsequent period because of 'reversal of the conditions' of disturbance, such as improved land management. Continued reduction of sediment means that lateral erosion will remove accumulated sediment, possibly revealing the interface between PSA and buried soil on stream banks.[19]

Vegetation and Sediments: Explanation, Scale, Causality

Combining ideas relating to vegetation and sediments into an excessively simple schematic may illustrate issues of spatial scale, evidence and causality (Figure 6.1). Environmental baselines for vegetation and sedimentation represent the initial point of historical inquiry. Time Future represents the endpoint; they may be separated by tens or hundreds of years. For simplicity, I have assumed that immediate causality is assigned only to events occurring inside the square, which represents the study region. Of course, causality can rarely be assigned to such bounded geographical spaces. But, for sake of argument, let us assume that these 'endogenous' causes include

17   Trimble (1998), pp. 284–95.
18   Trimble (1995), p. 201.
19   *Ibid.*, pp. 203–4.

local manifestations of factors such as government policies, labour relations and environmental ideologies, which are located outside the square.

Figure 6.1: Schematic of Spatial Scale and Causality in Vegetation and Sedimentation-Based Models of Environmental History

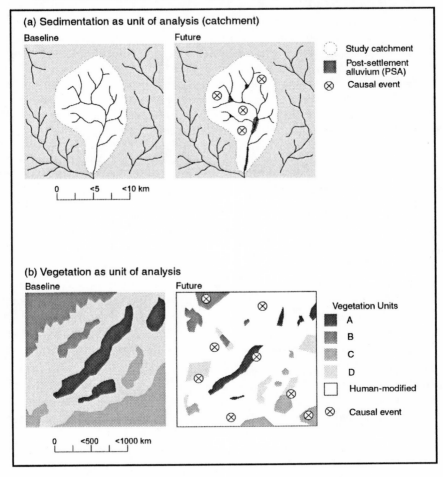

The baseline for the vegetation model could be generated from biogeographical studies that rely on written descriptions of past vegetation and field study. The four vegetation units could represent vegetation communities distributed over spatial scales ranging from 10,000 to 1,000,000 square kilometres, although analysis at more restricted spatial scales may occur. For the Time Future period, vegetation cover is dominated by the simple 'human modified' category, determined by aerial photography, satellite data or qualitative descriptions. Comparing the Baseline and Future, we may claim that certain events occurring within the area of study are immediate causes of the observed change in vegetation. These endogenous events may include sawmill operations, fuelwood demand, conversion of forest to agricultural land uses, the local manifestations of public policies and acts of conservation or preservation, or low human interference, perhaps because of poor suitability of resources, poor market opportunities or inappropriate technology.

The baseline for sediment dynamics is a much reduced spatial scale, from tens of square kilometres to 1,000 square kilometres. Reduced spatial scale is a function of the phenomenon of sediment production and transport, as I suggested earlier. Most eroded soil probably has not left the catchment and remains somewhere in storage, on alluvial fans, stream banks or in stream channels. Researchers must determine the extent of sedimentation in existence at the Baseline, and the nature of the benchmark soil horizon that will be used to determine the depth and volume of PSA. At the Time Future period researchers must determine the location and characteristics of PSA on the basis of field and laboratory analyses. Events endogenous to the catchment may be located, such as removal of original vegetation, planting of erosive crops, lack of soil conservation techniques and depopulation.

This excessively simple schematic illustrates how vegetation and sedimentation differ as evidence of environmental change. Sediment characteristics reveal soil erosion and land uses in relatively small catchments, which are used to infer environmental change more broadly in spatial terms. By contrast, measurement of vegetation changes, often covering relatively larger areas, supports claims for general environmental change. Overall, they are two modes of explanation that have tangible differences in that they support distinct environmental narratives or explanations. These points shall become clearer in a discussion of the environmental history of western São Paulo State, Brazil.

Talking to Sediments: a Case from Twentieth-Century Western São Paulo, Brazil

Thus far I have discussed conceptual questions relating to two types of biophysical evidence that environmental historians may use. To further develop the argument I need to explain how vegetation and sediments may be used to support environmental narratives, and how narratives may inform (but not necessarily influence) debates on public policies for environmental resources. The environmental history of the Western Plateau of

São Paulo, and the Middle Paranapanema River Valley (Table 6.1, Figure 6.2, Figure 6.3) will illustrate the conceptual points I have been making. The Western Plateau is highly urbanised (88.5 per cent of 5.6 million inhabitants). Vegetation in the late nineteenth century, before mass migration, was a mosaic of semi-deciduous mesophytic forest known as Atlantic Forest, tropical savanna (*cerrado*) and savanna woodland (*cerradão*) presently covering only 5.2 per cent of its land area. The main land use is pasture (59.8 per cent), followed by semi-permanent crops (13.9 per cent), permanent crops (7.8 per cent), and annual crops (7.4 per cent).[20]

Table 6.1: Summary of Selected Characteristics of Middle Paranapanema River Valley, São Paulo, Brazil

	Land-Suitability Region (see Figure 6.3)		
	A	**B**	**C**
Total Area (hectares)	521,583	978,992	145,808
Soil-Relief Characteristics	Oxisols >60% clay Well-drained Slopes 5 < 10%	Oxisols + Ultisols >80% sand Well-drained Slopes < 15%	Alfisols + Mollisols A: >80% sand B: > 25% clay Slopes > 15%
Soil Erosion Susceptibility	Low	Medium	High
Present Land Uses	Annual and semi-permanent crops	Semi-permanent crops; forestry; pasture	Pasture

Note: Soils in the Western Plateau are derived from Mesozoic-age sandstone formations (Bauru Group) and intrusive lava flows (Serra Geral Formation). The region's sandstone-derived soils, which not only are erosive and highly erosive but also dominate the region, are divided into two general types: (1) flat uplands (~48,000 km2) have coarse-textured Oxisols with >80% sand-sized particles in A horizons; (2) on sloping land (~46,000 km2) a complex of highly erodible Mollisols, Alfisols and Ultisols exists, in which B horizons, with >25% clay-sized particles, appear beneath A horizons with >85% sand-sized particles. Soils derived from Serra Geral basalt occur much less extensively and are less erodible. Well-drained Oxisols, with >60% clay-sized particles, are found on landscapes with rolling topography and flat uplands (Brasil, 1960; Instituto de Pesquisas Tecnológicas [IPT], 1981a; IPT, 1981b; Oliveira et al., 1999).

20   São Paulo (1999).

Figure 6.2: São Paulo State

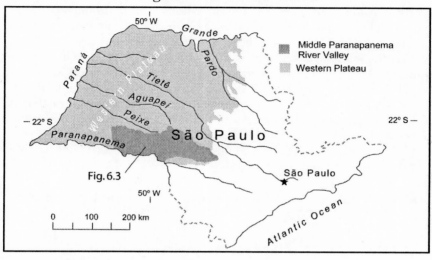

Shaded areas show (A) Western Plateau (126,171 km^2) and (B) Middle Paranapanema River Valley (see Figure 6.3) (IPT, 1981b; São Paulo, 1994; 1999).

Figure 6.3: Middle Paranapanema River Valley (16,763 km^2), with locations of case studies and three regions: (A) 5,216 km2; (B) 9,790 km^2; (C) 1,458 km^2 (reservoir area accounts for 299 km^2)

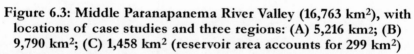

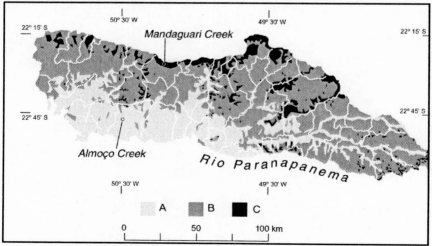

White lines show county (município) boundaries. See text and Table 1 for explanation of regions. Map redrawn from 1:250,000 data produced by the CDVale (cdvale@femanet.com.br).

Environmental Narratives

Environmental narratives are interpretations of environmental issues, often leading to public policies. The concept of environmental narrative has been used to show how policies are often designed to suit contentious conceptions of environmental issues.[21] In the case of vegetation-based understandings of the study region, environmental narratives stress the rapid deforestation of the 1.2 million square kilometre Atlantic Forest, presently reduced to less than eight per cent of its original area (Figure 6.4).[22] Dean's *Broadax and Firebrand* stresses mining, coffee production, fuel wood cutting and cattle ranching as causes for the rapid decline in forest cover; evidence for deforestation in several sub-regions is generalised for the entire Atlantic Forest region.[23]

Figure 6.4: Area of the Brazilian Atlantic Forest in 1500 and 1990

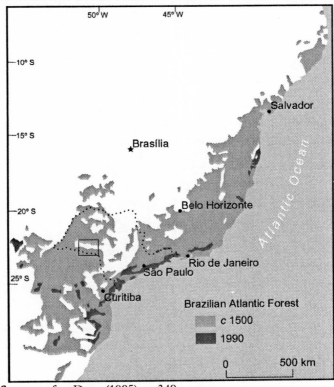

Source: after Dean (1995), p. 349.

21　Fairhead and Leach (1995; 1998); Hoben (1995); Roe (1995); Nygren (2000); Campbell (2002).

22　Dean (1995), pp. 3, 6–18; Fundação SOS Mata Atlântica (1998).

23　Dean (1995); Fonseca (1985); Victor (1975); Brannstrom (2002).

Claims for the rapid destruction of the Atlantic Forest are closely related to a narrative for environmental conservation. The Atlantic Forest ranked highly in recent hotspot analysis[24] and in the competing 'regional' approach,[25] both of which claim to satisfy the imperative that scarce funds should achieve greatest biodiversity conservation. Significantly, both models rely heavily on the existence of a greater Atlantic Forest as a 'single organism, with different organs playing complementary roles',[26] an idea that potentially strengthens existing policy instruments, most notably Brazil's National Atlantic Forest Policy.[27] Although the 1988 Brazilian Constitution had designated the Atlantic Forest as 'national patrimony', its location had to be determined later on a 1:5,000,000 government map.[28]

The recognition of sedimentation as an environmental indicator of past land uses differs in subtle but important ways from the forest-cover conceptualisation of environmental history.[29] This approach adopts a more comprehensive view of land uses, distinguishes among destructive capacity of different land uses on soils and the spatial distribution of land degradation. Although findings may be generalised for similar soil, topography and land use situations, this approach necessarily operates at a more reduced spatial scale than vegetation-based analysis.

The environmental narrative that begins with sedimentation as evidence would lead to analysis of past erosion and sediment accumulation rates in particular stream valleys. In addition, this approach recognises the significant regional variability of land degradation, because of the highly spatially heterogeneous nature of soil susceptibility to erosive processes and sediment storage in catchments. Overall, this approach focuses on a 'long view' of land uses, some destructive and others less so, stressing the impact of land uses that followed deforestation.

Environmental Public Policy Debates

Evidence of vegetation and sedimentation support at least two different stories about environmental change and public policies. The deforestation narrative for the greater Atlantic Forest, for example, supports the idea that increasing forest cover is the single most important environmental policy objective for rural areas. Three recent initiatives are exemplary.

---

24 Myers et al. (2000).

25 Dinerstein et al. (1995).

26 Joly et al. (1999), p. 339.

27 Dean (1995), pp. 338–40; Hodge et al. (1997), pp. 335–48.

28 Brasil (1999); IBGE (1993).

29 In comparison to the state of knowledge on land-cover change, little is known about the recent sedimentation history of the Western Plateau. Geomorphological and pedological surveys misrepresented PSA as Tertiary or Cenozoic deposits (Lepsch et al., 1977).

Firstly, narratives of a devastated greater Atlantic Forest support the creation of protected areas by government purchase, especially in coastal regions where surviving fragments are most significant. Exorbitant expropriation costs have perverted the state government's attempts to establish protected areas among private landholdings in the coastal Atlantic Forest. Careful legal and technical work, which uncovered numerous irregularities by landowners and their attorneys, saved the state US$1 billion during the creation of five conservation units.[30]

Secondly, the idea of a greater Atlantic Forest has supported the Brazilian government's top-down Atlantic Forest policy, which has caused considerable resource-governance problems for state governments. Federal legislation and decrees in the early 1990s prohibited clearing of the various stages of regrowth of several Atlantic Forest formations. In Santa Catarina, a southern Brazilian state, the policy made all forests — 16 per cent of the state's total area — off-limits. This sweeping decision increased deforestation and encouraged conflict among groups using forest resources. As a result, forest management became a much more difficult task.[31]

Thirdly, the deforestation narrative supports reforestation toward compliance of the 1965 Forest Code, which, for this region of Brazil, required that all rural properties have a forested 'Legal Reserve' (LR) of at least 20 per cent of area. The same Forest Code required that stream banks and other sensitive environments have forest cover as 'Permanent Protection' (PP) areas.[32] In São Paulo, proposed forest legislation would have forced landowners to reforest Permanent Preservation and Legal Reserve areas at their own expense. Landowners without forested PP areas would have ten years to reforest, and would be allowed to remove products from PP areas only if part of a 'sustainable' project registered with Forest Police. Landowners in violation of the 20 per cent LR requirement would have 20 years to reforest, but could plant commercial species.[33] To date, only the provision for mandatory reforestation has become law, but has met significant organised opposition by landowner groups.[34]

Deforestation is a hugely significant transformation of the environment; however, the focus on deforestation has marginalised soil, water and sediment issues from mainstream environmental policy debates. In contrast to evidence and narratives for the greater Atlantic Forest, the sediment narrative emphasises post-deforestation land uses. Major impacts to soils occurred after deforestation and have left a legacy of PSA in stream

30   Schwenk and Azevedo (1998).
31   Hodge, Queiroz and Reis (1997).
32   Brazil (1965).
33   São Paulo (1996).
34   São Paulo (1998); Brannstrom (2001a). The State of Paraná (1999) recently passed similar legislation, which allows for 20 years for landowners to meet LR obligations.

valleys.[35] This evidence and narrative not only support a critique of the reforestation proposal, but also encourage consolidation of recent initiatives to decentralise water management to river-basin committees.[36]

The sediment narrative suggests spatially heterogenous land degradation patterns and the prioritisation of catchments for policy intervention on the basis of soil, topography and past and present land uses. For example, reforestation of PP areas in the Middle Paranapanema River Valley (Figure 6.3; Table 6.1) would be highly problematic to implement. Difficulties in planting seedlings in riparian environments, the main PP target areas in the region, begin with the region's spatially variable drainage density.[37] At the 1:50,000 map scale, typical small catchments (between 20 and 30 km^2) in Region A (Figure 6.3) contain two first-order streams and one second-order stream. But in Region C (Figure 6.3) the same size catchment typically has between 25 and 30 first-order streams. This simple difference in geomorphology not only would magnify the area and cost of reforestation, but also would demand the type of flexible techniques and incentives omitted from the state's proposed legislation.

The characteristics of riparian environments, a product of post-settlement land uses, also vary among regions.[38] In Region A, presently dominated by annual crops and sugarcane, soil erosion caused by post-1970 agricultural mechanisation created large, poorly-drained alluvial fans that cannot be reforested. In Regions B and C (Figure 6.3), where pasture is more than 70 per cent of rural land cover, presettlement riparian surfaces have widened considerably because of upstream soil erosion. In these regions, reforestation policy should promote stream fencing, which would encourage natural regeneration of PP areas. Land tenure and landowner capitalisation, which strongly affect land uses, also vary significantly among the three regions. Reforestation strategies and incentives should differentiate among the relatively capitalised soybean, maize and sugarcane farmers (Region A), the poorly capitalised and part-time cattle ranchers (Region C) and the well-capitalised and large-scale ranchers (Regions A and B) (Figure 6.3; Table 6.1). A recent bottom-up proposal has attempted to convert this dilemma into a public policy for reforestation of PP areas;[39] however, resistance from technocrats who control the catchment committee has impeded further discussion.

The sediment-based environmental narrative supports recent water-resources policies that have created decentralised and participatory drainage-basin committees.[40] In the mid 1990s, state legislation created 22

35   Brannstrom and Oliveira (2000).
36   São Paulo (1994); Porto (1998).
37   Dunne and Leopold (1978), pp. 499–500.
38   Brannstrom and Oliveira (2000).
39   Brannstrom (2001a).
40   São Paulo (1994).

watershed management districts. In each district, committees of elected officials (municipal heads or *prefeitos*), state technicians and civil society representatives (organised as unions, industrial associations or non-governmental
organisations, for example) make some water-resources decisions and set priorities for certain water-resources investments. This new water-resources
management scheme, which depends on future water tariffs, repeats the key
words of contemporary development: 'integrative, decentralised and participatory'.[41] The main problems with the new system include variable technical
capacities, which state technicians often monopolise, and the tendency of
elected officials to excessively politicise the committees.

The sediment narrative would support concerns central to the new
water-resources management scheme. For example, the threat of eroding
PSA should promote extreme caution in the expansion of urban land uses
without adequate management of urban runoff. This argument is congru-
ent with recent recommendations for improved regulation of land subdivision for new housing or industries.[42] Populist housing programmes
notoriously lack proper surface-water control. Large areas of bare soil are
exposed during construction and downstream PSA is easily eroded by
increased runoff from paved surfaces. The results include mobilisation of
stored sediment and destruction of downstream infrastructure. Emphasis
on rural land uses as a factor in water management would reduce the present bias toward urban infrastructure projects.

Thus, there are potentially two different stories to be told from evidence of vegetation destruction or sedimentation. Two specific environmental histories will illustrate how evidence of vegetation and sediment
may lead to divergent environmental narratives, and thus to support different public policy initiatives.

Case I: The Mandaguari Creek
The vegetation-focused narrative would consider the Mandaguari Creek, a
31 square kilometre catchment, by analysing aerial photographs from 1962
(Figure 6.5) compared with the earliest known aerial photograph, from
1940 (Figure 6.6). The images indicate decline in forest and *cerradão* from
uplands and side slopes, and the comparison confirms the hypothesis that
the catchment's forests were replaced quickly by coffee or other land uses,
while the settlement frontier pushed relentlessly westward, similar to other
places in south-eastern Brazil.[43] Forest cover was destroyed quickly in the
1930s and 1940s, replaced initially by low-quality coffee plantations and
later by unproductive cattle pastures by the late 1960s. Most landowners
are in violation of the 1965 Forest Code's provision for 20 per cent of the

41   *Ibid.*, p. 5.
42   CPTI (1999).
43   Dean (1995); Monbeig (1952).

property to be maintained as Legal Reserve of native vegetation. Riparian areas of many properties, which fall under the Permanent Protection category, lack native flora.

Figure 6.5: Section of ~1:25,000 Aerial Photograph West of Echaporã, 1962 (22° 25' S, 50° 15' W), Image no. 8085

Source: Instituto Agronômico de Campinas, São Paulo.

Figure 6.6: Oblique Aerial Photograph of Bela Vista (Echaporã), 1940, Image no. 3388

Source: Instituto Geográfico e Cartográfico, São Paulo.

However, a different story might be told if we look at sediments in the bottom of stream valleys. Investigation reveals a distinct PSA unit, often thicker than two metres, which has buried a pre-settlement A horizon (Figure 6.7). Wood fragments are commonly embedded at the PSA-A horizon interface, and 'mobile cultural debris' such as rubber and plastic, may be pulled out of PSA at various depths. If we look more closely at the 1962 aerial photograph, rill and gully erosion are visible on side slopes; a reconnaissance of soils there would indicate that between 25 and 60 centimetres of extremely sandy soil are found above a clay-textured soil horizon. The side slopes are important because they supplied the soil particles that became deposited as sediment on alluvial fans and stream banks. Yet it would be difficult to determine precisely when the PSA developed, although radiocarbon dating suggests strongly that PSA is only a few decades old, thus confirming the hypothesis that massive soil erosion followed deforestation.[44] More sophisticated, and significantly more expensive, techniques might find pollutants, such as arsenic and radionuclides, bound to soil particles.

Figure 6.7: PSA and Benchmark Paleosol A Horizon in the Mandaguari Creek, Near Echaporã, São Paulo State, Brazil

Photograph by author, 1997.

What land uses followed removal of forest cover? Because the 1962 aerial photograph only captures one moment, it is necessary to turn to oral histories and written documents, such as judicial proceedings from a local courthouse, to determine land uses. Here we are confronted with evidence

44   Brannstrom and Oliveira (2000).

that cotton farming, practised under share-tenant contracts, existed on highly erosive slopes; furthermore, we find that claimants to land used landless workers, known as *prepostos*, to secure possession of contested landholdings.[45] Thus, turning to the stream banks and alluvial fans in small catchments raises questions that would not have been inspired by studying vegetation change. Did deforestation or cotton farming cause the most severe damage to soils? Was labour most exploited while claiming land, clearing forests or planting cotton? Returning to forest policies, evidence from sediments suggests that sites designated as 'Permanent Protection' are in fact recently created, with unknown stability, and thus very unlikely targets for the considerable expense of inputs and opportunity cost required of reforestation schemes.

Case II: The Almoço Creek

Approximately 50 kilometres south of the Mandaguari Creek, the Almoço Creek, a 20 square kilometre catchment, is presently used for mechanised soya–maize double-cropping on commercial farms. For the vegetation-focused environmental history approach, good evidence is available. An early-twentieth-century surveyor's map shows nearly total cover of mesophytic semi-deciduous forest, with only small areas of riparian vegetation and few clearings made for crops (Figure 6.8). Compare this with a 1962 aerial photograph showing only miniscule remnants of forest cover amidst coffee groves, annual crops and pasture (Figure 6.9). Devastation appears to have been nearly complete in the Almoço catchment, proving once again that Dean was right: the Atlantic Forest was removed quickly, unceremoniously and well before 1962.[46] In addition, many farms in the Almoço Creek lack the 20 per cent Legal Reserve that the 1965 Forest Code required.[47]

A different story emerges, however, when looking for sediment in the alluvial fan and stream banks in the catchment. PSA is also here, but its characteristics are very different than the Mandaguari because of the Almoço's soils, which are Oxisols containing 60 per cent clay-sized particles. PSA here is a mucky layer of clay found as much as 1.2 metres above the pre-settlement soil horizon. The pre-settlement soil is bright blue because iron has been reduced in anaerobic conditions and contains different clay particles than upland soils (Figure 6.10). Growing on the PSA is a species from the *Typha* genus, a water-loving invasive plant. When did the PSA form? This question demands oral evidence from farmers, several of whom were born on the farmsteads, and written evidence, mainly from judicial proceedings.

45   Brannstrom (2001b).
46   Dean (1995).
47   Recent policies have increased riparian forest cover to meet Permanent Protection requirements.

**Figure 6.8: Section of ~1:25,000 Aerial Photograph South of
Cândido Mota, 1962 (22° 50' S, 50° 25' W), Image no. 8684**

Source: Instituto Agronômico de Campinas, São Paulo.

Figure 6.9: Land Cover in the Queixadas Valley (84 km²), 1916

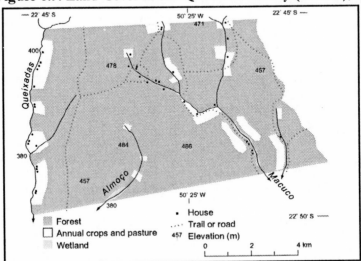

Source: Bernardo de Souza Murça v. João Laurinado Pereira et al., 'Divisão do 3o
Lote de Terras na Fazenda Queixadas' (1913), Caixa 2-ci, f 93, Centro de
Documentação e Apóio à Pesquisa, Arquivo do Fórum da Comarca de Assis,
Cartório do Segundo Ofício.

Figure 6.10: PSA and Benchmark Cg Horizon in Almoço Creek, near Cândido Mota, São Paulo State, Brazil

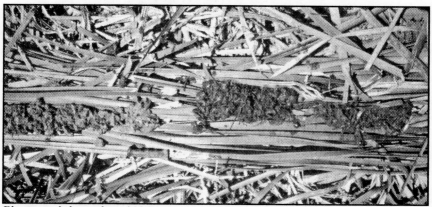

Photograph by author, 1996.

Between 1920 and 1970 floodplains and alluvial fans were planted in rice, if cultivated at all, because coffee was planted on the highest elevations of farms. Coffee groves occupied approximately 29 per cent of the area of coffee farms, and often were planted in interrow food crops as a means to attract labour without paying cash wages.[48] This situation changed dramatically in the mid-1970s, when farmers purchased tractors and soil-preparation equipment to double-crop soya and wheat. Conservative agricultural modernisation policies of the Brazilian military regime (1964–85) subsidised land owners with negative real interest rates (the inflation rate was higher than the interest rate) for production and infrastructure, adapted soy cultivars and soy processing and marketing facilities.[49]

Until the mid 1980s, however, soil conservation techniques were not included among policies for soya farmers. As a result, Oxisols developed a compact and dense sub-surface horizon beneath the upper 10-15 centimetre cultivated soil zone. Soil compaction dramatically reduced water infiltration and altered key soil characteristics.[50] Farmers in the Almoço reported that summer rainstorms would remove a saturated soil layer downslope, revealing the compacted horizon described as 'ribs' and a 'skeleton' that 'was so hard that you could hit it with a hoe and you couldn't break it apart'. Another farmer reported that runoff removed plants and seeds and creating a soil horizon 'as hard as a tabletop'.[51]

48 Brannstrom (2000).
49 Carrière (1991); Soskin (1988).
50 Torres et al. (1994).
51 Brannstrom (1998), pp. 142–3.

Significantly, soya-wheat double cropping is not part of the vegetation narrative because relatively little Atlantic Forest in western São Paulo was felled to plant soya. Soil erosion significantly altered streams, thus redefining how riparian areas are understood as Permanent Protection sites. The narratives point to different situations: a deforested landscape and a crop-producing landscape. The deforestation narrative, however, ends with the last forest fragment. The sediment-based narrative shifts the focus to the environmental implications of rapid agricultural mechanisation during the 1970s and, more recently, of no-tillage cultivation currently being practised. The problem for environmental historians is then to compare the consequences of deforestation and coffee production to soya-wheat double cropping.

Summary

An environmental narrative in the case of the Western Plateau of São Paulo, if based on sediments as evidence, would stress post-deforestation land uses and the uneven spatial distribution of land degradation. The vegetation-based narrative, by contrast, extrapolates from limited cases to all 1.2 million square kilometres of the Atlantic Forest.[52] The sediment counter-narrative uses environmental measures at smaller geographical scales, but could be extrapolated to encompass larger areas with similar soil-landscape and land-use conditions. Certainly, large areas of south-eastern Brazil have similar histories of agricultural settlement and soil characteristics.

Vegetation and sedimentation narratives potentially, but not necessarily, inform either side of contradictory policies within São Paulo's forestry and water resources bureaucracies. While the water-resources law stresses regional participation of different actors in catchment committees, a recent forestry proposal forces land users to engage the state directly as individuals. Regional decision-making is key to water policy, but the forestry officials have made a crude top-down attempt to coerce compliance to Permanent Protection and Legal Reserve areas. The forestry proposal originated in a consultative group dominated by the paper-pulp industry; the water-resources legislation was the result of international research on existing management strategies.

Why 'Talk' to Sediments?

Should environmental historians 'talk' to sediments instead of vegetation? Is it more effective or insightful to 'talk' to sediments? We cannot examine environmental evidence in precisely the same way as documentary evidence, but, according to Oldfield and Clark, the structure of interpreting documentary and field evidence is 'remarkably similar'.[53] What they did not consider fully

52　Dean (1995); Victor (1975); Fonseca (1985).
53　Oldfield and Clark (1990), p. 155.

were differences among competing types of field evidence. Thus, this inquiry is analogous to exploring the epistemological issues involved with, for example, census data, post-mortem property inventories or travellers' accounts as sources of evidence for environmental history.

A sediment-based focus I have explored also raises relevant issues for Latin American environmental history. Firstly, the river basin should be further explored as a category of analysis, not only for testing broad hypotheses about environmental change, but also because of its restricted area and objective location, which makes it convenient and viable as a research setting. North American environmental historians have success-fully made river basins the topics of fascinating studies that link water, public policies, environmental ideologies and economic activities.[54] Secondly, the sediment narrative I have stressed encourages renewed attention to the role of agricultural technologies, especially the profound impact of agricultural mechanisation on land and water resources. The full environmental implications of Latin America's twentieth-century agricul-tural modernisation have yet to be explored completely.

When we create narratives from environmental evidence, it is impor-tant to realise that we probably create different meanings depending on our choice of environmental evidence; hence, what we mean by 'environ-ment' in environmental history might require more consideration. Selecting to work with evidence of vegetation change, as a measure of the human impact on the environment, allows us to speak to such timely issues as biodiversity loss, indigenous knowledge and carbon emissions. Such a focus might support policy imperatives to increase forest cover or protect biodiversity 'hotspots'.[55] PSA is no more 'truthful' as a measure of environmental change than vegetation, but this is not the point. Interrogating sediments would probably result in different environmental narratives, stressing soil erosion and changing streams, usually at relatively small geographical scales; this epistemological claim might support initia-tives to manage soil and water resources at the scale of small catchments in rural, peri-urban and urban settings.

We often do not have a choice about which environmental variables to choose. These usually are determined by factors outside of our control. At minimum, however, we should be aware of the limitations and biases of the environmental variables available. It is not an unproblematic task to decide what to measure in the environment, nor is it a simple task to inter-pret what other scholars have measured. More careful consideration of this issue might reveal biases in how we prioritise the many aspects of the natural world and the complexity of human relationships with them.

54 Taylor (1999); Gumprecht (1999).
55 Myers et al. (2000).

PART III

Knowledges: New Technologies and Organisms

CHAPTER 7

Bananas, Biodiversity and the Paradox of Commodification

John Soluri

A banana seed, which the great majority of banana-eaters in temperate countries have never seen, is about a quarter of an inch in diameter, black in color, and very hard. Naturally, the presence of these seeds in the fruit would not enhance its market value. (*Science* 78 [14 July 1933])

Introduction

In May 1927 several dozen squatters occupied a piece of land near the town of La Masica, on the north coast of Honduras. The land, a property held by the New Orleans-based Standard Fruit Company, had previously been planted in bananas, but when the soil became heavily infected with Panama disease (a soil fungus) the company abandoned the farm. In a letter written to Honduran President Miguel Paz Barahona, Jacobo P. Munguía explained that the squatters sought to collaborate, not fight with the company: 'these men [the squatters] say, that they want to grow that [disease] resistant banana and that if the company finds a market for it, they will sell their output to the company with pleasure'.[1] Munguía enclosed a petition bearing the names of 108 individuals who expressed a desire to 'work independently' by growing a variety of banana known as the 'lakatan'. In one sense, there was nothing extraordinary about this incident; struggles between landowners and squatters were common enough in export-banana zones during the twentieth century.[2] However, the petition from La Masica is noteworthy because it reminds us that land is not the only resource needed by farmers. The plants themselves — in this case disease-resistant banana varieties — are also vital, a point perhaps so obvious as to have escaped the attention of the many scholars who have written about Latin America's agroexport economies.

Economic historians have written extensively on the 'boom and bust' cycles that characterised Latin American export economies, but less attention has been paid to how the process of commodification shaped, and was shaped by, the plant resources that formed the basis of international

---

1   Jacobo P. Munguía to President Miguel Paz Barahona, Esparta, 16 May 1927; Honduran National Archive (Tegucigalpa), leg. Correspondencia particular, año 1921.
2   For land conflicts in export banana zones, see LeGrand (1986); Soluri (2000); and Striffler (2002).

trade.[3] This situation can be attributed in part to the challenges of locating and interpreting sources — farmers generally spend more of their time nurturing plants than recording information about them. The movement of plant material — with a few notable exceptions — seldom produces paper trails.[4] The fact that influential explanatory models in Latin American studies, including modernisation and dependency theories, generally do not acknowledge the environmental rootedness of agriculture has further contributed to the prevalence of historical narratives that marginalise biological processes. Fortunately, researchers writing from diverse disciplinary backgrounds are beginning to examine the environmental history of tropical commodities.[5]

One of the most important biological dynamics in the case of the export banana industry has been the appearance and spread of plant pathogens. In the early twentieth century, the expansion of export banana monocultures triggered outbreaks of Panama disease, a fungal pathogen that lowered yields throughout the Caribbean and Central America. Panama disease epidemics prompted both the British government and the United Fruit Company to establish breeding programmes in the 1920s with the shared goal of developing a variety with disease resistance. The idea seemed plausible enough at the time; during the 1920s, the sugar industries in Cuba and Puerto Rico overcame diseases and dwindling yields by introducing hybrid canes from Java and elsewhere.[6] However, obstacles posed by both the banana's unusual biology and the structures and aesthetics of mass markets in the United States (the largest banana importer between 1890 and 1960) impeded the creation of successful hybrids. Mass markets for bananas had been built around a single variety — Gros Michel — whose physical characteristics set the trade's quality standard for at least 60 years. Any disease-resistant hybrid that produced fruits whose shape, colour, taste, texture and ripening qualities did not closely resemble those of Gros Michel fruit would not be a commercial success. Further complicating matters for banana breeders was the fact that Gros Michel bananas — along with many other varieties — were extremely infertile and rarely produced seed. This

---

3   See the otherwise impressive works by Bulmer-Thomas (1987) and Topik and Wells (1998). Economic historians are not alone in this regard. For important publications on specific commodities incorporating a range of disciplinary perspectives that downplay things environmental, see Mintz (1985); Moberg and Striffler (2003); and Roseberry, Gudmundson and Samper (1995).

4   For the celebrated case of rubber (*Hevea brasiliensis*), see Dean (1987).

5   The most comprehensive study to date is Tucker (2000). On Caribbean banana production, see Grossman (1998), pp. 1–33; on sugar, see McCook (2002), pp. 77–104; on Costa Rican banana production, see Marquardt (2001). Also see Funes (this volume) and Gallini (this volume).

6   On the introduction of sugarcane hybrids, see McCook (2002), pp. 77–104.

rather odd condition of seedless fruit has played a central role in shaping the twentieth-century history of the export banana trade.

Unfortunately, the evidence that I have examined to date sheds little light on small-scale grower attempts to cultivate disease-resistant bananas. This makes it difficult to determine the frequency of initiatives such as those taken by the La Masica squatters. On the other hand, the efforts of researchers employed by both the British government and the United Fruit Company to find a substitute for Gros Michel are well documented. Drawing on both published and unpublished papers and correspondence produced primarily by scientists (botanists, geneticists, cytologists and pathologists), this chapter traces the history of institutional banana breeding in the British Caribbean and Central America. My interest in writing about this seemingly obscure topic is to explore the tension between the intrinsic variability of biological organisms and the standardisation of mass market structures and quality standards historically associated with the production and consumption of agricultural commodities. This tension, in turn, helped to give rise to a key paradox of the nineteenth and twentieth century Latin American agroexport economies: mass production processes simultaneously reduced and appropriated the biological diversity necessary to sustain themselves.

The Diffusion of *Musa* and the Beginnings of the Caribbean Export Trade

Scientists currently recognise about 30 to 40 species of *Musa* including *Musa acuminata* Colla (AA), or dessert banana, and *Musa balbisiana* Colla (BB), or cooking banana. Scientists believe that most edible varieties are genetically related to these two species. Banana cultivation first took place in South-east Asia and the western Pacific, where human selection produced both diploid (AA, BB) and triploid (AAA) cultivars that were relatively seed-free.[7] South-east Asian cultivators were also the first to cross *M. acuminata* cultivars (AA) with *M. balbisiana* (BB), yielding both hybrid diploids (AB) and triploids (AAB, and ABB) that tended to be hardier and more drought tolerant than pure *M. acuminata* varieties. From these regions, bananas and plantains diffused to India, Africa and Polynesia. When the Portuguese reached the Atlantic coast of Africa, they encountered a well established banana culture. Portuguese sailors introduced bananas to the Canary Islands in the early fifteenth century; Spanish colonisers carried many varieties to the Americas a century later. Evidence also suggests that

---

7   The designations 'diploid' (AA), 'triploid' (AAA) and 'tetraploid' (AAAA) used throughout this chapter correspond to the number of chromosomes found in the cell nuclei of a given variety: a diploid has 22 chromosomes, a triploid 33 chromosomes and tetraploid 44 chromosomes (Jones, 2000, pp. 1–36).

Musa cultivars reached South America via Polynesian travellers.[8] Bananas and plantains spread throughout the American tropics during the sixteenth and seventeenth centuries. In Brazil and the Caribbean, *Musa* occupied a prominent spot in slave provision grounds.

Gros Michel bananas (AAA) do not enter the historical record until the early nineteenth century. In 1830 a French-born botanist named Jean Francois Pouyat transplanted a single Gros Michel plant from Martinique to his coffee plantation in Jamaica. The variety became extremely popular on the island where it was known as the 'Martinique banana' or 'banana Pouyat'.[9] From the Caribbean, the variety spread throughout Central America and beyond. In 1892 Colombian officials arranged to import Gros Michel from Jamaica. Given the well-documented migrations of workers from Jamaica to the Central American isthmus, there can be little doubt that the variety spread via unofficial routes as well during the late nineteenth century.[10] By the beginning of the twentieth century, Gros Michel was the most sought after variety in the rapidly expanding banana trade between the Caribbean and the United States.[11] Shippers favoured Gros Michel because of its ability to withstand the rigors of transport due to its relatively thick peel, compact bunches and uniform ripening. For a contemporary reader accustomed to seeing bananas packed in cardboard boxes, the importance of these features may seem mysterious. However, for nearly a century, bananas exported to the United States travelled on their full stem with only minimal padding (Figure 7.3). Also, the first shippers carried bananas in wind-powered schooners, making the length of the ripening process a crucial consideration when assessing the suitability of varieties for export. Gros Michel fruit also appealed to consumers; under favourable growing conditions, the plant produced large, yellow fruits whose flavour and texture had mass appeal across lines of race, class, age, gender and region in the United States. Although other kinds of bananas occasionally reached US markets in the late nineteenth century, Gros Michel was the variety around which shippers, wholesalers, retailers and consumers formed their sense of what constituted a proper banana.

Mass Production, Environmental Change and Panama Disease

The ability of fossil fuel-powered steamships and locomotives to transport bulky and highly perishable commodities over great distances helped to make bananas the first inexpensive, 'seasonless' fresh fruit widely available to consumers in the United States and, to a lesser degree, Europe. Between

8   Langdon (1993).
9   Rodríquez (1955), pp. 11–12.
10   On Caribbean migrations to Central American banana zones, see Chomsky (1996); Putnam (2002); and Echeverri-Gent (1992).
11   Jenkins (2000), pp. 14–15; Higgins (1904), p. 42.

1875 and 1894 the value of US banana imports increased ten fold (from less than US$500,000 to US$5.1 million). During this period, production was primarily in the hands of small-scale growers. In 1899 a dozen-odd shipping companies merged to form the United Fruit Company, marking an era of export production characterised by large-scale plantations, extensive railroad networks, and accelerating rates of resource use. Between 1902 and 1914 the value of US banana imports rose from US$7.3 million (29 million bunches) to nearly US$16.4 million (45 million bunches). By the outbreak of the Great War, the banana had become an 'everyday' food in the United States where per capita consumption neared nine kilogrammes. Following a decline in trade linked to wartime shipping restrictions, banana imports soared, peaking in 1929 when US$36 million (65 million bunches) entered US ports.[12] Although small-scale producers persisted in both the Caribbean and Central America, by the end of the 1920s two US companies — United Fruit and Standard Fruit — dominated the trade by controlling farms, railroads, steamship lines and marketing firms. In 1926 United Fruit, the largest banana company in the world during the first half of the twentieth century, owned approximately 650,000 hectares (1.6 million acres) of land including 70,000 hectares (172,000 acres) of banana plantations in the Caribbean and Latin America.[13]

The dramatic expansion of export banana cultivation reworked a significant portion of the humid, tropical lowlands that stretch along the Caribbean coast from Guatemala to Colombia (Figure 7.1). Thousands of workers felled forests, drained wetlands, established banana farms and built infrastructure including port facilities, railroads and labour camps. The banana plantations rarely contained anything but Gros Michel clones and weeds, mostly grasses. This rapid transformation of lowland tropical environments in Central America provided the agroecological context in which Panama disease emerged.[14] The soil-borne pathogen (*Fusarium oxysporum f cubense*) associated with the disease entered through the root structure before eventually making its way to the foliage where it caused the leaves to cease functioning. Over time, infected farms suffered declining yields. The densely planted monocultures of Gros Michel clones, linked by railroads, drainage systems, migrant workers and pack mules, contained few barriers at either the genetic or landscape level capable of slowing the fungus's spread.[15] Reports of Panama disease-like symptoms circulated in Panama as early as the 1890s. By the 1910s the disease was making major

12   Palmer (1932), p. 265.
13   Cutter (1926), p. 494.
14   For a contemporary botanist's assessment of the change in plant diversity following the establishment of banana plantations in Honduras, see Standley (1931).
15   For a general discussion of the correlation between plant density and disease incidence, see Mundt (1990).

inroads in Costa Rica and Surinam. Epidemics broke out in Honduras and Guatemala during the 1920s, and in Jamaica during the 1930s.

Figure 7.1. Twentieth-Century Banana-Producing Regions in Central America and United Fruit Company Trading Routes

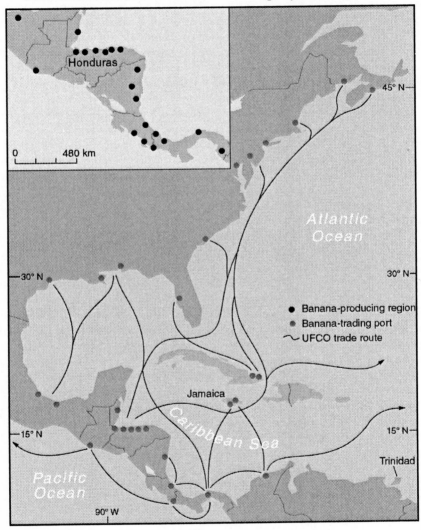

Sources: United Fruit Company (1931); West and Augelli (1976), p. 389.

As early as 1910 some scientists suggested that the long-term solution to Panama disease lay in finding a banana variety with resistance to the pathogen. A US researcher based in Cuba recommended cultivating the 'Chinese banana', a Cavendish variety (AAA) grown and traded in Asia, Hawaii and the Canary Islands.[16] That same year, United Fruit provided the Dutch government in Surinam with a Cavendish cultivar known as 'Congo'. However, only modest amounts of Congo bananas reached US consumers before United Fruit informed Dutch officials that the fruit was not marketable due to the variety's comparatively short shelf life and its tendency to ripen unevenly.[17] The experience in Surinam would be repeated over the next decade in Central America and the Caribbean. During the 1920s, United Fruit and its principal competitors exported small quantities of Lacatan bananas, a Cavendish cultivar from the Philippines, but the fruit failed to find a mass market due to resistance on the part of wholesalers and consumers who complained about its ripening colour, flavour and texture.[18] In 1924 a researcher in Jamaica reported on efforts to cultivate other Cavendish cultivars including Bumulan, Robusta and Bout Rond.[19] However, Cavendish varieties failed to find a market because the structures and aesthetic sensibilities of mass markets in the United States had evolved around Gros Michel bananas. The myriad varieties of *Musa* found in tropical regions were not a viable alternative in the minds of most US shippers, jobbers, retailers and consumers. The rigidity of mass markets and the banana's peculiar biology would place significant constraints on twentieth-century banana breeding projects.

Institutional Breeding Programmes, 1920s–1940s

In 1922 the British government founded the West Indian Agricultural College (later renamed Imperial College of Tropical Agriculture) in Trinidad. The following year, E.E. Cheesman joined the college faculty and initiated a banana-breeding programme. The British established a second banana research operation in Jamaica in 1924. Plant materials, including seeds and accessions were initially supplied by colonial officers stationed in tropical regions. In the mid-1920s, the British government financed two collecting expeditions to South Asia.[20] Around the same time, the United Fruit Company initiated breeding experiments on the Caribbean coast of Panama. Between 1925 and 1927 the company sponsored a banana col-

16 McKenney (1910).
17 Fawcett (1921 [1913]), pp. 230–4.
18 For an extended discussion of the problems associated with marketing the Lacatan during the 1920s, see Soluri (2002).
19 Ashby (1924).
20 Howes (1928), p. 305.

lecting trip conducted by Dr Otto A. Reinking who travelled extensively in South and South-east Asia. Reinking visited markets and homegardens in order to find a Panama disease-resistant variety whose fruit resembled that of Gros Michel. He appears to have concentrated his efforts on finding Cavendish-type bananas and other triploids.[21] Evidence suggests that this initial period of banana breeding involved a significant level of co-operation between United Fruit and the Imperial College. For example, before departing for Asia in 1925 a British researcher visited United Fruit's laboratory in Panama where he viewed the company's collection and exchanged ideas about breeding strategies.[22]

The first generation of scientific breeders undertook their experiments possessing limited knowledge about the cytology, genetics and taxonomy of the genus *Musa*.[23] However, researchers were well aware of one critical trait shared by Gros Michel and most other banana cultivars: the plants are parthenocarpic, meaning that they do not have to be fertilised by pollen in order to produce fruit. As a result, their fruit tends to be seedless, a trait for which human cultivators presumably selected over the course of centuries. As a consequence, banana cultivars reproduce themselves through vegetative propagation, or 'cloning', a trait that has facilitated their production by small-scale cultivators who benefit by not having to invest labour time replanting their fields on an annual basis.[24] The seed-free fruit pulp has also contributed to the enduring and widespread popularity of bananas across cultures.

But, parthenocarpy posed a major challenge to plant breeders who struggled to obtain seeds and pollen from the highly infertile Gros Michel. Banana breeding was possible only because Gros Michel plants could be induced to set seeds in small numbers using pollen from 'wild' (i.e., seeded) bananas(Figure 7.2). Claude Wardlaw's description of crossing experiments carried out at the Imperial College during the 1920s conveys the challenge that the banana's biology presented to scientists.[25] Pollination trials were carried out with six varieties of bananas, including the Gros Michel. Edible varieties were crossed when possible but due to their low pollen production, many crosses were made with two seed-bearing species.

---

21 Rowe and Richardson (1975), pp. 7–8.
22 Correspondence between Otto A. Reinking and John R. Johnston, 1924–27, Fundación Hondureña de Investigación Agrícola (hereafter FHIA), La Lima, Honduras, Guarumas Files, Folder Reinking, O.A., Banana Variety Correspondence, 1924–27.
23 Shepherd (1974), p. 482.
24 Farmers in the tropics never plant banana 'seed' *per se*. Instead, they plant rhizome material (i.e., bulbs) that over time send out lateral shoots, which, in the absence of pruning, develop into new banana plants. Export growers prune most of these shoots, or suckers, leaving one or two to mature into a fruit-bearing plant.
25 Wardlaw (1935), p. 116.

About 20,000 pollinated flowers yielded fewer than 200 seeds, 50 of which were empty. The remaining seeds came from just two varieties, Gros Michel and Silk (AAB); all had been pollinated by one of the seeded varieties. Only 17 seeds germinated and a mere five survived to the fruit-bearing stage. The work of early banana breeding, therefore, was tedious and full of uncertainty. It was also fairly expensive: maintaining experiments with giant herbaceous plants required rather large plots of land.

Figure 7.2: Banana with Seed

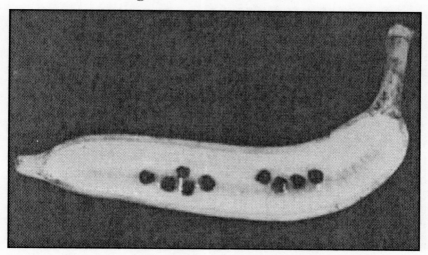

Source: Rowe and Richardson (1975), p. 15.

British researchers adopted three strategies in order to breed for disease resistance: repeated crosses of the triploid Gros Michel with a range of resistant 'male' diploids; repeated crosses using specific male parents on a range of triploids; and backcrossing tetraploid hybrids with their parents. Only the first strategy succeeded in producing progeny that potentially possessed the requisite phenotype (i.e., resistance to Panama disease and marketing qualities similar to the Gros Michel).[26] Diploids tended to possess disease resistance, but their fruits often diverged significantly from the morphology, size and colour of Gros Michel fruit. Therefore, British

---

26   Researchers attributed this to a genetic abnormality: when crossed with diploids, Gros Michel did not undergo normal meiosis, but instead contributed an unreduced triploid gamete. The diploid pollinators, on the other hand, underwent meiosis thus yielding tetraploid hybrids (Rowe, 1984, p. 140).

breeders began to focus on crossing diploids with diploids in order to create hybrid lines with 'improved' fruit quality that could subsequently be crossed with Gros Michel. This approach would dominate banana breeding during the twentieth century.[27]

Figure 7.3: Fruit Jobbers Suspending Gros Michel Bunches in Ripening Room

Source: United Fruit Company (1931), p. 16.

Imperial College breeders created two promising varieties in the early 1930s — the IC1 and the IC2 — that after six years of testing showed resistance to Panama disease.[28] The ripening behavior of the IC1 was said to be similar to that of Gros Michel. British researcher Wardlaw described the hybrid's other important qualities: 'The colour when ripe was excellent, the flavour pleasing but probably an acquired taste while the texture was noticeably delicate'.[29] As for the shipping qualities, Wardlaw noted that the fingers resisted bruising and mechanical injury and possessed a bunch symmetry 'similar to the Gros Michel and such as to make for easy storage under the usual trade conditions'. However, the major 'commercial disad-

27   Ortiz, Ferris and Vuylsteke (1995), pp. 112–3.
28   Wardlaw (1935), p. 116.
29   *Ibid.*, p. 118.

vantage' was that the fruit occasionally bore seeds when grown under 'ordinary banana-field conditions'. Wardlaw's assessment of the IC1 reveals the extent to which the Gros Michel phenotype set the market standard for export bananas; hybrid fruit that did not closely approximate that of the Gros Michel would not be considered for commercial production.

A 1929 United Fruit bulletin reveals that the company's breeding objectives differed little from those of the British programme. The bulletin's author, J.H. Permar, noting the continued inability to find a practical cure for Panama disease under 'existing cultural conditions', considered the possibility of breeding a disease-resistant banana with the characteristics of Gros Michel to be 'well worth considerable effort'.[30] Experiments carried out by the company between 1925 and 1928 crossed banana varieties with distinct chromosome counts 'which when combined might be expected to produce the chromosome counts [i.e., 33] of the edible, commercial varieties'.[31] The trials yielded 14 sterile varieties with edible, seedless fruit pulp. However, Permar lamented that the hybrids had little economic value since, 'in no case is their quality equal to the fruits that are generally recognised by the public as "bananas"'.[32] His assessment, like those of his British contemporaries, revealed the tension between biological variation and product standardisation that shaped the trajectory of banana breeding.

In 1930 United Fruit ended its breeding experiments in Panama and transferred its *Musa* collection to Lancetilla, the company's experimental garden in Tela, Honduras.[33] The move came at a time when the company was scaling back its operations on the Caribbean Coast of Panama in response to the spread of Panama disease and the Great Depression. In addition, the company's lack of success with marketing Lacatan fruit in the United States likely served to heighten scepticism about the ability to breed a marketable hybrid. Finally, United Fruit's management and stockholders had little reason to doubt that the company's vast land holdings and bulging cash reserves — the 1920s brought record rates of return — would ensure a supply of disease-free soils for the foreseeable future. From the vantage point of United Fruit's Boston-based management then, there was absolutely no reason to replace the cherished Gros Michel variety.[34]

Consequently, for the first half of the twentieth century, United Fruit — along with its primary competitors in Central America — adopted a strategy of abandoning diseased and/or low yielding soils and shifting

---

30   J.H. Permar, 'Banana Breeding,' *United Fruit Company Research Department Bulletin*, vol. 21 (1929), p. 1 (unpublished report held by FHIA Library).

31   *Ibid.*, pp. 2–3.

32   *Ibid.*, p. 13.

33   At the time, the collection consisted of 81 parthenocarpic cultivars, 27 seeded diploids and 26 plantains. See Rowe and Richardson (1975), p. 7.

34   On United Fruit's profit margins during the 1920s, see Dosal (1995).

UNIVERSITY OF WINCHESTER LIBRARY

production to locations with no previous history of banana cultivation. During the 1930s and 1940s Panama disease was a central factor in United Fruit's decision to abandon entire company divisions on the Caribbean coasts of Costa Rica and Panama. In Honduras the company closed down an entire division in the early 1940s. Its primary competitor, the Standard Fruit Company, also shifted its production dramatically, abandoning the Caribbean coast of Nicaragua and relocating its operations in Honduras. In general, export banana production in Central America shifted from the wet, Caribbean side of the isthmus to the Pacific coast. All told, prior to 1960 United Fruit abandoned at least 50,000 hectares of land in the Caribbean lowlands of Central America. Shifting plantation agriculture enabled the fruit companies to maintain overall production levels and reap profits, but it also perpetuated the spread of Panama disease and recurring cycles of deforestation, monocultural production and abandonment.[35]

The seemingly endless supply of banana lands available to United Fruit contrasted sharply with conditions in the British Caribbean where both capital and land were scarce. This difference, along with the rapid advance of Panama disease in Jamaica during the 1930s, helps to explain why the British continued to support breeding programmes throughout the 1930s and 1940s.[36] The need for disease-resistant varieties became even greater during the 1930s when a second epidemic, Sigatoka, or leaf spot disease, struck the Caribbean and Central America. The airborne pathogen (*Mycosphaerella musicola* Leach) associated with Sigatoka spread much more rapidly than the soil-dwelling fungus linked to Panama disease. Sigatoka-infected plants usually produced a mature fruit bunch, but the bananas grew soft and tended to ripen quickly — too quickly for the fruit to reach export markets in saleable condition. In 1936 United Fruit developed a control system that utilised high-volume applications of Bordeaux mixture (copper sulphate) applied by workers with high-pressure hoses. The system provided adequate protection when applied frequently (10 to 26 applications per year), but the capital- and labour-intensive process drove many small-scale producers out of the business and created a very unpleasant and potentially hazardous environment for field workers.[37]

In Jamaica, the effects of Sigatoka and Panama diseases, along with the Second World War's shipping restrictions, led to a sharp decline in banana cultivation from some 77,000 hectares in the mid-1930s to 24,000 hectares in 1947. By that point, Panama disease-free soils on the island had dwindled to the point where government banana breeders struggled to main-

35 The social effects of the cycle included acute local economic crises and elevated health risks for farm workers; see Marquardt (2001)and Soluri (2000).
36 Rodríquez (1955), pp. 18–19.
37 For a recent summary of Sigatoka disease, see Jones (2000), pp. 79–91. For the impact of the Bordeaux spray system on workers in Costa Rica, see Marquardt (2002).

tain disease-free populations for breeding experiments. However, important changes taking place in the British market enabled Jamaican banana production to recover. The foundation for the post-war market transition was laid in 1932, when the British government began to subsidise 'empire produced bananas' imported to the United Kingdom. Growers in Jamaica and the Windward Islands responded by rapidly dropping out of the US trade and reorienting toward the UK market. By 1938 Jamaica accounted for 83 per cent of the British banana supply.[38] The onset of the Second World War led to a suspension of banana imports into Britain and a concomitant drop in Jamaican production. Following the war, the British ministry of food became the sole importer of bananas. In 1947 the British government approved the shipment of Lacatan fruit, the Panama disease-resistant, Cavendish cultivar that had failed to find a market in the United States during the 1920s. Six years later, Lacatan bananas covered more than 40,000 hectares of farms in Jamaica.[39]

The end of the Gros Michel era in the British Caribbean, then, resulted not from a breakthrough in breeding but due to changes in the conditions under which bananas were produced and marketed. Dwindling amounts of suitable soils in Jamaica, combined with a rupture in market structures following the war-time intervention of the British government, enabled banana growers to turn to a well known variety in order to overcome at least some of their pathogen problems. In contrast, the United Fruit-dominated Central American industry continued to produce and export Gros Michel fruit into the 1950s.

Institutional Banana Breeding, 1950s–1980s

The post-war shift in market standards did not escape the attention of British banana breeders. In 1951 Norman Simmonds and his colleague Richard Baker noted that market acceptance of Cavendish cultivars such as Lacatan was compelling banana breeders to modify their criteria: 'now that the standards have fallen and Lacatan is acceptable to the trade, IC2 would in all probability prove a commercial success'. A breeding programme's 'minimal aims,' the authors added, 'can therefore be narrowed down to producing a banana as good as Lacatan but resistant to leaf-spot, or as resistant to disease as IC2 but better in quality. The "ideal banana" is still one with the characteristics of Gros Michel and resistance to both diseases.'[40]

In his 1959 monograph on bananas, Simmonds contrasted the shipping and marketing qualities of Lacatan and Gros Michel cultivars:

38   Grossman (1998), p. 38.
39   Rodríquez (1955), p. 19.
40   Baker and Simmonds (1951), p. 44.

At ripening, Gros Michel turns an excellent deep yellow, Lacatan a paler and less attractive colour — it will be remembered that tropically ripened fruit of members of the Cavendish group is distinctively green in colour. In flavour, Lacatan is not at all inferior to Gros Michel, as judged by tasting panels established in England some years ago to assess the results of trial shipments; this is true only of good quality, well-ripened fruit — doubtless the average quality of Lacatan ripened in England is lower than that of Gros Michel by reason of Lacatan's susceptibility to fungal wastage in transport. In texture, Gros Michel is (to most tastes) superior to Lacatan, having a slightly drier and more 'mealy break'.[41]

The comparison reveals the extent to which highly subjective aesthetic considerations shaped the work of banana breeders. Simmonds concluded that the Lacatan represented 'the irreducible minimum of quality in characters other than disease resistance'.[42] However, he also noted that consumer tastes could 'probably be educated' to accept varieties whose flavours and textures differed somewhat from that of Gros Michel. Simmonds therefore, recognised that consumer tastes were mutable, yet he retained a fixed notion of the ideal banana that would continue to shape banana breeding into the 1950s.

Following the end of the Second World War, a new Banana Research Scheme merged the Jamaica and Trinidad breeding programmes and provided funding for a collecting expedition to Asia. However, 'political considerations' in 1948 compelled the British research team to conduct a smaller survey in East Africa.[43] The trip yielded two diploid varieties that were soon incorporated into breeding trials. Six years later, the Colonial Office sponsored an expedition to South-east Asia and the western Pacific.[44] According to Simmonds, the trip had two principle objectives:

(1) to discover and collect wild and edible strains of *Musa acuminata* which, on the basis of bunch shape, fruit size, and disease resistance, might be of value in banana breeding; and (2) to amass all the scientific information about the bananas both wild and cultivated ... with a view both to improving fundamental knowledge of the group and to meeting future practical problems.[45]

These objectives reflected the British researchers' adherence to a breeding strategy based on crossing 'improved' diploid pollinators with Gros Michel

41   Simmonds (1962), p. 411.
42   *Ibid.*, p. 412.
43   This was not the first time that a banana collecting trip became entangled in geopolitics. Cheesman intended to tour Southeast Asia in 1939, but warfare in the Pacific forced him to cancel his trip.
44   Collecting was carried out in Australia, India, Malaysia, Papua New Guinea, Samoa and Thailand; Indonesia and Burma were left off the itinerary on 'political grounds' (Simmonds, 1956, p. 251).
45   *Ibid.*, p. 252.

in order to produce tetraploids. Consequently, the main objective of the 1954 expedition was to find both seeded and seedless varieties of *M. acuminata* that could help to improve the quality of the diploid pollinators used to fertilise the Gros Michel.[46]

Simmonds collected specimens of *Musa* from a wide range of environments including mountains, river valleys, foothills, savannas and forests. He reported a tendency to find *Musa* in open areas such as deforested valleys, sunny hillsides and riverbanks. The eight-month trip yielded *Musa acuminata* specimens from Samoa, Queensland, Papua New Guinea and Malaysia. However, collecting germplasm in South-east Asia was one thing; transplanting it in Caribbean soils was quite another. The seeds and suckers travelled to Trinidad via Kew Gardens, where they were studied and quarantined before being shipped to the Caribbean. By 1956 more than half of the collection had arrived at the Imperial College, but many of the plants did not adapt to their new environment. For example, Simmonds described the status of some seedless diploids from Malaysia and Papua New Guinea as 'very variable'. Some were 'excellent', but 'many' died and still others were susceptible to Sigatoka disease. Most of the samples collected at high altitudes appeared to be 'ill adapted' to lowland environments. There was nothing unusual about the mixed fate of the accessions collected by Simmonds; introduced *Musa* species often failed to thrive in Caribbean environments: by 1960, 585 specimen introductions had been registered in Imperial College's collection, but only 60 distinct cultivars survived.[47] That same year, the British government shifted its entire banana-breeding programme to Jamaica, bringing to a close 38 years of activity at the Imperial College in Trinidad.

Meanwhile, in Central America, the US fruit companies' shifting plantation agriculture had reached its practical limits. In Honduras, then the world's leading exporter of bananas, United Fruit abandoned more than 16,000 hectares between 1939 and 1953.[48] Faced with an impending shortage of pathogen-free soils, company engineers undertook large-scale 'land reclamation' projects that employed an extensive series of dykes along the Ulúa River to divert silt-laden flood waters to wetlands where the silt eventually settled, forming new soils (Figure 7.4). One of the largest silting projects undertaken

---

46   Although Cavendish cultivars succeeded in entering British markets, they did not replace Gros Michel in breeding experiments because they were sterile and seldom produced seeds when crossed with diploids.

47   In a 1974 paper the director of the Banana Breeding Research Scheme in Jamaica noted that researchers succeeded in establishing '[r]ather little' of the Southeast Asian material. The losses resulted from several factors, including the failure of more than half of the seeds to germinate. Other introductions succumbed to Panama disease, low altitudes and the dry season in Trinidad. See Shepherd (1974), p. 484.

48   United Fruit Company, Division of Tropical Research, Annual Reports (1939–53); unpublished reports held by the FHIA Library.

was a 4,500 hectare site known as El Pantano.[49] The first stage consisted of building levees, the longest of which extended almost five miles and was capable of holding water to a depth of three to four metres. In 1947 the company drained the land using a battery of turbine-driven pumps to remove standing water and to ensure that groundwater did not rise to unacceptable levels, no easy task in a lowland area situated between two rivers.

Figure 7.4: United Fruit Company Banana Plantation under Flood Fallow, Sula Valley, Honduras, 1949

Source: United Fruit Company Photograph Collection, Baker Library, Harvard Business School.

United Fruit also implemented large scale 'flood fallowing' projects that attempted to drown soil pathogen populations. Company engineers oversaw the construction of artificial lakes that were filled with water for several months prior to being drained and replanted with disease-free Gros Michel rhizomes. By 1953 some 5,700 hectares in Honduras had undergone the flood fallow process.[50] The El Pantano project and flood fallowing revealed United Fruit's engineering prowess, but also the rising costs and heightened ecological impacts associated with growing Gros Michel

49   Graham S. Quate, Tegucigalpa, 'The Agricultural Operations of the Tela RR Company,' 17 September 1947, pp. 6–8, United States National Archives, US .Foreign Agricultural Service, Narrative Reports, 1946–49, Box 743, Folder 'Finance-Fruits'.
50   Stover (1962), p. 96; United Fruit Company (1958), pp. 4–6.

on former wetlands that had once sustained a variety of flora and fauna.[51] The company's financial resources, combined with its access to subsidised soil and water resources, enabled it to extend the commercial life of Gros Michel several years after growers in the British Caribbean converted their farms to Cavendish varieties.

In fact, the first company to adopt resistant varieties in Central America was Standard Fruit. By the late 1940s, Standard Fruit was annually losing 10 to 15 per cent of its productive land in Honduras. In 1947 company executives decided to lease about 7,500 hectares of government land located in the Aguán River Valley for flood fallowing, but they halted the project in the early 1950s due to its high costs.[52] At that point, Standard Fruit decided to concentrate on finding a disease resistant banana that could replace Gros Michel. The company had been testing varieties since the mid-1940s, when it initiated trials with the IC2 (supplied by the Imperial College), the Bout Rond (a Cavendish variety that Simmonds considered to be the same as Lacatan), and the Giant Cavendish (a Cavendish cultivar from Brazil).[53] Standard shipped modest quantities of the IC2 between 1944 and 1954, but the hybrid's small fruit bunches and short-fingered bananas found little acceptance in US markets, a result that must have disappointed Simmonds and his colleagues at the Imperial College.

Standard Fruit officials were more excited about the marketing potential of Bout Rond and Giant Cavendish. Although they admitted that neither variety ripened in the manner of Gros Michel, company executives noted that the fruits of both varieties developed 'very nicely' when ripened at proper temperatures and exposed to ethylene gas.[54] Initially, Standard's Cavendish exports faced high rates of rejection and discounting in US markets due to the ease with which its delicate peel bruised. However, the company overcame this problem through a technological innovation: packing bananas in cardboard boxes prior to shipping from the tropics. On-farm boxing cut down on rejection rates and helped to ensure a market for Cavendish bananas. By 1958 Standard Fruit had completed its conversion to Panama

51   For a description of the impacts on local flora and fauna of wetland drainage, see Peters (1929), pp. 397–9.
52   Standard Fruit Company, 'Memorandum of conference held in the board room on the afternoon of January 3, 1947, for discussion of various matters concerning our Honduras and Nicaragua Divisions,' p. 1, Tulane University, Howard-Tilton Memorial Library, Standard Fruit and Steamship Company Papers, Box 8, Folder 26; and Henry O. Muery, 'Historical Overview,' typed manuscript, 17 May 1984, p. 1. I thank José P. Sanchez of La Ceiba, Honduras, for providing me with a copy of this unpublished account of Standard Fruit's research activities.
53   Hord (1966), pp. 269–75. On the Bout Rond, see Simmonds (1954), pp. 126–30.
54   P.C. Rose to S.D. Antoni, 24 September 1943, and A.J. Chute to P.C. Rose, 6 May 1944, Tulane University, Howard-Tilton Memorial Library, Standard Fruit and Steamship Company Papers, Box 8, Folders 14–15.

disease-resistant varieties. The company subsequently converted all of its farms to Giant Cavendish because the variety was higher yielding and less susceptible to wind damage than the Bout Rond.[55]

United Fruit continued to grow and export Gros Michel fruit through-out the 1950s, but by the middle of the decade nearly 50 per cent of the company's Honduran production came from flood fallow land, an indication that disease-free soils were becoming scarce. In addition, enthusiasm for flood fallowing began to wane when company researchers reported that treated soils yielded only five years of decent production before Panama disease reappeared.[56] In 1957 United Fruit's director of research noted that the company could no longer 'avoid problems by moving to new land'.[57] Two years later, the company's head plant pathologist wrote that banana breeding was 'the only hopeful long-term approach to the solution of the banana disease problem'.[58] That same year, the research division added a department of 'Plant Breeding and Genetics'.[59]

One of the first actions taken by the new department was to increase its collection of breeding material. The company enlisted the aid of tropical botanists Paul Allen and J.J. Ochse to lead trips to South-east Asia and the western Pacific to gather Musa germplasm.[60] The company assigned the Dutch-speaking Ochse to Indonesia, a region in which he had worked for decades (Ochse assisted Reinking's collecting work in the 1920s). Paul Allen initiated his collecting in the Philippines where he received logistical support from the College of Agriculture at Los Baños. Two months into the trip, Dorothy Allen — Paul's wife and a botanical illustrator — joined her husband.[61] Seldom acknowledged in scientific publications, Dorothy Allen played an important role in documenting, cleaning, packing and shipping the accessions. In a letter to Wilson Popenoe, Paul Allen described their work in the Philippines as a 'river-by-river, mountain-by-mountain and island-by-island search' in order to assemble a comprehensive collection of accessions for breeding purposes.[62] He added that after

55   'Giant Cavendish' was a misnomer; the plant was shorter than Gros Michel and Bout Rond.
56   Stover (1962), pp. 97.
57   United Fruit Company, 'Research meetings: summary of discussions and reports,' 29–31 August 1957, p. 4, FHIA Pamphlet 6603.
58   United Fruit Company, Division of Tropical Research, *Research Extension Newsletter*, vol. 6, no. 4 (November 1959), p. 10.
59   United Fruit Company, Division of Tropical Research, Annual Report (1959).
60   Rosales, Arnaud and Coto (1999), p. v.
61   See Dorothy Allen to Wilson Popenoe, 25 February 1961, Hunt Institute for Botanical Documentation Archive (hereafter HIBD Archive, Pittsburgh, Pennsylvania), Wilson Popenoe Collection, Correspondence.
62   Paul Allen to Wilson Popenoe, 21 February 1960, HIBD Archive, Wilson Popenoe Collection, Correspondence.

five months of collecting in the Philippines, he and his companions had recorded some 500 common names for bananas! The Allens spent eight months in the Philippines before travelling to Malaysia and Indonesia. All told, United Fruit's collectors spent 27 months sampling, processing and shipping *Musa* specimens.

As was the case with Simmonds's fieldwork, Paul Allen collected specimens from a range of landscapes, but he appears to have had the most success in and around human settlements. For example, in a letter describing his initial findings in the Philippines, Allen noted that bananas 'tend to replace our [Central American] Heliconias in the ecological scheme, and are seldom found anywhere except on cleared land and near people'.[63] He added that 'Unusual banana varieties are often spotted in back yards and must be purchased almost always through the aid of a single or sometimes double translation'.[64] Several months later, his team travelled to Kuala Lumpur, Malaysia 'where they collected so many seeds and bits it nearly floored us all caring for the material'.[65] Allen also visited Malay indigenous communities in his quest for *Musa* cultivars. In Dutch New Guinea, Ochse's team 'looked through the backyards of the Papuans' for signs of novel varieties. Elsewhere in Indonesia, John Womersley (a botanist enlisted to assist Allen after Ochse failed to live up to expectations) walked through Kampong gardens, paying local people for permission to take *Musa* specimens of interest. These descriptions of the botanising carried out by United Fruit-sponsored collectors lack precision, but they strongly suggest that *Musa* varieties were most often found in places — including urban areas like Kuala Lumpur — shaped by human activities.[66] In other words, the banana cultivars assembled by Allen were as much (agri)cultural artefacts as they were biological resources.

While the Allens were travelling through South-east Asia, changes taking place in the Americas prompted a shake up of United Fruit. By 1959 the conjuncture of increased rates of Panama disease, a glutted market for bananas (created in part by the dramatic rise in exports from Ecuador), escalating labour costs and legal troubles at home produced a sharp reduction in United Fruit's annual earnings and stock value.[67] As the decade

63   *Ibid.*
64   Paul Allen to Putnam Payne, Los Baños, 1 November 1959, FHIA Guarumas Files, Folder 37/2.
65   Dorothy Allen to Wilson Popenoe, 25 February 1961, HIBD Archives, Popenoe Collection, Correspondence.
66   See respectively, Paul Allen to Dr I.Y. Carey, Kuala Lumpur [no date], Folder 22/2; Nader Vakili to Putnam Payne, Holandia, New Guinea, 5 October 1960, Folder 16/2; and John S. Womersley, 5 March 1960, Folder 22/3; FHIA Guarumas Files.
67   Between 1950 and 1960, earnings fell from US$66 million to US$2 million and share prices plummeted from US$70 to US$15. Over the same period, banana exports from Ecuador increased from eight million bunches to about 36 million. See Simmonds (1962), p. 324.

came to a close, Thomas Sunderland replaced long-time company executive Kenneth Redmond as chief executive officer.[68] Noting that Panama disease was costing the company millions of dollars a year, Sunderland wasted little time before calling for increased production of Cavendish-type bananas.[69] In 1960 United Fruit's research department reported that no further experiments would be conducted with Gros Michel; the department's energies shifted to testing various Cavendish cultivars (including Giant Cavendish, Valery and Grand Nain) for disease resistance and ability to ship in cardboard boxes. Three years later, the company had 4,500 hectares planted in Valery bananas and 29 boxing plants in Honduras.[70]

By 1965 United Fruit had converted all of its Central American production to Panama disease-resistant varieties. As had been the case with both growers in the British Caribbean and the Standard Fruit Company, United Fruit eventually overcame the problem of Panama disease by modifying its production practices in order to plant Cavendish cultivars from the Asian tropics.[71] After decades of profiting from a production system that severely reduced plant diversity on a regional scale, United Fruit took advantage of the pan-tropical diversity within the *Musa* genus in order to overcome one of its most enduring production problems.

In 1961 Paul Allen returned to Honduras where he devoted two years to the daunting task of cataloguing and studying the 700 accessions that his team had collected.[72] The collection included *Musa* from at least 17 countries, but the vast majority came from just four: Indonesia, Malaysia, Papua New Guinea and the Philippines. Between 1965 and 1975 United Fruit breeders, working with one of the largest collections of *Musa* in the world, developed an 'elite' line of diploids that possessed both disease resistance and agronomic and aesthetic qualities that began to approach those found in commercial varieties.[73] One particularly promising hybrid diploid resulted from crosses made with accessions from Papua New

---

68   Arthur, Houck and Beckford (1968), p. 146.
69   *Ibid.*, p. 150.
70   Tela Railroad Company (1964), p. 2. FHIA Library, Pamphlet 6644.
71   Otto Reinking collected Valery plants in 1925 while travelling in Saigon. Rowe and Richardson (1975), pp. 7–8.
72   Paul Allen died in 1963. Paul Allen to Wilson Popenoe, 3 Dec. 1961, HIBD Archive, Paul H. Allen Papers, Box 2. The total number of accessions grew to 850 in 1964 before it was revised downward to 574 following a 1970 review of the collection. United Fruit breeders Philip Rowe and D.L. Richardson attributed the reduction to the toll taken by plant diseases and the elimination of duplicate specimens.
73   Identifying disease resistance among diploids proved to be relatively easy: researchers found resistance to fusarium races 1 and 2 and Sigatoka in *M. acuminata* subspecies *malaccensis* and *burmannica*. Burrowing nematode resistance was found in *Pisang jari buaya* group of *M. acuminata*. Many of the cultivars produced small bunches of fruit or failed in some other way to meet market standards.

Guinea, Java, Malaysia and the Philippines —another example of how commercial breeders in Central America utilised the diversity of *Musa* found throughout the tropical world.[74] Company breeders subsequently used the hybrid diploids in crosses with Highgate, a Gros Michel dwarf mutant found in Jamaica, and other triploids.

The industry-wide conversion to boxed Cavendish varieties led to a redefinition of what constituted an ideal export banana. The need for disease resistance remained crucial, but the list of pathogens and pests expanded to include two strains of Panama disease in addition to Sigatoka, bacterial wilt (*Pseudomonas solanacearum*) and burrowing nematodes (*Radopholus similis*).[75] The 1960s were also marked by heightened emphases on increasing yields, reducing losses due to wind damage and retailing blemish-free bananas. The aesthetics of standardisation became even more exacting and led to a sharp increase in the use of irrigation water, fertilisers and an array of pesticides (Figure 7.5). Ironically, the new standards rendered obsolete some of the hybrids produced by breeding programmes in the 1960s that might have been accepted on export markets in the pre-Cavendish era. For example, United Fruit breeders produced a Panama and Sigatoka disease-resistant tetraploid plant that produced Gros Michel-like fruit, but researchers did not consider the hybrid to be commercially viable on account of its comparatively tall stature and low yields. Company breeders created other tetraploids that outyielded many Cavendish varieties, but the hybrids tended to have short shelf lives or other characteristics considered to be marketing defects.

The British programme in Jamaica achieved similar results during this period. Researchers carried out extensive breeding trials using Highgate and a synthesised diploid whose lineage included some of the accessions collected by Simmonds in Borneo, India, Malaysia, Samoa and Zanzibar.[76] The crosses produced several tetraploids that possessed resistance to Panama disease and Sigatoka. Taste panels found tetraploid bananas to be comparable in flavour to Cavendish fruit, but they had a shelf life that was considerably shorter than that deemed necessary to be a commercial success on British markets. Nearly 60 years after the founding of a British breeding programme in the Caribbean, an export-quality, disease-resistant hybrid remained an elusive goal.

In 1984 the management of United Brands (formerly United Fruit), apparently frustrated that 25 years of breeding had failed to yield a commercially successful cultivar, donated its breeding programme to the Fundación Hondureña de Investigación Agrícola (FHIA) in La Lima,

---

74   Rowe and Richardson (1975), p. 28.
75   The spread of Black Sigatoka in Honduras in the mid-1970s added yet another pathogen to the list; see Rowe and Richardson (1975), pp. 22–7.
76   Simmonds (1962), pp. 421–2.

Honduras. Supported by international donor agencies, FHIA's research agenda expanded to include breeding varieties of bananas and plantains consumed by people living in the tropics. In the 1990s, the breeding programme at FHIA started to yield tangible results building on past decades' efforts to improve diploids. Today, a handful of FHIA tetraploid hybrids, including one with resistance to both Panama disease and Black Sigatoka, are being produced for domestic markets in Brazil, the Caribbean and Central America. Cavendish cultivars continue to dominate US mass markets.[77]

Figure 7.5: Inspection of Boxed Cavendish Bananas

Source: *Baltimore Sun*, 14 June 1962; copy from Henry B. Arthur Papers, Harvard Business School Archives.

---

77   For recent developments in both 'conventional breeding' and emerging genetic engineering programmes, see Rowe and Rosales (2000) and Sági (2000).

People, Plants and the Boundaries of Environmental History

The history of twentieth-century banana breeding is most noteworthy for what 80 years of scientific efforts failed to produce: an export quality, disease-resistant hybrid. The strange condition of seedless fruit, combined with international markets' preference for Gros Michel bananas, prevented the introduction of disease-resistant varieties for 40 years, a delay that had significant consequences for tropical landscapes and livelihoods. Export banana production reduced biological diversity at local and regional levels: thousands of hectares of lowland forests and wetlands — along with their resident flora and fauna — disappeared, replaced by banana monocultures and related infrastructure. When banana growers finally replaced Gros Michel, they did not plant hybrids; instead, they planted Cavendish varieties with long cultivation histories in South-east Asia. In a very real sense, the roots of modern export banana production in the Caribbean and Latin America extend across continents into a pre-modern past.

The story of export bananas illustrates how tracing the movement of plants across continents and cultures raises new possibilities for linking the histories of tropical peoples and places in precise and meaningful ways.[78] It also opens up novel ways to understand the historical agency of non-literate, politically marginal cultivators who over the course of centuries nurtured the plant resources that have been appropriated by states and companies bent on the mass production and consumption of commodities. The challenge for researchers studying Latin American agro-export commodities, then, is to integrate transnational frameworks with evidence harvested from the local places where people-plant ties have been made, severed and refashioned. In so doing, we can begin to formulate new explanatory models of the region's past whilst simultaneously redefining the geographical and conceptual boundaries of 'Latin American' environmental history.

78　The pioneering work in this area is Crosby (1972). For an example of nineteenth- and twentieth-century Pacific exchanges, see Tyrell (1999).

CHAPTER 8

Zebu's Elbows: Cattle Breeding and the Environment in Central Brazil, 1890–1960[*]

Robert W. Wilcox

Close observers of the Brazilian livestock industry witnessed a transition in attitudes toward cattle ranching and its relationship with the environment in the late twentieth century. As ranching in the Amazon Basin at the time received its share of legitimate criticism from inside and outside the country, several interests responded by attempting to address some of the business's more egregious aspects and its impact on the environment. In addition to laws regulating pasture burning and serious enforcement of the 1964 Forest Code that requires some ranch land to be maintained in forest reserves, both of which had mixed results, one non-governmental response was the creation of the so-called '*boi ecológico*', or ecological steer. While a part of the organic agricultural movement in various countries of the world, in Brazil such an exotic beast was new and was promoted primarily by the Associação Brasileira de Criadores de Zebú (ABCZ) in Uberaba, Minas Gerais. In breeding terms it is the zebu, the most ubiquitous cattle grazing Brazilian pastures today (Figure 8.1; Figure 8.2; Figure 8.3).

While debate is inevitable over the applicability of 'ecological' to any breed of cattle, the rationale behind its promotion lay primarily in the desire to enter or expand access to the international meat market, especially in the European Union and the United States. This marketing priority was nothing new to the Brazilian cattle industry, since it was this that drove the expansion of ranching into the Amazon Basin, in large part facilitated by the availability of government subsidies. In virtually all cases, the animals involved were zebu.[1]

[*]   Many thanks to the numerous persons and organisations who kindly provided their help and expertise to make the research and writing of this chapter possible. In Brazil I am especially indebted to the staffs of EMBRAPA–Gado de Corte, Campo Grande, Mato Grosso do Sul, the Museu do Zebú, Uberaba, Minas Gerais, and Senhora Elza Gonçalves Dória Passos and Doutor Abílio Leite de Barros in Campo Grande. Research would not have been possible without the generous funding of the Social Sciences and Humanities Research Council of Canada, and Northern Kentucky University sabbatical and project grants.
[1]   For some information on the impact of ranching on the Amazon rainforest, see the various articles in Schmink and Wood (1984) and Parsons (1993).

Figure 8.1: Cattle Movements and Vegetation in Mato Grosso do Sul, Brazil

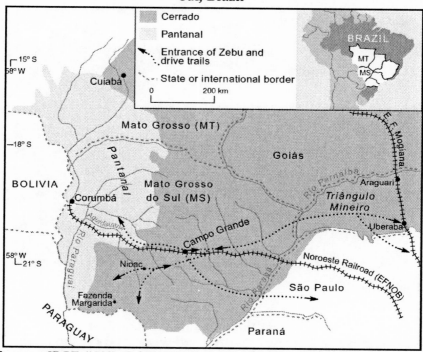

Sources: IBGE (1993); Galvão (1960), p. 120; Abreu (1976), p. 214.

Zebu often were touted as 'ecological' thanks to reliance on natural grass in their diet, which produces a lean meat with no residues of chemicals or agrotoxins. There was also the argument that avoidance of the application of growth hormones and antibiotics to the animals, and the absence of marbled flesh, make zebu meat healthier for consumers. And the identification of BSE (*Bovine spongiform encephalopathy* or 'mad cow' disease) and return of foot-and-mouth disease to Europe in the late 1990s and 2001 caused a significant increase in the demand for organic beef. In addition, raising animals on extensive or semi-extensive properties arguably had minimal impact on ranching ecosystems. In other words, the zebu was considered a 'healthy' animal that satisfied both the health and environmental concerns of European and US consumers.[2]

2 Santos (2000), pp. 392, 401; Gonçalves (2001a; 2001b). According to Gonçalves, even Conservation International, the environmental organisation, in partnership with other interests such as the Bank of Brazil and the International Development Bank, among others, supports several ranches in raising organic beef in the Pantanal of Mato Grosso do Sul.

Figure 8.2: Award-Winning Specimen of Zebu Heifer (Nellore), ABCZ National Exposition, Uberaba, Minas Gerais, 2001

Author's photo.

Figure 8.3: Zebu Bull, Londrina, Paraná, July 2002

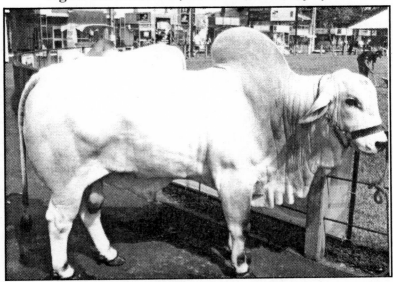

Photograph by Christian Brannstrom

Deliberate breeding of all livestock has been an integral part of cattle raising in the Americas since at least the nineteenth century, and while breed
selection based on environmental conditions has been a part of this from
the beginning, only rarely has breeding entered into environmental debates
over ranching, whether in terms of ranching's ecological impact or the
influence the environment has had on ranching practices. Key to successful breeding are the environmental conditions that determine choice of
breed and the impact of adoption on the local ecosystem. Combined with
breeding, familiar aspects of ranching such as introduction of planted
grasses, fencing, provision of dietary supplements and animal health care,
where applied with solely business outcomes in mind, often lead to unin-
tended consequences for regional ecosystems and the broader environment. This dynamic, which I call 'zebu's elbows', is the focus on this essay.
I have chosen Mato Grosso do Sul and the distinctive humped-back zebu
cattle because zebu, primarily the pure white Nellore, is dominant in Brazil,
with the exception of Rio Grande do Sul. Historically southern Mato
Grosso, by 2000 Mato Grosso do Sul hosted the largest beef herd in the
country, over 20 million head of almost exclusively zebu.[3]

The Zebu Revolution

Although often perceived in Brazil and most of the western world as a different breed from European-origin cattle, zebu is effectively a distinct species
that reproduces readily with non-zebu cattle. The European-origin animal is
classified as *Bos taurus taurus* or *Bos taurus* and is recognised to have developed
in southern Europe, although its initial origin was probably west Asia or
northern Africa. Zebu, native to the Indian subcontinent, and classified as
either *Bos taurus indicus* or *Bos indicus*, developed separately, although likely
from similar obscure origins.[4] This discussion will follow the Brazilian prac-

3   Instituto Brasileiro de Geografia e Estatística (IBGE) figures for 1997, as quoted in
     Santos (2000), p. 33. I draw the concept of elbows from Evan Eisenberg's (1998, p.
     8) insightful discussion of the necessity of teamwork among humans and their
     domesticates in expansion into ecosystems. Mato Grosso do Sul was created in 1979
     out of the state of Mato Grosso. Historically, cattle ranching dominated in the south-
     ern part of that state. Brazil has the second-largest bovine herd in the world and is
     the biggest beef raiser in history, with potentially over 160 million head in produc-
     tion. While most of the animals are zebu, it should be noted that the southern state
     of Rio Grande do Sul, until recently Brazil's major cattle region and where European
     breeds and breeding have dominated since the colonial period, has not hosted zebu
     to the same extent as most other regions due to its temperate climate. For an excel-
     lent discussion of this issue and much more, see Bell (1998).

4   Santiago (1985), pp. 8, 12–5. If we accept the more common classifications of *Bos
     taurus* and *Bos indicus*, zebu is a distinct species from the European-origin animal, while
     the different variations within each species are varieties or breeds. For the sake of
     consistency, I will maintain common usage of the term 'breed' to refer to zebu.

tice of calling the Asiatic animal 'zebu', the name allegedly of French origin, which was in turn probably borrowed and corrupted from Tibetan.[5]

There is no record of when the first zebu entered Brazil, but evidence indicates that such entry occurred regularly, if uncontrolled, during the colonial era. Some have speculated that the first were imported during the slave trade with Africa, but Brazil also had irregular contact with Portuguese colonies in India (Goa) and East Asia (Macao), where varieties of zebu reigned supreme. Nevertheless, most cattle were imported from Portugal itself, and those few zebu that did enter Brazil were soon absorbed into the national herd through natural crossbreeding, losing their identifying characteristics, particularly the hump behind the neck. Only in the late nineteenth century did the importation of zebu become an organised effort.[6]

Alberto Santiago has recorded several imports of zebu through the nineteenth and into the twentieth century, noting that until the 1870s there was no organisation and isolated animals, breeder pairs, or small groups came to the country more by chance than by design and had minimal impact on cattle raising in the country. Still, some observers did note their rapid adaptability to the Brazilian tropical or semi-tropical milieu, prompting a few ranchers in Rio de Janeiro in the 1870s, driven by a growing need for hardier draught animals in the coffee plantations and in part by periodic fresh meat shortages in the capital, to begin commercial importation from India. Over the next two decades several lots of animals were imported into Brazil. Exact numbers are unknown, but probably no more than a few dozen animals actually entered the country during this time. The impact on ranching was slight, at least initially, but by the 1880s ranchers began to notice the adaptability of zebu in an unlikely region of the country.[7]

Over the course of the late eighteenth and early nineteenth centuries, ranching had spread into the far western panhandle of Minas Gerais, the 'Triângulo Mineiro' (Figure 8.1). This is a plateau region of abundant natural grasses, but its climatic extremes of wet summers and dry winters

5   Norris (1975), p. 1488. Skeat (1961 [1910], p. 730) suggests that the usage came into English from the French perversion by Buffon of the Tibetan *zobo*, meaning a male hybrid between a yak bull and a common cow. While I am highly sceptical, another opinion suggests that zebu originates from Hindi in the form of 'Zri Bhu', meaning approximately 'the coming to earth of the spirit of god'. 'Bhu', which by itself means the Earth where god lives a human experience, or the presence of the spirit at the carnal moment, is also applied to the cow, since it is the instrument which permits the fecundation of the Earth and is the gift of god. Applied to bovine cattle, this might explain their sacredness as a key part of Hindu belief. My thanks to Rinaldo dos Santos in Uberaba, Minas Gerais, for this speculation.

6   Santiago (1985), p. 176.

7   *Ibid.*, pp. 114–5, 168–71; Taunay cited in Domíngues (1966), pp. 27–8, 31; Anon. [*O Zebú na Pecuaria*] (1931), pp. 32–3.

were sufficiently harsh that Iberian-origin breeds were susceptible to degeneration, especially in drought years when forage was limited. But with the establishment of a military headquarters in Uberaba during the Paraguayan War (1864–70), the region attracted a wave of settlers. In an attempt to deal with local environmental limitations, ranchers in the later 1870s began to buy zebu breeder animals from Rio de Janeiro. The reasons were largely based on the clear adaptability of zebu to semi-tropical conditions on the ranches of Rio de Janeiro. This included such characteristics as skin colour and thickness that resisted the hot tropical sun and ticks, the latter otherwise requiring tick baths, a sudoriferous (sweat) system that permitted zebu to endure the often intense humidity in certain areas of the country and the ability of zebu to thrive on nutritionally-poor pasture that other animals rejected or otherwise were not well suited. Size and meat gains were alleged to be impressive, much more than those of the small 'native' cattle in the region [see *Breeds in Mato Grosso* below], and compared well to some European breeds in more temperate regions of the country, while the zebu's calm temperament was well-suited to handling. The stocking of the Triângulo with the species was enormously successful over the next two decades, but left local ranchers subject to supply and price dictated by either ranchers in Rio de Janeiro or foreign import houses. This led one rancher, Teófilo de Godoy, to make the expensive and risky voyage to India himself in 1893–94.[8]

Godoy began the first of a series of direct imports of zebu by ranchers in the Triângulo, stimulated by the expanding cattle market in São Paulo and the arrival of the Mogiana railroad at Uberaba in 1895, and Araguari the following year. Between 1893 and 1914 over 2,000 breeder zebu were imported into Brazil from India, one-half destined directly for the Triângulo. The animals travelled in specially constructed pens on the upper decks of ships carrying jute for coffee sacks. Between 60 and 90 animals could be accommodated by the ships, and they were usually accompanied by Indian cowherders, who were then repatriated after arrival in Santos. As the Triângulo became the focus of zebu raising in Brazil, the region became completely reliant on the breed. Even the advent of the First World War did not deter importers, and between 1914 and 1921, when extensive imports ended, over 3,300 zebu were brought into the country, most heading to the Triângulo (Figure 8.4).[9]

8   Santiago (1985), pp. 169–71; Lopes and Rezende (1985), pp. 17–9, 22–3; Barcelos (1943), p. 31. The prices charged Triângulo ranchers by the importers were high, between 100 and 400 *milréis* (US$55 to 220) each in 1875, depending on the age, quality and sex of the animal.

9   Lopes and Rezende (1985), p. 31; Santiago (1985), pp. 119–34, 143, 168–71.

Figure 8.4: Movement of Zebu from India and Brazil

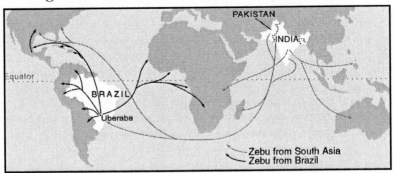

Source: Santiago (1985), p. 16.

Importation was aided by support from both the federal and the Minas Gerais state governments for pedigree cattle raising beginning in 1907. Federal laws in that year, and in 1911, 1912 and 1913, loosened import regulations and offered subsidies, while the Minas government encouraged the display of zebu at the first national agricultural exhibition in 1908 and stimulated imports in 1908–09, despite objections by some veterinarians and ranchers. In 1910 the federal ministry of agriculture subsidised the import of 242 animals, most destined to Minas. While there was a heated debate at the time concerning the value of zebu as a breeder animal, Minas state president, João Pinheiro, reflected a utilitarian attitude when he declared: 'I do not want to know if the science of zootechnicians recommends the zebu or not; what I know is that the ranchers of Uberaba and other regions of Minas Gerais are getting rich with zebu, and that's enough for me.'[10]

Considering the geographical proximity of Mato Grosso to the Triângulo, it is no surprise that zebu soon saw their way into that state. Previously, however, Mato Grosso ranchers had relied on several varieties of breeds, with little attention to scientific selection or other forms of choosing their animals, and what entered the region first came to be the basis of herd development virtually throughout the region.

Breeds in Mato Grosso

The breeds of cattle entering Mato Grosso with the first neo-European settlers were those familiar to ranchers throughout the Americas. These were the descendents of varied Iberian stock that had populated the hemisphere from southern Chile to Texas during the colonial era. Those most

---

10   Santiago (1985), pp. 168–71; Lopes and Rezende (1985), pp. 27–8; Silva (1947), pp. 71–2.

sought-after were muscular, heavily-boned animals with short legs, long, curved horns and powerful front quarters (including the head), suited to draught labour. In Brazil, these animals were often called *alemtejano*, or *minhoto*, after regions in Portugal, but were hardly distinguishable from the *correntino* and *criollo*, which dominated in the interior regions of Argentina and Paraguay.[11] With time, a series of national breeds began to develop, including random mix with the odd animal from Africa or Goa, but these crosses were unplanned and had only slight impact on the regional breeds then emerging in the Americas. As decades and centuries passed, cattle adapted to local conditions and developed characteristics unknown to their ancestors. Most noticeable were the enlargement of horns, necessary in an extensive ranching system for defence against predators such as wildcats and wolves. As a result of this type of ranching, cattle became semi-feral, shied from humans and were not indisposed to putting up a fight at roundup time. These animals are comparable to the famed longhorn that roamed the North American range in the nineteenth and early twentieth centuries. But the Brazilian beasts were more suited to the tropics, developing wider hooves, thick hides and strong constitutions. These were the animals that entered and populated Minas Gerais and Mato Grosso from the eighteenth through the nineteenth centuries.[12]

In Mato Grosso, the most common breeds seem to have been the *pantaneiro* or *cuiabano* in the Pantanal floodplain, and the *chino* or *curraleiro* and *franqueiro* in the drier upland savanna (*cerrado*), although these were not mutually exclusive. In the Brazilian *cerrado*, traditional breeds included *caracú, franqueiro, chino* and *mocho*, but both *caracú*, a breed largely developed in São Paulo, and *mocho* (a hornless breed) were rare in Mato Grosso throughout the period, although they were sometimes crossed with others, usually more by chance than by design. Similar to *correntino* cattle, the *franqueiro* often had exceptionally long horns (when removed, each horn was said to be capable of holding as much as five to six litres of liquid), a powerful head and strong front quarters, making the breed ideal as draught labour. It also carried a thick, highly-prized hide, used for leather. But it was a small animal, had a low meat-to-bone ratio and was a poor reproducer, lowering its value in the meat market, especially with the increase in the demand for beef during the First World War. Thereafter, the *franqueiro* was gradually crossbred with zebu and no longer exists in its original form.[13]

11   According to John E. Rouse, both Spanish and Portuguese America received Iberian cattle that were similar, what he generalises as 'criollo'. Rouse (1977, pp. 291–3) speculates that the Portuguese breed most commonly brought to Brazil was the *mertolengo*, which was 'closely related to the Retinto of Spain'. Interestingly, the *retinto* is subject to preservation programmes in both Spain and Argentina today.

12   Ayala and Simon (1914), pp. 288–9; Cotrim (1913), p. 135; Cavalcanti (1928), pp. 33–4.

13   Endlich (1902), pp. 742–4; Lisboa (1909), pp. 137–9; Cotrim (1913), pp. 136–45.

More widespread and useful was the *chino* or *curraleiro*, an animal found not only in Mato Grosso but in Minas Gerais, Goiás and São Paulo. The origins of this breed are uncertain, with some arguing that it was a cross between Iberian and Indian cattle, others that it carried *franqueiro* and *correntino* genes. Allegedly brought to Mato Grosso by post-Paraguayan War settlers from Minas Gerais (as was probably the case with the *franqueiro*), it was prized for its rapid growth, good proportion of meat to bone (up to 50 per cent), well-developed hooves and high fertility. The *chino* had short horns and was skittish if left on its own, but became docile after a short time around humans. And the breed was hardy enough to survive the long and exhausting three-month drives to Minas and São Paulo. Its major drawbacks, however, were the small stature, with correspondingly low amounts of meat, and its tendency to become commercially less desirable if subsequent generations were not regularly crossbred with more corpulent animals. Similar to most other 'native' breeds of Brazil, the chino disappeared into zebu crosses.[14]

In the Pantanal, the *pantaneiro* (*tucura* in the local vernacular) was the result of crossbreeding between the *caracú* and *franqueiro*, although there is evidence to suggest that the animal may have descended from crosses between Brazilian, Paraguayan and *correntino* cattle. Until ranchers in the Pantanal began purchasing zebu in significant numbers during the 1930s and 1940s, the *pantaneiro* dominated ranching in the region because it was well adapted to the unusual conditions of the Pantanal. It was small and agile, sported large, narrow horns, had a thick hide and had adapted well to regular flooding of its adopted habitat. Its rate of survival under arduous conditions was remarkably high, with close to 20 per cent annual herd growth, a characteristic that guaranteed increases with little effort on the part of the rancher. The conditions under which the *pantaneiro* was raised were hardly conducive to weight gain, however. The animal's slow maturation, light weight and allegedly weak hindquarters were mentioned by observers as the principal results of the breed's 'degeneration' in the region. It also was an aggressive animal, known to attack even men on horseback, a temperament hardly ideal for the raising of cattle on a commercial scale.[15]

14   Endlich (1902), pp. 745–6; Lisboa (1909), p. 140; Cotrim (1913), pp. 136–45; Carvalho (1906), pp. 159–60. The name 'chino' did not come from China, but probably from the practice in Spanish America of calling crossbreeds or mestizos 'chino', which also suggests the breed's place of origin. Drives covered extensive distances, from 600 to 1,000 kilometers, comparable to the famous nineteenth-century trail drives of the Chisholm Trail in the USA. See Abreu (1976); Wilcox (1992b), pp. 158–60.

15   Lisboa (1909), pp. 136–7; Rondon (1972), pp. 58–9; Cotrim (1913), pp. 136–45; Andrade (1936), p. 7; Domingues and Abreu (1949), p. 17. The *pantaneiro* is rare today, though one ranching family in the northern Pantanal still raises purebred *tucura*, and there is a government programme to maintain its gene pool, in much the same manner as with *caracú* in São Paulo.

As a result, ranching in the Pantanal was poorly developed compared to other regions of the country. The *pantaneiro* was raised for its hide or, after the beginning of the twentieth century, also for its meat as jerky. Initially, both products were produced on ranches in the Pantanal and then shipped to Corumbá or Cuiabá for sale and export. Later, they were supplied to the various jerky factories (*charqueadas*) that sprang up along the Paraguay and Aquidauana rivers in response to demand in Cuba and north-eastern Brazil during the First World War as traditional jerky production in Rio Grande do Sul and Uruguay shifted to refrigerated meat. Animals were frequently rounded up *a bala* (by the bullet), due to their feral nature. Only once zebu entered the Pantanal and crossed with the *pantaneiro* did the structure of ranching in the region change, transforming an essentially subsistence activity into a thriving business.[16]

While there were occasional drives to Minas in the late nineteenth century, the 'native' breeds of cattle in Mato Grosso supported a local ranching industry mainly centred on production of hides, beef for limited regional consumption, jerky or, in the northern Pantanal, for beef bouillon. This meant that ranching was primarily extensive, with animals often left to raise themselves. Ranches were relatively large, with fencing only near the ranch house or line camps, and pasture was usually native grasses and legumes. Care was limited to roundup for drives, castration and branding. Often animals were missed, while the income generated was limited. For most, it was a precarious business without much profit, a situation that elicited concern from observers, particularly those who believed in the potential for ranching in Mato Grosso to generate substantial revenue for cattlemen and the state. While there were periodic calls among government officials, ranchers, veterinarians and even presidents of the state for improvement, these were directed principally to the importation of European breeds (Hereford, Durham, Polled Angus), taking the phenomenal success of cattle raising in Argentina as the model worthy of emulation. There was a clear recognition that the Mato Grosso ranching industry required more modern methods if it was to provide greater income, but there was less understanding of the character of tropical ranching and the suitability of certain breeds to the region.[17]

The first and only major effort systematically to import European breeds into Mato Grosso was by Brazil Land, Cattle and Products

16 Oliveira (1941b), p. 65; Maciel (1922), pp. 22, 29; Carvalho (1906), p. 162; Dr Cassio Leite de Barros, interview by author, Corumbá, Mato Grosso do Sul, 9 June 1990. For a relevant discussion on the marketability of various beef products in Argentina and Uruguay, particularly in terms of distance from market, see Crossley and Greenhill (1977), chapter 8.

17 Mato Grosso (1887); Lisboa (1909), p. 140; Travassos (1898), pp. 35–6; Ruffier (1917), pp. 58–9, 65–6.

Company, part of the US-owned Percival Farquhar syndicate, which introduced 1,000 purebred Durham and Shorthorn to one of its ranches in southern Mato Grosso just before the First World War. This experiment was copied by a few ranchers in the region, particularly other foreign interests, but was an abysmal failure. The breeds were hardly acclimatised to the Mato Grosso environment, finding the local forage unpalatable and constantly suffering from the intense sun and insect plagues. In the end they succumbed to the extremely harsh winters of 1917 and 1918. It may have been that the animals did not receive the care they required, but the experience convinced Brazil Land of the need to raise more hardy breeds, particularly zebu, and other ranchers of the inadvisability of importing more European animals. The inability of the railroad to provide regular livestock transport also contributed to this decision. The solution chosen by Brazil Land was reinforced by the company's US veterinarian, Dr MacNeill, who had been in charge of the import experiment, and who by 1918 supported zebu as his first choice for breeding under Mato Grosso conditions. This, of course, was a path already travelled by some ranchers in the state. Despite some diehard attempts to continue European imports, including by the government of Mato Grosso as late as 1930, with the First World War the oft-disparaged zebu received the stimulus needed to consolidate its penetration of Mato Grosso, creating in the process a cattle ranching revolution in the state.[18]

The first zebu was said to have arrived in 1880, although this appears to have been an isolated case. More regular introduction of the breed into Mato Grosso probably began after 1895, although only after the turn of the century did this expand. Several ranchers, particularly in the Campo Grande area, bought zebu in Minas for resale in Mato Grosso or for their own ranches. Paulo Coelho Machado reported that in response to a national economic recession his grandfather, Antônio Rodrigues Coelho, drove a herd of local cattle to Uberaba for sale in 1906, but could not sell the animals and was forced to trade them for 400 zebu. These he brought back to his ranch near Nioac, keeping half for himself and selling the rest. Coelho later declared that this was the best investment he had ever made, since the quality of his stock improved significantly when the imports were crossed with 'degenerated' local cattle. They were also admired for their endurance on the long drives to market in São Paulo. And the introduction of zebu into Mato Grosso extended across the border to Paraguay, where as early as 1911 that country's northern regions had a

18   Corrêa Filho (1926), pp. 48–50; Ruffier (1919), pp. 7–10; Barros (1922), pp. 12, 17–21; Campo Grande (1944), p. 36; Campo-Grande (n.d.), pp. 15–6; Conti (1945), p. 19; Coelho Machado (1990), p. 94. MacNeill expressed his change of mind in a letter to Conti after he had returned to the United States.

considerable number of zebu crosses, and some ranchers were even importing breeder zebu from Brazil.[19]

Yet ranchers in Mato Grosso did not always acquire zebu as a matter of choice. Until just a few years before the First World War, the most heavily travelled route for the export of Mato Grosso cattle was through Minas, also the major source for breeder animals. As a result, drovers from Minas would arrive in Mato Grosso for the annual cattle drives, trailing herds of breeder zebu as part or full payment. In many cases, ranchers in Mato Grosso had little option but to accept zebu blood in the rejuvenation of their herds, since other breeds were almost impossible to find or prohibitively expensive. But few Mato Grosso ranchers could afford purebred animals, nor even the periodic purchase of new halfbreed cattle. The result was a gradual decline in animal precocity, average weight and resistance to the extensive ranching conditions under which they lived. As early as 1907 Miguel Lisboa noticed that after four or five generations the zebu's initial hardiness in the local environment had disappeared, and the cattle were degenerating in all respects, especially in terms of body weight. They were still considered ideal as traction animals and for their ability to tolerate the long drives, but no longer were they producing as they had. This observation overlapped with a growing national controversy over the suitability of zebu to Brazilian conditions.[20]

Zebu 'Suitability'

As zebu came to dominate the pastures of the Triângulo Mineiro, and its apparent phenomenal success attracted attention in other regions of Brazil, ranchers and zooscientists began to direct their attention to the animal's value for the Brazilian ranching sector. Such attention ultimately generated a heated debate over the zebu's suitability to Brazilian pastures, in particular compared to European and native breeds. For some, the imports from Asia were seen as better suited to a zoo than to the pasture; for others, zebu were the saviour of central Brazilian ranching, including in Mato Grosso.

Part of what came to be an anti-zebu lobby, centred largely in São Paulo, had to do with concern among some ranchers that the zebu did not live up to its expectations after the first or second generation. Led by Dr Luis Pereira Barreto, a respected São Paulo physician, breeder and amateur zootechnician, the anti-zebu group admitted that the first generation was 'truly splendid'. But succeeding generations, Pereira Barreto argued, declined rapidly:

19   Andrade (1936), p. 6; Endlich (1902), pp. 744–5; Coelho Machado (1990), p. 94; López Decoud (1911), pp. ciii–cix; Crossley and Greenleaf (1977), p. 333; Wilcox (1992b), pp. 155–8.
20   Lisboa (1909), pp. 139, 152–3; Endlich (1902), p. 745.

the second is already much inferior; the third very bad; the fourth is a juvenile goat herd; the fifth a herd of long-eared hares; the sixth, finally is of debilitated rats, wretched, infertile ... Zebu meat has the rankness of capybara [*Hydrochoerus capybara*]; cows don't have enough milk to raise their young; males and females are wild beasts.[21]

The basis of Pereira Barreto's argument was that zebu degenerated rapidly over the generations, in comparison to the hardier native breeds, in particular *caracú*, of which he was a tireless promoter. This opinion was seconded by Dr Assis Brasil, a renowned ranching specialist and politician from Rio Grande do Sul. Assis Brasil saw the infatuation with zebu as based on superficial external characteristics only, with no attention paid to zooscience, calling it the 'Asiatic plague' and characterising its champions as having succumbed to 'collective hysteria'. Less strident in his criticism was the respected Eduardo Cotrim, whose experience with cattle was extensive, if largely confined to Rio Grande do Sul and Rio de Janeiro. In his highly-regarded manual on cattle raising, published in 1913, Cotrim opined that the immense popularity of this 'Hindu idol' in recent years had produced a painful experience for Brazilian ranchers, who did not understand that in the course of countless centuries in India the zebu had 'proven' it was incapable of improvement. While admitting that it was suitable as a traction animal, he disparaged zebu meat, saying that it was of secondary quality because the breed did not adapt well to 'luxurious' pastures. And he warned that zebu milk production was exceptionally low, calf care by cows minimal and the procreation rate well below that of national breeds, such as *caracú*. The addition of Cotrim's voice to the discussion gave great legitimacy to the anti-zebu lobby.[22]

The animal's defenders argued that its critics did not understand the difficult nature of ranching in central Brazil. Carlos Fortes, an animal expert from Minas Gerais, noted in 1903 that the state ranching industry was poorly developed, little cattle care was practiced, there were few government supports and exports were low as a result. He explained that zebu was the best selection for remote regions, either as purebreds or as scientifically-controlled crosses. His point was that the animal's rusticity and productivity under less-than-ideal conditions made it a natural choice for ranchers in regions like western Minas Gerais, Goiás and Mato Grosso. Others, including some federal government technicians, argued that the

21 Lopes and Rezende (1985), p. 34. Pereira Barreto was a coffee planter and public health expert in São Paulo and a major figure in the movement for agricultural improvement in the state, at one time serving as the state's secretary of agriculture.
22 Lisboa (1909), p. 154; Cotrim (1913), p. 135; Cotrim (1912:), pp. 71–92. The Rio Grande do Sul Breeder's Union journal, *A Estância*, published between 1913–27, was also a major source of anti-zebu articles and analysis; see Bell (1998), pp. 92–3.

zebu was ideally adapted to the tropical climate of Brazil, produced better than its detractors made out and was especially resistant to diseases that frequently incapacitated European breeds.[23]

Fortes's points were supported by Joaquim Travassos, a powerful member of the National Agricultural Society in Rio. Travassos studied the zebu in Brazil and in India even before the anti-zebu forces launched their attack. He noticed that while zebu meat production was markedly less than that of European breeds in ideal conditions, the Indian animal was best adapted to the local climate in a number of ways: longer ears to sweep away flies; usually light hair colour, reflecting sun; darker skin pigmentation that increased resistance to ultraviolet light; resistance to tropical parasites; less sweating, therefore greater absorption of heat by droplets. Travassos relied heavily on a study undertaken by British zooscientist Robert Wallace in India in the 1870s. Wallace, who made the first scientific study of zebu, concluded that European cattle were unsuited to the tropics, and that to improve local zebu, breeder stations and veterinary schools should be established. Travassos argued that the same should be done in Brazil.[24]

This was the crux of the problem, as several observers pointed out during the course of the debate. As a breed, zebu was not prone to inevitable 'degeneracy' as its detractors claimed, but as in all animal raising inadequate care leads to a commercial quality decline over several generations. Fernand Ruffier, a French veterinarian who had settled in Brazil, argued during the war that crosses between *Bos taurus* and *Bos indicus* were more akin to hybridisation than to crossbreeding in that sterility did not occur, but it was necessary to crossbreed regularly to avoid degeneration. Although not a supporter of zebu importation, he and others argued that the best way to improve cattle quality in Brazil (as always, compared to the success of Argentina) was to create conditions under which the animals could prosper, including better pastures, closer attention by ranchers and the establishment of zootechnical education facilities. Allegedly, this was not understood by Brazilian ranchers, who believed that by simply injecting some zebu blood into their herds they would produce some miraculous breed requiring no further care. Without doubt this attitude did exist, but more likely high expense explains the reluctance of remote ranchers to practice such crossbreeding, particularly in regions such as Mato Grosso. Until the First World War, the financial reward from such care was virtually non-existent and as such only the richest ranchers could afford the investment.[25]

---

23 Fortes (1903), pp. 4–7, 11–2, 18–24; Lopes and Rezende (1985), pp. 35–6.
24 Travassos (1903), pp. 257–96, 321–3, 330–2. Except for the role of sweating, which functions opposite to the manner they believed, Travassos and Wallace's observations have been supported by present-day zooscience.
25 Ruffier (1917), pp. 39–42, 58–9, 65–6, 72–8; Neves (1918), pp. 58–9, 63–8.

In Mato Grosso zebu grew in importance, particularly in cross breeding with local breeds like the *franqueiro* and *chino*. In cases where ranchers provided little care, however, these animals became so wild they posed a risk to humans and more docile cattle, forcing some owners to destroy them. Still, zebu was the breed of choice by the First World War, primarily because of its ability to withstand the long, arduous drives to São Paulo. This advantage became even more clear during the wartime cattle boom, when most ranchers throughout central Brazil accepted zebu as the breed best adapted to the Brazilian savanna. Extensive exports of frozen zebu meat to warring Europe also convinced many doubters of the product's marketability and its place in the national economy. The zebu was already on the way to predominating in Campo Grande and the most southerly zones of the state, and ranchers in the Pantanal first began to import zebu breeders during and after the war. The controversy diminished, and even Eduardo Cotrim accepted the inevitability of zebu for central Brazil's ranching industry, although he cautioned the need for selection and breeding care.[26]

The debate did not die, however, as anti-zebu opinion was backed up for a time from London, where the issue of zebu meat came to dominate. Arguing that zebu meat was unpalatable for the European consumer due to its unusual fat distribution, in 1918 the London Board of Trade banned imports. The response from the more extremist anti-zebu *paulista* lobbyists was a call for a permanent ban on imports of zebu and the slaughter of all remaining zebu stock in the country. Such action was reinforced by European decisions in 1920 and 1921 to limit or downgrade Brazilian beef, in part due to its 'inferior' quality, but also because there were excessive stocks of beef in the market after the wartime demand declined. Most importantly, the ban was challenged by several zooscientists, notably Fernand Ruffier, who argued that it was the result of a combination of poor preparation of the meat in the São Paulo refrigerated meat packing plants to meet the feverish wartime demand, and politics, the latter to protect British cattle interests in Argentina and in Britain. Zebu production suffered a potentially fatal blow in 1921, however, when a lot of breeder animals imported from India through São Paulo was found to be infected with rinderpest.[27]

Mineiro breeders pushed on with importations of breeder zebu from India through 1919–21, bringing in over 3,000 head in that three-year peri-

26 Corrêa Filho (1926), pp. 44–6; Anon. ['A creação'] (1916), pp. 362–3; Rondon (1920), p. 19; Barros (1987), p. 63; Correio Paulistano (1916), pp. 3–4. According to Ruffier, Brazil exported 33,661 tonnes of frozen meat in 1916, corresponding to roughly 374,000 head at 180 kilograms of marketable meat per animal. There was no attempt to distinguish how much was of zebu origin (Ruffier, 1918, p. 39; Bell, 1998, pp. 153–4).

27 Ruffier (1919), pp. 7–10, 18–28; Domingues (1966), pp. 40, 43; Downes (1986), pp. 474–6; Embrapa (2000), pp. 4–5.

od, by far the largest number ever. Rinderpest was discovered in one of the lots, and while the federal government prohibited further imports of zebu, neighbouring countries and some European nations banned the entry of Brazilian animals and meat. The outbreak, which did not spread beyond São Paulo city, was controlled by the Brazilian authorities, who not only destroyed some 3,300 head of cattle but also dogs and ravens in the vicinity, disinfected rail cars, stock and packing areas, and temporarily closed the meat packers. Naturally, the issue was exploited by the anti-zebu lobby, which argued that not only were zebu rachitic and degenerate but were also repositories of a disease that could decimate the national herd.[28]

The short-term impact was to depress further an already stagnant post-war ranching sector. After a boom in imports between 1917 and 1921 only one significant batch was imported from India until the 1950s, involving 192 animals. Meat production picked up by 1923, however, and impressive expansion of the internal market in the 1920s and development of a 'national' zebu breed, the Indubrasil, served to mute zebu disparagers. This was partly aided by improved treatment of cattle and meat by the meat packers and by an unexpected source, a representative of the British ministry of agriculture who visited the country in the late 1920s. The official, John Lamb Frood, visited Uberaba and São Paulo and was impressed by the quality of zebu and meat processing. He suggested that greater cross-breeding with breeds like Hereford or Polled Angus might be beneficial, but assured Brazilian ranchers that he was returning to Britain convinced of the value of zebu in providing beef for the European market. Frood's opinion was echoed by Sir Edmund Vestey, head of the British conglomerate that controlled a number of Brazil's meat-packing plants, who visited Mato Grosso in 1927 and admitted that the problem was with the processing of the meat, not the breed. These visits legitimised zebu as a viable animal in the production of export beef, albeit with the caveat that more scientific breeding methods be employed.[29]

Frood and Vestey's opinions were reinforced by the Sociedade Rural Brasileira, an organisation begun in 1919 primarily by cattle interests, which urged government support for using zebu to 'improve' herds in Mato

28   Santiago (1985), pp. 145, 170; United States, Department of Agriculture, Trade Report no. 173, by W.L. Schurs, US commercial attaché, Rio de Janeiro, 12 April 1921, 'Cattle Plague in State of São Paulo'; and Trade Report no. 292, by Bernard H. Noll, US trade commissioner, Rio de Janeiro, 7 January 1922, 'Imports of Zebu Cattle Suspended,' Record Group 166 — Records of the Foreign Agricultural Service, Narrative Agricultural Reports, 1904–54. Brazil, entry 5, box 64, United States National Archives [USNA–RG 166], Washington, DC.

29   Santiago (1985), pp. 169–70; 'Propaganda de Matto Grosso,' in *Almanaque Illustrado* (Campo Grande, n.p., n.d.), pp. 243–6; *Gazeta de Commercio* (1927). Vestey had three meat-packing plants in Brazil, at Barretos and Santos in São Paulo and Mendes near Rio de Janeiro. For meat packer production in the 1920s, see Downes (1986), p. 480.

Grosso, Goiás and Minas Gerais. And a Sociedade questionnaire sent to the major packing houses in 1929 and 1930 revealed considerable satisfaction with zebu meat amongst the companies. They emphasised that their production was based on zebu and suggested that ranchers should breed purebred animals, or at least crossbreed using purebred zebu bulls. While admitting that zebu meat was considered inferior in Europe, and that the price of zebu beef ranged from three-quarters to one-half as much as beef from Argentina and Uruguay, the interviewees emphasised their conviction that the breed was the most suitable for central Brazilian environmental conditions.[30]

By the 1930s, the 'suitability' debate had been resolved in favour of zebu, and between 1920 and 1950 the central Brazilian cattle industry became increasingly sophisticated in developing several zebu crosses (Figure 8.5). This involved importing and raising several different breeds of zebu, particularly Nellore, Gir and Guzerá, as well as developing a distinctly Brazilian zebu breed called Indubrasil, which was the product of various zebu crosses. While at times making the mistake of selecting animals more on external appearance than on productivity, the business expanded dramatically.[31]

Such expansion required some additional inputs from zooscience and cattle politics, however. By the late 1930s observers noticed that the stocks of purebred Indian cattle were precariously low in Brazil. This prompted the federal government to act. Between 1934 and the early 1940s, federally-funded experimental ranches were set up in the Triângulo and in São Paulo. The 1930s saw the development of a national Genealogical Registry Service through the Rome Agricultural Conference of 1936, and zebu registry was authorised two years later. These measures were instrumental in guaranteeing zebu a permanent place in Brazilian ranching circles, and in preserving the small numbers of purebred stock still in existence. At the same time, by the 1950s it was recognised that the general quality of Brazilian-bred animals was insufficient and there was a need to inject new blood into the industry. Between 1955 and 1962 official and unofficial imports consolidated zebu breeding in Brazilian herds, making it unnecessary for further significant imports of zebu since. By the 1970s, the industry had become sophisticated enough to engage in its own breeding programme, leading to the overwhelming predominance of Nellore in the national herd. Based largely on the Brazilian experience, zootechnicians from other countries such as South Africa and Australia have affirmed Nellore's superiority in large-scale tropical ranching. It is highly fertile and

---

30   Anon. [*O Zebú na Pecuaria*] (1931), pp. 39–40; Anon. ['Inquerito'] (1930), pp. 1–5.
31   Santiago (1985), pp. 72–3, 81, 86, 468; Menezes (1937), p. 8. Illustrating the importance ranchers placed on appearance, at the height of purchases in India, the Brazilian belief that animals with long ears were purer breeds prompted Indian cattle traders to jocularly refer to the Brazilians as 'buyers of cattle ears' (Menezes, 1937).

gains weight easily, while the beast's normally light hair colour plays a key role in its adaptability to tropical conditions of hot sun and little shade.[32]

Figure 8.5: Exaggerated Example of Size Differences between Zebu ('Goliath') and the *Curraleiro* ('David')

The text claims that horns are the only 'advantage' the *curraleiro* possesses over the zebu.

Source: *Zebú*, August 1943, p. 12.

For central Brazil, the result was that between 1921 and the 1940s, zebu came to dominate, with a significant presence in São Paulo. In Mato Grosso, zebu were the main breed by the 1930s, particularly in Campo Grande, although it took another two decades to dominate in the Pantanal (Figure 8.6). Andrade explained that reasons for adoption were simple: hardiness; precocity of calves; resistance to parasites; and easy ability to swim, essential in the fording of rivers and streams during drives. The capacity to endure the long drives to market with minimal deleterious effects and to regain weight quickly was central in the decisions of Mato

32 Menezes (1940), p. 18; Lopes and Rezende (1985), pp. 63–5; Brazil (1978), pp. 2–3; Santiago (1985), pp. 170–1. Until the 1970s it was impossible to know with any degree of certainty the percentage of zebu in the Brazilian herd.

Grosso ranchers to opt for zebu, despite the controversy surrounding its value. The expansion of jerky production in the state during and after the First World War, although largely a response to external market factors in Brazil and the Río de la Plata, was facilitated by zebu introduction, since these animals were on average much larger than the *pantaneiro* or *chino*. And leaner zebu meat was appreciated by the *charqueadas* because it spoiled less in transit, especially since most was sent downriver through Montevideo to northeast Brazil and Cuba. In addition, the animal's resistance to hide-damaging parasites and flies made the hide a natural for the leather industry, which in Brazil began its expansion after the Second World War. By 1940 Mato Grosso reportedly had a higher proportion of zebu in its herd than any other region of Brazil, including Minas and Goiás.[33]

Figure 8.6: Zebu and Zebu Cross Cattle at Fazenda Margarida, circa 1928

From collection of Senhora Elza Gonçalves Dória Passos, Campo Grande, Mato Grosso do Sul (with permission).

33 Conti (1945), p. 20; Andrade (1936), p. 7–8; Leite (1942), pp. 9–11; Oliveira (1941a), pp. 184–5; Crossley and Greenhill (1977), pp. 296–9. There was some debate over whether Mato Grosso had a higher percentage of zebu blood in its herds than other regions. Durval Menezes argued in 1940 that Goiás produced more beef per animal because there was a higher concentration of zebu in that state than in Mato Grosso (Menezes, 1940, p. 21; Ruffier, 1918, p. 352); United States. Department of State. Report by C.R. Cameron, US Consul, São Paulo, 'São Paulo Livestock Industry and Exposition,' 26 June 1929, Record Group 166. Records of the Foreign Agricultural Service, Narrative Agricultural Reports, 1904–54, Brazil, Entry 5, Box 64, USNA–RG 166.

At the same time, Brazilian zebu breeders exported breeder animals to other countries of the Americas (Figure 8.4). The first organised exportations were between 1923 and 1925, when over 800 zebu were sent to Mexico, though due to the political situation the majority ended up in the southern USA. According to Santiago, these lots were influential in the development of the American Brahman breed. Exports to Mexico were repeated in 1945 and 1946, with a few bulls also entering the USA. Other countries that received significant numbers of Brazilian breeder zebu were Argentina, Bolivia, Colombia, Paraguay and Venezuela, while there were several exports to Africa, particularly the former Portuguese colonies of Angola and Mozambique. Most of the major Brazilian exports were in the 1940s, with some sporadic sales in the 1950s and 1960s. And the bulk were bulls, largely Nellore, Gir and Indubrasil. By the 1970s, export was largely semen, and had expanded to Central America and the Caribbean.[34]

Despite such demand, zebu alone could not be the salvation of the central Brazilian cattle industry. In his address to the general assembly of the Brazilian National Agricultural Society in 1916 Dr Ezequiel Ubatuba expressed a growing view of the day that the development of the '*sertão*' (interior) of Brazil required, among agricultural inputs, the essential ranching requirements of: 'wire, vaccine, salt, forage, veterinarians, zebu cattle'.[35] Ubatuba's address indicated the view that the introduction of a cattle breed without 'improvement' of the land and animal care had little value. Such future development would have profound impact on the relationship of ranching and the local ecosystem in Brazil. The arrival of a new breed onto the pastures of Mato Grosso thus brought with it the introduction or intensification of activities that would lead to prosperity for many ranchers, but also much greater pressure on the land, ultimately shifting the relationship between ranching and the regional environment.

'Zebu's Elbows' in Ranching Ecosystems

Although beef cattle ranching throughout the Americas, including the United States, has been extensive, by the early twentieth century the pro-

34   Santiago (1985), pp. 106–7, 611–47, 709, Anon. (1931), p. 32. Although Brazilian animals contributed to the pedigree of American Brahman, this breed was largely developed in the USA and with stock brought from India or bred in the USA itself. The Brahman is similar to Indubrasil, but the product of a more meticulous programme that has continued to this day. With the exception of some of Brazil's closer neighbours, most infusions of zebu into Latin American herds originated in the United States as Brahmans or Santa Gertrudis. Brazilian exports today include embryos and some limited live breeder animals. And one of the ironies of the long-term Brazilian breeding programme is that in recent years concern in India for the purity of zebu has led to Brazil becoming a potential repository for export to India!

35   Ubatuba (1916), p. 10. Ubatuba was a veterinarian originally from Rio Grande do Sul who had become a convert to the value of zebu for the Brazilian pastoral economy.

vision of salt and mineral supplements, fencing and the controlled productivity of animals, and introduction of non-native forage ('exotics'), became an important aspect of ranching in North America north of the Rio Grande river and in southern South America. Only recently has this become the case in the American tropics, where most of the cattle have been semi-feral and roundup often amounted to organised 'hunting' of the animals. The application of selective breeding and other inputs such as the provision of salt and fencing, or introduction of exotic grasses, was either not possible or seen as unnecessary by most ranchers until well into the twentieth century. As a result, ranching in Mato Grosso tended to rely on native grasses into mid-century, and was dependent on climatic predictability.[36]

In terms of central Brazilian cattle raising, the two most important biomes are the Pantanal and the highland savanna (*cerrado*). As expected, the environmental impact of ranching has varied depending on the structure of ecosystems within these biomes. Annual flooding in the Pantanal creates conditions for ranching that are in contrast to the long dry season and relatively infertile soil conditions of the highlands. Ranching appears to have had less of a direct impact on the Pantanal than in the Cerrado, which has prompted some observers to suggest that ranching was instrumental in 'saving' the Pantanal from the uncontrolled development and environmental degradation threatening the rest of southern Mato Grosso and much of Brazil today. Elsewhere, I have discussed in some detail the environmental impact on both the Pantanal and the Cerrado.[37] Here, my intent is to examine the production roles of zebu introduction and directly-related inputs such as guided diet and regular provision of salt, fencing and planted pasture in putting pressure on Mato Grosso ecosystems over the period under study.

It is often said by cattle raisers throughout Brazil that half of a breed is made through the mouth. This maxim indicates how much successful ranching depends on breeding combined with other essential inputs, particularly the provision of forage. With this in mind, in the late 1930s, a member of the Secretariat of Agriculture for the state of Minas Gerais, F.P. Cardoso, visited the Hudgins Ranch in Texas to view their experiments with zebu breeding. The ranch was well known worldwide for the breeding of zebu, which included using stock imported from Brazil in 1923. What Hudgins offered the Brazilians was a systematic method of cattle raising, which included strictly-controlled breeding, a dietary regime based on breed and environment, differential treatment of cows, bulls and calves, specific treatment of diseases and pests, construction of fences and water troughs and regulated planting of alfalfa and other forage. This was a breeder ranch, thus there was a relatively heavy stocking of pasture: 1.06 head per acre (0.45 head per hectare). By

36   Corrêa Filho (1926), pp. 50–2.
37   Wilcox (1992a), pp. 244–6; Wilcox (1999).

comparison, the well-known King Ranch, also of Texas, pastured some 125,000 head (20 per cent zebu cross known as Santa Gertrudis) on over 500,000 hectares, about one animal per four hectares. The organisation of both these ranches indicates the intensity with which zebu raising had developed in an important ranching region of the United States.[38]

Many of these measures were not absent in Brazil, of course, and in fact had been advocated by various observers and zootechnicians over the years, including Assis Brasil, Ruffier, Travassos, Lisboa and others, but the organisation of the Texans was what most interested the visitors. Observations there confirmed the opinions of the officials, who were bent upon influencing ranchers in Brazil of the commercial benefits of such investment in order to stimulate a stagnated Brazilian cattle industry. This visit is key to understanding the priorities that came to dominate the debate about raising and breeding cattle in Brazil during the period.

The concern of the Brazilians becomes even clearer through examination of the Brazilian 'cattle crisis' of 1942–43. The number of animals available to the market declined significantly in those years, causing costs to rise and consumption to fall. Several reasons were given, including excessive general slaughter or slaughter of cows and calves stimulated by the demands of the Second World War, internal overconsumption and the transition of beef jerky production from Rio Grande do Sul to central Brazil (Mato Grosso, Goiás and Minas Gerais). A study carried out by noted São Paulo animal scientist, Oscar da Silva Brito, while recognising these as valid contributions to the crisis, presented revealing statistics that indicated the real reason was overproduction in general because the number of animals available was greatly exaggerated throughout the country. Indeed, the estimate of 50 million head for Brazil at the time probably was inflated by almost twice the actual number, a situation that naturally would have led to the mistaken assumption that little control over production was necessary. Brito recommended the extension of more credit and greater technical assistance to ranchers, including a 'rationalisation of their work methods; in the selection of breeders; in hygiene and feed for the herd; in the "improvement" [*melhoria*] of fields and pastures, etc.' What Brito was saying was that the ranchers of central Brazil in particular had been operating within a generally extensive regime, but one which by the 1940s required more organised ('scientific') inputs in order to satisfy market demands. Zebu were an integral part of this modernisation process.[39]

---

38   Cardoso (1943), pp. 38–41; Carneiro (1943), p. 11. The Hudgins ranch was located near Hungerford, Texas, about 80 kilometres southwest of Houston. The King Ranch group also invested in ranching around the world in later years, including in Brazil in the Amazon and the state of São Paulo from the 1950s to the 1980s. Most of the animals raised were Santa Gertrudis-zebu crosses. For more, see Murphy (1969).

39   Brito (1944), pp. 7–16.

These observations were reinforced earlier by a study published in 1941 that applied findings in the USA to cattle raising in Mato Grosso. Jorge Ramos de Otero, an animal scientist with the ministry of agriculture who was commissioned to report on ranching conditions in southern Mato Grosso in 1939, argued that in Brazil heavy concentration on quantity of animals meant that feed had been largely ignored in favour of an obsession with breed improvements. This, he said, was not how US ranchers saw the process, for they had been experimenting with several different types of African grasses, including rhodes grass (*Chloris gayana Kunth.*), elephant grass (*Pennisetum purpureum Schum.*) and kikuyu grass (*Pennisetum clandestinum Hochst.*). However, US ranchers had even come to Brazil to observe the performance of native species in Brazilian pastures, including Mato Grosso, with the possibility of the introduction of such native forage (particularly legumes) into the USA. With this in mind, Otero was commissioned to collect samples of grasses and legumes in Mato Grosso to better understand the botanical makeup of the region's pastures leading to potential future cultivation.[40]

Travelling through a region acclaimed throughout Brazil for its abundant and nutritious natural pastures, Otero and his team noticed the utilisation of native grasses on most ranches, but also the growing presence of unpalatable invaders, above all the despised *barba de bode* (goat's beard; *Aristida pallens Cav.*). And some wealthier ranchers were introducing exotics such as *capim jaraguá* (*Hyparrhenia rufa*), *gordura* (molasses grass; *Melinis minutiflora*), elephant and kikuyu grass, all aggressive invaders originally from Africa seen in other regions of Brazil. Native grasses were still apparent, although in gradual decline when in competition with exotics, while native legumes, particularly of the various *Arachis* species, abounded throughout the state, with cattle apparently consuming them regularly. Yet while highly appreciated by Otero for their resistance to trampling and fire, as well as nutritional value, apparently there was no attempt by ranchers to cultivate legumes.[41]

Otero also reported how several ranches in diverse ecological regions were raising zebu, such as Fazenda Pacurí (Margarida; see Figure 8.1 and Figure 8.6) near the Paraguayan border, owned by the *erva mate* (*Ilex paraguariensis*; Paraguayan tea) giant Empresa Mate Laranjeira. Here, as well as on wealthier ranches located on the savanna of the upper Pantanal and near Campo Grande, zebu were raised in conditions that saw clearing and planting of exotic grasses such as *jaraguá*, *gordura* and elephant. Kikuyu also was a commonly-introduced forage by ranchers who could afford the expense of upkeep. Part of the reason for these introductions was the grow-

---

40   Otero (1941), pp. 3–5.
41   *Ibid.*, pp. 6, 12–15, 17–29. For more on the role of Africa in supplying most of the pasture grasses of Brazil and elsewhere in tropical America since colonial times, see Parsons (1942), pp. 12–7; Filgueiras (1990), pp. 57–63.

ing presence of *barba de bode*, which was spreading with other invaders due to trampling and overgrazing. The introduction of new grasses was an attempt to replace native grasses with exotics that could offer cattle, especially newly-introduced zebu, more abundant and nutritious alternatives. Considering this and the time and expense of breeding animals, such introductions were perceived as necessary to protect one's investment.[42]

Otero had few recommendations for ranchers in terms of selection of grass or legume species for planting, but he made a couple of observations that reveal his perceptions. He decried pasturing animals almost immediately after burning, a practice that had been a part of ranching in Brazil for centuries, because it led inevitably to overpasturing and destruction of valuable and nutritious grasses, especially those native to the region. Otero also stressed the need to divide pastures to avoid overuse, and in particular to apply 'improvements' to the specific ranching ecosystems of each region in the nation. This fit neatly into the growing perception that ranching production could only be expanded through breeding and selection of planted pasturage.[43]

However, until the 1940s or even later, the expensive inputs of planting pasture and fencing were most viable for only one type of cattle raising — fattening for slaughter. While São Paulo benefited in the regions surrounding the slaughterhouses, which until the 1940s maintained fattening pastures near their facilities, Mato Grosso and other regions only began to introduce this step in cattle raising when rail transport replaced drives and local markets grew. This meant that the quality of animals driven from Mato Grosso had been less important than the forage consumed once at final destination. Only in the 1940s and the 1950s did significant opportunities for fattening and easier transport of animals by rail develop. This was the time when regular planting of pasture grasses became a part of the Mato Grosso cattle regime, especially near the railway. Indeed, observers noted in the early 1950s that planted jaraguá was going 'native' in the region. In fact, planting was widespread enough by that time that in the *cerrado* the ratio of animals to land on many planted pastures was two per hectare, comparable to the average of three per hectare on heavily-utilised São Paulo fattening pastures and substantially more than 0.33 to 0.14 per hectare on extensive operations (three to seven hectares per head). Since zebu breeding was well underway in the state, the addition of these and other essential economic inputs signalled significant change for ranching ecosystems.[44]

42   Otero (1941), pp. 14–8, 20, 23–4, 28.
43   *Ibid.*, pp. 42–3, 53. For recent discussions of burning in the history of ranching in Brazil, see Dean (1995), pp. 112–5, 203–4; Wilcox (1992a; 1999).
44   Montserrat and Gonçalves (1954), pp. 10, 18, 51, 53.

The introduction of planted pasture required several specialised inputs, not least of which was the construction of fencing and provision of easily-accessible water and feed troughs. Otero mentions the latter as common for the wealthier and more developed ranches of the Campo Grande region, indicating a greater concentration of cattle on the properties as economic opportunities became available. However, two of the most difficult obstacles for ranchers throughout Brazil have been accessing regular water sources for the animals and the cost of fencing. In Mato Grosso such inputs came slowly or partially. In 1916, after a trip through the Triângulo Mineiro and the states of Goiás and Mato Grosso, where zebu were becoming dominant, Ezequiel Ubatuba addressed the annual congress of the National Agricultural Society in Belo Horizonte on the value of zebu for the *sertão* (interior) of Brazil. Ubatuba extolled the attributes of zebu and urged the federal government to support cattle raisers by encouraging pasture rotation and reducing import taxes on smooth and barbed wire, posts, nails, grass seeds, vaccines, windmills, well diggers and anti-tick chemicals for the ranchers, 'all, finally, necessary for the ranching industry to achieve its maximum development'. Such action was affirmed by comparison to the United States and Argentina, where similar policies were in place, with obvious positive effects. Ubatuba also underlined the necessity of such inputs as silos to store feed (he suggests maize, as was done in Argentina) due to the sometimes severe droughts experienced in the *sertão*. These suggestions, which were seldom acted on by Brazilian governments, indicate the importance seen by some of the ranching industry for the national economy, while making it clear that breed introduction could only be successful with such interventions, which in the end constituted '... the best defence of zebu cattle'.[45]

Most Mato Grosso cattlemen understood and were willing to follow suggestions for improvement of their operations, but even when transport and market opportunities expanded there was still a major problem to overcome. Despite the Estrada de Ferro Noroeste do Brasil (EFNOB) railroad that had been completed between the Paraguay River and São Paulo through Campo Grande in 1914, until the 1950s most commerce was conducted by rudimentary roads or trails and by river. This resulted in high costs that worked against 'improvements' in fencing and salt provision, essential in controlled ranching and ultimately in permitting the number of animals to increase to the point of having a noticeable impact on the regional ecosystem. Wire fencing, particularly barbed wire, which had such a profound impact on cattle ranching worldwide, came to Mato Grosso as early as the late nineteenth century, although it was not regularly employed until after the 1920s. However, government subsidies on importation

45   Otero (1941), p. 48; Ubatuba (1916), pp. 45–8.

beginning with the Vargas regime of the 1930s and 1940s, as well as serv-ices for the sanitary care of animals through zootechnical ranches, such as that established at Campo Grande in 1936, offered the possibility for cat-tlemen to import their needs more regularly and at prices they could afford. Shipping records indicate that wire entered the state largely by way of the Paraguay River up to the 1940s. But both wire and salt still were expensive for local ranchers compared to other regions of the country into the 1940s and 1950s. And when government tariff relief on the import of barbed wire ended with the fall of the Vargas regime in 1945, prices soared. Even as late as the mid-1950s a roll of 400 metres cost four times the price before entry into the country. Considering the nature of exten-sive ranching in Mato Grosso and limited prices for finished animals in the market, minimal purchase of these items made economic sense.[46]

With the expansion of zebu raising and more regular planting of pas-ture, however, wire and salt use increased. And most importantly, there was the realisation and desire among Mato Grosso's ranchers for opportunities to string more fencing. This was clear to cattlemen who saw not only the immediate economic value of wire but also the merit in separating herds in extensive ranching. By the mid-1950s, ranchers' desires for cheaper wire led to demands for lower tariffs on barbed wire, although lower costs were satisfied only by the expansion of Brazilian production of barbed wire in the 1960s and 1970s. Once such fencing became common, however, the environmental impact was soon apparent.[47]

Lucídio Rondon wrote that due to the great Pantanal flood of 1974 some 300,000 head of cattle were lost. However, he did not attribute these losses to nature alone. A native of the region who had lived in the city but returned home to write, Rondon argued that the introduction of modern ranching methods involving indiscriminate forest cutting and the stringing of kilometres of fencing caused the floods to be more damaging than they otherwise would have been. The ecosystem was modified by overdevelop-ment, thus was more prone to silting leading to more extensive flooding, while cattle and wild animals were trapped by the fences and drowned:

46   Alfândega de Corumbá, Capatazia and Mesa de Renda Alfandegada de Porto Murtinho and Porto Esperança, *Guias de importação, 1895–1944*, microfilm rolls 41–4, Núcleo de Documentação e Informação Histórica Regional, Universidade Federal de Mato Grosso [NDIHR–UFMT]; Oliveira (1941a); Lisboa (1909), pp. 142–5; Correa Filho (1926), pp. 50–2; Andrade (1936), pp. 8, 11; Pinho (1957), pp. 65–6. Until the 1950s railroad interest was largely directed to São Paulo and the coffee economy. See Queiroz (1999), pp. 391–406 and Azevedo (1950), pp. 128–9. The ranch at Campo Grande, though originally established in 1918, only became operational during the Vargas period. In the 1960s it became the national centre of beef cattle experimen-tation and study in the form of the Empresa Brasileira de Pesquisa Agropecuária — Gado de Corte (EMBRAPA–GC).
47   Pinho (1957), pp. 23, 33–5.

'Thus, with the arrival of civilisation and in its name, deforestation, ripping out this and that, fencing here and there, they modified a beautiful landscape, rivers dried up, fauna were weakened, and in this way nature was saddened [*entristecida*].'[48]

Finally, one other important aspect of the concentration of animals in the Brazilian ranching sector is salt. In this case, I mean salt also to represent the directed provision of various supplements in the cattle diet, including other minerals, hay, grains or animal and bone meal. Salt itself, however, stands at the top of the list of requirements and one that constantly plagued cattle raisers over the many centuries of ranching in Brazil. While in some areas of Brazil, including parts of Mato Grosso, there were abundant natural sources of salt, such as dirt licks (*barreiros*), salt ponds (*salinas*) or high salt content of native forage, these were insufficient for cattle needs, especially where more controlled raising was undertaken. The result was that artificial salt licks had to be built, in order to provide between 400 grams and 1.2 kilograms per animal per month, depending on the region and season. In Mato Grosso, this was particularly necessary in the Cerrado, where there were no *barreiros* and where planted pasture provided inadequate amounts of salt. But salt also had to be protected from the elements, above all in the rainy season, also the season when grasses and legumes have the least amount of salt content. This required the construction of troughs with small roofs in various parts of the pasture. It was recommended that these be placed sporadically around pastures so as to avoid too heavy a concentration of animals at any one time. Over time, the increase in the number of animals pastured meant demand for salt rose, a situation that was not fully satisfied by the national salt industry until the 1950s. The reason was simple — imported salt was cheaper, especially if it came as ballast in ships from Europe, but the market was primarily the jerky factories in Mato Grosso and Rio Grande do Sul. With the Second World War, salt imports dropped precipitously, while the national industry could not satisfy demand, even by the *charqueadas*. This same industry was stimulated by the war and was able to supplant imports by 1945, but only in the 1950s was it able to provide sufficient stocks to ranchers at reasonable prices. Ultimately, it is in this decade that we see the expansion of salt provision and its attendant impact in Mato Grosso.[49]

The impact of salt and other supplements on cattle raising of course was related closely to planted pasture and fencing. As ranchers developed opportunities for a more economically viable business, the numbers of animals multiplied, increasing their concentration on the range. Between

48   Rondon (1974), p. 115.
49   Anon. ['Almanaque'] (1916), p. 180; Anon. ['Sal para os animais'] (1943), pp. 195–6; Fernandes (1939), pp. 57–60.

1920 and the late 1950s, the Mato Grosso cattle population grew from roughly 2.8 million to 8.5 million, while stocking rates increased from one head per 3.9 hectares in 1920 to one head per 1.8 hectares by the 1950s, although there were wide differences between regions, especially if planted pastures near the rail line are taken into account. By the latter date, virtually all were zebu. At the same time, improved breeding technology and conditions contributed to a dramatic increase in the average size of animals over the decades, from less than 400 kilos live weight at four years in the early 1920s to over 600 kilos live weight at two years by the 1960s. This combination of more and larger animals on the land, and what was clear success in raising more beef for both national and international markets, set the precedent for transfer of zebu breed technology to other parts of Brazil and abroad. The decade of the 1970s experienced tremendous expansion of the beef herd in Brazil, most visibly in the Amazon Basin, and almost all animals were zebu or zebu crosses. By that decade, pressure on various ranching ecosystems throughout the country was widespread, only intensifying over the following decades as new grasses, raising techniques and breed experiments have expanded throughout the country. Zebu's contribution was fundamental.[50]

Epilogue

In his recent article on organic beef in the São Paulo financial newspaper *Gazeta Mercantil*, José Alberto Gonçalves quotes the president of the São Paulo packing house Independência, Antônio Russo Neto, on the significance of the 'boi orgânico' to ranching in central Brazil: 'The ecological steer is the third revolution in ranching in the last 30 years, after the success of [the introduction of] brachiaria [*Brachiaria decumbens* and *humidicola*] as pasture and the reduction in the age of slaughter'. Russo's statement is striking because he seems to take zebu for granted. Indeed, his conclusion of the essential inputs in the recent history of Brazil's tropical and semi-tropical ranching sector were made possible largely by the earlier introduction of zebu, including into regions previously seen as marginal for beef cattle raising.[51]

Readers acquainted with recent Brazilian history will notice that the expansion of zebu in Mato Grosso corresponded to the period of the officially-promoted 'March to the West' (*Marcha para o Oeste*) during the Vargas

---

50   Brazil (1926), p. 401; Vieira (1960), pp. 196, 198, 207; Nash (1926), p. 255; Ruffier (1918), p. 36; Santiago (1985), p. 409. The average weights here combine males and females. On average, females weigh between two-thirds and three-quarters as much as males.

51   Gonçalves (2001b). *Braquiária* was indeed a revolution. It was introduced into Brazilian pastures beginning in the 1970s, and today is the preferred forage planted in most of the country.

government of the 1930s and 1940s. Located in the far west, Mato Grosso was an integral part of the push for incorporation of the oft-ignored interior into the Brazilian nation. This was not a new concept, but was the most complete in conception and implementation to that time, and would serve as a precedent for policies in subsequent decades. Cattle ranching became a significant part of the process, even though the original intent of planners was to base the expansion on agricultural cultivation.

Although the politics of the *marcha* ended with Vargas's overthrow in 1945, the forces it unleashed continued. The occupation of the *sertão* became a national obsession beginning in the 1950s with the building of the new capital of Brasília, and extended through governmental agricultural and transport subsidies designed to expand Brazil's export options during the 1964–85 military dictatorship. The process was most intense during the 1970s and 1980s, as it included direct fiscal support for the establishment of large cattle operations in the Amazon Basin, in conscious disregard for environmental impact, and which have become the target of justifiable national and international criticism. The vast majority of animals placed into this tropical zone were zebu. It is hard to imagine how the process could have proceeded without the experiments and knowledge gained in previous decades in Minas Gerais and Mato Grosso. Indeed, one can argue that zebu breeders contributed indirectly to the occupation and environmental degradation of the Brazilian Cerrado and Amazon today, inadvertent proponents of a process with extensive unexpected consequences.[52]

The introduction of zebu, then, inevitably brought with it zebu's elbows — the almost simultaneous introduction of new techniques and other inputs perceived as necessary to make the business of cattle raising economically viable. With production as the first priority, environmental pressure was unavoidable. More animals led to planted pasture, which attracted additional animals, encouraging further inputs. It is ironic, then, to see at the end of the twentieth century yet another innovation in the reinvention of zebu as a 'boi ecológico' that, it was assumed, would promote Brazilian beef in markets abroad, as well as buffer cattle ranching from the exigencies of environmentalists. That story is not finished, of course, but if there is an environmental lesson in the history of the Brazilian zebu, it is that breed innovation based on economic benefit inevitably carries with it a combination of related ramifications that have a significant cumulative impact on the land. In this context, it is highly advisable that any promotion of a breed of animal be viewed with considerable circumspection on the part of researchers, ranchers and the public as a whole.

---

[52] For a 'Marxist' interpretation of this process in Mato Grosso and elsewhere, see Foweraker (1981).

CHAPTER 9

Individual Agency and Ecological Imperialism: Aimé Bonpland in Southern South America[*]

Stephen Bell

One who has travelled through diverse parts of the Americas is astonished and saddened by the landscapes of the Buenos Aires Pampas. As much as nature has been lavish in almost all parts of the New World, it has been equally parsimonious in this part here. The Buenos Aires countryside presents a picture of the greatest sterility, destitute as it is of trees and bushes ... It is truly shameful to see that the European Spanish, in the space of three centuries, have left this land so short of trees. (From Aimé Bonpland's manuscript plans for an integrated agricultural project, Buenos Aires, 21 June 1832)

The essay which follows, part of a larger project on the French-born botanist and traveller Aimé Bonpland (1773–1858), draws much of its immediate stimulus from Alfred Crosby's 1986 study *Ecological Imperialism*.[1] By placing his focus on the ecological consequences of European expansion, marrying sociopolitical concerns with those of the biophysical realm, Crosby greatly advanced the research agenda for the historical geography of the environment. As numerous observers have noted, his influential study opened the way for the comparative environmental history of the developing world. Increasingly, however, researchers have found a more complex reality than that depicted by Crosby. It was not simply that European ecology was transferred pell-mell into regions such as southern South America, but the plant resources of these world peripheries were also increasingly key to the economic development plans of the metropolitan countries. The traffic in plants and animals was emphatically no one-way movement out from Europe. As scholars have probed the melding of imperial concerns with local circumstances, a more complex picture of the mechanisms of transfer has also emerged.[2] These mecha-

---

[*] The research for this chapter was supported by the Social Sciences and Humanities Research Council of Canada and through the Academic Senate of the University of California, Los Angeles.
1 Crosby (1986).
2 Richard Drayton's ideas about natural science and British imperialism (Drayton, 2000, p. 171) could be usefully extended to some other parts of Europe.

nisms are a major focus of the present chapter. While texts are quick to remember the famous examples of the movement of plant materials across the globe for explicit imperial purposes, of which cinchona and rubber provide excellent examples, the record of environmental change also needs to consider the sometimes unwitting actions of individuals. An emphasis on their work can be useful, not least through the reconstruction of the scientific networks in which they worked. Some of these networks are explicit, others remain deeply hidden. They will only reemerge through more archival research. Following the argument of Karl Butzer, this is a kind of environmental history requiring sustained study, one that 'cannot be proclaimed from a hilltop by the sweep of a hand'.[3]

The present chapter seeks to illustrate the above points by reexamining parts of the career of the French-born botanist and traveller Aimé Bonpland (1773–1858) (Figure 9.1). While almost forgotten today, Bonpland was a figure of considerable fame in the nineteenth century, mainly for the value of the botanical work he undertook in equinoctial America from 1799–1804 in collaboration with Alexander von Humboldt. After an interlude of mainly botanical work in France, Bonpland resided from early 1817 until his death in various parts of southern South America (Figure 9.2). There he combined a wide range of occupations, including the practice of medicine, pharmacy, botany, including its economic components, and breeding of merino sheep. In contrast to Humboldt, his activities on South American soil have been slow to attract sustained research attention.

Although he published very little, Bonpland has been recognised as a pioneer in the development of geographical knowledge in southern South America.[4] He provides an interesting example of an individual who devoted decades to the study of southern South American physical environments. His capacity to revisit many sites of description set him apart from most other European scientific travellers. The surviving manuscripts from his South American career, still mainly unpublished, run to over 4,000 pages. Demonstrating the important role of historical contingencies in plant exchanges, the present chapter aims to illuminate the wide variety of circumstances where he was involved in species exchange at a variety of geographical scales. Some of this work was intensely local (his planting records survive for a series of South American locations, including the hills of southern Paraguay), while other initiatives took place on a global canvas. While Bonpland presented himself mainly as a disinterested actor furthering science, the chapter shows how the French government apparatus eventually came to steer his work to a greater degree than earlier appreciated. This study works deliberately with selective examples. After a

---

3   Butzer (1992), p. 362.
4   Rodríguez Esteban (1991), pp. 25–6.

South American career that lasted more than four decades, a chapter is not enough to synthesise the breadth of Bonpland's interests in plant geography. In particular, his sustained and extensive studies of yerba mate or Paraguayan tea (*Ilex paraguariensis*) merit a study apart.[5]

Figure 9.1: Aimé Bonpland at São Borja, Brazil, c. 1845

Lithograph by Achille Devéria, based on a drawing made by Alfred Demersay and published in the atlas accompanying the latter's *Histoire physique, économique et politique du Paraguay et des établissements des Jésuites*, 2 vols. and a large-format atlas (Paris: L. Hachette, 1860–64): 'Through the repeated and insistent entreaties of my venerable friend M. Bonpland, I took up the crayon again, something I had ceased to use at the same time I left college; I had not forgotten how to use it.'

This chapter concentrates selectively on three phases where Bonpland was especially open to international influences. First, it considers his background and circumstances when recruited by Argentina's revolutionaries

5   On Bonpland and *yerba mate* see, for example, Linhares (1969), pp. 50–55, 100–01; and Whigham (1991a), pp. 48–49, 85–90.

to Buenos Aires in late 1816, an interesting chapter in the mixing of ecological with political concerns. A second phase of particular interest includes
his work at Buenos Aires in 1832, following almost a decade where he, a
famous scientist, was held hostage in José Gaspar de Francia's Paraguay.
Finally, the chapter describes the work he did for the French government
during the final five years of his life, a chapter of activity that still merits further research.[6] While Bonpland has been written up thus far mainly in the
context of France and Germany (through Humboldt), this chapter also
shows he held a wider web of scientific contacts from South America than
has commonly been assumed. In fact, he provides an excellent example of
David Lowenthal's point that collaboration in the exchange of environmental knowledge involved the commingling of national interests.[7]

Aimé Bonpland came from a background where he was used to working
on a vast canvas. This derived in part from his fieldwork with Humboldt. Not
long after his return to South America in late 1816, the professors of the
Jardin des Plantes in Paris praised highly his comparative studies of cinchona,
for example.[8] Had he still been in France, he would have received strong official encouragement to continue these. The scale of Bonpland's work in
France after the return in 1804 with Humboldt to Europe has not always
been appreciated as fully as it deserves. His work for the Empress Josephine
at Malmaison was on a truly grand scale. In the catalogue prepared for the
1997 exhibition on the French empress and natural sciences, Christian
Jouanin usefully reminds us that of the three botanists associated with
Malmaison, Pierre Ventenat (1757–1808), Charles François Brisseau de
Mirbel (1776–1854) and Bonpland, the last had by far the heaviest and most
diverse duties.[9] Like Ventenat, Bonpland assumed the task of publishing
descriptions of the rare plants on Josephine's properties; as with Mirbel, he
had the responsibilities of managing a vast project of plant acclimatisation,
but in his case on two properties, Malmaison and Navarre. Josephine's considerable financial resources served as a platform for Bonpland to propose
journeys directed to plant exchanges. These took him to various parts of
France, to Vienna, but most importantly to London. In short, well before
Bonpland decided to settle in the Americas, he was accustomed to making
plant exchanges and scouring for new materials.[10] And he was used to the

6   Even the best of Bonpland's earlier biographies make only fleeting mentions of the
     Algerian work. See, for example, Hamy (1906), pp. lxxxiv, 188–9; and Hossard (2001),
     p. 140. The theme escaped all mention in Sarton's generally thorough 1943 essay.
7   Lowenthal (1997), p. 229.
8   See the report made by the botanist René Louiche Desfontaines, 23 December 1818,
     Archives Nationales de France [hereafter AN], F17, 3974.
9   Jouanin (1997), pp. 54–9.
10   There is mention in one of Bonpland's manuscripts that he was already sending seeds
     of useful trees and forage grasses to Buenos Aires as early as September 1814, before
     he left Europe. See Muséum d'Histoire Naturelle, Paris [hereafter MHN], ms. 214,
     'Listes de plantes données (1814–1820)'.

work of seeking to determine the practical elements of specific plants. These were among the skills that made him an extraordinary immigrant when he sought to reach the waters of the Plata in late 1816.

Entering the Plata

When Bonpland arrived at Buenos Aires, there were high expectations of what he could achieve there. A newspaper report noted in February 1817 that he enriched the country from his first arrival 'with a multitude of seeds, and with two thousand living plants'.[11] All of these were judged valuable 'in a country where the vegetable kingdom is in its first infancy', a comment which reads strangely today. It reminds us that the political struggle for independence was perhaps seen as having an ecological counterpart. Immigrants came in more than human form. As for the humans, there is no doubt that Bonpland was viewed as an especially valuable arrival, belonging to the 'class of men' who held themselves apart from political controversies. He would not succeed in doing that for long. In a country of immense and fertile lands, here was an individual devoted to adorning nature with more alluring qualities through the addition of more plant life. Part of the dividend would come through medicinal plants. Another component of the project was agricultural, so that Bonpland was expected to 'put into execution a method of practical agriculture, the fruit of all his observations in England, France and America'. The authorities at Buenos Aires also held in mind a plant conservatory, to be based on Bonpland's introductions, what was known in the region already and what he could find through future researches. Given the political upheavals that would shortly follow, such idealism makes almost painful reading today.

We do not learn all the plant materials that accompanied Bonpland to the Plata from the contemporary newspaper account. But even a summary description points to a vast labour, which included fruit trees, vegetables, plants with medicinal properties, pasture grasses, 150 species of vines from the Jardin du Luxembourg and various types of willow useful for making baskets. In addition, the material included the Spanish carob-tree, whose fruits were much appreciated to feed livestock, especially horses, and all of the sour-fruit trees of France. As the newspaper editors opined, 'we hope that our compatriots will know how to make use of this rich acquisition and propagate it in all of the provinces"[12]

A few days later there came a further summary, outlining Bonpland's 'eminent' scientific background in Europe, mainly on account of the work he accomplished in the Americas with Humboldt. Botany was his forte,

11   *La Crónica Argentina*, 1 February 1817, quoted in Domínguez (1929), p. 14.
12   *Ibid.*

but the country would have made a 'singular acquisition' if Bonpland were
to communicate his researches to other sciences, 'especially medicine, with
which botany has an immediate connection'.[13] It was clear that Buenos
Aires had gained the talents of an immigrant of great scientific merit, with
concrete achievements in both Europe and the Americas. As a friend of
Simón Bolívar, he was also viewed positively as the first botanist and zool-
ogist to visit Argentina since it declared its Independence.

The records that survive point to much energy on Bonpland's part. He
was herborising by February 1817.[14] The marginal notes in French in his
botanical registers are rich in detail on the historical geography of plants.
In Buenos Aires the blacks smoked marijuana in their pipes as a substitute
for tobacco.[15] Asparagus had only been cultivated at Buenos Aires for two
years, grown from seeds introduced from London.[16] And the registers are
thick in comparative considerations about earlier botanical work undertak-
en with Humboldt. By 17 March 1817 he was planting seeds, many of
them gathered at Malmaison two or three years earlier.[17] Others were given
by individuals — great and small — resident in Buenos Aires. In June
Bonpland took possession of the Quinta de los Sauces on the fringes of
the city, where he immediately began experimenting with the cultivation of
indigenous plants. Although the government at Buenos Aires was
favourable to his plan of establishing a botanical garden there, the election
to take on this particular property soon became highly problematical. The
Bethlehemite fathers, who were the previous owners, did not wish to cede
control. This drew Bonpland into a bitter legal struggle.[18] However, within a year, he was able to send a consignment of southern South American
seeds to Paris through the hands of Roguin and Meyer, the leading French
merchants at Buenos Aires in the period. Other shipments sent through
Hullet Brothers were presumably destined for London.[19]

On 22 June 1818 Bonpland asked for the chair in natural history left
vacant by the sudden death of Tadeus Haenke at Cochabamba.[20] He laid
out his objectives in three parts. First, he promised to conclude the work
of gathering all of the plants indigenous to Buenos Aires and its environs.
Then he would begin the work of publishing a description of the regional flora based on dry specimens. He would take his model from the vol-

13   *La Crónica Argentina*, 5 February 1817, quoted in Domínguez (1929), p. 15.
14   See MHN, ms. 203. This comprises Bonpland's botanical registers for the period
     1817–21.
15   *Ibid.* See the entry no. 23, 'Cannabis sativa'.
16   *Ibid.* See the entry no. 36, 'asparagus officinalis?'.
17   See the folder no. 27 in MHN, ms. 215.
18   The matter is reviewed in Ruiz Moreno, Risolía and d'Onofrio (1955), pp. 19–20.
19   MHN, ms. 214 contains extensive records of seed exchanges, listing species, dates and
     recipients.
20   Ruiz Moreno, Risolía and d'Onofrio (1955), p. 31.

umes on American plants published in collaboration with Humboldt. These had appeared in a vastly expensive folio edition.[21] As a concession to cost, the engravings would not appear in colour. On the other hand, this volume would differ from Bonpland's earlier work by printing the observations on plant properties in Spanish, so that local readers without command of French or Latin could draw benefit from the work. As a final point, he announced his readiness to begin journeys to the interior. By this means, he could increase the number of species present in his garden, designed to become the future botanical garden of the United Provinces (an ambition that would never be realised). Collections of dried plants, minerals, insects, birds, shells and fossils could be deposited in the national library, the university or wherever else the government saw fit. He concluded with the observation that work of this nature would motivate him to fix his residence 'forever in this country'.[22]

Bonpland was appointed to the chair in natural history, but there was no salary.[23] Although he would never meet his publication objectives, there is no doubt whatsoever that he held to a design building on the work accomplished earlier with Humboldt and at Malmaison. Surviving coloured drawings of insects and butterflies in Buenos Aires are testimony of concrete achievements from his early work at that city. We have only cryptic references about how much manuscript material was lost from Buenos Aires during the period when Bonpland was later held prisoner in Paraguay. When he told a French colleague, the botanist Alire Raffeneau Delile, in 1821 that he was ready to publish the flora of the United Provinces (presumably meaning of the Buenos Aires region and of the Upper Plata), there is no ground to disbelieve this.[24] Like much else in his career, this project was a casualty of politics.

Bonpland's manuscripts also point to a vigorous programme of seed exchanges, with a high degree of internationalism. While earlier authors may be partly correct in claiming he sold fruit and vegetables to live at

21   In Humboldt and Bonpland's *Plantes équinoxiales* (1805–17) the 144 plates were published in black and white. The 17 fascicles comprising this study were mainly Bonpland's work. In their *Monographie des mélastomacées* (1806–23), part of which was also prepared by Bonpland, the 120 engravings were prepared in colour. On the complicated publishing history of the above works, see Fiedler and Leitner (2000), pp. 250–72.

22   Ruiz Moreno, Risolía and d'Onofrio (1955), p. 34.

23   Domínguez (1929), p. 17.

24   Bonpland to Delile, Santa Ana, 1821, printed in Hamy (1906), pp. 79–80. This letter to Delile, a close friend of Bonpland's in France, was written from a former Jesuit mission on the borders of Paraguay. Alire Raffeneau Delile (1778–1850) is remembered mainly as the author of the *Flore d'Egypte* (Paris, n.p., 1824). After his travels with Napoleon's forces to Egypt, and a spell as a representative of the French government to the United States, he spent many years as the occupant of the chair in botany in the Faculty of Medicine at Montpellier.

Buenos Aires, it is clear that much more than market gardening was taking place.[25] Many of the names in his records of seed exchanges are easily traceable. As earlier at Malmaison, there is a heavy focus on elites. The list of recipients includes major politicians (such as Juan Martín de Pueyrredón, Manuel Belgrano, José de San Martín), the British (Robert Staples, the unofficial British consul, and William Bowles, commander of the South Atlantic squadron of the Royal Navy) and the French (including General Dauxion Lavaysse, a high-profile Napoleonic refugee in Buenos Aires, and the naturalist Félix Louis L'Herminier in Guadeloupe). We learn that Bonpland received pineapples from Rio de Janeiro from a letter he wrote there in November 1818, where he announced his plans to construct a glasshouse in Buenos Aires, yet another echo of life at Malmaison.[26] He also received indigo from Rio de Janeiro.[27] He would publish a description of this plant from the Upper Plata in Buenos Aires.[28] By means of such exchanges, Bonpland established a network where people widely recognised his authority and brought him natural history materials, from locations as diverse as the battlefield at Chacabuco and the Atlantic coast of what is now Uruguay.[29] Oral accounts often kindled curiosity to see particular species in situ. In 1818 Bonpland was given seeds of the giant water lily (a few decades later, one of the wonders of the Royal Botanic Gardens in Kew) brought down from Santa Fe. Although he would soon observe this plant in person, he worked immediately from a verbal description to arrive at his sense of where to classify it.[30]

No plant caught his attention more than yerba mate, or Paraguayan tea, the staple beverage of the region. Once planted by the Jesuits in their missions, the yerba supply depended on collecting following their expulsion from South America. Supply in the leading market, the Río de la Plata, was further compromised once Francia's Paraguay held the virtual monopoly of this commodity but 'interest in Upper Platine yerba remained avid in

25   Wilson (1994), p. 40; Kirchheimer (1993), p. 125.
26   Bonpland to Acard, Buenos Aires, 18 November 1818. See Ruiz Moreno, Risolía and d'Onofrio (1955), p. 60. I have thus far been unable to gain any biographical details about Acard and his work at Rio de Janeiro. I speculate, however, that he may have had links to the French cultural mission to Brazil of 1816. Remembered mainly in the spheres of art and architecture, this was designed originally to include practical components, including agriculture. The members of the mission were chosen following advice received from Alexander von Humboldt. Bonpland was in contact with some of the members of the mission from Buenos Aires. See Taunay (1983), pp. 9–11.
27   See MHN, ms. 203, entry no. 138, 'indigofera tinctoria conf.'
28   *El Argos* (Buenos Aires), 10 November 1821.
29   The famous battle of Chacabuco was fought on 12 February 1817 between Chilean independence forces and Spanish troops. It took place just north of Santiago.
30   MHN, ms. 203, entry no. 147, 'Nelumbium conf. *mayz de agua.*'

Buenos Aires'.[31] There was a longstanding interest in Buenos Aires in the question whether yerba grew closer to the city, with various contemporary claims that it grew on islands in the Paraná and mentions of its presence near the Uruguay River.[32] Reminiscent of his work with Humboldt on the various species of cinchona, the study of yerba had obvious strategic and commercial components. Visiting the island Martín García in December 1818 he found a small stand of yerba, which led to the earliest description of this by a European scientist.[33] He returned there again in August and September of 1819. An obsession with the characteristics of this plant was taking hold. On 11 August 1820 Bonpland asked the authorities in Buenos Aires for a passport to go to the Upper Plata on a scientific journey.[34] That led to a fascinating trip to the former Jesuit mission area on the disputed borders of Paraguay (present-day Misiones). But the successful resuscitation of a former Jesuit planted *yerbal* also led Bonpland into the hands of Francia. In December 1821 he was dragged by force into Paraguay, where his books, instruments and freedom to connect with a broader world would be taken away for a long spell.

The nature of Bonpland's confinement in Paraguay has been the subject of many accounts but it lies beyond the confines of this chapter.[35] While it provided obvious scope for the close examination of plant materials, it also represented a long hiatus from books and from significant journeyings.

Revisiting Buenos Aires

With his sudden release from captivity in Paraguay, Bonpland's options broadened, but not to the degree that earlier researchers have assumed. He was pursued by debts contracted in Europe or in Buenos Aires, including for the books he supplied far back in 1816 for what was planned by London-based revolutionaries to be Argentina's national library.[36] He needed to find a source of income, an objective most readily dealt with once his brother at La Rochelle had sent medical instruments to replace those taken away by order of Francia. And he was emphatically no friend

31 Whigham (1991b), p. 120.
32 Bonpland made extensive notes based on the local claims; Museo de Farmacobotánica 'Juan Aníbal Domínguez,' Facultad de Farmacia y Bioquímica, Universidad de Buenos Aires [hereafter MFJAD], Archivo Aimé Bonpland [hereafter AAB], *carpeta* [docket] 6. The natural distribution of yerba mate remains a topic for scientific study even today. See Giberti (1995), pp. 289–300.
33 See Giberti (1990), p. 663.
34 Ruiz Moreno, Risolía and d'Onofrio (1955), p. 79.
35 Among the many treatments see Pérez Acosta (1942); Williams (1972), pp. 114–8.
36 See the letter from Bonpland to the Paris publisher Barrois l'aîné, Corrientes, 28 March 1838, which discusses a debt assumed on 14 October 1816; AAB, carpeta 4.

of Juan Manuel de Rosas and his political system. After arranging a place to live and work in the former Jesuit mission area of Rio Grande do Sul, Bonpland paid an extended visit to Buenos Aires, the city in southern South America where he could most readily communicate with the authorities and with scientific friends in Europe.

Buenos Aires also offered more clearly the scope for reading and for writing. Using the library of Pedro de Angelis, scholar, journalist and, effectively, the minister of propaganda for the Rosas government, he was able to read extensively from earlier travel accounts dealing with the Upper Plata.[37] He also consulted more recent published works, including those of Humboldt, and made scientific notes on a wide range of topics. The contents of these notes are too extensive to report in their totality, but the following brief examples will serve to demonstrate their diversity.[38] Reading a report about Peruvian cotton made by the South Carolina Agricultural Society, Bonpland speculated whether this would resemble the cotton grown in Paraguay that he had seen. In the newspaper *El Lucero*, no doubt an organ of ready access, since it was published by de Angelis from 1829 to 1833, he read about the Chaco region. Elsewhere, he consulted newspaper reports made by the British consul Joseph Barclay Pentland at Arequipa, Peru about the measurement of the highest peaks in the Andes, learning for the first time that Chimborazo was not the tallest peak in the cordilleras. Bonpland had not accompanied the highest climb in the world after all.[39] In addition, there are records on subjects as diverse as cholera and palaeontology. On a topic such as the transport of woody plants from and to the Rio de Janeiro botanical garden, the level of detail is especially rich. In Buenos Aires, Bonpland could also finally read some of the key publications that had emerged during his long period of captivity in Paraguay. Devouring the fifth volume of Humboldt's travel account of their shared journey to the Americas and his *Tableaux de la nature*, this reader's interests mainly concerned crops and the subject of how easily authors rendered indigenous names incorrectly.[40] Criticism of Humboldt's errors was mild in comparison with those supposedly made by Auguste de Saint-Hilaire in his books on Brazil. Bonpland considered that what Saint-Hilaire

37　On Pedro de Angelis, see especially the excellent study by Sabor (1995).

38　They are taken from the scientific journal Bonpland kept for June 1832; AAB, carpeta 7.

39　The ascent of Chimborazo volcano took place on 23 June 1802. Humboldt provided several accounts of this dramatic event in his letters, but see especially those to his brother Wilhelm from Lima, 25 November 1802 and to Thomas Jefferson, Philadelphia, 24 May 1804, published in Humboldt (1993), pp. 211, 292.

40　The themes noted included Humboldt's discussions of coffee cultivation at Caracas, the vague discussion of the timing of Otaheiti cane's diffusion into South America and cereal yields in the tropics. The page references in Bonpland's notes are to Humboldt and Bonpland (1820), pp. 82, 94, 104, 132, 134, and to Humboldt (1828), p. 257.

had to say about the cultivation of cotton and of tobacco was useless, presumably in the sense of anybody seeking to follow the written advice.[41]

On 7 May 1832 Bonpland paid a visit to Santa Catalina, the site of the former Scottish colony Monte Grande developed by the Scottish merchants John and William Parish Robertson in the 1820s with Bernardino Rivadavia's encouragement.[42] Today, the trees planted there by the Scottish immigrants form part of a protected ecosystem distinctive in the whole of South America, which is located on the grounds of an agronomy school. Although the colony was presumed a casualty of politics after 1829, there was still some activity there in 1832.[43] We have no direct testimony beyond a plant description, but it may be that Santa Catalina stimulated Bonpland to think once more about the prospects for extending cultivation in and around the city of Buenos Aires.[44]

Through the agency of his Neapolitan-born host Pedro de Angelis, Bonpland opened communication in June 1832 with Michel Tenore, the director of the botanical garden at Naples.[45] He sent 32 species of plants to Tenore, with very specific comments about the properties of indigenous plants. He also made clear that he had selected a subset of what he sent on to Paris, by choosing items particularly suitable to the climate of Naples. In return, Bonpland wanted two things, particularly herbaceous cotton. It is on record that Tenore sent this to South America, but the fate of the cotton is not known.[46] It was probably a casualty of the recipient's inability to revisit Buenos Aires before a five-year interval.

In the same month, Bonpland completed a manuscript on a scheme for the agricultural development of the area around Buenos Aires.[47] It is unclear today what stimulated him to write this, but his recent visit to Santa Catalina may have had some bearing. The document provides an important window into Bonpland's preoccupations. His paper begins by singing the praises of the tropics for cultivation, of which he had gained direct

41   He took notes on Auguste de Saint-Hilaire's recently published *Voyage dans les provinces de Rio de Janeiro et Minas Geraes* (1830), using a copy borrowed from Henry Stephen Fox, the British minister resident at Buenos Aires.
42   See Robertson and Robertson (1839), p. 91.
43   Grierson (1925), p. 67. There is an interesting brief review of the Scottish colonisation in Fernández-Gómez (1993, pp. 95–100), who points out that this was the first homogeneous ethnic (in the sense of non-Spanish) settlement in the Río de la Plata, and of huge importance in studying the roots of agricultural improvement in the region. The Robertson brothers sank a considerable capital into the scheme.
44   MHN, ms. 205, entry no. 1215, 'Yucca gloriosa conf'. I have established the timing of this visit through Bonpland's meteorological records; AAB, carpeta 5.
45   See Bonpland to Michel Tenore, Buenos Aires, 4 June 1832; AAB, carpeta 2.
46   Tenore to Bonpland, Naples, 4 April 1836; AAB, carpeta 2.
47   Aimé Bonpland, 'Nottes pour servir à un ètablissement agricole dont les fruits doivent être consomés pour la plus part dans la Capitale de B. ayres,' Buenos Aires, 21 June 1832; AAB, carpeta 5.

experience in the Upper Plata, including Paraguay. He then says he will pass in silence over the colder regions, in order to see what could be done in a temperate climate, such as Buenos Aires.

There is an implicit understanding of the concept of land rent in Bonpland's paper, which is set out as a series of three interlocking types of rural establishment, where the intensity of land use was at its highest close to the city. Zone three was to be a carefully-managed *estancia*. No doubt impressed by the growth of the city since he left it over a decade before, he comments on the already immense daily consumption of the city, observing that 'the population of Buenos Aires is already very large and susceptible to increase in a progression that nobody can calculate'. When James Scobie wrote about urban change in Buenos Aires, it was still a *gran aldea* in 1870; we need to remember that Bonpland's most immediate residence patterns before sounding so optimistic about Buenos Aires hinged around a series of former Jesuit mission settlements, whose small populations were but a fraction of what they had been in the first half of the eighteenth century.[48] He clearly saw potential for doing much more to furnish the growing domestic market, maintaining there was profit from the near beginning with fruits and vegetables. Crops such as maize, wheat, tobacco and sweet potatoes were seen as better cultivated in fields than in gardens. Pumpkins in particular would yield a quick income. Planting trees for firewood was a less easy economic proposition; they needed more time to render a stream of income. At the time, Buenos Aires drew only on peach-trees for firewood. He seemed keen to work with a managed forest of these, from which could be drawn 'a true Kirschwasser drink'. Distillation was another echo of his period of captivity in Paraguay. Beyond working with plants already in Argentina, Bonpland stressed the importance of making further introductions. Once a model rural property was established, he said, it would be easy to make direct contacts with various parts of France, with Britain, the United States, Mexico and Brazil in the search for further useful vegetable material. These were precisely the main countries where Bonpland had correspondents.

Phase two of the scheme was about milk cows and merino sheep. With work and perseverance Bonpland thought that the wool of Buenos Aires could conquer the markets of Europe, in the way that Saxony wools were sought to a greater degree in 1832 than those from Spain. Here, his optimism had some concrete foundation. He noted that the value of cross breeding could be seen in the beauty of the wool produced by Peter Sheridan, whose animals were supposedly not treated with greater care than the creole flocks. Bonpland was something of an authority on merinos.[49] He had managed an important flock for Josephine at Malmaison.

48   Scobie (1974), p. 14.
49   Bell (1995).

He also knew Sheridan, the famous sheep pioneer on the Pampas, in person. Sheridan supplied Bonpland with merino breeding stock for his experiments in south-eastern Corrientes during the later 1830s.[50]

According to Bonpland, the only forage plant cultivated around Buenos Aires in 1832 was some alfalfa. He called for research into forage grasses, concerned mainly about the winter feeding of his projected large flocks of merinos. Alfalfa would not serve here. He had seen entire flocks of merinos perish when inflated by gas. Whether this was on the grasslands of Argentina or in Napoleonic France is not specified.

Other crops worthy of closer attention included cotton. When Levant cotton arrived from Naples (a hidden reference to Michel Tenore and the botanical garden he headed), it needed to be sown with great care. In an age still dependent on candles, Bonpland saw potential great economy in using cotton in the manufacture of candle wicks. Tobacco was also destined to become important with time. He based this judgement on the success of his own planting experiments in Buenos Aires in 1819. In addition, tobacco was in cultivation on Governor Rosas's ranches; in 1832, it was supposed that 'everybody' knew of the success of this. Ornamental flowers deserved to be encouraged for pharmaceutical purposes.

There is a particularly revealing passage in the manuscript where Bonpland made clear his displeasure with what he saw as the sterility of the landscape around Buenos Aires, showing his continuing enthusiasm for tropical vegetation. In his words, nature had been miserly, and human initiative on the part of the Spanish during the colonial era had been lacking. The ombú (*Phytolacca dioica*), one of the world's largest trees, and the tala (*Celtis tala*) were almost the only native species. He saw little economic potential for either. While he thought that the *tala* could serve only as firewood, its modern uses are broader. Today it is a focus for conservation efforts on the Pampas.

The agricultural manuscript provides details of a series of desirable exotic tree species, some of which are viewed as pests today in Argentina. Bonpland was also an enthusiast for bringing trees from the interior into Buenos Aires, but he did not specify what he held in mind. The first exotic species he recommended was the carob-tree (*Ceratonia siliqua*), whose fruits, known as St John's Bread, could serve as seasonal food for livestock. By the early twentieth century, the carob-tree was described as covering 'immense stretches' of the northern Pampas.[51] After reviewing different types of willows and poplars, Bonpland said he had seen two examples of

50 See Peter Sheridan to Bonpland (letter written in Spanish), Buenos Aires, 4 July 1841; AAB, carpeta 4. I was still unaware of this important connection when I published my 1995 article on Bonpland and sheep.
51 Maudit (1909), p. 270.

European oaks in the Barracas district of Buenos Aires. These had grown fairly large, he noticed, and he claimed they would have grown bigger if they had not been maltreated by animals. He took these oaks as a certain index that it was worth trying all the variant species in Buenos Aires, whether from Europe, the United States or Mexico. The common ash was seen as providing wood of the first rank for Buenos Aires, as in Europe. Brought from France in 1817, very probably by Bonpland himself, the species was doing well in 1832, which encouraged further introductions. This was not the only tree for which Bonpland seems to have been responsible. All the examples of the Honeylocust (*Gleditsia triacanthos*) present in Buenos Aires were obtained from seeding done in 1817. It is interesting to see how far the many types of tree mentioned had come into use by the 1908 census.

In summary, a present-day reader of Bonpland's manuscript on agricultural development around Buenos Aires will be struck by his energy for change and by his extraordinary level of empirical knowledge about the regional vegetation systems. He never questioned for a moment the wisdom of trying exotic introductions. The optimism in his report reminds us of why Bonpland was considered good company throughout his time in South America, but the idealism is rarely much grounded. For example, when he proposed the planting of 'immense artificial prairies', or planted pastures, who was to pay for the cultivation? Bonpland was no more capable of seeing the future than any of us, but it is interesting to reflect that Argentina by around 1920 devoted a greater area to alfalfa than any other nation on earth.[52] His idealism contrasts with the cautious experimentation of Rosas, such as the cultivation of alfalfa along the river banks.[53] Diversification of land use was not yet a major consideration in Buenos Aires in the 1830s. The few persons mentioned by name in Bonpland's paper represent an avant-garde. Apart from a buried reference to Michel Tenore in Naples, four other individuals are mentioned by name. Three of these are British pioneers in Argentina's agriculture, whose activities in the first half of the nineteenth century are worthy of more research. The final example is Rosas himself. Domingo F. Sarmiento's famous barb that all he cared for was land has perhaps obscured Rosas's practical concerns for its management.

A long confinement in Paraguay helped Bonpland become more aware of the ecological consequences of some of his actions. Writing to Mirbel (the professor in charge of cultivation at the Jardin des Plantes) from Buenos Aires in 1837, he recalled that when he arrived in the Plata he brought with him around 2,000 living plants. At that time, the number of plants in the region was viewed as limited, whether indigenous or exotic.

52   Alfalfa accompanied the successful emergence of large-scale wheat cultivation. See
      Scobie (1964), p. 46; Bell (1998), p. 129.
53   On Rosas and agriculture, see Slatta (1983), p. 151-2.

Today one could see immense gardens with plants from all countries: 'The soil of Buenos Aires, bare in 1818, is rich today in vegetables, of which several offer a concrete use'.[54]

During his second visit to Buenos Aires post-Paraguay, Bonpland received a portion of his French state pension for the first time during his South American residency. He soon returned to the Upper Plata, where he sought land in Santa Ana in south-eastern Corrientes (Figure 9.2). He held the ambition to render this property a second Malmaison, but his efforts at merino breeding and experimental cultivation were rapidly undercut by the struggle of Corrientes against Rosas. The later 1830s and the 1840s were more about survival than experimentation. The famous battle of Pago Largo of 1839, which Corrientes lost, was fought very close to Bonpland's land. As a supporter of the losing forces, Bonpland was fortunate that he did not meet the same fate as many of his neighbours. Some authors have argued that his scientific credentials spared him, but the hard evidence is lacking.[55]

Figure 9.2: Regions of Southern South America Visited by Aimé Bonpland, 1817–58

54   Bonpland to Mirbel, Buenos Aires, 25 January 1837; AAB, carpeta 2.
55   Pioli de Layerenza and Artigas de Rebes (1990), p. 61.

Reemerging from Montevideo

The political instability of the later 1830s and the 1840s obstructed scientific work on Bonpland's part and these years were not conducive to travel. It is a clear sign of how much his activity patterns were broken that E.T. Hamy's major biography of Bonpland found no letters to publish for the years between 1841 and 1849. However, in 1849 Bonpland made a major journey by land across the Serra of Rio Grande do Sul, descending from southern Brazil to Montevideo by sea (this city was still besieged on land), from where he was able to renew old links and foster new ones with Europe.[56]

An important link renewed at some point in 1849 was with Sir William Hooker, the director of the Royal Botanic Gardens at Kew, a person Bonpland had met in Paris decades earlier through Humboldt, shortly before departing for South America. William Hooker had published in 1816 the cryptogams brought back from the Americas by Bonpland and Humboldt.[57] Hooker and Bonpland had some further contacts in the 1830s, when the former was the regius professor of botany at Glasgow University. He wrote to Bonpland in the hope of gaining South American plant materials, and also offering to be of help as a collaborator for possible publications.[58] A letter conserved in Buenos Aires provides concrete evidence that at least some exchange of species was attempted between Scotland and the Río de la Plata.[59]

In Bonpland's patterns of receipt of correspondence, long delays occasioned by political instability were frequent. In 1849 Bonpland's name came up in England again in the search for a South American plant cure for hydrophobia. The British government sought further examples of guaco (*Mikania guaco*), described by Humboldt and Bonpland along their journey, and thought to be growing 'more or less in the environs of São Borja' where Bonpland was living.[60] Following this overture, Bonpland conveyed an offer to send plant materials to Kew through Robert Gore, the British consul in Montevideo.

56   This portion of Bonpland's travel manuscripts has been published. See Bonpland (1978).
57   See Fiedler and Leitner (2000), pp. 320–1.
58   William Jackson Hooker to Bonpland, Glasgow University, 25 May 1835; AAB, carpeta 2. This letter is published in abbreviated form in Cordier (1914), p. 10.
59   Hooker to Bonpland, Glasgow, at some point in the 1830s (the exact year is indistinguishable in the manuscript); AAB, carpeta 2. Hooker sent Bonpland the heliotrope plant, the small jasmine and the orange-tree with myrtle leaves.
60   Kew's message to Bonpland was relayed through a British private citizen. See Henrique [Henry] Symonds to Bonpland, Montevideo, 14 March 1849 (letter written in Spanish); AAB, carpeta 4. Symonds wrote this letter on the point of leaving South America, following commercial failure. Tied to Liverpool mercantile interests, he provides an interesting example of early British investment in land in the interior of South America. In the 1830s, Symonds was active in ranching in Corrientes, where his links to Bonpland developed. As with Bonpland, his efforts to develop the fine wool industry were a casualty of political instability. Bonpland published his description of *Mikania guaco* in Humboldt and Bonpland (1805–17), vol. 2, pp. 84–7 and Plate 105.

Hooker was quick to respond to Bonpland's offer 'to transmit to the Royal Gardens of Kew duplicates of … rare specimens of plants, bulbs, fruits and seeds', assuring him this was 'already spoken of at the Foreign Office with much satisfaction'.[61] As with other European institutions, Bonpland seems to have sought a catalogue from Kew, in order to avoid sending duplicate materials. Hooker sought to put his mind at rest. Barring the most common and universal species, Bonpland had

> … been exploring quite a new territory. Except what Mr. Tweedie has sent us from Buenos Ayres, *we* know nothing of the vegetation of the regions you have visited and therefore all that you have thought worth collecting will be sure to be valuable to us and you need make no particular *selection*. I had hopes at one time of receiving plants from a man of the name of Barclay but he preferred brandy to fulfilling his duties as collector, and we got nothing from him.

> I often reflect on the pleasant interview I had with you in Paris, when our mutual friend Humboldt introduced me to your personal acquaintance. Since then your researches up the Paraná and the Paraguay must have been peculiarly interesting and valuable.[62]

The remainder of Hooker's letter provided a brief account of the travels of his son Joseph, who promised 'to be as great a traveller (in point of extent of country) as you and Humboldt have been'.[63] After five years accompanying Sir James Ross to Antarctica, Joseph Hooker would now spend three years chiefly devoted to the exploration of the wonders of the Sikkim Himalayas, including Tibet: 'He explored Kinchinjunga, the loftiest of all mountains (28,167 feet) and has twice penetrated into Tibet. A note on the first of these excursions, I take the liberty of enclosing for your acceptance.'[64] What Sir

---

61 Hooker to Bonpland, Royal Gardens, Kew, 1 December 1849; AAB, carpeta 2.
62 *Ibid.* James Tweedie (1775–1862) had a background in garden planning in Scotland. He originally came to Buenos Aires as the main gardener at the Scottish colony of Monte Grande (Santa Catalina), founded by the Robertson brothers on the fringes of Buenos Aires. He was still present there in the later 1820s, but also travelled to collect plant species in the Plata. Tweedie sent extensive materials to Hooker. See Barreto (1976), pp. 1366–7; Grierson (1925), pp. 43, 56. George Barclay was sent out from Kew to South America, 1836–41; Desmond (1995), pp. 141, 432.
63 Hooker to Bonpland, Royal Gardens, Kew, 1 December 1849; AAB, carpeta 2.
64 *Ibid.* Joseph Hooker had visited Paris in 1845, from where his letters were full of pungent opinions about French scientists. In preparation for his extensive travels he also visited Humboldt, whose physical appearance did not meet the levels of distinction he predicted: 'I expected to see a fine fellow six feet without his boots, who would make as few steps to get up Chimborazo as thoughts to solve a problem. I cannot now at all fancy his trotting along the Cordillera as I once supposed he would have *stalked*. However, he received me most kindly and made a great many enquiries about all at Kew and in England' (Huxley, 1918, p. 180).

William communicated here was that his son had overtaken Humboldt and Bonpland in making the highest climb in the world, not that this record would hold for long.

Partly through Humboldt, Bonpland's life was still registering with the Hookers. It remains unclear what exactly he sent to Kew, beyond a late 1855 reference that he had sent numerous seeds of the giant water lily (*Victoria regia*), a species that first received a partial description in his botanical registers as long back as September 1818.[65] His English was extremely limited for reading catalogues or publications. But William Hooker's repeated efforts to contact Bonpland are an interesting example of Kew's orbit extending beyond obvious channels in the search for material.[66]

While Paraguay had the capacity to excite intellectuals in Europe, mainly on account of its closed nature while under Francia's dictatorship, Bonpland showed considerable interest in the French colony Algeria, a place he perceived as opening to development. France occupied Algiers around the time that Bonpland was released from Paraguay. French colonial ambitions in Algeria entered the popular consciousness in the 1830s. Bonpland seems to offer a confirmation of this, from the distance of South America. Shortly after leaving Paraguay, he included plants for Algeria, including Paraguayan tobacco, in a shipment of specimens in May 1831 to the Jardin des Plantes. Writing to Mirbel there in 1837 he noted that some seeds taken from the shipment in Buenos Aires already formed large trees six years later. However, the climate in Buenos Aires was less suited to the growth of these plants than that of Algiers: 'In order to have a certain guide, I would like to know the plants that grow under the climate of our new African colony, whether indigenous or exotic.'[67] Bonpland was clearly thinking about Algeria's potential in economic botany, but he had no direct links to the colony from the interior of South America.

Deprived of French-language materials during his Paraguayan confinement, it seems probable that Bonpland would have taken a keen interest in

65   Bonpland to William Gore Ouseley, Montevideo, 18 December 1855; AAB, carpeta 3. Bonpland's earliest description of what the South Americans called 'water maize', on account of the food value of its seeds, was made in September 1818 in Buenos Aires, based on material sent to him from Santa Fe. He first saw the plant in person during May 1821 in Corrientes, along his journey to the former Jesuit missions. See entries no. 147 and 543 in MHN, ms. 203.

66   On the character of Sir William Hooker's global grasp for botanical materials, see Grove (1995), p. 426. Before William Gore Ouseley left England for a South American diplomatic posting, Hooker charged him expressly to seek out Bonpland. On this occasion, as earlier, Hooker conveyed the message he wished to see Bonpland publish the results from his 'long study of nature in these countries.' Ouseley to Bonpland, Encarnación [Itapúa], Paraguay, 1 April 1855 (letter written in French); AAB, carpeta 3.

67   Bonpland to Mirbel, Buenos Aires, 25 January 1837; AAB, carpeta 2.

the progress of Algerian colonisation from reading the French newspapers circulating in South America. One influential commentator was Alexis de Tocqueville. In his 'Essay on Algeria' of October 1841 he opined that the city of Algiers was the centre of French power in Africa: 'It is there that the plow was first put to the soil and the work of colonisation begun; it is there that we must prove we can colonise Africa'.[68] However, after a period of intense urban speculation around Algiers, the rural colonisation moved extremely slowly. In his 1847 report, Tocqueville himself described the goal that would guide France's project in Algeria: 'We should set out to create not a colony properly speaking in Algeria, but rather the extension of France itself across the Mediterranean'. The project involved 'implanting in Africa a population that resembles us in everything'.[69] Part of this meant support for introductions of exotic plants.

The 1848 French Constitution declared Algeria 'an integral part of France', so that it could be eventually absorbed into the metropolitan administrative structure.[70] By November 1853 the needs of the French metropolitan government were communicated to South America in a document dealing with general concerns of French commerce in the Plata, which also included 'an enumerative note of a number of plants native to Uruguay and to Paraguay, [but] unknown for the greater part in our latitudes'.[71] The acclimatisation of these plants in Algiers was seen as offering potential great advantages, by building up the economy there, and eventually saving the metropole from importing specific things from beyond French colonial possessions. The minister of war sought seeds from Montevideo and Buenos Aires in order to foster the agricultural development of Algeria. Paris wanted to know the geography of where seeds were drawn from, including some account of geological and climatic conditions. The costs of plant transfers were to be assumed by the ministry.

Demonstrating the importance of contingencies, these specific requests for help from Paris arrived in Montevideo at one of those infre-

68 Tocqueville (2001), pp. 84–5.
69 *Ibid.*, pp. 161–2.
70 See Jennifer Pitts's introduction in Tocqueville (2001), p. xxxvii. There is an interesting review of the different French ideas about North African colonisation in Heffernan (1989).
71 Édouard Drouyn de Lhuys, the minister of foreign affairs, to Consul-general Maillefer [Daniel-Pierre Martin-Maillefer], Paris, 30 November 1853; Ministère des Relations Extérieures, Paris [hereafter MRE], Correspondance consulaire et commerciale [hereafter CCC], Montevideo, 1843–56, tome 5, fols. 279–80. Around this time Bonpland was also invited to accompany the United States' Plata–Paraná–Paraguay survey; see Page (1859), pp. 295–8. Since he was very positive about the idea, it remains unclear why he did not act upon it. Other work, including the new plant mission for Algeria, probably stood in the way. On the considerable significance of the US naval survey of the Plata, see Fifer (1991), especially pp. 13–8.

quent times when Bonpland was visiting there. As soon as he gained wind of the seed transfer project, probably from the French consul Maillefer, he wrote to Napoleon III offering his services. His letter to the emperor even carries an earlier date than Consul Maillefer's official reply to Paris about the scheme.[72]

In writing to Napoleon III, Bonpland began by referring to 36 years of forced residence in South America, where he reckoned he had done nothing to jeopardise his nationality. What he meant by 'forced residence' is not easily determined. In any legal sense, he was free to return to France. Any sense of force was probably psychological; he felt he had work to complete in South America. As late as 1856, at his birthday celebration in São Borja in Brazil, he was calling for four more years to complete his South American studies.[73] After referring to the brilliant reign of Napoleon I, Bonpland reminded the new emperor that he had seen employment at the 'incomparable' Malmaison and Navarre for nine years. The experiences of what he termed 'that short phase' working with Josephine had left their mark for life. Although now 82, 'the new order of things' left Bonpland wishing to revisit Paris. He would be happy to find an opportunity to present his South American researches to the emperor, in the same way he presented to Napoleon I those made in the equinoctial regions 'in concert with [Humboldt], the most famous of travellers'.[74] There was perhaps some room for sentiment when seeking imperial preference, since Bonpland had held the new emperor as a baby.[75]

On the same day he wrote the piece of flattery above, Bonpland returned to Consul Maillefer the 'nomenclature' of the trees of Paraguay and Uruguay, sent to South America in the search for seeds for the experimental botanical garden at Algiers: 'It is unfortunately very common to find foreign names, and above all those of plants poorly described, even in published works. The naming system that we have on hand provides a very striking example of this.' Thus Bonpland had seen fit to revise the

72   Bonpland to Napoleon III, Montevideo, 12 January 1854; AAB, carpeta 2. There are both a draft and a copy of the letter sent in the Bonpland archive at Buenos Aires. As often with Bonpland, the content varies. My wording is based on the draft. A transcription of the letter sent is published in Hossard (2001), pp. 195–6. Maillefer to Drouyn de Lhuys, Montevideo, 2 February 1854; CCC, Montevideo, tome 5, fol. 282.

73   This is according to the testimony of his close friend at São Borja, the French-born priest and scholar Jean-Pierre Gay. See Jean-Pierre Gay's manuscript 'Le naturaliste Mr. Aimé Bonpland,' São Borja, 29 August 1858. This manuscript of 19 numbered pages is in AN, F17 3974.

74   Bonpland to Napoleon III, Montevideo, 12 January 1854; AAB, carpeta 2.

75   See Gay, 'Le naturaliste Mr. Aimé Bonpland'. Gay also claimed to learn from Bonpland's oral testimony that the latter was present at Napoleon III's birth. Jean-Pierre Gay to the Baron d'Ornano, French vice-consul at Porto Alegre, São Borja, 15 October 1856; MRE, Affaires Diverses, République Argentine, 1841–67, carton 2.

list. He repeated the names sent from France, but included the earlier idea of what was under consideration, the botanical names, 'whether using the Linnean or natural systems', and a series of practical observations directed toward issues of acclimatisation: 'I imagine I have been too prolix in my explication of the indigenous names and in the observations that I made about each plant. My firm desire is to be useful to science and to my country.'[76] Shortly after his release from Paraguay, he pointed out, the materials he sent to the Paris museum included a collection of seeds supposed useful for Algeria, a place, as he phrased it, that had always fixed his regards. The difficulty of communicating with France from the South American interior had suspended all of his plans for Algeria. We know Bonpland had sent materials for Algeria to Paris in the 1830s at his own initiative; he told Humboldt that he never received a response about these.[77] Thus the minister of war's project, with its clear mechanisms for transfer, held much appeal for him. He promised to work at this scheme, gathering both seeds from species in the plant catalogue and others he considered potentially useful in North Africa. In his properties at Santa Ana, Corrientes and São Borja, Rio Grande do Sul, both located on the banks of the Uruguay River, Bonpland told the consul he constantly sowed seeds as fast as they came to him. He also pointed out that he was in the longstanding habit of taking all the necessary precautions for their germination and growth. Part of a request for catalogues from the experimental garden at Algiers was to avoid duplication. In addition, by knowing what grew there, it would be possible to work by analogy, so that shipments could be more complete and useful.[78]

In response to this offer of help, Consul Maillefer was able to send by the return mailboat to France 'a valuable work by Mr. Aimé Bonpland, the most competent man in South America' in the matter of seed exchanges.[79] No doubt the offer of practical help was a boon to an overburdened French consul. The services of the consulate were provided to draw up the table sent to France, where the minister was alerted he would find 'corrected indigenous names, botanical names, the places of origin and a good

76 Bonpland to Maillefer, Montevideo, 21 January 1854; CCC, Montevideo, tome 5, fols. 284–85v

77 See Bonpland to Humboldt, Montevideo, 29 January 1854, published in Hamy (1906), p. 182. In the following month, Bonpland already described the Algerian work to Humboldt as 'an immense task', while in October he claimed there was nobody competent to whom he could delegate. Bonpland to Humboldt, Montevideo, 3 February 1854 and Restauración [Paso de los Libres], 2 October 1854, published in Hamy (1906), pp. 186, 188–9.

78 Bonpland to Maillefer, Montevideo, 21 January 1854; CCC, Montevideo, tome 5, fols. 284–285v.

79 Maillefer to Drouyn de Lhuys, Montevideo, 2 February 1854; CCC, Montevideo, tome 5, fol. 282.

number of observations even more practical than academic'.[80] Maillefer forwarded the request for catalogues, both from Paris and Algiers, so that Bonpland would be able to better direct his operations. He also pointed out that Bonpland was working without self interest. Some flattering words from the imperial government were perhaps in order? Consul Maillefer showed his understanding of how to use the French government apparatus in order to stimulate Bonpland's work.

The first shipment came from Concordia, Entre Ríos, in March.[81] It comprised two boxes filled with fully ripe fruits of the yatay palm (*Butia yatay*), a species Bonpland considered valuable. In the 1850s, he observed, it still formed extensive woods in Entre Ríos and Corrientes, growing in sandy terrain, almost invariably formed of hills that followed no constant direction. While common on the western bank of the Uruguay River, there were scarcely any trees on the eastern side.[82]

The character of the leaves of the yatay meant that it served more than any other grass to make the roofs of houses and huts. The numerous bitter-sweet fruits were also of use. When mature, the inhabitants made daily visits to the yatay forests. Oxen, cows and pigs, whether feral or domesticated, fattened promptly on this fruit. As for the seeds, people laid in ample provisions of these for the winter, feeding themselves on the hard and oily perisperm. As of yet, nobody had tried to make oil from the almonds, even though these were rich in the substance. From the young and undeveloped shoots of this palm, people made *eau-de-vie*. Bonpland deplored this habit because it destroyed the forests. He advised instead the fermenting of the ripe fruits as an alternative method.

After giving this palm's potential economic uses, Bonpland explained how to conserve the seeds. He wanted them stratified in new earth in Montevideo, suggesting that Margat, a French-born gardener resident there, was the person who could best achieve this.[83] In Algiers, since the number of samples was large, he suggested that local authorities should find some sandy terrain to plant a palm forest (very specific planting instructions were given). In closing, he lamented that the excessive dryness of the summer had limited his first shipment to a single species.

When Maillefer wrote to the minister of foreign affairs from Montevideo in July 1854, his themes were many, including French diplo-

80   *Ibid.*
81   Bonpland to Maillefer, Concordia, Entre Ríos, 4 March 1854; CCC, Montevideo, tome 5, fols. 295–6.
82   This South American palm is today a focus for conservation in Argentina's Parque Nacional El Palmar, Entre Ríos.
83   Pedro Antonio Margat (1806–1890), a naturalised Uruguayan, arrived at Montevideo from Versailles in 1838. His career in the horticultural transformation of Montevideo's gardens and parks was important. See Pivel Devoto (1977), pp. 473–501.

matic representation about to be established in Paraguay. After observing it was hard to find Uruguayan official newspapers of the kind sought by the ministry of agriculture and commerce in France, he continued: 'On the other hand, I have the satisfaction of sending ... a third case of seeds for our Algerian colony. Gathered with care by the celebrated Mr. Bonpland, who sent them to me from Entre Ríos, these seeds of useful vegetables have been packed under my supervision by Mr. Margat, [Uruguay's] leading horticulturalist.'[84] However, there were signs that the seeds appeared to be suffering even by the time they reached Montevideo.

Catalogues arrived from France in September 1854. The consul forwarded them to Bonpland by a sure route, accompanied by a letter of thanks outlining the high opinion the departments of war and of foreign affairs held of his 'learned and useful researches'.[85] The official stimulus for greater things was clear.

Shipments of plant materials from Montevideo to Algiers via France turned regular, despite the frequent difficulties of transport between the Upper Plata and the coast, and the problem of finding appropriate material in season. At the beginning of 1856 Maillefer asked the French government once again for some new words of satisfaction and encouragement for 'Humboldt's companion'. Earlier ones had fed his ardour and seemed to knock a half-century from his age.[86]

Writing from Paris in November 1856, the minister of foreign affairs communicated that the Algerian plantings based on Bonpland's shipments of yatay and date palms (*Phoenix dactylifera*) had already succeeded, but it was now thought desirable to extend the plantation. Paris sought a new shipment of at least 2,000 seeds of each species.[87]

During Bonpland's visits to Montevideo, made mainly to renew the paperwork connected with his French pension, he came to know the French consul and his family well. Thus the tone of their correspondence turned more familiar. Writing from Corrientes in April 1857, Bonpland recorded he was sending seeds down river with Ernest Mouchez, the commander of the *Bisson*, a French warship. He had recently joined this vessel on a journey to Paraguay. At Asunción, he made a botanical excursion with Mouchez 'and we used all possible means to procure useful plants for

---

84 Maillefer to Drouyn de Lhys, Montevideo, 4 July 1854; CCC, Montevideo, tome 5, fol. 305.

85 Maillefer to Drouyn de Lhys, Montevideo, 2 October 1854; CCC, Montevideo, tome 5, fol. 338.

86 Maillefer to Alexandre, the Comte Walewski, Montevideo, 1 January 1856; CCC, Montevideo, tome 5, fols. 384 and 384v.

87 Walewski to Maillefer, Paris, 7 November 1856; CCC, Montevideo, tome 5, fol. 450v. As the example of the date palm shows, not everything Bonpland sent to Algeria was indigenous to South America.

Algeria. I am working without pause to gather new useful seeds'.[88] These would accompany the new shipments of seeds of the yatay and date palms that he planned to send very soon. On the same date, Bonpland sent a second letter to Maillefer, announcing that he would not be able to visit the consul in Montevideo for around a year. During this time, he planned to mark animals in Santa Ana and would make new plantings on his property there. In addition, he would gather seeds for Algeria and work in governor Juan Pujol's museum of natural history in Corrientes (Bonpland was the founding director of this institution; it is named after him today). Perhaps he would find the chance to return to Asunción once more, he speculated.[89] Then he referred to Maillefer's own trip on the *Bisson* on the Uruguay River, making comments that reveal his continuing wonderment at subtropical vegetation. He regretted the consul's short journey had not been extensive enough to let him appreciate 'the beauty of the South American vegetation'. On the Uruguay, it was necessary to ascend as far as the Piratini River in Rio Grande do Sul to find exciting vegetation. On the Paraná, vistas grew interesting beginning at Candelaria. A better idea still was to ascend the Paraguay River to Asunción, 'the Chamonix [near the foot of Mont Blanc, and visited by Bonpland in 1805] of tropical vegetation'.[90] Maillefer had baptised the small towns of Paysandú and Arroyo de la China [Concepción del Uruguay] in the Uruguay valley as a budding Venice and an Amsterdam. Bonpland was impressed by neither of these places, which he viewed as sad and backward. His judgment stemmed foremost from the vegetation. The towns were surrounded by nothing but 'very small trees', of which people made nothing more than 'a savage use'.[91] Here we have another clear example of his preference for tropical areas.

---

88 Bonpland to Maillefer, Corrientes, 6 April 1857; AAB, carpeta 4. Ernest Mouchez accomplished important hydrographic work along the Atlantic coast of South America. According to Maillefer, the idea of offering Bonpland an official French passage to Paraguay came from him; he enjoyed the notion that Bonpland could herborise for Algeria above the tomb of his former persecutor Francia. See Maillefer to Walewski, Montevideo, 4 June 1857; CCC, Montevideo, 1857–1864, tome 6, fols. 26 and 26v.

89 There was an unsuccessful effort by Maillefer to send Bonpland on a repeat visit accompanying the *Bisson* to Paraguay in late 1857, with the hope that he could reach Mato Grosso, 'so vast, so fertile and so little known'. Illness prevented Bonpland from making this second journey. However, since Mouchez had been unable to ascend the rivers above Asunción, Maillefer later related to Paris, Bonpland would have less cause to miss 'the virgin forests of Cuiabá' with which the consul 'had nourished his botanical imagination'. See Maillefer to Walewski, Montevideo, 1 December 1857 and 27 April 1858; CCC, Montevideo, tome 6, fols. 64v.–65 and 82–84v.

90 Bonpland visited the Chamonix valley during August 1805 in the company of the famous botanist and biogeographer Augustin Pyramus de Candolle; see the latter's memoirs (Candolle, 1862, p. 155).

91 Bonpland to Maillefer, Corrientes, 6 April 1857; AAB, carpeta 4.

This interesting account of life was followed a month later by a further missive from Corrientes, documenting a new shipment of seeds 'for our Algerian colony'.[92] When yet more material arrived at Montevideo in September, Maillefer showed signs that he was emotionally affected by the shipments and their results. He pointed out to the minister of foreign affairs that should he survey Bonpland's accompanying notes in detail, he could not help but be struck by the efforts this octogenarian was making on behalf of France. Despite the matters of expense, fatigue (and sometimes personal dangers), correspondence and requests too often unanswered, plus trips in primitive forests and the Chaco desert, Bonpland spared nothing to enrich the 'vegetable treasure' of France's Algerian colony.[93]

By April 1858 the minister of war agreed that Bonpland should be informed of the results of his work. At last a report was forwarded by the director of the experimental garden in Algiers, documenting the success of a large part of the material sent from South America. In addition, the French government wished to systematise exchanges of plant materials between Algeria and southern South America, with a particular focus on Paraguay. The means of communication would involve 'serres de voyage', or travelling hot-houses. The first item on the list of desiderata was manioc, a staple food.[94]

By the time this report arrived at Montevideo, Bonpland was dead. Maillefer stressed the irony that he would never see its account of the success of his shipments. France still sought material for Algiers from southern South America, above all from Paraguay. But Maillefer was unsure whether the con-sul there, Alfred de Brossard, 'with all of his taste for intellectual things', would be able to conquer the apathy Bonpland had complained about on the part of his Asunción correspondents.[95] With Bonpland's death, the project of plant exchange between Paraguay and Algeria was suspended, although not before the Comte de Brossard attempted a catalogue of plants indigenous to Paraguay drawn in part from the deceased's manuscripts.[96]

92 Bonpland to Maillefer, Corrientes, 30 May 1857; CCC, Montevideo, 1857–1864, tome 6, fols. 45 and 45v.

93 Maillefer to Walewski, Montevideo, 1 September 1857; CCC, Montevideo, tome 6, fols. 48–49.

94 Walewski to Maillefer, Paris, 7 April 1858; CCC, Montevideo, tome 6, fols. 80–81v.

95 Maillefer to Walewski, Montevideo, 28 June 1858; CCC, Montevideo, tome 6, fols. 89–91v.

96 Consul Brossard compared a recently-published catalogue prepared by Vicente Estigarribia, earlier Francia's doctor (and notable beyond his role in the history of Paraguayan science as the sole individual trusted with unlimited rights of access to the dictator's private rooms), with what he found in Bonpland's manuscripts. Although Brossard wrote patronisingly about the quality of Estigarribia's knowledge of indigenous plants, and with only lukewarm enthusiasm about Bonpland's, he sent a huge list of 206 species drawn from their manuscripts from Paraguay considered of potential value for acclimatisation in Algeria. See Brossard to Walewski, Asunción, 4 November 1858; CCC, Assomption, 1854–62, tome 1, fols. 316–7. On Estigarribia, see Chaves (1946), pp. 180–1.

Botanists resident in South America played important roles in linking a much wider web of places than commonly assumed. While he did much that can be characterised as disinterested science, Aimé Bonpland also provides a clear example of how allegedly non-political professionals could be readily drawn into colonial projects. Working for France became a more important theme of the last years of his life than previously recognised. While E.T. Hamy summarised Bonpland's South American achievements in his important biography by viewing them as strictly technical, of interest mainly to botanical specialists, nineteenth-century French official opinion saw things differently.[97] For Consul Maillefer in Montevideo, Bonpland raised himself above what he termed 'the usual vanity of science' to offer much of truly practical value. He did not confine himself to arid classifications and purely technical descriptions. He put the results of 40 years of experience and observation from different parts of South America into the notes accompanying his shipments.[98] The force of Maillefer's argument will probably strike anyone reading Bonpland's still unpublished comments today.[99] Thus the Nestor of botany was also a utilitarian above all (perhaps today we could say a developmentalist). In pharmacy, medicine and cultivation, allied with domestic, rural and industrial economy, Bonpland drew on all fields of science. His considerable and underappreciated record of plant and seed exchanges is only one of many aspects of his South American career still open to revision in the literature.

97　Hamy (1906), p. xcv
98　See Maillefer to Walewski, Montevideo, 1 September 1857; CCC, Montevideo, tome 6, fol. 49.
99　As one example of the extraordinary level of detail he provided, see for example his extensive comments on the ombú tree (*Phytolacca dioica*), the emblematic species for the Pampas, in an account written to accompany a shipment of materials for Algeria. After reviewing the many South American uses of this species (for its shade, ashes and medical properties), the description continues as follows: 'I have known for years that there is a single example of this tree at Cádiz. Since it is dioecious, it will not have been able to multiply from seed. All the recent information I have been able to gather leads me to believe this truly useful tree does not exist in Europe.' December 1855; AAB, carpeta 5.

Bibliography

Aagesen, David L. (1998) 'On the Northern Fringe of the South American Temperate Forest: the History and Conservation of the Monkey-Puzzle Tree,' *Environmental History*, vol. 3, pp. 64–85.

Abad, L.V. de (1945) *Azúcar y caña de azúcar. Ensayo de orientación cubana* (La Habana: Ed. Mercantil Cubana).

Aboites, Luis (1998) *El agua de la nación: una historia política de México (1888–1946)* (México, DF: Centro de Investigación y Estudios Superiores en Antropologia Social).

Abreu, Dióres Santos (1976) 'Comunicações entre o sul de Mato Grosso e o sudoeste de São Paulo. O comércio de gado,' *Revista de História* (São Paulo), vol. 53, no. 105, pp. 191–214.

Academia de Ciencias de Cuba (1989) *Nuevo Atlas Nacional de Cuba* (La Habana: Instituto de Geografía de la Academia de Ciencias de Cuba; Instituto Geográfico Nacional, Spain).

Academia de la Investigación Científica (1995) *El agua y la ciudad de México* (México, DF: Academia Mexicana de la Ciencia).

Acuña Ortega, V.H. (ed.) (1994) *Historia general de Centroamérica: las repúblicas Agroexportadoras (1870–1945)*, vol. 4 (San José, Costa Rica: FLAC-SO).

Adams, Frederick (1914) *Conquest of the Tropics* (Garden City, NJ: Doubleday).

Albores, Beatriz (1995) *Tules y sirenas: el impacto ecológico y cultural de la industrialización en el Alto Lerma* (México, DF: El Colegio Mexiquense).

Alegret, Juan L. (1985) 'La Comarca de Cabo Gracias a Dios,' *Encuentro*, vols. 24–25, pp. 65–94.

Altieri, M.A. (1991) 'Traditional Farming in Latin America,' *The Ecologist*, vol. 21, pp. 93–6.

Amaral, Samuel (1998) *The Rise of Capitalism on the Pampas: The Estancias of Buenos Aires 1785–1870* (Cambridge: Cambridge University Press).

Andrade, Dolor F. (1936) *Mato Grosso e a sua pecuária* (São Paulo: Universidade de São Paulo).

Andrews, Anthony P. (1983) *Maya Salt Production and Trade* (Tucson: University of Arizona Press).

Anon (1875) *Apuntes estadísticos del Estado Zulia tomados de orden del ilustre americano, General Guzmán Blanco, Presidente de la Republica* (Caracas: Imprenta de La Opinión Nacional).

Anon (1892) 'The Moskito Coast,' *Periodical Accounts, Moravian Missions*, vol. 1, no. 12, pp. 639–40.

Anon (1900) *Informe sobre el censo de Cuba, 1899* (Washington, DC: Imprenta del Gobierno.

Anon (1906) 'Rubber Plantations Injured,' *The India Rubber World*, vol. 35, p. 63

Anon (1907) *Censo de la República de Cuba, 1907. Bajo la administración provisional de los Estados Unidos* (Washington, DC: Oficina del Censo de los Estados Unidos).

Anon (1907a) 'Nicaragua — the Moskito Coast,' *Proceedings of the Society for Propagating the Gospel* [no volume], pp. 87–9.

Anon (1907b) 'Nicaragua Wind and Rubber,' *The India Rubber World*, vol. 35, p. 113

Anon (1908) 'Recent Disturbances — Sam Pitts,' *Periodical Accounts of the Moravian Missions*, vol. 7, no. 73, pp. 38–9.

Anon (1909) 'Nicaragua,' *Bulletin of the International Bureau of the American Republics* (July), pp. 218–28

Anon (1916) *Almanaque comercial 'Matto-Grossense'* (São Paulo: publisher unknown).

Anon (1916a) 'A creação em Matto Grosso.' *Brasil Agrícola* (Rio de Janeiro), vol. 1, December, pp. 362–3.

Anon (1919) *Censo de la República de Cuba. Año de 1919* (La Habana: Maza, Arroyo y Caso Impresores).

Anon (1930) 'O inquerito sobre o gado zebu, "Precisamos julgar definitivamente o gado zebu",' *Rural: Orgam [sic] da Sociedade Rural de Cuiabá (Cuiabá)*, vol. 1(August), pp. 1–5

Anon (1931) *O Zebú na pecuaria* (São Paulo: Livraria Liberdade).

Anon (1943) 'Sal para os animais,' *Boletim de Indústria Animal*, vol. 6 (October), pp. 195–6.

Aranda, Gaspar de (1995) *La administración forestal y los montes de Ultramar durante el siglo XIX* (Madrid: ICONA).

Arnold, David (1996) *The Problem of Nature: Environment, Culture and European Expansion.* (Oxford: Blackwell).

Arnold, David and Guha, Ramachandra (eds.) (1995) *Nautre, Culture, Imperialism: Essays on the Environmental History of South Asia* (Delhi: Oxford University Press).

Arthur, Henry B., Houck, James P. and Beckford, George L. (1968) *Tropical Agribusiness Structures and Adjustments — Bananas* (Boston: Graduate School of Business Administration, Harvard University).

Ashby, S.F. (1924) 'Bananas Resistant to Wilt (Panama Disease),' *Tropical Agriculture*, vol. 1, pp. 172–3.

Ayala, César J. (1999) *American Sugar Kingdom: The Plantation Economy of the Spanish Caribbean 1898–1934* (Chapel Hill: University of North Carolina Press).

Ayala, S. Cardoso and Simon, Feliciano (1914) *Album graphico do Estado de Matto Grosso (E.E.U.U. do Brazil)* (Corumbá/Hamburg: publisher unknown).

Azevedo, Fernando de (1950) *Um trem corre para o oeste; estudo sobre a noroeste e seu papel no sistema de viação nacional* (São Paulo: Livraria Martins Editora).

Bahre, Conrad J. (1991) *A Legacy of Change: Historic Human Impact on Vegetation in the Arizona Borderlands* (Tucson: University of Arizona Press).

Baker, R.E.D. and Simmonds, Norman W. (1951) 'Banana Research — Changes in Outlook,' *Tropical Agriculture*, vol. 28, pp. 43–5.

Balboa Navarro, Imilcy (2000) *Los brazos necesarios: inmigración, colonización y trabajo libre en Cuba, 1878 – 1898* (Alzira, Valencia: Centro Francisco Tomás y Valiente, UNED).

Balée, William (1998) 'Historical Ecology: Premises and Postulates,' in William Balée (ed.), *Advances in Historical Ecology* (New York: Columbia University Press), pp. 13–29.

Baptista, Federico (1964) 'El esfuerzo pionero,' *El Farol* (April, May, June), pp. 4–7.

Barberii, Efrain (1997) *De los pioneros a la empresa nacional 1921–1975, La Standard Oil of New Jersey en Venezuela* (Caracas: Lagoven).

Barcelos, Adão R (1943) 'De norte a sul do Brasil, o Zebú entrou em nossos rebanhos, dando côice na seringa do veterinário,' *Zebú* (Uberaba, Minas Gerais, December), pp. 28–32.

Barham, Bradford L., and Coomes, Oliver T. (1996) *Prosperity's Promise: the Amazon Rubber Boom and Distorted Development* (Boulder, CO: Westview Press).

Barreto, Abeillard (1976) *Bibliografia sul-riograndense: a contribuição portuguesa e estrangeira para o conhecimento e a integração do Rio Grande do Sul,* vol. 2 (Rio de Janeiro: Conselho Federal de Cultura).

Barros, José de (1987 [?]) *Lembranças para os meus filhos e descendentes* (São Paulo: n.p.).

Barros, Paulo de Moraes (1922) *O sul de Matto Grosso e a pecuaria* (N.l.: n.p.).

Bassett, Thomas J. and Crummey, Donald (eds.) (2003) *African Savannas: Global Narratives and Local Knowledge of Environmental Change* (Oxford: James Currey).

Bassett, Thomas J. and Zuéli, Koli Bi (2000) 'Environmental Discourses and the Ivorian Savanna,' *Annals of the Association of American Geographers,* vol. 90, no. 1, pp. 67–95.

Bataillon, Claude (1968) Les *régiones géographiques au Mexique* (Paris: Institut de Hautes Etudes de l'Amérique Latine).

Bataillon, Claude (1971) *Ville et campagnes dans la région de México* (Paris: Anthropos).

Bates, Henry Walter (1882) *Central America, the West Indies and South America,* 2nd ed. (London: E. Stanford).

Behling, Hermann (1998) 'Late Quaternary Vegetational and Climatic Changes in Brazil,' *Review of Paleobotany and Palynology,* vol. 99, pp. 143–56.

Beinart, William (2000) 'African History and Environmental History,' *African Affairs,* vol. 99, pp. 269–302.

Beinart, William, and McGregor, JoAnn (eds.) (2003) *Social History and African Environments* (Oxford: James Currey).

Bell, Charles Napier (1862) 'Remarks on the Mosquito Territory its Climate, People, Productions, etc., etc. with a Map,' *The Journal of the Royal Geographic Society* (Great Britain), vol. 32, pp. 242–68.

Bell, Charles Napier (1989 [1899]) *Tangweera. Life and Adventures among Gentle Savages* (Austin: The University of Texas Press).

Bell, Stephen (1995) 'Aimé Bonpland and Merinomania in Southern South America,' *The Americas,* vol. 51, no. 3, pp. 301–23.

Bell, Stephen (1998) *Campanha Gaúcha: a Brazilian Ranching System, 1850–1920* (Stanford: Stanford University Press).

Bellingeri, M. (1981) 'Las estructuras agrarias bajo el *Porfiriato,*' in C. Cardoso (ed.), *México en el siglo XIX* (México, DF: Nueva Imagen), pp. 97–118.

Bello, Lourdes, Díaz, Judith and Pernalete, Luisa (1980) *El fin de los pueblos de agua y el petróleo* (Caracas: Biblioteca de Trabajo Venezolana, Colección Raíces Mi Pueblo), vol. 7, Cooperativa Laboratorio Educativo.

Belt, Thomas (1985 [1874]) *The Naturalist in Nicaragua* (Chicago: The University of Chicago Press).

Benet, F. (1929) *Guía general de Venezuela 1929*, vol. 1 (Caracas: Imprenta de Oscar Brandstetter Leipzig).

Bennett, Hugh H., and Allison, Robert V. (1962 [1928]) *Los suelos de Cuba* (Havana: Comisión Nacional Cubana de la UNESCO).

Berchon, Charles (1910) *A través de Cuba. Relato geográfico, descriptivo y económico* (Paris: SCEAUX, Imprenta de Charaire).

Bergad, Laird W. (1992) *Cuban Rural Society in the Nineteenth Century: the Social and Economic History of Sugar Monoculture in Matanzas* (Princeton: Princeton University Press).

Bergquist, Charles (1986) *Labor in Latin America: Comparative Essays on Chile, Argentina, Venezuela and Colombia* (Stanford: Stanford University Press).

Bevilacqua, Piero (1996) *Tra natura e storia* (Rome: Donzelli).

Bevilacqua, Piero (1998) *Venezia e le acque: una metafora planetaria* (Rome: Donzelli).

Bevilacqua, Piero (2001) *Demetra e Clio: uomini e ambienti nella storia* (Rome: Donzelli).

Bevilacqua, Piero (2002) *La mucca è savia: ragioni storiche della crisi alimentare europea.* (Rome: Donzelli).

Birrichaga, Diana (1998) 'Las empresas de agua potable en México: 1887–1930,' in Blanca Suárez C. (ed.), *Historia de los usos del agua en México. Siglos XIX y XX* (Mexico City: Instituo Mexicano de Tecnologia del Agua, Centro de Investigación y Estudios Superiores en Antropologia Social), pp. 183–223.

Bogue, Margaret Beattie (2000) *Fishing the Great Lakes: an Environmental History, 1783–1933* (Madison: University of Wisconsin Press).

Bohem, Briggite (1994) 'La desecación en la ciénega de Chapala y las comunidades indígenas: el triunfo de la modernización en la época porfiriana,' in Carmen Viqueira and Lydia Torre (eds.), *Sistemas hidráulicos, modernización de la agricultura y migración* (Mexico City: UIA–El Colegio Mexiquense), pp. 339–84.

Bohorquéz, Lenin (1994) 'Pérez Soto y la rehabilitación en el Zulia 1926–1935,' Magister Historia, Universidad del Zulia.

Bonpland, Aimé (1978) *Journal voyage de Sn. Borja a la cierra y a Porto Alegre: diário viagem de São Borja à serra e a Porto Alegre*, transcription of original manuscripts, notes and revision by Alicia Lourteig (Porto Alegre and Paris: Instituto de Biociências, Universidade Federal do Rio Grande do Sul; Centre National de la Recherche Scientifique).

Bortz, J., and Haber, S. (2002) *The Mexican Economy, 1870–1930: Essays on the Economic History of Institutions, Revolution and Growth* (Stanford: Stanford University Press).

Botting, Douglas (1988) *Humboldt, un savant democrate,1769–1859* (Paris: Belin).

Boyer, Richard E. and Davies, Keith A. (1973) *Urbanization in 19th Century Latin America: Statistics and Sources* (Los Angeles: Latin American Center, University of California).

Brannstrom, Christian (1995) 'Amost a Canal: Visions of Interoceanic Communication across Southern Nicaragua,' *Ecumene*, vol. 2, no. 1, pp. 65–87.

Brannstrom, Christian (1998) 'After the Forest: Environment, Labor, and Agro-Commodity Production in Southeastern Brazil,' PhD dissertation, University of Wisconsin–Madison.

Brannstrom, Christian (2000) 'Coffee Labor Regimes and Deforestation on a Brazilian Frontier, 1915–1965,' *Economic Geography*, vol. 76, pp. 326–46.

Brannstrom, Christian (2001a) 'Conservation-with-Development Models in Brazil's Agro-Pastoral Landscapes,' *World Development*, vol. 29, no. 8, pp. 1345–59.

Brannstrom, Christian (2001b) 'Producing Possession: Labour, Law and Land on a Brazilian Agricultural Frontier, 1920-1945,' *Political Geography*, vol. 20, no. 7, pp. 859–83.

Brannstrom, Christian (2002) 'Rethinking the "Atlantic Forest" of Brazil: New Evidence for Land Cover and Land Value in Western São Paulo, 1900–1930,' *Journal of Historical Geography*, vol. 28, no. 3, pp. 420–39.

Brannstrom, Christian, and Antônio Manoel dos Santos Oliveira (2000) 'Human Modification of Stream Valleys in the Western Plateau of São Paulo, Brazil: Implications for Environmental Narratives and Management,' *Land Degradation and Development*, vol. 11, no. 6, pp. 535–48.

Brazil (1960) *Levantamento de reconhecimento dos solos do Estado de São Paulo* (Rio de Janeiro: Centro Nacional de Ensino e Pesquisas Agronômicas).

Brazil (1965) 'Lei No. 4.771 de 15 de setembro de 1965, alterada pela Lei No. 7803 de 18 de julho de 1989'.

Brazil (1999) *Constituição da República Federativa do Brasil; Constituição do Estado de São Paulo* (São Paulo: Imprensa Oficial).

Brazil (Ministério da Agricultura) (1978) *Manual técnico para criação de gado de corte em Mato Grosso* (Campo Grande: Embrater).

Brazil (Ministério da Agricultura, Commercio e Obras Públicas, Directoria Geral de Estatística) (1926) *Recenseamento realizado em 1 de Setembro de 1920, vol. 3, pt.1, Agricultura* (Rio de Janeiro: Typ. da Estatística).

Brechin, Gray (1999) *Imperial San Francisco: Urban Power, Earthly Ruin* (Berkeley: University of California Press).

Brimblecombe, Peter (1987) *The Big Smoke: a History of Air Pollution in London since Medieval Times* (London: Methuen).

Brito, Oscar da Silva (1944) 'A pecuária do Brasil Central e sua produção de bovinos de corte,' *Boletím de Indústria Animal* (São Paulo), vol. 7, no. 1–2, pp. 7–16.

Brooks, Andrew P. and Brierley, Gary J. (1997) 'Geomorphic Responses of Lower Bega River to Catchment Disturbance, 1851–1926,' *Geomorphology*, vol. 18, pp. 291–304.

Bulmer-Thomas, Victor (1987) *The Political Economy of Central America since 1920* (Cambridge: Cambridge University Press).

Bulmer-Thomas, Victor (1994) *The Economic History of Latin America since Independence* (Cambridge: Cambridge University Press).

Burns, E. Bradford (1980) *The Poverty of Progress* (Berkeley: University of California Press).

Burns, E. Bradford (1991) *Patriarch and Folk. The Emergence of Nicaragua, 1798–1858* (Cambridge: Harvard University Press).

Butzer, Karl W. (1992) 'The Americas before and after 1492: an Introduction to Current Geographical Research,' *Annals of the Association of American Geographers*, vol. 82, no. 3, pp. 345–68.

Butzer, Karl W. (1993) 'No Eden in the New World,' *Nature*, vol. 362, no. 4 March, pp. 15–17.

Butzer, Karl W., and Butzer, E.K. (1997) 'The "Natural" Vegetation of the Mexican Bajio: Archival Documentation of a 16th-Century Savanna Environment,' *Quaternary International*, vol. 43, no. 4, pp. 161–72.

Cabrera, Luis (1972) *Obras completas: obra jurídica* (México, DF: Oasis).

Cabrera, Ramiro (1897) 'Los recursos naturales de Cuba y sus perspectivas para el capital americano,' *Cuba y América* (New York), vol. 1, no. 9, pp. 2–4.

Callejas, Santiago (1896) 'Development of Eastern Nicaragua,' *Consular Reports, United States*, vol. 50, pp. 523–4.

Camacho Pichardo, Gloria (1998) 'Proyectos hidráulicos en las Lagunas del Alto Lerma (1880–1942),' in Blanca Estela Suárez Cortez (ed.), *Historia de los usos del agua en México: Oligarquia, empresas y ayuntamientos (1840–1940)* (Mexico City: Instituto Mexicano de Tecnologia del Agua, Centro de Investigación y Estudios Superiores en Antropologia Social), pp. 229–80.

Campbell, Lisa M. (2002) 'Conservation Narratives in Costa Rica: Conflict and Co-existence,' *Development and Change*, vol. 33, no. 1, pp. 29–56.

Campo Grande (Estado de Matto Grosso), Prefeituria Municipal de (1944) *Relatório 1943* (Rio de Janeiro: Imprensa Nacional).

Campo-Grande (Matto Grosso), Municipio de (no date) *Relatório do anno de 1922, Apresentado á Camara Municipal pelo Intendente Geral Arlindo de Andrade Gomes* (São Paulo: Comp. Melhoramentos).

Canabal, Beatriz (1997) *Xochimilco: una identidad recreada* (Mexico City: Universidad Autónoma Metropolitana, Universidad Autonoma Chapingo).

Candolle, Augustin Pyramus de (1862) *Mémoires et souvenirs* (Geneva: Joël Cherbuliez).

Cardoso, Ciro F.S. (1975) 'Historia económica del café en Centroamérica (siglo XIX): Estudio comparativo,' *Estudios Sociales Centroamericanos*, vol. 12, pp. 9–40.

Cardoso, Ciro Flamarion Santana and Pérez Brignoli, Héctor (1981) *Historia económica de América Latina* (Barcelona: Crítica).

Cardoso, F.P. (1943) 'A seleção do gado Zebú no Rancho Hudgins,' *Zebú* (September), pp. 38–41.

Carmack, Robert M. (1973) *Quichean Civilization: the Ethnohistoric, Ethnographic and Archaeological Sources* (Berkeley: University of California Press).

Carneiro, Geraldo G. (1943) 'O problema da criação de gado nas regiões tropicais,' *Zebú* (November), pp. 9–12.

Carney, Judith A. (2001) *Black Rice: the African Origins of Rice Cultivation in the Americas* (Cambridge: Harvard University Press).

Carrasco, P. (1979) 'La aplicabilidad a Mesoamérica del modelo andino de verticalidad,' *Revista de la Universidad Complutense*, vol. 27, pp. 237–43.

Carrière, Jean (1991) 'Some Thoughts on the Political Dynamics of Brazilian Soya Policy,' in Geert A. Banck and Kees den Boer (eds.), *Sowing the Whirlwind: Soya Expansion and Social Change in Southern Brazil* (Amsterdam: CEDLA), pp. 61–73.

Carvalho, Ricardo Ernesto Ferreira de (1906) *Indústria pastoril: promptuario de noções geraes e especias de zootecnia* (São Paulo: publisher unknown).

Casals, Vicente (1989) 'Las ideas sobre la protección del bosque en Cuba y Filipinas durante el siglo XIX,' in José Luis Pesset (eds.), *Ciencia, vida y espacio en Iberoamérica* (Madrid: CSIC), pp. 357–88..

Castellanos Cambranes, J. (1996) *Café y campesinos: los orígenes de la economía de plantación moderna en Guatemala, 1853–1897* (Madrid: Catriel).

Castro Herrera, Guillermo (1994) *Los trabajos de ajuste y combate* (La Habana: Casa de las Américas).

Castro Herrera, Guillermo (1997) 'The Environmental Crisis and the Tasks of History in Latin America,' *Environment and History*, vol. 3, no. 1, pp. 1–18.

Cavalcanti, Manuel Paulino (1928) *Raças de carne* (Rio de Janeiro: Ministerio da Agricultura, Industria e Commercio).

Caviedes, César N. (2001) *El Niño in History: Storming Through the Ages* (Gainesville: University Press of Florida).

Centro de Estadísticas (1864) *Noticias estadísticas de la Isla de Cuba en 1862: dispuestas y publicadas por el Centro de Estadística* (Havana: Imprenta del Gobierno).

Chamorro B., Cristiana (1991) 'Paraíso busca tiempo perdido,' *La Prensa*, 27 October.

Chaves, Julio César (1946) *El supremo dictador; biografía de José Gaspar de Francia*, 2nd ed. (Buenos Aires: Editorial Ayacucho).

Chew, Sing C. (2001) *World Ecological Degradation: Accumulation, Urbanization, and Deforestation, 3000 B.C.–A.D. 2000* (Walnut Creek, CA: AltaMira).

Chomsky, Aviva (1996) *West Indian Workers and the United Fruit Company in Costa Rica, 1870 – 1940* (Baton Rouge: Louisiana State University Press).

Cioc, Mark (2002) *The Rhine: An Eco-Biography, 1815–2000* (Seattle: University of Washington Press).

Clark, William J. (1898) *Commercial Cuba; a Book for Business Men* (New York: C. Scribner Sons).

Coates, Peter (1998) *Nature: Western Attitudes since Ancient Times* (Cambridge: Polity Press).

Coatsworth, John H. (1984) *El impacto económico de los ferrocarriles en el Porfiriato* (Mexico City: ERA).

Coatsworth, John (1990) *Los orígenes del atraso: nueve ensayos de historia económica de México en los siglos XVIII y XIX* (Mexico City: Alianza Editorial Mexicana).

Coe, Michael D., and Flannery, Kent V. (1967) *Early Cultures and Human Ecology in South Coastal Guatemala* (Washington, DC: Smithsonian Press).

Coelho Machado, Paulo (1990) *A Rua Velha, Vol. 1 de Pelas Ruas de Campo Grande* (Campo Grande, MS: Tribunal de Justiça de Mato Grosso do Sul).

Collinson, John (1868) 'Explorations in Central America, Accompanied by Survey and Levels from Lake Nicaragua to the Atlantic Coast,' *Proceedings of the Royal Geographical Society of London*, vol. 12, pp. 25–48.

Colquhoun, Archibald Ross (1895) *The Key of the Pacific. The Nicaraguan Canal* (Westminster: Archibald Constable and Company).

Colten, Craig E., and Skinner, Peter N. (1996) *The Road to Love Canal: Managing Industrial Waste before EPA* (Austin: University of Texas Press).

Commission for Historical Clarification (1999) *Memory of Silence. Tz'Inil Na'Tab'Al. Conclusions and Recommendations* at hrdata.aaas.org/ceh/report/english/default.html, accessed 20 June 2002.

Conolly, Priscilla (1987) *El contratista de don Porfirio: obras públicas, deuda y desarrollo desigual* (Mexico City: Fondo de Cultura Económica).

Constanza, Robert (2000) 'The Dynamics of the Ecological Footprint Concept,' *Ecological Economics*, vol. 32, no. 3, pp. 341–5.

Conti, Pedro (1945) 'Zebús, cobras e lagartos,' *Zebú* (May), pp. 13–20.

Cordier, Henri (ed.) (1914) *Papiers inédits du naturaliste Aimé Bonpland conservés à Buenos Aires* (Buenos Aires: Jacobo Peuser).

Corral Alemán, José Isaac del (1936) *Derecho forestal cubano. disposiciones fundamentales*, vol. 1 (Havana: Imp. P. Fernández y Cía).

Corrêa Filho, Virgílio (1926) *A propósito do Boi pantaneiro, monographias cuiabana*, vol. 6 (Rio de Janeiro: Ponghetti e Cia.).

Correio Paulistano (1916) 'Congresso de Pecuaria,' *Correio Paulistano* (23 September).

Costa, Maria de Fátima (1999) *História de um país inexistente: o pantanal entre os séculos XVI e XVIII* (São Paulo: Editora Estação Liberdade; Livraria Kosmos Editora).

Cotrim, Eduardo A. (1912) 'Contribuição para o estudo das vantagens ou desvantagens da introducção do sangue do gado Zebú nas nossas manadas,' in *Inquerito sobre o gado Zebú* (Rio de Janeiro: Typ. Serviço Estatístico), pp. 71–92.

Cotrim, Eduardo (1913) *A fazenda moderna: guia do criador de gado bovino no Brasil* (Brussels: Typ. V. Verteneuil et L. Desmet).

CPTI [Cooperativa de Serviços, Pesquisas Tecnológicas e Indústrias] (1999) 'Diagnóstico da situação dos recursos hídricos da UGRHI 17–Médio Paranapanema,' Assis, São Paulo: Consórcio Intermunicipal do Escritório da Região do Governo de Assis; Comitê de Bacia Hidrográfica do Médio Paranapanema.

Crawley, J.T. (1917) 'El cultivo de la caña de azúcar en Cuba,' *Boletín, Estación Experimental Agronómica*, vol. 35 (February).

Crespo, M. (1956) 'Títulos indígenas de tierras,' *Antropología e Historia de Guatemala*, vol. 8, pp. 10–12.

Cronon, William (1983) *Changes in the Land: Indians, Colonists, and the Ecology of New England* (New York: Hill and Wang).

Cronon, William (1991) *Nature's Metropolis: Chicago and the Great West* (New York: W.W. Norton and Co.).

Cronon, William (1993) 'The Uses of Environmental History,' *Environmental History Review*, vol. 17, no. 3, pp. 1–22.

Cronon, William (1995) 'The Trouble with Wilderness; or, Getting Back to the Wrong Nature,' in William Cronon (ed.), *Uncommon Ground: Toward Reinventing Nature* (New York: W.W. Norton), pp.69–90..

Crosby, Alfred W. (1972) *The Columbian Exchange: Biological and Cultural Consequences of 1492* (Westport, CN: Greenwood Press).

Crosby, Alfred W. (1986) *Ecological Imperialism: the Biological Expansion of Europe, 900–1900* (Cambridge: Cambridge University Press).

Crosby, Alfred W. (1995) 'The Past and Present of Environmental History,' *American Historical Review*, vol. 100, no. 4, pp. 1177–89.

Crossley, J. Colin and Greenhill, Robert (1977) 'The River Plate Beef Trade,' in D.C.M. Platt (ed.), *Business Imperialism, 1840–1930: an Inquiry Based on British Experience in Latin America* (Oxford: Oxford University Press), pp. 284–334.

Crumley, Carole L. (1998) 'Foreward,' in William Balée (ed.), *Advances in Historical Ecology* (New York: Columbia University Press), pp. ix–xiv.

Cuba (Ministerio de Agricultura) (1951) *Memoria del censo agrícola nacional, 1946* (Havana: P. Fernández y Cía.).

Cuba (Secretaría de Agricultura, Comercio y Trabajo) (1914) *Portfolio azucarero. Industria azucarera de Cuba, 1912–1914* (Havana: Librería e Imprenta la Moderna Poesía).

Cuba, Gobierno Militar de la Isla de (Secretaría de Agricultura, Comercio e Industria) (1900) *Memoria de los trabajos realizados en el año fiscal que comenzó en 1° de julio de 1899 y terminó en 30 de junio de 1900* (Havana: publisher unknown).

Cuba, República de (1904) *Breve reseña para la Exposición Universal de St. Louis, Missouri, USA* (Havana: Imprenta de Rambla y Bouza).

Cuba, República de (1925) *El Libro de Cuba* (publisher unknown).

Cunill Grau, Pedro (1999) 'La geohistoria,' in Marcello Carmagnani, Alicia Hernández Chávez and Ruggiero Romano (eds.), *Para una historia de América: I. Las estruturas* (Mexico: El Colegio de México; Fondo de Cultura Económica), pp. 13–159.

Cutter, Victor M. (1926) 'Caribbean Tropics in Commercial Transition,' *Economic Geography*, vol. 2, pp. 494–507.

Dana, Peter H. (1999) 'Diversity in Descriptions of a Destroyed Place: Greytown, Nicaragua,' PhD dissertation, The University of Texas.

Davis, Mike (1998) *Ecology of Fear: Los Angeles and the Imagination of Disaster* (New York: Metropolitan Books).

Davis, Mike (2001) *Late Victorian Holocausts: El Niño Famines and the Making of the Third World* (New York: Verso).

Davis, S. (1970) 'Land of our Ancestors: a Study of Land Tenure and Inheritance in the Highlands of Guatemala,' PhD thesis, Harvard University.

De Kalb, Courtney (1893) 'Nicaragua: Studies on the Mosquito Shore in 1892,' *Journal of the American Geographical Society of New York*, vol. 25, pp. 236–88

Dean, Warren (1987) *Brazil and the Struggle for Rubber: a Study in Environmental History* (Cambridge: Cambridge University Press).

Dean, Warren (1989) 'The Green Wave of Coffee: Beginnings of Tropical Agricultural Research in Brazil (1885–1900),' *Hispanic American Historical Review*, vol. 69, no. 1, pp. 91–115.

Dean, Warren (1992) 'The Tasks of Latin American Environmental History,' in Harold K. Steen and Richard P. Tucker (eds.), *Changing Tropical Forests: Historical Perspectives on Today's Challenges in Central and South America* (Durham: Forest History Society), pp. 5–15.

Dean, Warren (1995) *With Broadax and Firebrand: the Destruction of the Brazilian Atlantic Forest* (Berkeley: University of California Press).

Dearing, John (1994) 'Reconstructing the History of Soil Erosion,' in Neil Roberts (ed.), *The Changing Global Environment* (Oxford: Blackwell), pp. 242–61.

Demeritt, David (2002) 'What is the "Social Construction of Nature"? A Typology and Sympathetic Critique,' *Progress in Human Geography*, vol. 26, no. 6, pp. 767–90.

Demeritt, David (1998) 'Science, Social Constructivism and Nature,' in Bruce Braun and Noel Castree(eds.), *Remaking Reality: Nature at the Millenium* (London: Routledge), pp. 173–93..

Denevan, William M. (2001) *Cultivated Landscapes of Native Amazonia and the Andes* (Oxford: Oxford University Press).

Depons, Francisco (1889) 'Viaje a la Parte Oriental de la Tierra Firme en la America Meridional, 1798–1799–1800,' *El Zulia Ilustrado* (30 August), no. 9, pp. 70–1.

Desmond, Ray (1995) *Kew: the History of the Royal Botanic Gardens* (London: The Harvill Press).

Diamond, Jared (2003) 'The Last Americans: Environmental Collapse and the End of Civilization,' *Harper's Magazine* (June), pp. 43–51.

Díaz-Briquets, Sergio and Pérez-López, Jorge F. (2000) *Conquering Nature: The Environmental Legacy of Socialism in Cuba* (Pittsburgh: University of Pittsburgh Press).

Dinerstein, Eric, Olson, David M., Graham, Douglas J., Webster, Avis L., Primm, Steven A., Bookbinder, Marmie P. and Ledec, George (1995)

A Conservation Assessment of the Terrestrial Ecoregions of Latin American and the Caribbean (Washington, DC: World Bank).

Dionisio Vives, Francisco (1829) *Cuadro estadístico de la Siempre Fiel Isla de Cuba correspondiente al año 1827* (Havana: Oficina de las Viudas de Arazoza y Soler).

Domíngues, Otávio (1966) *O gado indiano no Brasil: historiografia, exterior e raças, reprodução e criação, melhoramento* (Rio de Janeiro: Planam and Sunab).

Domingues, Otavio and Abreu, Jorge de (1949) *Viagem de estudos à Nhecolandia, Publicação No. 3* (Rio de Janeiro: Instituto de Zootecnia).

Domínguez, Juan A. (1929) *Aimé Bonpland: su vida en la América del sur y principalmente en la República Argentina (1817–1858)* (Buenos Aires: Imprenta y Casa Editorial Coni).

Domínguez, Lourdes, Febles, Jorge and Rives, Alexis (1994) 'Las comunidades aborígenes de Cuba,' in Instituto de Historia de Cuba (ed.), *Historia de Cuba. La colonia. Evolución socio económica y formación nacional. De los orígenes hasta 1867* (Havana: Editora Política), pp. 5–57..

Dominguez, M. (1977) 'Desarrollo de los aspectos tecnológicos y científicos de la industria del café en Guatemala, 1830–1930,' *Anuario de Estudios Centroamericanos* (Costa Rica), vol. 3, pp. 97–114.

Dore, Elizabeth (2000) 'Environment and Society: Long-Term Trends in Latin American Mining,' *Environment and History*, vol. 6, no. 1, pp. 1–29.

Dosal, Paul J. (1995) *Doing Business with the Dictator: a Political History of United Fruit in Guatemala* (Wilmington, DE: Scholarly Resources).

Doughty, Robin W. (2000) *The Eucalyptus: a Natural and Commercial History of the Gum Tree* (Baltimore: The Johns Hopkins University Press).

Dovers, Stephen R. (2000a) 'On the Contribution of Environmental History to Current Debate and Policy,' *Environment and History*, vol.. 6, no. 2, pp. 131–50.

Dovers, Stephen (2000b) 'Still Settling Australia: Environment, History, and Policy,' in Stephen Dovers (ed.), *Environmental History and Policy: Still Settling Australia* (Victoria: Oxford University Press), pp. 2–23..

Dovers, Stephen, Edgecombe, Ruth and Guest, Bill (eds.) (2003) *South Africa's Environmental History: Cases and Comparisons* (Athens: Ohio University Press).

Downes, Earl Richard (1986) 'The Seeds of Influence: Brazil's "Essentially Agricultural" Old Republic and the United States, 1910–1930,' PhD dissertation, The University of Texas at Austin.

Dozier, Craig L. (1985) *Nicaragua's Mosquito Shore: the Years of British and American Presence* (Tuscaloosa: University of Alabama Press).

Drayton, Richard (2000) *Nature's Government: Science, Imperial Britain, and the 'Improvement' of the World* (New Haven and London: Yale University Press).

Dunlap, Thomas R. (1981) *DDT: Scientists, Citizens, and Public Policy* (Princeton: Princeton University Press).

Dunlap, Thomas R. (1999) *Nature and the English Diaspora: Environment and History in the United States, Canada, Australia, and New Zealand* (Cambridge: Cambridge University Press).

Dunne, Thomas and Leopold, Luna B. (1978) *Water in Environmental Planning* (New York: W.H. Freeman).

Dussel, Patricia and Herrera, Roberto (1999) 'Repercusiones socioeconómicas del cambio de curso del río Salado en la segunda mitad del siglo XVIII,' in Bernardo García Martínez and Alba González Jácome (eds.), *Estudios sobre historia y ambiente en América I: Argentina, Bolivia, México, Paraguay* (Mexico City: Instituto Panamericano de Geografia e Historia; El Colegio de México), pp. 137–49.

Dye, Alan (1998) *Cuban Sugar in the Age of Mass Production: Technology and the Economics of the Sugar Central, 1899–1929* (Stanford: Stanford University Press).

Eakin, Marshall C. (1999) 'The Origins of Modern Science in Costa Rica: the Instituto Físico-Geográfico Nacional, 1887–1904,' *Latin American Research Review*, vol. 34, no. 1, pp. 123–50.

Earle, F.S. (1905) 'La caña de azúcar,' *Boletín, Estación Central Agronómica de Cuba*, vol. 2.

Ebel, Roland H. (1969) *Political Modernization in Three Guatemalan Indian Communities* (New Orleans: Middle American Research Institute, Tulane University).

Echeverri-Gent, Elisavinda (1992) 'Forgotten Workers: British West Indians and the Early Days of the Banana Industry in Costa Rica and Honduras,' *Journal of Latin American Studies*, vol. 24, pp. 275–308.

Eisenberg, Evan (1998) *The Ecology of Eden* (New York: Alfred A. Knopf).

Ellner, Steve (1995) 'Venezuelan Revisionist Political History,' *Latin American Research Review*, vol. 30, no. 2, pp. 91–121.

Ely, Roland T. (1963) *Cuando reinaba su majestad el azúcar: estudio histórico sociológico de una tragedia latinoamericana: el monocultivo en Cuba. Origen y evolución del proceso* (Buenos Aires: Ed. Sudamericana).

Embrapa (2000) 'Cresce, no Brasil, o número de adeptos de programas de cruzamento animal,' *Gado de Corte Informa* (Empresa Brasileira de Pesquisa Agropecuária [Embrapa], Gado de Corte, Campo Grande), vol. 12, no. 4, pp. 4–5.

Endfield, Georgina, and O'Hara, Sarah L. (1999) 'Degradation, Drought, and Dissent: an Environmental History of Colonial Michoacán, West Central Mexico,' *Annals of the Association of American Geographers*, vol.. 89, no. 3, pp. 402–19.

Endlich, Rodolpho (1902) 'A criação do gado vaccum nas partes interiores da America do Sul,' *Boletim da Agricultura*, vol. 3, no. 12, pp. 742–4.

Erickson, Clark L. (2000) 'An Artificial Landscape-Scale Fishery in the Bolivian Amazon,' *Nature*, vol. 408, no. 6809, pp. 190–3.

Espinosa, Gabriel (1996) *El embrujo del lago* (México, DF: Universidad Nacional Autónoma de México).

Everall, W. (1912) 'De cómo empezó la industria cafetera en Guatemala,' *Centroamérica: organo de publicidad de la Oficina Internacional Centro-Americana*, vol. 4, pp. 147–51.

Ewell, Judith (1984) *Venezuela: a Century of Change* (Stanford: Stanford University Press).

Ezcurra, Exequiel (1990) 'The Basin of Mexico,' in B.L. Turner, II, William C. Clark, Robert W. Kates, John F. Richards, Jessica T. Mathews and William B. Meyer (eds.), *The Earth as Transformed by Human Action: Global and Regional Changes in the Biosphere over the Past 300 Years* (Cambridge: University of Cambridge Press), pp. 577–88.

Ezcurra, Exequiel, Mazari-Hiriart, Marisa, Pisanty, Irene and Aguilar, Adrián Guillermo (1999) *The Basin of Mexico: Critical Environmental Issues and Sustainability* (Tokyo: United Nations University Press).

Fairhead, James and Leach, Melissa (1995) 'False Forest History, Complicit Social Analysis: Rethinking some West African Environmental Narratives,' *World Development*, vol. 23, no. 6, pp. 1023–1035.

Fairhead, James and Leach, Melissa (1998) *Reframing Deforestation: Global Analysis and Local Realities: Studies in West Africa* (London: Routledge).

Fawcett, William (1921 [1913]) *The Banana: its Cultivation, Distribution, and Commercial Uses* (London: Duckworth and Co.).

Feldman, Lawrence. H. (1992) *Indian Payment in Kind: the Sixteenth Century Encomiendas in Guatemala* (Culver City, CA: Labyrinthos).

Fernandes, J. Sampaio (1939) *Indústria do Sal* (Rio de Janeiro: Serviço de Publicidade Agrícola).

Fernández-Gómez, Emilio Manuel (1993) *Argentina: gesta británica: revalorización de dos siglos de convivencia*, vol. 1 (Buenos Aires: Editorial L.O.L.A. [Literature of Latin America]).

Fiedler, Horst and Leitner, Ulrike (eds.) (2000) *Alexander von Humboldts Schriften: bibliographie der selbstständige erschienenen Werke. Vol. 20, Beiträge zur Alexander-von-Humboldt-Forschung* (Berlin: Akademie Verlag).

Fiege, Mark (1999) *Irrigated Eden: the Making of an Agricultural Landscape in the American West* (Seattle: University of Washington Press).

Fifer, J. Valerie (1991) *United States Perceptions of Latin America, 1850–1930: a 'New West' South of Capricorn?* (Manchester and New York: Manchester University Press).

Filgueiras, Tarciso de Sousa (1990) 'Africanas no Brasil: Gramíneas introduzidas da África,' *Cadernos de Geociências*, vol. 5 (July), pp. 57–63.

Florescano, Enrique (1986) *Precios del maíz y crisis agrícolas en México, 1708–1810* (Mexico City: ERA).

Fonseca, Gustavo A.B. da (1985) 'The Vanishing Brazilian Atlantic Forest,' *Biological Conservation*, vol. 34, pp. 17–34.

Foreign Policy Association (1935) *Problemas de la Nueva Cuba. Informe de la Comisión de Asuntos Cubanos* (New York: Foreign Policy Association).

Fortes, Carlos Pereira de Sá (1903) *Industria pastoril; relatorio apresentado à commissão fundamental do Congresso Agricola, Commercial e Industrial de Minas* (Belo Horizonte: publisher unknown).

Foster, David R. (2002) 'Insights from Historical Geography to Ecology and Conservation: Lessons from the New England Landscape,.' *Journal of Biogeography*, vol. 29, pp. 1269–75.

Foweraker, Joe (1981) *The Struggle for Land: a Political Economy of the Pioneer Frontier in Brazil from 1930 to the Present Day* (Cambridge: Cambridge University Press).

Frasquieri, Tranquilino (1933) 'Nuestra crisis forestal,' *Revista de Agricultura, Comercio y Trabajo*, vol. 14, no. 18, pp. 3–8.

Fryirs, Kirstie and Brierley, Gary J. (1999) 'Slope-Channel Decoupling in Wolumla Catchment, New South Wales, Australia: the Changing Nature of Sediment Sources following European Settlement,' *Catena*, vol. 35, pp. 41–63.

Fundação SOS Mata Atlântica, Instituto Nacional de Pesquisas Espaciais and Instituto Socioambiental (1998) *Atlas da evolução dos remanescentes florestais e ecossistemas associados no domínio da mata atlântica no período 1990–1995* (São Paulo: Fundação SOS Mata Atlântica, Instituto Nacional de Pesquisas Espaciais, Instituto Socioambiental).

Funes Monzote, Reinaldo (1998) 'Los conflictos por el acceso a la madera en La Habana: 1774–1815. Hacendados vs. Marina,' in José Antonio Piqueras Arenas (ed.), *Diez nuevas miradas de historia de Cuba* (Castellón: Universitat Jaume I), pp. 67–90.

Funes Monzote, Reinaldo (1999) 'El fin de los bosques y la plaga del marabú en Cuba. Historia de una venganza ecológica,' paper presented at the Conference 'História e Meio-Ambiente: o Impacto da Expansão Europeia,' Funchal, Madeira.

Gadgil, Madhar, and Guha, Ramachandra (1993) *This Fissured Land: an Ecological History of India* (Delhi: Oxford University Press).

Gall, F. (1978) *Diccionario geográfico de Guatemala*. 4 vols (Guatemala: Instituto Geográfico Nacional).

Gallini, Stefania (2002) 'La rivoluzione del caffè in un agrosistema Maya, Guatemala 1830–1902: Una storia ambientale,' PhD thesis, Università di Genova.

Galvão, Marília Velloso (ed.) (1960) *Geografia do Brasil, grande região centro-oeste* (Rio de Janeiro: IBGE).

Gandy, Matthew (2002) *Concrete and Clay: Reworking Nature in New York City* (Cambridge: MIT Press).

Garbrecht, Luis (1920) 'New Mining Fields in Northeastern Nicaragua,' *Engineering and Mining Journal*, vol. 109, pp. 791–97.

García Acosta, Virgina (ed.) (1996) *Historia y destastres en América Latina* (Bogotá: La Red/CIESAS).

García de León, Antonio (1988) *Historia de la cuestión agraria mexicana* (Mexico City: Siglo XXI).

Gazeta de Commercio (1927) 'Uma opinião sobre o gado zebu,' *Gazeta de Commercio* (Tres Lagoas, Mato Grosso), vol. 7, no. 27 (July).

Genin, A. (1910) *Notes sur le Mexique 1908* (Mexico City: Imprenta Lacaud).

Gerbi, Antonello (1985) *Nature in the New World: from Christopher Columbus to Gonzalo Fernandez de Oviedo*, translated by Jeremy Moyle (Pittsburgh: University of Pittsburgh Press).

Giberti, Gustavo C. (1990) 'Bonpland's Manuscript Name for the Yerba Mate and *Ilex Theezans* C. Martius ex Reisseck (Aquifoliaceae),' *Taxon*, vol. 39, no. 4, pp. 663–5.

Giberti, Gustavo Carlos (1995) 'Aspectos oscuros de la corologia de *Ilex paraguariensis* St. Hil,' in Helga Winge et al. (eds.), *Erva-mate: biologia e cultura no Cone Sul* (Porto Alegre: Editora da Universidade Federal do Rio Grande do Sul), pp. 289–300.

Gilmore, A.B. (1928) *Manual de la industria azucarera cubana. The Cuba Sugar Manual* (Havana and New Orleans: Ed. Metropolitana).

Ginzburg, Carlo (1980) *The Cheese and the Worms: the Cosmos of a Sixteenth-Century Miller*, translated by John and Anne Tedeschi (Baltimore: Johns Hopkins University Press).

Gismondi, Michael and Mouat, Jeremy (2002) 'Merchants, Mining and Concessions on Nicaragua's Mosquito Coast: Reassessing the American Presence, 1893–1912,' *Journal of Latin American Studies*, vol.. 34, pp. 845–79.

Glacken, Clarence J. (1967) *Traces on the Rhodian Shore: Nature and Culture in Western Thought from Ancient Times to the End of the Eighteenth Century* (Berkeley: University of California Press).

Glantz, Margo (1982) *Viajes en México: Crónicas extranjeras* (Mexico City: Secretaría de Educación Publica).

Gonçalves, José Alberto (2001a) 'De olho no boi "natural",' *Gazeta Mercantil* (23 August), A3.

Gonçalves, José Alberto (2001b) 'Exportadores investem em carne orgânica,' *Gazeta Mercantil*, 7 August, B–20.

González Fuentes, Pascual (1849) *Memoria presentada a la H. Legislatura del Estado de México* (Toluca: Imprenta de J. Quijano).

González Jácome, Alba (1999) 'El paisaje lacustre y los procesos de desación en Tlaxcala, México,' in Bernardo García Martínez and Alba González Jácome (eds.), *Estudios sobre historia y ambiente en América I: Argentina, Bolivia, México, Paraguay* (Mexico City: Instituto Panamericano de Geografia e Historia; El Colegio de México), pp. 191–218.

González, J.H. (1994) 'History of Los Altos, Guatemala: a Study of Regional Conflict and National Integration, 1750–1994,' PhD dissertation, Tulane University.

González, Juan Manuel (2001) 'Una aproximación al estudio de la transformación ecológica del paisaje rural colombiano: 1850–1990,' in

UNIVERSITY OF WINCHESTER LIBRARY

Germán Palacio (ed.), *Naturaleza en disputa: ensayos de historia ambiental de Colombia, 1850–1995* (Bogotá: Universidad Nacional de Colombia), pp. 75–115..

Gosling, Ronald (1893) 'Report on the Coffee Industry in Guatemala, FO Misc. Series No. 255,' *Parliamentary Papers* (H.C. London), vol. 41, pp. 1–8.

Gould, Jeffery L. (1998) *To Die in This Way. Nicaraguan Indians and the Myth of Mestizaje, 1880–1965* (Durham: Duke University Press).

Grandin, Greg (2000) *The Blood of Guatemala: a History of Race and Nation* (Durham: Duke University Press).

Graziosi, F. Falcinelli (ed.) (1898) *Guia ilustrada del Estado de Nicaragua* (Rome: publisher unknown).

Green, Ronas Dolores (1984) *Las viejas historias de los Sumus* (Managua: CIDCA).

Grierson, Cecilia (1925) *Colonia de Monte Grande, Provincia de Buenos Aires: primera y única colonia formada por escoceses en la Argentina* (Buenos Aires: Jacobo Peuser).

Griffiths, Tom, and Robin, Libby (eds.) (1997) *Ecology and Empire: Environmental History of Settler Societies* (Edinburgh: Keele University Press).

Grossman, Lawrence S. (1998) *The Political Ecology of Bananas: Contract Farming, Peasants, and Agrarian Change in the Eastern Caribbean* (Chapel Hill: University of North Carolina Press).

Grossmann, Guido (1909) 'Rev. G. Grossmann's Visit to the Goldmines in the Pispis District, 2–21 Nov. 1908,' *Periodical Accounts of the Moravian Missions*, vol. 7, no. 77, p. 261.

Grossmann, Guido (1988 [1940]) *La Costa Atlántica* (Managua: Editorial la Ocarina).

Grove, Richard G (1995) *Green Imperialism: Colonial Expansion, Tropical Island Edens, and the Origins of Environmentalism, 1600–1860* (Cambridge: Cambridge University Press).

Grove, Richard H. (1997) *Ecology, Climate and Empire: Colonialism and Global Environmental History, 1400–1940* (Cambridge: White Horse Press).

Grove, Richard H., Damodaran, Vinita and Sangwan, Satpal (eds.) (1998) *Nature and the Orient: the Environmental History of South and Southeast Asia* (Delhi: Oxford University Press).

Guatemala (1880) *Censo de la República de Guatemala* (Guatemala: Tipografía el Progreso).

Guatemala (1890) *Recopilación de Leyes Agrarias de Guatemala* (Guatemala: Tipografía La Unión).

Guatemala (Secretaría de Fomento, Sección de Estadística) (1883) *Anales estadísticos de la República de Guatemala, año de 1882* (Guatemala: Ministerio de Fomento).

Gudmundson, L. (1996) 'Tierras comunales, públicas y privadas en los orígines de la caficultura en Guatemala y Costa Rica,' *Mesoamérica*, vol. 31, pp. 41–56.

Guerra, F. (1988) *México: del antiguo régimen a la revolución* (Mexico City: Fondo de Cultura Económica).

Guerra, Ramiro (1970 [1927]) *Azúcar y población en las Antillas* (Havana: Ed. Ciencias Sociales).

Gumprecht, Blake (1999) *The Los Angeles River: its Life, Death, and Possible Rebirth* (Baltimore: Johns Hopkins University Press).

Guyosa, J.M. (1892) *El Valle de Mexico: ventajas que resultarian a la salud publica con el desagüe* (Mexico City: Imprenta de Joaquín G. Campos y Comp.).

Haber, Stephen (1992) *Industria y subdesarrollo: la industrialización en México,1890–1940* (MexicoCity: Alianza Editorial).

Hajer, Maarten A. (1995) *The Politics of Environmental Discourse: Ecological Modernization and the Policy Process* (Oxford: Clarendon Press).

Hall, Carolyn (1982) *El café y el desarrollo histórico-geográfico de Costa Rica*, 3rd ed. (San José: Editorial Costa Rica).

Hamy, E.T. [Ernest Théodore] (1906) *Aimé Bonpland, médecin et naturaliste, explorateur de l'Amérique du Sud. Sa vie, son oeuvre, sa correspondance* (Paris: Librairie Orientale & Américaine E. Guilmoto).

Hardoy, Jorge E., Mitlin, Diana and Satterthwaite, David (eds.) (1992) *Environmental Problems in Third World Cities* (London: Earthscan Publications).

Harrison, Peter D., and Turner, B.L. II (eds.) (1978) *Pre-Hispanic Maya Agriculture* (Albuquerque: University of New Mexico Press).

Hays, Samuel P. (1998) *Explorations in Environmental History: Essays by Samuel P. Hays* (Pittsburgh: University of Pittsburgh Press).

Hays, Samuel P. (2001) 'Toward Integration in Environmental History,' *Pacific Historical Review*, vol. 70, no. 1, pp. 59–67.

Heckenberger, Michael J., Kuikuro, Afukaka, Tabata Kuikuro, Urissapá, Russell, J. Christian, Schmidt, Morgan, Fausto, Carlos and Franchetto, Bruna (2003) 'Amazonia 1492: Pristine Forest or Cultural Parkland?' *Science*, vol. 301 (19 September), pp. 1710–14.

Heffernan, Michael J. (1989) 'The Parisian Poor and the Colonization of Algeria during the Second Republic,' *French History*, vol. 3, no. 4, pp. 377–403.

Herrera, Ricardo (1984) 'El origen de las sabanas cubanas,' in Leo Waibel and Ricardo Herrera (eds.), *La toponimia en el paisaje cubano* (Havana: Ed. Ciencias Sociales), pp. 49–97.

Higbee, E. (1947) 'The Agricultural Regions of Guatemala,' *Geographical Review*, vol. 37, pp. 177–201.

Higgins, J.E. (1904) *The Banana in Hawaii*, Bulletin No. 7, Hawaii Agricultural Experiment Station (Honolulu: Hawaiian Gazette Company).

Hill, Robert T. (1898) *Cuba and Porto Rico, with the Other Islands of The West Indies. Their Topography, Climate, Flora, Products, Industries, Cities, People, Political Condition* (New York: The Century Co.).

Hoben, Allan (1995) 'Paradigms and Politics: the Cultural Construction of Environmental Policy in Ethiopia,' *World Development*, vol. 23, no. 6, pp. 1007–1021.

Hodge, Sandra S., Queiroz, Maike Hering de and Reis, Ademir (1997) 'Brazil's National Atlantic Forest Policy: a Challenge for State-Level Environmental Planning,' *Journal of Environmental Planning and Management*, vol. 40, no. 3, pp. 335–48.

Hord, H.H.V. (1966) 'The Conversion of Standard Fruit Company Banana Plantations in Honduras from Gros Michel to the Giant Cavendish Variety,' *Tropical Agriculture*, vol. 43, pp. 269–75.

Horst, O. (1995) '1902, año de caos: El impacto sociopolítico y económico de las catastrofes naturales en Guatemala,' *Mesoamerica*, vol.. 30, pp. 308–26.

Hossard, Nicolas (2001) *Aimé Bonpland (1773–1858), médecin, naturaliste, explorateur en Amérique du Sud; à l'ombre des arbres* (Paris: L'Harmattan).

Hostnig, Rainer (1991) *Monografía del Municipio de Ostuncalco* (Quezaltenango: CCIC).

Hostnig, Rainer (1993–96) *El Curato de San Juan Ostuncalco*, 2 vols. (Quezaltenango: CCIC).

Hostnig, Rainer (ed.) (1997) *Esta tierra es nuestra* (Quezaltenango: CCIC).

Houwald, Götz von (1975) *Los alemanes en Nicaragua* (Managua: Banco de Nicaragua).

Howes, F.N. (1928) 'The Banana in some Tropical Eastern Countries — its Forms and Variations,' *Kew Bulletin of Miscellaneous Information*, pp. 305–36.

Huerta, Rodolfo (1993) 'Identidad y clase obrera: los papeleros de San Rafael, 1918–1936,' in Alejandro Tortolero V. (ed.), *Entre lagos y volcanes: Chalco-Amecameca: pasado y presente* (Mexico City: El Colegio Mexiquense), pp. 451–80.

Huerta, Rodolfo (1999) 'Agua y capitalismo en el valle de México,' unpublished manuscript.

Humboldt, Alexander von (1828 [1808]) *Tableaux de la nature, ou, Considerations sur les déserts, sur la physionomie des végétaux, et sur les cataractes de l'Orénoque*, translated from the German by J.B.B. Eyriès, vol. 1 (Paris: Gide Fils).

Humboldt, Alexander von (1993) *Briefe aus Amerika, 1799–1804*, edited by Ulrike Moheit. Vol. 16, *Beiträge zur Alexander-von-Humboldt-Forschung* (Berlin: Akademie Verlag).

Humboldt, Alexandre de (1997) *Essai politique sur le royaume de la Nouvelle-Espagne du Mexique* (France: Utz).

Humboldt, Alexander von and Bonpland, Aimé (1805–17) *Plantes équinoxiales, recueillies au Mexique, dans l'île de Cuba, dans les provinces de Caracas, de Cumana et de Barcelone, aux Andes de la Nouvelle-Grenade, de Quito et du Pérou, et sur les bords du Rio Negro, de l'Orénoque et de la rivière des Amazones*, 2 vols (Paris: Tübingen: F. Schoell; J.G. Cotta).

Humboldt, Alexander von and Bonpland, Aimé (1806–23) *Monographie des mélastomacées*, 2 vols (Paris: Librairie Grecque-Latine-Allemande; Gide Fils).

Humboldt, Alexander von and Bonpland, Aimé (1820) *Voyage aux régions équinoxiales du nouveau continent, fait en 1799, 1800, 1801, 1802, 1803 et 1804, par Al. de Humboldt et A. Bonpland*, vol. 5 (Paris: N. Maze).

Huxley, Leonard (ed.) (1918) *Life and Letters of Sir Joseph Dalton Hooker*, vol. 1 (London: John Murray).

IBGE [Fundação Instituto Brasileiro de Geografia e Estatística] (1993 [1988]) 'Mapa de vegetação do Brasil' (Rio de Janeiro: IBGE).

Iglesias, Fe (1998) *Del ingenio al central* (San Juan: Ed. Universidad de Puerto Rico).

Intercontinental Railway Commission (1898) *Report of Surveys and Explorations Made by Corps 1 in Guatemala, El Salvador, Honduras, and Costa Rica, 1891–93: Texts and Tables*, vol. 2 (Washington, DC: Government Printing Office).

IPT (1981a) *Mapa geológico do Estado de São Paulo*, 2 vols (São Paulo: IPT).

IPT (1981b) *Mapa geomorfológico do Estado de São Paulo*, 2 vols (São Paulo: IPT).

Ireland, Gordon (1971 [1941]) *Boundaries, Possessions, and Conflicts in Central and North America and the Caribbean* (New York: Octagon Books).

Irias, Juan Francisco (1853) 'Río Wanks and the Mosco Indians,' *Transactions of the American Ethnological Society* (New York), vol. 3, pp. 159–66.

Isenberg, Andrew C. (2000) *The Destruction of the Bison: An Environmental History, 1750–1920* (Cambridge: Cambridge University Press).

Jarosz, Lucy (1996) 'Defining Deforestation in Madagascar.' in Richard Peet and Michael Watts (eds.) *Liberation Ecologies. Environment, Development, Social Movements* (New York: Routledge), pp. 148–64.

Jenkins, Virginia Scott (2000) *Bananas: an American Story* (Washington, DC: Smithsonian Institute).

Jenks, Leland H. (1966) *Nuestra colonia de Cuba* (Havana: Ed. Revolucionaria).

Jiménez, Michael F. (1995) '"From Plantation to Cup": Coffee and Capitalism in the United States, 1830–1930,' in William Roseberry, Lowell Gudmundson and Mario Samper Kutschbach (eds.), *Coffee, Society, and Power in Latin America* (Baltimore: Johns Hopkins University Press), pp. 38–64.

Joly, C.A., Aidar, M.P.M., Klink, C.A., McGrath, D.G., Moreira, A.G., Moutinho, P., Nepstad, D.C., Oliveira, A.A., Pott, A. Rodal, M.J.N. and Sampaio, E.V.S.B. (1999) 'Evolution of the Brazilian Phytogeography Classification Systems: Implications for Biodiversity Conservation,' *Ciência e Cultura*, vol.. 51, no. 5/6, pp. 331–48.

Jones, Chester Lloyd (1940) *Guatemala, Past and Present* (Minneapolis: University of Minnesota Press).

Jones, David R. (ed.) (2000) *Diseases of Banana, Abacá, and Enset* (New York: CABI Publishing).

Jouanin, Christian (1997) 'Bonpland,' in Musée National des Châteaux de Malmaison & Bois-Préau (ed.), *L'impératrice Joséphine et les sciences naturelles* (Paris: Éditions de la Réunion des Musées Nationaux), pp. 54–67.

Juárez, Orient Bolívar (ed.) (1995) *Maximiliano von Sonnenstern y el primer mapa oficial de la República de Nicaragua* (Managua: INETER).

Kahle, Günter and Potthast, Barbara (eds.) (1983) *Der Wiener Schiedsspruch von 1881. Eine Dokumentation zur Schlichtung des Konfliktes Zwischen Grossbritannien und Nicaragua um Mosquitia* (Köln: Böhlau Verlag).

Karnes, Thomas L. (1978) *Tropical Enterprise. The Standard Fruit and Steamship Company in Latin America* (Baton Rouge: Louisiana State University Press).

Kirchheimer, Jean-Georges (1993) 'Bonpland et la conspiration française de 1818 à Buenos Aires,' in Jeanine Potelet and Joseph M. Farré (eds.), *Mundus Novus-Nouveaux Mondes (XVIe–XXe S.)* (Paris: Centre de Recherches Ibériques et Ibéro-Américaines, Université de Paris X–Nanterre), pp. 123–30.

Klepeis, Peter, and Turner, B.L. II (2001) 'Integrated Land History and Global Change Science: the Example of the Southern Yucatán Peninsular Region Project,' *Land Use Policy*, vol. 18, pp. 27–39.

Knox, James C. (2002) 'Agriculture, Erosion, and Sediment Yields,' in Antony R. Orme (ed.), *The Physical Geography of North America* (New York: Oxford University Press), pp. 482–500.

Konrad, Edmond G. (1995) 'Nicaragua durante los 30 años de gobierno conservador (1857–1893): la familia Zavala,' *Mesoamérica*, vol. 30, pp. 287–308.

Kroeber, C. (1994) *El hombre, la tierra y el agua: las políticas en torno a la irrigación en la agricultura de México,1885–1911* (Mexico City: Instituto Mexicano de Tecnología del Agua, Centro de Investigación y Estudios Superiores en Antropología Social).

Land, Myrick and Barbara (1957) *Jungle Oil, the Search for Venezuela's Hidden Treasure* (New York: Coward-McCann).

Langdon, Robert (1993) 'The Banana as a Key to Early American and Polynesian History,' *Journal of Pacific History*, vol. 28, pp. 15–35.

Lazo Arriaga, A. (1903) 'Contestación al cuestionario presentado por el señor don Federico de la Madriz,' in *Memoria de Fomento* (Guatemala: Ministerio de Fomento), pp. 130–41.

Leach, Melissa and Mearns, Robin (eds.) (1996) *The Lie of the Land: Challenging Received Wisdom on the African Environment* (London: International African Institute).

Ledru, Marie-Pierre, Salgado-Labouriau, Maria Lea and Lorscheitter, Maria Luisa (1998) 'Vegetation Dynamics in Southern and Central Brazil during the Last 10,000 yr B.P,' *Review of Paleobotany and Palynology*, vol. 99, pp. 131–42.

LeGrand, Catherine (1986) *Frontier Expansion and Peasant Protest in Colombia, 1830–1936* (Albuquerque: University of New Mexico Press).

Leite, Gervásio (1942) *O gado na economia matogrossense* (Cuiabá: Escolas Profissionais Salesianos).

Lentz, David L. (2000) 'Summary and conclusions,' in David L. Lentz (ed.)*Imperfect Balance: Landscape Transformations in the Precolumbian Americas* (New York: Columbia University Press), pp. 493–505.

Lepsch, I.F., Buol, S.W. and Daniels, R.B. (1977)'Soil-Landscape Relationships in the Occidental Plateau of São Paulo State, Brazil: I. Geomorphic Surfaces and Soil Mapping Units,' *Soil Science Society of America, Journal*, vol. 41, no. 1, pp. 104–9.

Lerch, Otto (1896) 'Eine Fahrt auf dem Prinzapulca und Banbana-Flusse (Nordost-Nicaragua),' *Globus*, vol. 70, pp. 181–4.

Levi, L.J. (1996) 'Sustainable Production and Residential Variation: a Historical Perspective on Pre-hispanic Domestic Economies in the Maya Lowlands,' in L. Scott Fedick (ed.), *The Managed Mosaic: Ancient Maya Agriculture and Resource Use* (Salt Lake City: University of Utah Press), pp. 94–8.

Lévy, Paul (1873) *Notas geográficas y económicas sobre La República de Nicaragua* (Paris: Librería Española).

Lieuwen, Edwin (1954) *Petroleum in Venezuela* (Berkeley: University of California Press).

Lieuwen, Edwin (1965) *Venezuela* (London: Oxford University Press).

Lindo Fuentes, H. (1993) 'Economía y sociedad (1810–1870),' in Edelberto Torres-Rivas (ed.), *Historia General de Centroamérica*, vol. 3 (Madrid: FLACSO; V Centenario), pp. 141–201.

Lindsay-Poland, John (2003) *Emperors in the Jungle: the Hidden History of the U.S. in Panama* (Durham, NC: Duke University Press).

Lines, William J. (1991) *Taming the Great South Land: a History of the Conquest of Nature in Australia* (Berkeley: University of California Press).

Linhares, Temístocles (1969) *História econômica do mate*. Vol. 138, *Coleção Documentos Brasileiros* (Rio de Janeiro: Livraria J. Olympio).

Lino, Baudillo Miguel, Erans, Mollins and Davis, Fidencio (1994) *Mayangna Sauni as. tradición oral de la historia mayangna* (Managua: The Nature Conservancy).

Lipsett-Rivera, Sonya (1993) 'Water and Bureaucracy in Colonial Puebla de los Angeles,' *Journal of Latin American Studies*, vol. 25, pp. 25–44.

Lisboa, Miguel Arrojado Ribeiro (1909) *Oeste de S. Paulo, sul de Mato-Grosso; geologia, indústria mineral, clima, vegetação, solo agrícola, indústria pastoril* (Rio de Janeiro: Typografia do 'Jornal do Commercio').

Lopes, Maria Antonia Borges and Rezende, Eliane M. Marquez (1985) *ABCZ, 50 anos de história e estorias* (Uberaba: Associação Brasileira de Criadores de Zebú).

López Decoud, Arsenio (1911) *Album gráfico de la República del Paraguay, 1811–1911* (Buenos Aires: publisher unknown).

Lowenthal, David (1997) 'Empires and Ecologies: Reflections on Environmental History,' in Tom Griffiths and Libby Robin (eds.), *Ecology and Empire: Environmental History of Settler Societies* (Edinburgh: Keele University Press), pp. 229–36.

Luckin, Bill (1986) *Pollution and Control: a Social History of the Thames in the Nineteenth Century* (Bristol: Adam Hilger).

Maciel, José de Barros (1922) *A pecuaria nos pantanaes de Matto Grosso. These apresentado ao 3o. Congresso de Agricultura e Pecuaria, 1922* (São Paulo: Imp. Metodista).

McAuliffe, J.R., Sundt, P.C., Valiente-Banuet, A., Casas, A. and Viveros, J. Luis (2001) 'Pre-Colombian Soil Erosion, Persistent Ecological Changes, and Collapse of a Subsistence Agricultural Economy in the Semi-Arid Tehuacán Valley, Mexico's "Cradle of Maize",' *Journal of Arid Environments*, vol. 47, no. 1, pp. 47–76.

McBeth, Brian (1983) *Juan Vicente Gómez and The Oil Companies in Venezuela, 1908–1935* (New York: Cambridge University Press).

McBryde, F.W. (1969) *Geografía cultural e histórica del Suroeste de Guatemala*, 2 vols. (Guatemala: Seminario de Integración Social Guatemalteca).

McCay, Bonnie J. (1998) *Oyster Wars and the Public Trust: Property, Law, and Ecology in New Jersey History* (Tucson: University of Arizona Press).

McCook, Stuart (2002) *States of Nature: Science, Agriculture, and Environment in the Spanish Caribbean, 1760–1940* (Austin: University of Texas Press).

McCreery, David (1994) *Rural Guatemala, 1760–1940* (Stanford: Stanford University Press).

McDermond, C.C. (1932) *Who's Who in Venezuela* (Maracaibo: Publication Office Apartado 331).

McEvoy, Arthur F. (1986) *The Fisherman's Problem: Ecology and Law in the California Fisheries, 1850–1980* (New York: Cambridge University Press).

McKenney, R.E.B. (1910) 'The Central American Banana Blight,' *Science*, vol. 31, no. 13 (May), p. 750.

MacKenzie, John M. (ed.) (1990) *Imperialism and the Natural World* (Manchester: Manchester University Press).

MacKenzie, John M. (1997) *Empires of Nature and the Nature of Empires: Imperialism, Scotland and the Environment* (Lothian: Tuckwell Press).

McNeill, John R. (1988) 'Deforestation in the Araucaria Zone of Southern Brazil, 1900–1983,' in John F. Richards and Richard P. Tucker (eds.), *World Deforestation in the Twentieth Century* (Durham, NC: Duke University Press), pp. 15–32.

McNeill, J.R. (2000) *Something New Under the Sun: an Environmental History of the Twentieth-Century World* (London: Penguin).

Marchand, Bernard (1971) *Venezuela: travailleurs et villes de petrole* (Paris: Institute des Hautes Etudes de L'Amerique Latine).

Marquardt, Steve (2001) '"Green Havoc": Panama Disease, Environmental Change, and the Labor Process in the Central American Banana Industry,' *American Historical Review*, vol. 106, no. 1, pp. 49–80.

Marquardt, Steve (2002) 'Pesticides, Parakeets, and Unions in the Costa Rican Banana Industry, 1938–1962,' *Latin American Research Review*, vol. 37, no. 2, pp. 3–36.

Marrero, Leví (1974–1984) *Cuba, economía y sociedad* (Madrid: Ed. Playor).

Martí, Carlos (1915) *Films cubanos, Oriente y Occidente. La República será agrícola o no será* (Barcelona: Sociedad General de Publicaciones).

Martín, Juan Luis (1944) *Esquema elemental de temas sobre la caña de azúcar como factor topoclimático de la geografía social de Cuba* (Havana: no publisher).

Martínez Moctezuma, Lucía (1996) 'D'Espagne au Mexique: I. Noriega Laso un entrepeneur dans la Vallée de Mexico 1868–1913,' PhD Thesis, Université de Paris–X Nanterre.

Martínez Moctezuma, Lucía (2001) *Iñigo Noriega Laso: un emporio empresarial* (Mexico City: UAM).

Martínez Moctezuma, Lucía and Tortolero V., Alejandro (2000) 'Chemin de fer et marché: les limites de la modernisation porfiriste,' *Cahiers des Amériques Latines*, vol. 34, pp. 123–44.

Martinez-Alier, Joan (1991) 'Ecology and the Poor: a Neglected Dimension of Latin American History.' *Journal of Latin American Studies*, vol. 23, pp. 621–39.

Mato Grosso (1887) *Relatório do vice-presidente Dr. José Joaquim Ramos Ferreira devia apresentar à Assembléa Legislativa Provincial de Matto Grosso, 2ª sessão da 26ª legislatura de Setembro de 1887* (Cuiabá: publisher unknown).

Matos, Eliseo (c. 1970) *Breve historia de los montes de Cuba*, unpublished manuscript (INDAF).

Maudit, Fernando (1909) 'Arboriculture in Argentina,' in Argentine Republic (ed.), *Stock-Breeding and Agriculture in 1908, Monographs*. Vol. 3, *Agricultural and Pastoral Census of the Nation* (Buenos Aires: Printing Works of the Argentine Meteorological Office), pp. 267–93

Megargel Publications (1927) *Megargel's Manual of South American Oil Companies* (New York: Megargel's Publications).

Melville, Elinor G.K. (1994) *A Plague of Sheep: Environmental Consequences of the Conquest in Mexico* (Cambridge: Cambridge University Press).

Melville, Elinor G.K. (1997) 'Global Development and Latin American Environments,' in Tom Griffiths and Libby Robin (eds.), *Ecology and Empire: Environmental History of Settler Societies* (Edinburgh: Keele University Press), pp. 185–98.

Menezes, Durval Garcia de (1937) *O Indubrasil; conferencia promunciada em 2 de Maio de 1937 no recinto da 3a Exposição Agro-pecuaria de Uberaba, em homenagem á 'Sociedade Rural do Triangulo Mineiro'* (Rio de Janeiro: Sociedade Rural do Triangulo Mineiro).

Menezes, Durval Garcia de (1940) 'O Zebú — riqueza paulista,' *O Zebu* 1 (August), pp. 14–26.

México (1911) *Memoria de la Secretaría de Fomento presentada al H.congreso de la Unión por el srio de Estado y del despacho del ramo Lic. Rafael Hernández* (Mexico City: Imp. y Fototipia de la Secretaría de Fomento).

México (Direccion de Estadística) (1920) *Tercer censo de población de los Estados Unidos Mexicanos verificado el 27 de octubre de 1910* (Mexico City: Dirección de Talleres Gráficos del Poder Ejecutivo).

Mierisch, Bruno (1893) 'Eine Reise nach den Goldgebieten im Osten von Nicaragua,' *Petermanns geographische Mitteilungen* , vol. 39, pp. 25–39.

Mierisch, Bruno (1895) 'Eine Reise quer durch Nicaragua, vom Managua-See bis nach Cabo Gracias á Dios,' *Petermanns geographische Mitteilungen*, vol. 41, pp. 57–66.

Miller, Arthur G. (ed.) (1983) *Highland-Lowland Interaction in Mesoamerica: Interdisciplinary Approaches* (Washington, DC: Dumbarton Oaks Research Library and Collection).

Miller, Char and Rothman, Hal (1997) 'Introduction,' in Char Miller and Hal Rothman (eds.), *Out of the Woods: Essays in Environmental History* (Pittsburgh: University of Pittsburgh Press), pp. xi–xvi.

Miller, Shawn William (2000) *Fruitless Trees: Portuguese Conservation and Brazil's Timber* (Stanford: Stanford University Press).

Miner, William Harvey (1915) *Bananas. The Story of a Trip to the Great Plantations of Nicaragua* (Sioux Falls, S.D.: The Sioux Plantation Co.).

Mintz, Sidney (1985) *Sweetness and Power: the Place of Sugar in Modern History* (New York: Penguin Books).

Moberg, Mark and Striffler, Steve (eds.) (2003) *Banana Wars: Production, Power, and History* (Durham: Duke University Press).

Molina Enríquez, Andrés (1981) *Los grandes problemas nacionales* (Mexico City: ERA).

Monbeig, Pierre (1952) *Pionniers et planteurs de São Paulo* (Paris: Librairie Armand Colin).

Monet, Rosalba (1986) *Sindicalizacion y conflictos laborales 1936–1941, aportes para el estudio del Movimiento Obrero Venezolano*, Magister Thesis, Department of History, UCV, Caracas.

Montserrat, Econ. J. and Gonçalves, Carlos A. (1954) *Observações sôbre a pecuária no Brasil Central* (Porto Alegre [?]: publisher unknown).

Moreno Fraginals, Manuel (1978) *El ingenio: complejo económico social cubano del azúcar*, vol. 1 (Havana: Ciencias Sociales).

Mosk, S. (1980) 'Economía cafetalera de Guatemala durante el periodo 1850–1918: su desarrollo y signos de inestabilidad,' in J. Luján Muñoz (ed.), *Economía de Guatemala 1750–1940* (Guatemala: USAC), pp. 161–82.

Moyano, Eduardo L. (1991) *La nueva frontera del azúcar: El ferrocarril y la economía cubana del siglo XIX* (Madrid: CSIC)

Mundt, Christopher C. (1990) 'Disease Dynamics in Agroecosystems,' in C. R. Carroll, John Vandermeer and Peter Rosset (eds.), *Agroecology* (New York: McGraw-Hill), pp. 263–99.

Murphy, Charles J.V. (1969) 'The King Ranch South of the Border,' *Fortune* (July), pp. 132–44.

Musset, Alain (1992) *El agua en el Valle de México* (Mexico City: Portico de la Ciudad de México; Centro de Estudios Mexicanos y Centroamericanos).

Musset, Alain (1999) 'Lo sano y lo malsano en las cuidades españolas de América (siglos XVI–XVII),' in Bernardo García Martínez and Alba González Jácome (eds.), *Estudios sobre historia y ambiente en América I: Argentina, Bolivia, México, Paraguay* (Mexico City: Instituto Panamericano de Geografia e Historia; El Colegio de México), pp. 1–22.

Myers, Norman, Mittermeier, Russell A., Mittermeier, Cristina G., Fonseca, Gustavo A.B. da and Kent, Jennifer (2000) 'Biodiversity Hotspots for Conservation Priorities,' *Nature*, vol. 403, no. 24 (February), pp. 853–8.

Nash, Roy (1926) *The Conquest of Brazil* (New York: AMS Press).

Naylor, Robert A. (1967) 'The Mahogany Trade as a Factor in the British Return to the Mosquito Shore in the Second Quarter of the 19th Century,' *The Jamaican Historical Review*, vol. 7, pp. 1–27.

Naylor, Robert A. (1989) *Penny Ante Imperialism: The Mosquito Shore and the Bay of Honduras, 1600 – 1914: A Case Study in British Informal Empire* (London: Associated University Press).

Nelson, Wolfred (1894) 'The Mosquito Reserve,' *Harper's Weekly*, 22 December, p. 1210–1.

Neves, Antonio da Silva (1918) *Primeira conferencia nacional de pecuária; origem provável das diversas raças que povoam o territorio patrio, alimentação racional, hygiene animal* (São Paulo: publisher unknown).

Newson, Linda A. (1986) *The Cost of Conquest: Indian Decline in Honduras under Spanish Rule* (Boulder: Westview Press).

Newson, Linda A. (1987) *Indian Survival in Colonial Nicaragua* (Norman: University of Oklahoma Press).

Nicaragua (1885) *Memoria de gobernación* (Managua: Gobierno de Nicaragua).

Nicaragua (1893) *Memoria de gobernación.* (Managua: Gobierno de Nicaragua).

Nicaragua (1897) *Memoria de gobernación.* (Managua: Gobierno de Nicaragua).

Nicaragua (1905) *Ley sobre conservación de bosques* (Managua: Tipografía Nacional).

Nicaragua (1907) *Memoria de relaciones exteriores* (Managua: Gobierno de Nicaragua).

Nicaragua (1920) *Memoria de relaciones exteriores* (Managua: Gobierno de Nicaragua).

Nicaragua (Ministerio de Agricultura y Ganaderia) (1976) *Zelaya progresa con Somoza* (Managua: Gobierno de Nicaragua).

Nicaragua. Presidencia de la República (1955) *La Comunicación con el Atlántico y la Información Pública* (Managua: Oficina de Información).

Nicol, John M.(1898) 'North-East Nicaragua.' *The Geographical Journal*, vol. 11, pp. 658–60.

Niederberger, Christine (1987) *Paleopaysages et archéologie pre-urbaine dans le bassin de Mexico* (Mexico City: Centre Français d'Études Mexicaines et Centramericaines).

Nieto Caicedo, M. (1946) 'Epidemia regional de malaria en la Cuenca del Lago de Maracaibo 1942–1943,.' Paper presented at the XII Conferencia Sanitaria Panamericana Cuadernos Amarillos (Caracas: Editorial Grafolit).

Norris, William (ed.) (1975) *The Heritage Illustrated Dictionary of the English Language* (New York: Heritage Publishing).

Norton, Albert J. (1900) *Norton's Complete Hand Book of Havana and Cuba. Containing Full Information for the Tourist, Settler and Investor* (Chicago: Rand E. Mc Nally Company).

Nygren, Anja (2000) 'Environmental Narratives on Protection and Production: Nature-Based Conflicts in Río San Juan, Nicaragua,' *Development and Change*, vol. 31, no. 4, pp. 807–30.

O'Connor, James (1997) 'What is Environmental History? Why Environmental History,' *Capitalism, Nature, Socialism*, vol.. 8, no. 2, pp. 3–29.

O'Hara, Sarah L., Street-Perrott, F. Alayne and Burt, Timothy P. (1993) 'Accelerated Soil Erosion around a Mexican Highland Lake caused by Prehispanic Agriculture,' *Nature*, vol. 362, no. 4 (March), pp.48–51.

O'Keefe, John F., and Foster, David R. (1998) 'An Ecological History of the Massachusetts Forests,' in Charles H.W. Foster (ed.) *Stepping Back to Look Forward: A History of the Massachusetts* Forest (Cambridge: Harvard University Press), pp. 19–66..

Oertzen, Eleonore von, Rossbach, Lioba and Wünderrich, Volker (eds.) (1989) *The Nicaraguan Mosquitia in Historical Documents 1844–1927* (Berlin: Dietrich Reimer Verlag).

Offen, Karl H. (1998) 'An Historical Geography of Chicle and Tunu Gum Production in Northeastern Nicaragua,' *Yearbook, Conference of Latin Americanist Geographers*, vol. 24, pp. 57–74.

Offen, Karl H. (1999) 'The Miskitu Kingdom. Landscape and the Emergence of a Miskitu Ethnic Identity, Northeastern Nicaragua and Honduras, 1600–1800,' PhD dissertation, University of Texas, Austin.

Offen, Karl H. (2000) 'British Logwood Extraction from the Mosquitia: the Origin of a Myth.,' *Hispanic American Historical Review*, vol. 80, no. 1, pp. 113–35.

Offen, Karl H. (2002a) 'Ecología Cultural Miskita en los Años 1650–1850,' *Wani*, vol. 30, pp. 42–59.

Offen, Karl H. (2002b) 'The Sambo and Tawira Miskitu: the Colonial Origins and Geography of Miskitu Differentiation in Eastern Nicaragua and Honduras,' *Ethnohistory*, vol. 49, pp. 319–72.

Offen, Karl H. (2004) 'Historical Political Ecology: an Introduction,' *Historical Geography*, vol. 32, in press.

Oldenburg, Christian (n.d.) *La villa de Altagracia y su comarca* (Maracaibo: Imprenta del Estado).

Oldfield, F., and Clark, R.L. (1990) 'Environmental History — the Environmental Evidence,' in P. Brimblecombe and C. Pfister (eds.), *The Silent Countdown: Essays in European Environmental History* (Berlin: Springer–Verlag), pp. 137–61.

Olien, Michael D. (1983) 'The Miskito Kings and the Line of Succession,' *Journal of Anthropological Research*, vol. 39, pp. 198–241.

Olien, Michael D. (1985) 'E.G. Squier and the Miskito: Anthropological Scholarship and Political Propaganda,' *Ethnohistory*, vol. 32, pp. 111–33.

Olien, Michael D. (1988) 'Imperialism, Ethnogenesis and Marginality: Ethnicity and Politics on the Mosquito Coast, 1845– 1964,' *The Journal of Ethnic Studies*, vol. 16, pp. 1–29.

Oliveira, Antonio Carlos de (1941a) *Economia pecuaria do Brasil Central: bovinos* (São Paulo: Departamento Estadual de Estatística de São Paulo).

Oliveira, Antonio Carlos de (1941b) 'Economia pecuaria do Brasil Central, bovinos (Estudo gêo-estatístico e político-económico), I Parte,' *Boletim do Departamento Estadual de Estatística (São Paulo)*, vol. 10 (October), pp. 9–66.

Oliveira, João Bertoldo, Camargo, Marcelo Nunes, Rossi, Marcio and Filho, Braz Calderano (1999) *Mapa pedológico do Estado de São Paulo* (Campinas; Rio de Janeiro: Instituto Agronômico; Embrapa Solos).

Opatrný, Josef (1996) 'Los cambios socio-económicos y el medio ambiente: Cuba. Primera mitad del siglo XIX,' *Revista de Indias*, vol. LVI, no. 207, pp. 367–86.

Orellana, Sandra L. (1995) *Ethnohistory of the Pacific Coast* (Lancaster, CA: Labyrinthos).

Ortiz, R., Ferris, R.S.B. and Vuylsteke, D.R. (1995) 'Banana and Plantain Breeding,' in Simon Gowan (ed.), *Bananas and Plantains* (London: Chapman and Hall), pp. 110–46.

Osgood, Wilfred H., and Conover, Boardman (1922) *Game Birds From Northwestern Venezuela*, publication 210, vol. XII, no. 3 (Chicago: Field Museum of Natural History).

Otero, Jorge Ramos de (1941) *Notas de uma viagem de estudos aos campos do sul de Mato Grosso* (Rio de Janeiro: Serviço de Informação Agrícola, Ministério da Agricultura).

Ovidio Quirós, Luis (1960) *Estudio sobre ejidos (ejidos del Estado Zulia)* (Caracas: publisher unknown).

Pádua, José Augusto (2002) *Um sopro de destruição: pensamento político e crítica ambiental no Brasil escravista, 1786–1888* (Rio de Janeiro: Jorge Zahar Editora).

Page, Thomas J. (1859) *La Plata, the Argentine Confederation, and Paraguay* (New York: Harper & Brothers).

Palacio, Germán (2002) 'Historia tropical: A reconsiderar las nociones de espacio, tiempo y ciencia,' in Germán Palacio and Astrid Ulloa (eds.), *Repensando la naturaleza* (Bogotá: Universidad Nacional Sede Letícia/IMANI/Colciencias), pp. 67–98.

Palacios, Marco (1983) *El café en Colombia, 1850–1970: una historia económica, social y política* (Mexico City: El Colegio de México/Él Áncora).

Palerm, Angel (1990) *México prehispánico: evolución ecológica del valle de México* (México: Consejo Nacional para la Cultura y las Artes).

Palmer, Jesse T. (1932) 'The Banana in Caribbean Trade,' *Economic Geography*, vol. 8, pp. 262–73.

Palmer, Meryvn (1945) *Through Unknown Nicaragua. The Adventures of a Naturalist on a Wild-Goose Chase* (London: Jarrolds Publishers).

Paraná, Estado do (1999) 'Decreto No. 387/99 que instituiu o SISLEG — Sistema de Manutenção, Recuperação e Proteção da Reserva Legal e Áreas de Preservação Permanente no Estado do Paraná,' *Diário Oficial*, 3 March.

Parsons, James J. (1942) 'Spread of African Pasture Grasses to the American Tropics,' *Journal of Range Management*, vol. 25, pp. 12–17.

Parsons, James J. (1955) 'The Miskito Pine Savanna of Nicaragua and Honduras,' *Annals of the Association of American Geographers*, vol. 45, pp. 36–63.

Parsons, James J. (1993) 'The Scourge of Cows,' in Susan E. Place (ed.), *Tropical Rainforests: Latin American Nature and Society in Transition* (Wilmington, DE: Scholarly Resources), pp. 36–48.

Pearson, Henry C. (1905) 'A Visit to Rubber Plantations in Nicaragua,' *The India Rubber World*, vol. 32.

Pedoya, Charles (1990) *La guerre de l'eau* (France: Frisson-Roche).

Peet, Richard and Watts, Michael (1996) 'Liberation Ecology: Development, Sustainability, and Environment in an Age of Market Triumphalism,' in Richard Peet and Michael Watts (eds.), *Liberation Ecologies: Environment, Development, Social Movements* (New York: Routledge), pp. 1–45..

Peluso, Nancy Lee (1992) *Rich Forests, Poor People: Resource Control and Resistance in Java* (Berkeley: University of California Press).

Peluso, Nancy Lee and Watts, Michael (eds.) (2001) *Violent Environments* (Ithaca: Cornell University Press).

Pepper, David (1996) *Modern Environmentalism: an Introduction* (London: Routledge).

Pera y Peralta, Rafael (1913) *Ensayo geográfico e histórico del término municipal de Santa Cruz del Sur* (Havana: Imp. y Papelería La Americana).

Pérez Acosta, Juan F. (1942) *Francia y Bonpland*. Vol. 79, *Publicaciones del Instituto de Investigaciones Históricas de la Facultad de Filosofía y Letras de la Universidad de Buenos Aires* (Buenos Aires: Jacobo Peuser).

Pérez Jr., Louis A. (1983) *Cuba between Empires, 1878–1902* (Pittsburgh: University of Pittsburgh Press).

Pérez Jr., Louis A. (2001) *Winds of Change: Hurricanes and the Transformation of Nineteenth-Century Cuba* (Chapel Hill: University of North Carolina Press).

Pérez Siller, Javier (ed.) (1998) *México-Francia: Memoria de una sensisbilidad común, siglos XIX–XX* (Mexico City: BUAP; El Colegio de San Luis; CEMCA).

Pérez-Valle, Eduardo (1995) 'Delineando la imágen de Nicaragua. Contribución de Sonnenstern a nuestra cartographía,' in Orient Bolívar Juárez (ed.), *Maximiliano von Sonnenstern y el primer mapa oficial de la República de Nicaragua* (Managua: INETER), pp. 7–18.

Perozo, Angel Fereira (1993) *La explotación petrolera y sus efectos en la sociedad Zuliana a través de testimonios orales, gráficos y sonoros 1920–1950* (Maracaibo: Universidad del Zulia, Centro de Estudios Históricos CONDES, Trabajo Ascenso).

Perpiña (Escolapio), P. Antonio (1889) *El Camagüey. Viajes pintorescos por el interior de Cuba y por sus costas con descripción del país* (Barcelona: Librería de J. A. Bastinos y Librería de Luis Niubó).

Peters, James L. (1929) 'An Ornithological Survey in the Caribbean Lowlands of Honduras,' *Bulletin of the Museum of Comparative Zoology*.

Pezzoli, Keith (1998) *Human Settlements and Planning for Ecological Sustainability: The Case of Mexico City* (Cambridge: MIT Press).

Pfister, C., and Brimblecombe, P. (1990) 'Introduction,' in P. Brimblecombe and C. Pfister (eds.), *The Silent Countdown: Essays in European Environmental History* (Berlin: Springer–Verlag), pp. 1–6.

Pim, Bedford and Seeman, Berthold (1869) *Dottings on the Roadside, in Panama, Nicaragua, and Mosquito* (London: Chapman and Hall).

Pimentel, David, Harvey, C., Resosudarmo, P., Sinclair, K., Kurz, D., McNair, M., Crist, S., Shpritz, L., Fitton, L., Saffouri, R. and Blair, R. (1997) 'Land Use, Erosion, and Water Resources,' in Asit K. Biswas (ed.) *Water Resources: Environmental Planning, Management, and Development* (New York: McGraw-Hill), pp. 37–71.

Pinho, Francisco Fortes de (1957) 'As Cêrcas,' *Cadernos A.A.B.B.* 23, nos. 65–66, pp. 7–66.

Pino Santos, Oscar (1973) *El imperialismo norteamericano en la economía de Cuba* (Havana: Ed. Ciencias Sociales).

Pioli de Layerenza, Alicia and Artigas de Rebes, María Isabel (1990) 'Amado Bonpland en el Plata,' *Hoy es Historia*, año 7, no. 41, pp. 54–63.

Pivel Devoto, Juan E. (1977) 'Diario del estabelecimiento de horticultura y aclimatación de Pedro Margat, 1846–1871,' *Revista Histórica* (Montevideo), vol. 50, pp. 473–501.

Pompejano, Daniele (1999) *La crisis del antiguo régimen en Guatemala (1839–1871)*, translated by Diana Jalul (Guatemala: Editorial Universitaria; Universidad de San Carlos de Guatemala).

Porter, Robert P. (1899) *Industrial Cuba. Being a Study of Present Commercial and Industrial Conditions, with Suggestions as to the Opportunities presented in the Island for American Capital, Enterprise and Labour* (New York: G.P. Putnam's Sons).

Porto, Monica (1998) 'The Brazilian Water Law: a New Level of Participation and Decision Making,' *International Journal of Water Resources Development*, vol. 14, no. 2, pp. 175–82.

Potthast-Jutkeit, Barbara (1994) 'El impacto de la colonización alemana y de las actividades misioneras moravas en la Mosquitia, durante el siglo XIX,' *Mesoamérica*, vol. 28, pp. 253–88.

Pruna, Isabel (1956) *Bosques y deforestación de Cuba a través de la historia* (Havana, unpublished manuscript).

Putnam, Lara Elizabeth (2002) *The Company they Kept: Migrants and the Politics of Gender in Caribbean Costa Rica, 1870–1960* (Chapel Hill: University of North Carolina Press).

Queiroz, Paulo Roberto Cimó (1999) 'Uma ferrovia entre dois mundos: A.E.F. Noroeste do Brasil na construção histórica de Mato Grosso (1918–1956),' PhD dissertation, Universidade de São Paulo.

Quintero, Julio (1991) 'Los campamentos petroleros de la costa oriental del Lago de Maracaibo: el sindicato como factor de integración comunitaria, caso Maraven,' Magister Thesis, Universidad del Zulia

Rackham, Oliver (1980) *Ancient Woodland: its History, Vegetation and Uses in England* (London: Edward Arnold).

Rackham, Oliver (1996 [1976]) *Trees and Woodland in the British Landscape* (London: Orion Books).

Radkau, J. (1993) '¿Qué es la historia del medio ambiente?' *Ayer: Historia y Ecología*, vol. 11, pp. 119–46.

Rangarajan, Mahesh (1996) *Fencing the Forest: Conservation and Ecological Change in India's Central Provinces 1860–1914* (Delhi: Oxford University Press).

Rebello, Carlos (1860) *Estados relativos a la producción azucarera de la Isla de Cuba* (Havana: no publisher).

Reed, Ruiz et al. (1880) *Memoria sobre un ingenio central en Puerto Príncipe* (Havana: La Propaganda Literaria).

Reeves, R.(1999) 'Liberals, Conservatives, and Indigenous People: the Subaltern Roots of National Politics in Nineteenth Century Guatemala,' PhD dissertation, University of Wisconsin, Madison.

Restrepo Forero, O. (1984) 'La Comisión Corográfica: un acercamiento a la Nueva Granada,' *Quipu*, vol. 1, pp. 349–68.

Reyes, Cayetano (1991) *Paisajes rurales en el norte de Michoacán* (Mexico City: El Colégio de México; Centre Français d'Études Mexicaines et Centraméricaines).

Risco Rodríguez, Enrique del (1995) *Los bosques de Cuba, su historia y características* (Havana: Editorial Científico Técnica).

Rivas, V.I. (1838) *Vindicación que hace Valerio Ignacio Rivas sobre la impostura que el C.Macario Rodas le suscitó en el Departamento de Quezaltenango* (Guatemala: **publisher?).

Robertson, John Parish and Parish Robertson, William (1839) *Francia's Reign of Terror, Being a Sequel to Letters on Paraguay*, vol. 2 (Philadelphia: E.L. Carey & A. Hart).

Rodríguez Esteban, José Antonio (1991) 'El conocimiento geografico en Argentina. Siglos XIX y XX,' *Ería. Revista de Geografía* (Oviedo), vols. 24–25, pp. 23–38.

Rodríguez Ferrer, Miguel (1876) *Naturaleza y civilización de la grandiosa Isla de Cuba, o estudios variados y científicos, al alcance de todos y otros históricos, estadísticos y políticos*, vol. 1 (Madrid: Imprenta de J. Noguera).

Rodríguez, L. et al. (1986) *Caracterización y diagnóstico del patrimonio agrario colectivo Las Mercedes, Colomba Costa Cuca, Quezaltenango* (Guatemala: Universidad San Carlos, Facultad de Agronomía).

Rodriguez, Mario (1964) *A Palmerstonian Diplomat in Central America: Frederick Chatfield* (Tucson: University of Arizona Press).

Rodriquez, D.W. (1955) *Bananas: an Outline of the Economic History of Production and Trade with Special Reference to Jamaica* (Kingston: The Government Printer).

Roe, Emery M. (1995) 'Except-Africa: Postscript to a Special Section on Development Narratives,' *World Development*, vol. 23, no. 6, pp. 1065–9.

Roig, Juan Tomás (1918) 'Breve reseña sobre una excursión botánica a Oriente,' *Memorias de la Sociedad Cubana de Historia Natural*, vol. 3, no. 4–6, pp. 168–75.

Roig, Juan Tomás (1965) *Diccionario botánico de nombres vulgares cubanos* (Havana: Ed. Consejo Nacional de Universidades).

Rojas, Teresa (1990) *La agricultura mexicana desde sus orígenes hasta nuestros días* (Mexico City: Consejo Nacional para la Cultura y las Artes).

Rondon, Cândido Mariano da Silva (1920) *Matto-Grosso, o que elle nos offerece e o que espera do nós. Conferencia realizada a 31 de Julho de 1920, pelo Exmo. Snr. General Cándido Mariano da Silva Rondon, perante a Sociedade Rural Brasileira no cidade de S. Paulo* (São Paulo: publisher unknown).

Rondon, J. Lucídio N. (1972) *Tipos e aspectos do Pantanal* (São Paulo: publisher unknown).

Rondon, J. Lucídio N. (1974) *No pantanal e na amazônia em Mato Grosso* (São Paulo: publisher unknown).

Rosales, Franklin, Arnaud, Elizabeth and Coto, Julio (eds.) (1999) *A Tribute to the Work of Paul H Allen: a Catalogue of Wild and Cultivated Bananas* (Montpellier, France: International Network for the Improvement of Banana and Plantain).

Roseberry, William (1991) 'To the Last Drop,' *NACLA Report on the Americas*, vol. 25, pp. 26–30.

Roseberry, William (1995) 'Introduction,' in William Roseberry, Lowell Gudmundson and Mario Samper Kutschbach (eds.) *Coffee, Society, and Power in Latin America* (Baltimore: Johns Hopkins University Press), pp. 1–37.

Roseberry, William, Gudmundson, Lowell and Kutschbach, Mario Samper (eds.) (1995) *Coffee, Society, and Power in Latin America* (Baltimore: Johns Hopkins University Press).

Rossbach, Lioba (1985) 'Ascenso y caida de Samuel Pitts (1894–1907),' *Encuentro*, vols. 24–25, pp. 55–64.

Rouse, John E. (1977) *The Criollo: Spanish Cattle in the Americas* (Norman, OK: University of Oklahoma Press).

Rousset, Ricardo V. (1918) *Historial de Cuba*, vol. 3 (Havana: Librería Cervantes).

Rowe, Phillip (1984) 'Breeding Bananas and Plantains,' *Plant Breeding Reviews*, vol. 2, pp. 135–55.

Rowe, Phillip and Rosales, F.E. (2000) 'Conventional Banana Breeding in Honduras,' in David R. Jones (ed.), *Diseases of Banana, Abacá, and Enset* (New York: CABI Publishing), pp. 435–48.

Rowe, Phillip R., and Richardson, Dewayne L. (1975) *Breeding Bananas for Disease Resistance, Fruit Quality, and Yield* (La Lima: SIATSA).

Rubio Sanchez, M. (1953–54) 'Breve historia del desarrollo del café en Guatemala,' *Anales de la Sociedad de Geografía e Historia de Guatemala*, vol. 27, pp. 169–238.

Ruffier, Fernand (1917) *Dos meios de melhorar as raças nacionaes. Primeira Conferencia Nacional de Pecuária. These n. 12* (Rio de Janeiro: publisher unknown).

Ruffier, Fernand (1918) *Manual practico de criação de gado no Brasil* (São Paulo: Empreza Editora de 'Chacaras e Quintaes').

Ruffier, Fernando (1919) *Guerra ao Zebu; um pouco de agua fria* (Castro, Paraná: publisher unknown).

Ruiz Moreno, Aníbal, Risolía, Vicente A. and d'Onofrio, Rómulo (1955) *Aimé Bonpland: aportaciones de carácter inédito sobre su actividad científica en América del Sud*, vol. 17, *Publicaciones del Instituto de Historia de la Medicina* (Buenos Aires: Universidad Nacional de Buenos Aires).

Russell, Edmund (2001) *War and Nature: Fighting Humans and Insects with Chemicals from World War I to Silent Spring* (Cambridge: Cambridge University Press).

Russell, Emily W.B. (1997) *People and the Land Through Time: Linking Ecology and History* (New Haven: Yale University Press).

Sabloff, Jeremy. A., and Henderson, John S. (eds.) (1993) *Lowland Maya Civilization in the Eighth Century A.D.* (Washington, DC: Dumbarton Oaks Research Library and Collection).

Sabor, Josefa Emilia (1995) *Pedro de Angelis y los orígenes de la bibliografía Argentina: ensayo bio-bibliográfico* (Buenos Aires: Ediciones Solar).

Sági, L. (2000) 'Genetic Engineering of Banana for Disease Resistance — Future Possibilities,' in David R. Jones (ed.), *Diseases of Banana, Abacá, and Enset* (New York: CABI Publishing), pp. 465–95.

Sagra, Ramón de la (1862) *Cuba en 1860 o sea cuadro de sus adelantos en la población, la agricultura, el comercio y las rentas públicas* (Paris: Lib. L. Hachette y Cia.)

Saint-Hilaire, Auguste de (1830) *Voyages dans les provinces de Rio de Janeiro et Minas Geraes*, 2 vols. (Paris: Grimbert et Dorez).

Samper Kutschbach, Mario (1994) 'Modelos vs. prácticas. Acercamiento inicial a la cuestión tecnológica en algunos manuales sobre caficultura, 1774–1895,' *Revista de Historia* (Costa Rica), vol. 30, pp. 11–40.

Sánchez, Efraín (1999) *Gobierno y geografía: Agustín Codazzi y la Comisión Corográfica de la Nueva Granada* (Bogotá: Banco de la República; El Ancora Editores).

Sánchez, Martín (2001) 'De la autonomía a la subordinación: Riego, organización social y administración de recursos hidráulicos en la cuenca del río Laja,Guanajuato,1568–1917,' PhD thesis, El Colegio de México.

Sanders, W.T., and Murdy, Carson N. (1982) 'Cultural Evolution and Ecological Succession in the Valley of Guatemala: 1500 B.C. — A.D. 1524,' in *Maya Subsistence: Studies in Memory of Dennis E. Puleston*, edited by Kent V. Flannery, pp. 19–64. (New York: Academic Press).

Santamaría, Antonio (1996) 'Caña de azúcar y producción de azúcar en Cuba. Crecimiento y organización de la industria azucarera cubana desde mediados del siglo XIX hasta la finalización de la Primera Guerra Mundial,' in C. Naranjo, M.A. Puig Samper and L.M. García Mora (eds.), *La nación soñada: Cuba, Puerto Rico y Filipinas ante el 98* (Madrid: Doce Calles), pp. 225–250.

Santamaría, Antonio (2000) 'Intensificación y economías de escala: la transformación tecnológico-organizativa de la industria azucarera cubana después de la primera guerra mundial, 1919–1930,' in Centro de Estudos de História do Atlântico (ed.), *História e tecnologia do açúcar* (Funchal: CEHA — Secretaria Regional do Turismo e Cultura), pp. 423–52.

Santamaría, Antonio (2001) *Sin azúcar no hay país: la industria azucarera y la economía cubana (1919–1939)* (Seville: CSIC, Escuela de Estudios Hispano-Americanos, Universidad de Sevilla).

Santamaría, Antonio and García, Luis M. (1998) 'Colonos. Agricultores cañeros, ¿clase media rural en Cuba?, 1880–1898,' *Revista de Indias*, vol. 8, no. 212, pp. 131–61.

Santiago, Alberto Alves (1985) *O zebu na Índia, no Brasil e no mundo* (Campinas: Instituto Campineiro de Ensino Agrícola).

Santos, Rinaldo dos (2000) *Zebu ano 2000* (Uberaba, Minas Gerais: Associação Brasileira dos Criadores de Zebu).

São Paulo (1994) *Legislação sobre recursos hídricos* (São Paulo: Departamento de Aguas e Energia Elétrica).

São Paulo (1996) *Anteprojeto de Lei Florestal do Estado de São Paulo* (São Paulo: Secretaria de Estado do Meio Ambiente).

São Paulo (1999) *Perfil ambiental do Estado de São Paulo* (São Paulo: Secretaria de Estado do Meio Ambiente).

São Paulo, Governador do Estado de (1998) 'Lei No. 9.989, de 22 de maio de 1998; dispõe sobre a recomposição da cobertura vegetal no Estado de São Paulo,' *Diário Oficial*, 23 May.

Sapper, K. (1897) *Sobre la geografía física, la población y la producción de la República de Guatemala* (Guatemala: Ministerio de la Educación Pública).

Sarton, George (1943) 'Aimé Bonpland (1773–1858),' *Isis* 34, no. 97, pp. 385–99.

Schmink, Marianne and Wood, Charles H. (eds.) (1984) *Frontier Expansion in Amazonia* (Gainesville: University of Florida Press).

Schwenck Jr., Paulo de Mello and Azevedo, Pedro Ubiratan Escorel de (eds.) (1998) *Regularização imobiliária de áreas protegidas. Vol. I. Coletânea de trabalhos forenses, relatórios técnicos e jurisprudências* (São Paulo: Secretaria de Estado do Meio Ambiente; Procuradoria Geral do Estado).

Scobie, James R. (1964) *Revolution on the Pampas: a Social History of Argentine Wheat, 1860–1910* (Austin: University of Texas Press).

Scobie, James R. (1974) *Buenos Aires: Plaza to Suburb, 1870–1910* (New York: Oxford University Press).

Scoones, I. (1999) 'New Ecology and the Social Sciences: What Prospects for fruitful engagement?' *Annual Review of Anthropology*, vol. 28, pp. 479–507.

Secreto, M.V. (2000) 'Dominando la floresta tropical: desbravamentos para el café paulista (Brasil siglo XIX),' *Theomai*, vol. 1, pp. 32–50.

Sheail, John (1985) *Pesticides and Nature Conservation: The British Experience 1950–1975* (Oxford: Clarendon Press).

Shepherd, K. (1974) 'Banana Research at ICTA,' *Tropical Agriculture*, vol. 51, pp. 482–90.

Showalter, William Joseph (1920) 'Cuba. The Sugar Mills of the Antilles,' *National Geographic Magazine*, vol.. 38 (July), pp. 1–33.

Sieboerger, Wilhelm (1891a) 'Letter Sieboerger to Rice, Quamwatla, Jan. 20 1891,' *The Moravian*, vol. 36, no. 8 .

Sieboerger, Wilhelm (1891b) 'Letter Sieboerger to Rice, Quamwatla, April 22, 1891,' *The Moravian*, vol. 36, no. 25.

Silva, Alexandre Barbosa da (1947) *O zebu na India e no Brasil* (Rio de Janeiro: publisher unknown).

Silva, Eduardo (1997) 'The Politics of Sustainable Development: Native Forest Policy in Chile, Venezuela, Costa Rica and Mexico,' *Journal of Latin American Studies*, vol. 29, no. 2, pp. 457–93.

Simmonds, Norman W. (1954) 'A Survey of the Cavendish Group of Bananas,' *Tropical Agriculture*, vol. 31, pp. 126–30.

Simmonds, Norman W. (1956) 'A Banana Collecting Expedition to South East Asia and the Pacific,' *Tropical Agriculture*, vol. 33, pp. 251–71.

Simmonds, Norman W. (1962) *The Evolution of Bananas* (London: Longman's).

Simmons, C.S., Tarano T., J.M. and Pinto Z., J.H. (1959) *Clasificación de reconocimientos de los suelos de la República de Guatemala* (Guatemala: Editorial José de Pineda Ibarra).

Sivaramakrishnan, K. (1999) *Modern Forests: Statemaking and Environmental Change in Colonial Eastern India* (Stanford: Stanford University Press).

Skeat, Walter W. (1961 [1910]) *An Etymological Dictionary of the English Language* (London: Oxford University Press).

Slatta, Richard W. (1983) *Gauchos and the Vanishing Frontier* (Lincoln, NE: University of Nebraska Press).

Sluyter, Andrew (2002) *Colonialism and Landscape: Postcolonial Theory and Applications* (Lanham, MD: Rowman & Littlefield).

Smith, Mark J. (1995) 'The Political Economy of Sugar Production and the Environment of Eastern Cuba, 1898–1923,' *Environmental History Review*, vol. 19, no. 4, pp. 31–48.

Smout, T.C. (2000) *Nature Contested: Environmental History in Scotland and Northern England since 1600* (Edinburgh: Edinburgh University Press).

Solis, I. (1979) *Memoria de la Casa de la Moneda de Guatemala y del desarrollo económico del país* (Guatemala: Ministerio de Finanzas de Guatemala).

Soluri, John (2000) 'People, Plants and Pathogens: the Eco-Social Dynamics of Export Banana Production in Honduras, 1875–1950,' *Hispanic American Historical Review*, vol. 80, no. 3, pp. 463–501.

Soluri, John (2002) 'Accounting for Taste: Export Bananas, Mass Markets, and Panama Disease,' *Environmental History*, vol. 7, no. 3, pp. 386–410.

Sonnenstern, Maximiliano (1938) 'Informe sobre la expedición al Río Coco por el ingeniero civil de la República [1869],' in Republic of Honduras (ed.), *Límites entre Honduras y Nicaragua: alegato presentado a su Majestad Católica El Rey de España en Calidad de Árbitro por las Representaciones de la República de Honduras, Madrid, Marzo de 1905* (New York: [no publisher]), pp. 227–44..

Soskin, Anthony B. (1988) *Non-Traditional Agriculture and Economic Development: the Brazilian Soybean Expansion, 1964–1982* (New York: Praeger).

Soulé, Michael E., and Lease, Gary (eds.) (1995) *Reinventing Nature? Responses to Postmodern Deconstructionism* (Washington, D.C: Island Press).

Squier, E.G. (1852) *Nicaragua: its People, Scenery, Monuments, and the Proposed Interoceanic Canal*, 2 vols (New York: D. Appleton & Co.).

Stadelman, R. (1940) 'Maize Cultivation in Northwestern Guatemala,' *Contribution to American Anthropology and History*, vol. 6, no. 33, pp. 83–265.

Standley, Paul C. (1931) 'The Flora of Lancetilla,' *Field Museum of Natural History — Botany*, vol. 10, pp. 8–49.

Stanfield, Michael Edward (1998) *Red Rubber, Bleeding Trees: Violence, Slavery, and Empire in Northwest Amazonia* (Albuquerque: University of New Mexico Press).

Stansifer, Charles (1977) 'José Zelaya Santos: a New Look at Nicaragua's Liberal Dictator,' *Revista Interamericana*, vol. 7, pp. 468–85.

Steinberg, Ted (2002) 'Down to Earth: Nature, Agency and Power in History,' *American Historical Review*, vol. 107, no. 3, pp. 798–820.

Steinberg, Theodore (1991) *Nature Incorporated: Industrialization and the Waters of New England* (Cambridge: Cambridge University Press).

Stelzner, Uli, and Walther, Thomas (1998) 'Los civilizadores: alemanes en Guatemala,' video produced by ISKA (Germany).

Stepan, Nancy Leys (2001) *Picturing Tropical Nature* (Ithaca: Cornell University Press).

Stover, Robert H. (1962) *Fusarial Wilt (Panama Disease) of the Banana and other Musa Species* (Kew: Commonwealth Mycological Institute).

Striffler, Steve (2002) *In the Shadow of State and Capital: The United Fruit Company, Popular Struggle, and Agrarian Restructuring in Ecuador, 1900–1995* (Durham: Duke University Press).

Sujo W., Hugo (1986) 'La Reincorporación de la Mosquitia,' *Wani*, vol. 4, pp. 17–22.

Taracena, A. (1997) *Invención criolla, sueño ladino, pesadilla indígena: Los Altos de Guatemala: de región a Estado, 1740–1840* (San José: Porvenir; CIRMA; Delegación Regional de Cooperación Técnica y Científica del Gobierno de Francia).

Tarr, Joel A. (1996) *The Search for the Ultimate Sink: Urban Pollution in Historical Perspective* (Akron: University of Akron Press).

Taunay, Afonso de E. (1983 [1956]) *A missão artística de 1816*, vol. 34, *Coleção Temas Brasileiros* (Brasília: Editora Universidade de Brasília).

Taylor III, Joseph E. (1999) *Making Salmon: an Environmental History of the Northwest Fisheries Crisis* (Seattle, WA: University of Washington Press).

Tela Railroad Company (1964) *Datos de 1963* (La Lima, Honduras: Tela Railroad Company).

Tenorio, Trillo Mauricio (1998) *Artilugio de la nación moderna: México en las exposiciones universales 1890–1930* (Mexico City: Fondo de Cultura Económica).

Termer, F. (1931) *The Archaeology of Guatemala* [translation of 'Zur Archäologie von Guatemala,' *Baessler Archiv*,vol. 14, pp. 167–91, n.p., 1939].

The Lamp (1927) 'What of Venezuela?' *The Lamp*, vol. 10, no. 4, p. 7.

Tiffen, Mary, Mortimore, Michael and Gichuki, Francis (1994) *More People, Less Erosion: Environmental Recovery in Kenya* (Chichester: John Wiley & Sons).

Tocqueville, Alexis de (2001) *Writings on Empire and Slavery*, edited and translated by Jennifer Pitts (Baltimore and London: Johns Hopkins University Press).

Topik, Steven C. (2000) 'Coffee Anyone? Recent Research on Latin American Coffee Societies,' *Hispanic American Historical Review*, vol.. 80, no. 2, pp. 225–66.

Topik, Steven C., and Wells, Allen (eds.) (1998) *The Second Conquest of Latin America: Coffee, Henequen, and Oil during the Export Boom, 1850–1930* (Austin: University of Texas Press).

Torre, Carlos de la, and Aguayo, A.M. (1928) *Geografía de Cuba* (Havana: Ed. Cultural).

Torres, E., Saraiva, O.F. and Galerani, P.R. (1994) 'Soil Management and Tillage Operations,' in EMBRAPA [Empresa Brasileira de Pesquisa Agropecuára] (ed.), *Tropical Soybean Improvement and Production* (Rome: FAO), pp. 131–43.

Tortolero V., Alejandro (1995) *De la coa a la máquina de vapor: actividad agrícola e innovación tecnológica en las haciendas mexicanas 1880–1914* (Mexico City: Siglo XXI).

Tortolero V., Alejandro (ed.)(1996) *Tierra, agua y bosques: historia y medio ambiente en el México Central* (Mexico City: CEMCA–I.Mora–Universidad de Guadalajara).

Tortolero V., Alejandro (1997) 'Les hommes et les ressources naturelles dans le bassin de Mexico: l'innovation technologique et son impact dans un milieu rural: Chalco (1890–1925),' *Annales: Histoire, Sciences Sociales*, vol. 52, no. 5, pp. 1085–1114.

Tortolero V., Alejandro (1999) *La agricultura mexicana: crecimiento e innovaciones* (Mexico City: Instituto Mora; UNAM; Colegio de Michoacán; Colegio de México).

Tortolero V., Alejandro (2000a) '¿Revolución agrícola en el valle de México? El caso de Iñigo Noriega,' in Lindón y Noyola Hiernaux (eds.), *El Valle de Chalco: la construcción social de un territorio emergente* (Mexico City: El Colegio Mexiquense), pp. 113–32.

Tortolero V., Alejandro (2000b) *El agua y su historia* (Mexico City: Siglo XXI).

Tortolero V., Alejandro (2002) 'Une banque francaise de l'ancien régime à la révolution: la Banque de Paris et des Pays-Bas,' in Albert Broder and Carlos Marichal (eds.), *Banque et investissements francaises en Amerique Latine* (Paris: Universite de Paris XIII; Creteil, forthcoming).

Tortolero V., Alejandro (2003a) 'Crecimiento y atraso: la vía mexicana hacia el capitalismo agrario,' *Historia Agraria* (Murcia, Spain) (April), pp. 123–52.

Tortolero V., Alejandro (2003b) 'Los caminos de agua en la producción y el comercio en el sureste de la Cuenca de México en la segunda mitad del siglo XVIII,' in R. Liehr (eds.), *Esfuerzos y fracasos de la modernización en México: de las reformas borbónicas al Porfiriato* (Madrid; Frankfurt am Main: Iberoamericana; Vervuert, forthcoming).

Travassos, J. Carlos (1898) *Indústria pastoril, Fasciculo n. 2* (Rio de Janeiro: Sociedade Nacional de Agricultura).

Travassos, J. Carlos (1903) *Monographias agrícolas* (Rio de Janeiro: publisher unknown).

Trimble, S.W. (1992) 'Preface,' in Lary M. Dilsaver and Craig E. Colten (eds.), *The American Environment: Interpretations of Past Geographies* (Lanham, MD: Rowman & Littlefield), pp. xv–xxii.

Trimble, Stanley W. (1995) 'Catchment Sediment Budgets and Change,' in Angela Gurnell and Geoffrey Petts (eds.), *Changing River Channels* (Chichester: John Wiley and Sons), pp. 201–15.

Trimble, Stanley W. (1998) 'Dating Fluvial Processes from Historical Data and Artifacts,' *Catena*, vol. 31, pp. 283–304.

Tucker, Richard P. (2000) *Insatiable Appetite: the United States and the Ecological Degradation of the Tropical World* (Berkeley: University of California Press).

Tyrrell, Ian (1999) *True Gardens of the Gods: Californian–Australian Environmental Reform, 1860–1930* (Berkeley: University of California Press).

Ubatuba, Ezequiel (1916) *O sertão e a pecuaria: papel economico do gado Zebú* (Bello Horizonte: Imprensa Official do Estado de Minas Gerais).

Uekoetter, Frank (1998) 'Confronting the Pitfalls of Current Environmental History: an Argument for an Organisational Approach,' *Environment and History*, vol. 4, no. 1, pp. 31–52.

United Fruit Company (1931) *About Bananas* (Boston: United Fruit Company).

United Fruit Company (1958) *Problems and Progress in Banana Disease Research* (Boston: United Fruit Company).

US Department of Commerce (1931) *Commercial and Industrial Development of Venezuela* (Washington, DC: Government Printing Office).

Vale, Thomas R. (ed.) (2002) *Fire, Native Peoples, and the Natural Landscape* (Washington, DC: Island Press).

Vega Bolaños, Andres (1944) *Cómo reincorporó Nicaragua su costa oriental. La Mosquitia, desde la colonia hasta su reincorporación definitiva. La lucha de Nicaragua con Inglaterra por la soberania en ese territorio. Lo que hicieron los patriotas nicaragüenses para lograr el triunfo de la República. Nicaragua vence a la Gran Bretaña con las armas del derecho* (Managua: Editorial Atlántida).

Veloz Goiticoa, N. (1924) *Venezuela-1924, reseña geográfica, flora, fauna, epoca colonial, Independencia, división político territorial* (Caracas: Ministerio de Fomento, Lit y Tip del Comercio).

Venezuela. Ministerio de Fomento (1928) *Memoria y cuenta que presenta a la Asamblea Legislativa del Estado Zulia el secretario general de gobierno 1927* (Caracas: Editorial Sur America).

Venezuela. Ministerio de Fomento (1929a) *Memoria del Fomento 1928, presentada al Congreso de los Estados Unidos de Venezuela*, vol. 1 (Caracas: Editorial Sur América).

Venezuela. Ministerio de Fomento (1929b) *Memoria y cuenta que presenta a la Asamblea Legislativa del Estado Zulia el Secretario General de Gobierno 1928* (Caracas: Editorial Sur America).

Venezuela. Ministerio de Fomento (1930) *Memoria y Cuenta que presenta a la Asamblea Legislativa del Estado Zulia el secretario general de Gobierno 1929* (Caracas: Editorial Sur America).

Venezuela. Ministerio de Fomento (1937) *Recopilación de leyes y reglamentos de hidrocarburos y demás minerales combustibles* (Caracas: Editorial Bolívar).

Venezuela. Ministerio Relaciones Interiores (1928) *Memoria Ministerio Interior 1927* (Caracas: publisher unknown).

Victor, Mauro A.M. (1975) *A devastação florestal* (São Paulo: Sociedade Brasileira de Silvicultura).

Vieira, Maurício Coelho (1960) 'A pecuária,' in Marília Velloso Galvão (ed.), *Geografia do Brasil, grande região centro-oeste* (Rio de Janeiro: IBGE), pp. 183–222.

Vitta, José (1946) 'La costa atlántica,' *Revista de la Academia de Geografía e Historia de Nicaragua*, vol. 8, pp. 1–46.

Vivó Escoto, Jorge A. (1964) 'Weather and Climate of Mexico and Central America,' in Robert C. West, *Handbook of Middle American Indians: Natural Environment and Early Cultures* (Austin: University of Texas Press), pp. 187–215.

Wackernagel, Mathias (1998) 'The Ecological Footprint of Santiago de Chile,' *Local Environment*, vol. 3, no. 1, pp. 7–25.

Wagner, R. (1996) *Los alemanes en Guatemala: 1824–1944* (Guatemala: published by author).

Wagner, R. (2001) *Historia del café de Guatemala* (Bogotá: Villegas).

Waibel, Leo (1984 [1943]) 'La toponimia como contribución a la reconstrucción del paisaje original de Cuba,' in Leo Waibel and Ricardo Herrera (eds.), *La toponimia en el paisaje cubano* (Havana: Ed. Ciencias Sociales).

Walling, D.E. (1983) 'The Sediment Delivery Problem,' *Journal of Hydrology*, vol. 65, pp. 209–37.

Wardlaw, Claude W. (1935) *Diseases of the Banana* (London: Macmillan and Company).

Watanabe, J.M. (1996) 'Los Mames.' in J. Luján Muñoz (ed.), *Historia general de Guatemala* (Guatemala: Asociación Amigos del País; Fundación para la Cultura y el Desarrollo), pp. 233–43.

Watts, David (1987) *The West Indies: Patterns of Development, Culture and Environmental Change since 1492* (Cambridge: Cambridge University Press).

Weinstein, Barbara (1983) *The Amazon Rubber Boom 1850–1920* (Stanford: Stanford University Press).

West, Robert C. and Augelli. John P. (1976) *Middle America: its Lands and Peoples*, 2nd ed. (Englewood Cliffs, NJ: Prentice Hall).

Whigham, Thomas (1991a) *La yerba mate del Paraguay (1780–1870)* (Asunción: Centro Paraguayo de Estudios Sociológicos).

Whigham, Thomas (1991b) *The Politics of River Trade: Tradition and Development in the Upper Plata, 1780–1870* (Albuquerque: University of New Mexico Press).

White, Richard (1985) 'American Environmental History: the Development of a New Historical Field,' *Pacific Historical Review*, vol. 54, no. 3, pp. 297–335.

White, Richard (1990) 'Environmental History, Ecology, and Meaning,' *Journal of American History*, vol. 76, no. 4, pp. 1111–6.

White, Richard (1995a) '"Are you an Environmentalist or do you Work for a Living?": work and Nature,' in William Cronon (ed.), *Uncommon Ground: toward Reinventing Nature* (New York: W.W. Norton), pp. 171–85.

White, Richard (1995b)*The Organic Machine* (New York: Hill and Wang).

White, Richard (2001) 'Environmental History: Watching a Historical Field Mature,' *Pacific Historical Review*, vol. 70, no. 1, pp. 103–11.

Whitmore, Thomas M. and Turner, B.L. II (2002) *Cultivated Landscapes of Middle America on the Eve of Conquest* (Oxford: Oxford University Press).

Whitney, Gordon G. (1994) *From Coastal Wilderness to Fruited Plain: a History of Environmental Change in Temperate North America 1500 to the Present* (Cambridge: Cambridge University Press).

Wilcox, Robert W. (1992a) 'Cattle and Environment in the Pantanal of Mato Grosso, Brazil, 1870–1970,' *Agricultural History*, vol. 66 (Spring), pp. 244–65.

Wilcox, Robert W. (1992b) 'Cattle Ranching on the Brazilian Frontier: Tradition and Innovation in Mato Grosso, 1870–1940,' PhD dissertation, New York University.

Wilcox, Robert W. (1999) '"The Law of the Least Effort": Cattle Ranching and the Environment in the Savanna of Mato Grosso, Brazil, 1900–1980,' *Environmental History*, vol. 4, no. 3, pp.338–68.

Wilken, Gene (1987) *The Good Farmers: Traditional Agricultural Resource Management in Mexico and Central America* (Berkeley: University of California Press).

Williams, John Hoyt (1972) 'Paraguayan Isolation under Dr. Francia: a Re-evaluation,' *Hispanic American Historical Review*, vol. 52, no. 1, pp. 102–22.

Williams, Michael (1989) *Americans and their Forests: a Historical Geography* (New York: Cambridge University Press).

Williams, Michael (1994) 'The Relations of Environmental History and Historical Geography,' *Journal of Historical Geography*, vol. 20, no. 1, pp. 3–21.

Williams, Michael (2003) *Deforesting the Earth: From Prehistory to Global Crisis* (Chicago: University of Chicago Press).

Williams, Robert G. (1986) *Export Agriculture and the Crisis in Central America* (Chapel Hill: University of North Carolina Press).

Williams, Robert G. (1994) *States and Social Evolution: Coffee and the Rise of National Governments in Central America* (Chapel Hill, NC: University of North Carolina Press).

Williams, S. and Self, S. (1983) 'The October 1902 Plinian Eruption of Santa Maria Volcano, Guatemala,' *Journal of Vulcanology and Geothermal Research*, vol. 16, pp. 35–56.

Wilson, Jason (1994) 'The Strange Fate of Aimé Bonpland,' *London Magazine*, April–May, 36–48.

Woodward, R.L. (1993) *Rafael Carrera and the Emergence of the Republic of Guatemala, 1821–71* (Athens, GA: University of Georgia Press).

Worster, Donald (1979) *Dust Bowl: the Southern Plain in the 1930s* (New York: Oxford University Press).

Worster, Donald (1988) 'Doing Environmental History,' in Donald Worster (ed.) *The Ends of the Earth: Perspectives on Modern Environmental History* (New York: Cambridge University Press), pp. 289–307.

Worster, Donald (1990a) 'Seeing beyond Culture,' *Journal of American History*, vol. 76, no. 4, pp. 1142–7.

Worster, Donald (1990b) 'Transformation of the Earth: Toward an Agroecological Perspective in History,' *Journal of American History*, vol. 76, no. 4, pp. 1087–1106.

Worster, Donald (1993) *The Wealth of Nature: Environmental History and the Ecological Imagination* (New York: Oxford University Press).

Woude, Van der (1987) 'Boserup's Thesis and the Historian,' in Antoinette Fauve-Chamoux (ed.), *Evolution agraire et croissance demographique* (Liege, Belgium: Editions Derouaux Ordina), pp. 381–4.

Wrigley, E.A. (1988) *Continuity, Chance and Change: the Character of the Industrial Revolution in England* (Cambridge: Cambridge University Press).

Wünderich, Volker (1996) 'La unificación nacional que dejó una nación dividida: el gobierno del Presidente Zelaya y la "reincorporación" de la Mosquitia a Nicaragua en 1894,' *Revista de Historia*, vol. 34, pp. 9–44.

Wynn, Graeme (1981) *Timber Colony: A Historical Geography of Early Nineteenth Century New Brunswick* (Toronto: University of Toronto Press).

Yarrington, Doug (1997) *A Coffee Frontier: Land, Society, and Politics in Duaca, Venezuela, 1830–1936* (Pittsburgh: University of Pittsburgh Press).

Zamora Acosta, Elías (1979) 'El control vertical de diferentes pisos ecológicos: aplicación del modelo al occidente de Guatemala,' *Revista de la Universidad Complutense*, vol. 27, pp. 245–72.

Zamora Acosta, Elías (1985) *Los Mayas de las tierras altas en el siglo XVI: tradición y cambio en Guatemala* (Seville: Diputación Provincial).

Zanetti, Oscar (1998) *Comercio y poder. Relaciones cubano-hispano-norteamericanas en torno a 1898* (La Habana: Casa de La Américas).

Zanetti, Oscar, and García, Alejandro (1987) *Caminos para el azúcar* (Havana: Editorial de Ciencias Sociales).

Zarrilli, Adrián Gustavo (2001) 'Capitalism, Ecology, and Agrarian Expansion in the Pampean Region, 1890–1950,' *Environmental History*, vol. 6, no. 4, pp. 561–83.

Zayas, Francisco (1904) *Política agrícola de la República. Nuevo método de siembras y cultivo de la caña de azúcar* (Havana: Imprenta La Prueba).

Zimmerer, Karl S. (1994) 'Human Geography and the "New Ecology": the Prospect and Promise of Integration,' *Annals of the Association of American Geographers*, vol.. 84, no. 1, pp. 108–25.

Zimmerer, Karl S. and Young, Kenneth R. (1998) 'Introduction: the Geographical Nature of Landscape Change,' in Karl S. Zimmerer and Kenneth R. Young (eds.) *Nature's Geography: New Lessons for Conservation in Developing Countries* (Madison: University of Wisconsin Press), pp. 3–34.

Zuñiga E., Melquisedec (1938) 'Descripción geográfica del Departmento de la Mosquitia practicada el año de 1875,' in Republic of Honduras (ed.), *Límites entre Honduras y Nicaragua: alegato presentado a su Majestad Católica El Rey de España en Calidad de Arbitro por las Representaciones de la República de Honduras, Madrid, Marzo de 1905* (New York: [no publisher]), pp. 197–226.

Zupko, Ronald E. and Laures, Robert A. (1996) *Straws in the Wind: Medieval Urban Environmental Law: the Case of Northern Italy* (Boulder: Westview Press).

UNIVERSITY OF WINCHESTER
LIBRARY

LIONAMI

Printed in the United Kingdom
by Lightning Source UK Ltd.
102740UKS00002BA/7-9